The Western Front, 1914 Trilogy

The Western Front, 1914 Trilogy
A Concise History of the Opening Campaigns of the First World War, 1914

Hacking Through Belgium

The Battle of the Rivers

The Battles in Flanders

Edmund Dane

The Western Front, 1914 Trilogy
A Concise History of the Opening Campaigns of the First World War, 1914
Hacking Through Belgium
The Battle of the Rivers
The Battles in Flanders
by Edmund Dane

FIRST EDITION

First published under the titles
Hacking Through Belgium
The Battle of the Rivers
The Battles in Flanders

Leonaur is an imprint of Oakpast Ltd
Copyright in this form © 2013 Oakpast Ltd

ISBN: 978-1-78282-227-1 (hardcover)
ISBN: 978-1-78282-228-8 (softcover)

http://www.leonaur.com

Publisher's Notes

The views expressed in this book are not necessarily those of the publisher.

Contents

Hacking Through Belgium   7
The Battle of the Rivers   109
The Battles in Flanders   249

Hacking Through Belgium

Contents

Prefatory Note	11
The "Scrap of Paper"	15
Liége	24
The Moral and Military Effect	31
The Belgian Army and Its Work	38
The German Tidal Wave	47
The Germans in Brussels	56
The Final Hack	65
The Crime of Louvain	73
The Politics of Rapine	86
The Agony of Antwerp	93
Chronology of Chief Events	103

Prefatory Note

It is the purpose of this book to show the great part played at a crisis in European history by a little People; the signal bravery of their decision; the vital importance, from a military standpoint, of their valiant defence of their Fatherland; and the moral effect in the struggle of that love of liberty which in the face of a devastation unparalleled in western Europe since the seventeenth century, has left their spirit unsubdued. Incomplete though at this juncture the record must be, the British people may be helped by it the more fully to appreciate the sacrifices made by the Belgians for those ideals of ordered independence and freedom on which the greatness of our own Empire has been reared; ideals whose reality has been tested and not found wanting in the fiery trial of war.

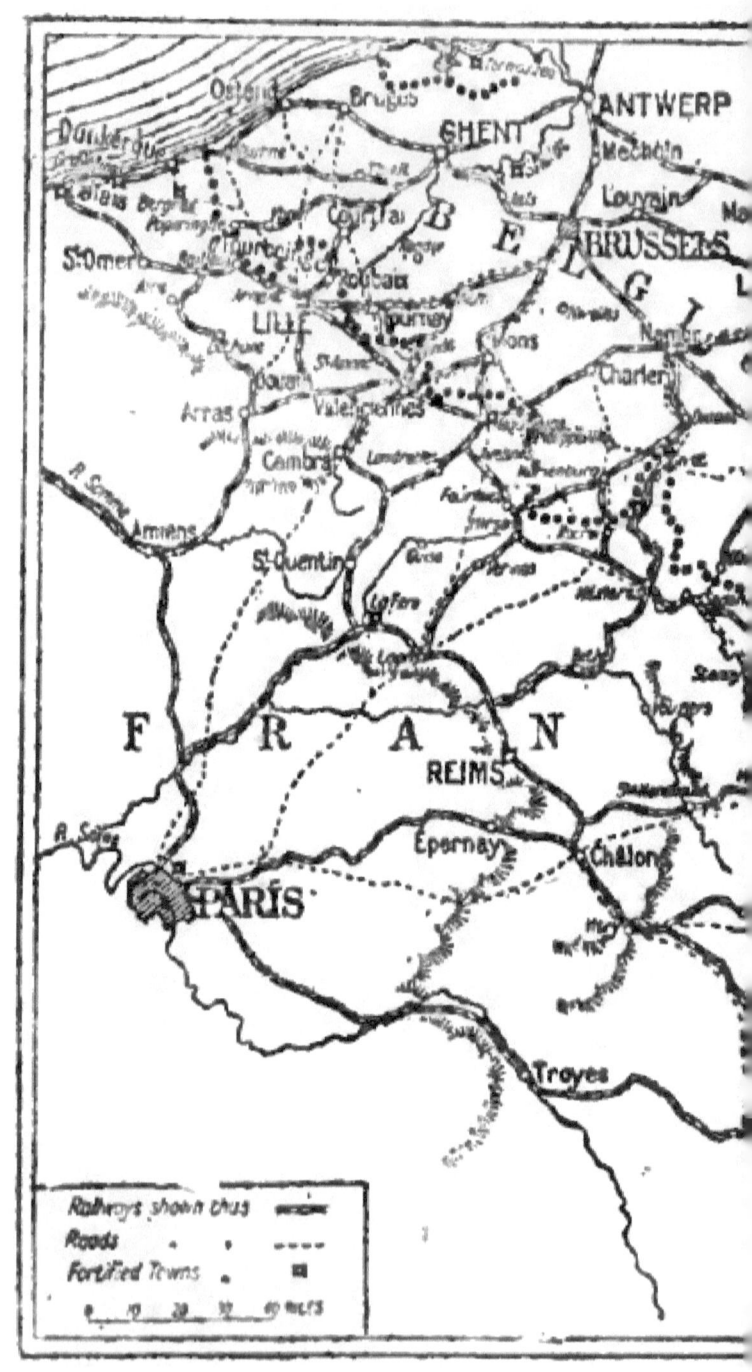

Chapter 1

The "Scrap of Paper"

At seven o'clock on the evening of Sunday, August 2, the German Minister at Brussels presented to the Belgian Secretary of State for Foreign Affairs the note from his government demanding as an act of "friendly neutrality" a free passage through Belgium for the German armies forming the main part of the expeditionary forces against France.

The note promised to respect the independence and integrity of Belgium at the conclusion of peace. It asked for the temporary surrender, on military grounds, of the fortress of Namur. In the event of refusal, the note added, Germany would be compelled to treat Belgium as an enemy. Twelve hours were given to the Belgian Government to reply.

The Belgian Cabinet were called together.

During those fateful hours the whole future of their country hung in the balance. Compliance with the demand meant that Belgium must sink to a dependency of the German Empire. If in the Great War, already opened by Germany's declaration on July 31 of hostilities against Russia, Germany prevailed, as the passive help of Belgium would assist her most materially to prevail, Belgium, in effect an ally of Germany, would be forced to look to Germany for protection, and to accept the conditions, whatever they might be, on which that protection would be given. In any event, that protection would afford an excuse for a continued, perhaps indefinite, occupation by German troops. That implied, forms apart, the annexation of Belgium. Forms apart, it implied the introduction of Prussian methods and Prussian rule. The native genius of Belgium read, in the brief and peremptory demand from Berlin, a destiny which would reduce 600 years' struggle for freedom to naught.

Not easy is it to measure the anxiety of that Sunday night during which King Albert and his ministers weighed their decision. Few meetings of statesmen have been more memorable or more momentous. Of the aims of Germany there could be no doubt. On April 18, 1832, Prussia with Austria had attached her signature to that guarantee of the neutrality and independence of Belgium which France and Great Britain had already signed, and which Russia signed sixteen days after the acquiescence of the Germanic Powers. By the Treaty of London in 1839, after the settlement of the Luxemburg question between Belgium and Holland the guarantee was solemnly ratified. In the meantime Germany had come to believe in what Count von Moltke the elder called "the oldest of all rights, the right of the strongest." Almost coincidently with the presentation of the note at Brussels the German Chancellor at Berlin was, in conversation with the British Ambassador, describing the guarantee as "a scrap of paper." Treaties and engagements are certainly scraps of paper, just as promises are no more than breaths. But upon such scraps of paper and breaths the fabric of civilisation has been built, and without them its everyday activity would come to an end.

Of what value then was the promise embodied in the ultimatum?

The promise had no value. Glance at the map of Belgium. It will be seen that the fortress of Namur is as nearly as possible the geographical centre of the country. What would be the substance of Belgian independence if, by "the oldest of all rights," that strong place was kept by Germany presumably as a barrier against France; actually as the central base of an occupation? Belgian independence would be a shadow.

In their extremity King Albert and his ministers turned to Great Britain. They had good reason. The independence of modern Belgium is the work of British statesmanship. Great Britain had, in 1831, initiated the guarantee although France was the first power to sign it, and Great Britain had always looked upon the guarantee as a solemn obligation. Lord John (then Earl) Russell said in the House of Lords in explaining the policy of the government in 1870:

> We are bound to defend Belgium, I am told that may lead us into danger. I deny that any great danger would exist if the country manfully declared her intention to stand by her treaties, and not to shrink from the performance of her engagements. When the choice is between infamy and honour, I cannot doubt that her Majesty's Government will pursue the course of honour; the

only one worthy of the British people. The main thing is how we can assure Belgium, assure Europe, and assure the world that the great name we have acquired by the constant observation of truth and justice shall not be departed from, and that we shall be in the future what we have been in the past.

Without distinction of party that embodies the consistent attitude British Ministers have taken up since the guarantee was signed. It proved, without distinction of party, to be the resolve of British statesmen and the British people still. In the exchange of despatches which took place between Brussels and London during this critical sitting of the Belgian Cabinet, one thing at any rate was clear. The undivided might and authority of Great Britain and her Empire was, come what may, to be cast on the side of international right and on the side of freedom. When the early light of that summer morning broke upon their deliberations the Belgian Ministry had made up their mind. The dawn after such a night symbolised the colours of their flag—through darkness and trial to liberty. They would face the worst. At 4 a.m. their answer was in the hands of the German Minister waiting to receive it. It was: "No."

The attack on the neutrality of Belgium, the reply declared, would be a flagrant violation of the rights of nations. To agree to the proposal of Germany meant a sacrifice of national honour. By every possible means Belgium was resolved to resist aggression. (See note following).

Note:—The text of the Belgian Government's reply was as follows;—

By its Note of August 2, 1914, the German Government makes it known that according to its certain information the French forces have had the intention of marching upon the Meuse by way of Givet and Dinant, and that Belgium, notwithstanding her good intention, would not be in a condition to repel without assistance an advance march of the French troops.

The German Government feels itself under the obligation to prevent that attack and to violate Belgian territory. Under these circumstances Germany proposes to the King's Government to adopt in reference to her a friendly attitude, and engages at the moment of peace to guarantee the integrity of the kingdom and its possessions in all their extent.

The note adds that if Belgium puts difficulties in the way of the forward movement of the German troops, Germany will be obliged to consider her as an enemy, and leave the final settlement between the two States, one with the other, to the decision of arms.

This note has provoked in the King's Government a profound and grievous astonishment.

The intentions it attributes to France are in contradiction with the formal declarations which have been made to us on August 1 in the name of the Government of the Republic.

Moreover, if, contrary to our expectation, a violation of Belgian neutrality should come to be made by France, Belgium would fulfil all her international duties and her army would oppose to the invader the most vigorous resistance.

The Treaties of 1839, confirmed by the Treaties of 1870, consecrate the independence and neutrality of Belgium under the guarantee of the Powers, and notably under that of his Majesty the King of Prussia.

Belgium has ever been faithful to her international obligations; she has accomplished her duties in a spirit of loyal impartiality; she has neglected no effort to maintain her neutrality and to have it respected.

The attempt upon her independence which the German Government threatens would constitute a flagrant violation of the rights of nations. No strategic consideration justifies violation of right.

Were it to accept the propositions that have been put to it, the Belgian Government would sacrifice the honour of the nations and at the same time go back on its duties towards Europe.

Conscious of the part that Belgium has played for more than eighty years in the world's civilisation, it refuses to believe that the independence of Belgium can be preserved only at the price of violation of her neutrality.

If that hope is ill-founded, the Belgian Government is firmly resolved to repel by every means in its power any attempt upon its right.

England agrees to co-operate as guarantor in the defence of our territory. The English fleet will assure the free passage of the Scheldt for the revictualling of Antwerp.

Any other answer was impossible. That fact, however, does not detract from the splendid bravery of the refusal. The Belgians have paid a high price for freedom. Ever since commerce and the arts found there their first foothold in Northern Europe, the flourishing cities and fertile fields of Belgium have been the lodestar of political adventurers and needy despoilers. They have been the sport of intrigues and royal marriages. They have been fought for by Burgundian, Spaniard, Austrian, Frenchman, Dutchman, and German. But throughout their chequered history the spirit of freedom, and the hope of shaping their own destinies was never crushed out.

In 1832 a new era began. This land, a marvel of human industry, where beautiful cities rich in monuments of art and devotion had sprung up amid ancient swamps; a land turned by patient labour from a desolation into a garden, was at length assured of peace. It was happy in the choice of public-spirited rulers. With unsparing energy and devotion to the common good, Leopold the First threw himself into the work of repairing the heavy ravages of war. He promoted the first railway on the Continent of Europe. He encouraged industry and education. He fostered commerce. Under his wise government the roads of Belgium became the best in Europe. The navigable waterways and canals were improved until they reached a total of over 1,000 miles. The rich mineral resources of the country were opened up. The work thus begun by the first King of the Belgians has been continued by his successors. No record of public spirit and public service has added greater lustre to a Royal House. an English statesman said:

> The people of Belgium have been governed with wisdom, with fairness, and with due regard to their national character, and they reward such treatment by devoted loyalty to their king and firm attachment to their constitution.

The decision now taken still to put freedom first meant undoing all the results laboriously won during nearly eighty years of tranquillity. Yet neither King Albert nor his ministers wavered. And the Belgian people were as firm as they. With Englishmen the love of liberty is commonly passive. They feel their freedom to be secure. Only when challenged does their love of freedom flame into passion. But the Belgians know that their freedom lives under challenge. The shadow of Prussian conscription lay athwart their door. That iron and materialistic system which takes its steady toll of a country's manhood, and crushes national spirit like a Chinese boot, has been the dread of Belgium, as it has been the dread of Holland for a generation. It was not forgotten that the designs of Prussia upon Belgium were no idea of yesterday. More than five months elapsed before diplomatic pressure brought Prussia in 1832 to put her name to the "scrap of paper" she has now repudiated. Count von Moltke made a special study of Belgium and Holland as of Poland. The inference is obvious. Had it not been for the firm front shown by Great Britain in 1870, the German occupation of Belgium would long ago have been an accomplished fact.

In 1870 Prussia did not feel herself strong enough to face France and Great Britain alone. Elated by the unexpected results of the war of 1870, and attributing them wholly to her own prowess instead of largely to the unpreparedness of France, her designs against the Netherlands were revived. Not France was the obstacle feared, but Great Britain. If we are to seek for the true reason of the anti-British spirit fostered in Germany, and certainly not discountenanced by official influence, it will be found in Great Britain standing in the way of this design. Colonies and *welt-politik* were the open talk of Pan-Germanism, but expansion east and west on the Continent of Europe was the definite objective of the plans so minutely prepared at Berlin; and of the costly and extensive apparatus of espionage spread like a network over Europe. This was the dream of riches before the eyes of the German subaltern as he ate the meal of a few pence which his "Spartan poverty" compelled him to take in a cheap *café*, and puzzled how to live without falling into debt.

We need not search far for evidence. If the reader looks at the map of western Germany he will see that a bunch of railway lines stretch to half a dozen points of the compass east of Aix-la-Chapelle like the extended fingers of a hand. They link Aix with eastern, northern, and southern Germany. Now Aix is not a great commercial centre. It is merely a watering-place. There is no more reason why Aix should be a huge railway-centre with vast sidings, and miles of platforms than, say, Wiesbaden. But these are not commercial railways. So far as ordinary traffic goes their construction represents almost a dead loss.

The railways are military and strategical. Regarding their construction one or two interesting facts have to be noted. The first is that their construction began just after the Boer War broke out; was almost coincident indeed with the famous telegram of the *Kaiser* on British reverses. The second fact is that the surveys, plans, and estimates for these railways must have been made long before, and been waiting in a pigeon-hole for a convenient opportunity.

Now ever since the days of the Great Elector Frederick William the affairs of Prussia have been administered with an economy which might almost be called parsimony. It is utterly foreign to Prussian spirit and tradition to spend millions of money without very good reason for it. Remarkably enough, another bunch of these railways, equally without ordinary traffic, converge upon the frontier of Holland.

Just as Scharnhorst was the inventor of the German universal service system, and von Hindersin the organiser of their artillery, so von Moltke was perhaps the first military man who appreciated thoroughly the importance of railways in war, and their value in that rapid hurling of masses of troops into a hostile country before its defence can be put upon a war-footing, which is the cornerstone of German strategy.

No doubt, then, can be entertained as to the true object of these railway enterprises. That they were not undertaken until it was believed Great Britain had ceased to be a serious obstacle, at all events in a land campaign, is confirmed by the nearly coincident change in naval policy which led Germany into heavy ship-building programmes. Great Britain was still a serious obstacle at sea. Therefore a navy had to be built big enough to render her acquiescent. Great Britain acquiescent, and Austria compliant, France and Russia, the remaining signatories to the guarantee, might be dealt with, it was thought, without fear of the result.

The outlay was heavy, but the hoped-for return was great. The Netherlands are a rich prize. Not merely their industrious and ingenious population, but their taxable capacity would make the German Empire easily the head State of Europe. If Holland has not the valuable coal and iron mines of Belgium, she has an important mercantile marine, and most valuable colonies, including a possession in India. The economic importance of the Netherlands to Germany, and possession of the ports of Amsterdam, Rotterdam, and Antwerp, is manifest. A vast expansion of over-sea trade; a host of new and lucrative employments for German bureaucrats, made this sacrifice by a parsimonious people seem well worth while.

But there are other considerations. Belgium has been the cockpit of Europe, because Belgium, as a military base, has almost unrivalled advantages. Possession or occupation of Belgium—they are much the same thing—means command of its wealth of resources, and of its 3,400 or more miles of excellent main roads. Seizure of these is a great weight in the scale. A powerful army based on Belgium dominates France and more especially Paris. France could be reduced by it to a state of tutelage. Conversely, of course, a great French army based on Belgium would have the Lower Rhine at its mercy, and could "bottle up" Germany more effectively even than a blockade of her coast. That was, in part, how Napoleon held down Prussia. Plainly the neutrality and independence of Belgium is the one commonsense solution; and not less plainly the interests of Great Britain are vitally involved.

Doubt as to the aims of Germany had long before been cleared up in responsible quarters informed of the facts. Mr. Asquith said in his speech at the Guildhall:

> The cynical violation of the neutrality of Belgium was after all but a step—the first step—in a deliberate policy of what, if not the *immediate*, the ultimate, and the not far distant aim was to crush the independence and the autonomy of the Free States of Europe. First Belgium, then Holland and Switzerland—countries, like our own, imbued with and sustained by the spirit of liberty—were one after another to be bent to the yoke.

It was hardly necessary for General von Bernhardi, in his book *The Next War*, to declare that the plan of the German General Staff was to march upon France through Belgium. In truth, he disclosed a secret that was as open as anything could be. The fortification by France of her eastern frontier, threatening to convert a campaign against France into a war of obstacles, at all events at the outset, defeated what has already been alluded to as the corner-stone of German strategy. A war of obstacles would not only allow France to gather her strength and to dispose of it where it would be most effective, but it would enable her to meet in the field a foe already shaken by the effort, and by the inevitably heavy losses incurred in breaking the barrier. In a word, the odds in such a campaign would be so much against the invader that for Germany an attack made upon those lines was as good as hopeless.

That, of course, was as well-known in Paris as in Berlin. It was no surprise, therefore, when von Bernhardi published his "disclosure." The real object of the disclosure was to prevent the statesmen concerned from taking it seriously. So long as such a plan was with good reason suspected of being entertained secretly at Berlin, it was to be reckoned with. When it was given to the world in a frothy and bombastic book, it would probably be felt to have lost its weight. The device apparently succeeded. France, relying upon the neutrality of Belgium, left her north-eastern frontier practically open. Of the barrier fortresses,

Maubeuge alone was adapted to resist a siege with modern artillery. As a fact, we know now that the device of giving away the secret did not succeed. On the contrary, it inspired the counter-plan which led the German armies to disaster.

Nevertheless, until the ultimatum was presented to the Government of Belgium few responsible men believed that Germany would go to the length of tearing up her own pledge.

In the face of that ultimatum, a country not more than one-eighth the area of Great Britain, and with a population less than that of Greater London, had to face a mighty military Empire which had sedulously spread the tradition that its armies were invincible. No wonder Germany reckoned on compliance, and all that compliance implied. It was much as if we ourselves had been suddenly challenged for national life and liberty by the world at large, with the certainty added of an immediate invasion. All the same, the Belgians did not flinch. They proved themselves worthy of the spirit of their fathers.

All this was involved in that "Scrap of Paper."

CHAPTER 2
Liége

Germany's rejoinder to Belgium was a declaration of war.

On August 3, German troops crossed the frontier at Dolhain, Francochamps, and Stavelot. Already on the previous day a German army, waiting at Treves, had crossed the Moselle at Wasserbillig, Besselbrieck, and Remich, and in defiance of protests occupied Luxemburg. These were the first military movements in the war.

Driving in the Belgian cavalry outposts along the frontier, the troops from Aix, three army corps under the command of General von Emmich, pushed forward to secure on the one hand a passage over the Meuse before effective opposition could be offered, and on the other to surprise Liége. The 9th corps was detached to seize Visé and the bridge at that place; the 10th marched by way of Verviers with the object of occupying the country to the south and approaching Liége along the level ground between the Vesdre and the Ourthe; the 7th corps followed the direct road from Aix to Liége.

On crossing the frontier, General von Emmich, in command of these troops, distributed to the civilian population a proclamation declaring the pacific intention of the invaders and promising protection for person and property if no hostility was shown. This proclamation, it is evident, had been drawn up and printed in anticipation of Belgian compliance, and no time had been afforded for amending it.

Since the Belgian Government had only on July 31 ordered a partial mobilisation, no considerable force, it was supposed, would be met with south of the Meuse, nor was Liége likely in so short a time to have been made ready for defence. The invading forces consequently brought forward no heavy siege guns. Their equipment in siege artillery was apparently limited to the twelve 5.9 howitzers, four to each army corps, which represented their ordinary field outfit. During the greater part of their advance, the 7th corps met with nothing more formidable than a weak screen of cavalry.

But the Belgian Government had taken prompt and energetic measures. The German troops sent to occupy Visé found on arrival there that, though the Belgians had evacuated the main part of the town lying on the south bank of the river, they had already blown up the bridge, and were prepared from the suburb on the opposite bank seriously to dispute the passage.

The Meuse at this point is fully 300 yards wide. Some sixty yards of the bridge had been destroyed. It was necessary, therefore, for the Germans to construct pontoon bridges, and to cover this operation by shelling the Belgians out of their positions.

From well-covered entrenchments and loopholed houses on the north bank, however, the Belgians kept up a galling fire, and, although out-weighted in the artillery duel, used their guns to good effect in hampering the German engineers. Repeatedly, when on the point of completion, the pontoon bridges were smashed by Belgian shells. The Belgians successfully contested the passage of the river for three days.

It was when this combat was at its hottest, on August 5, that a detachment of German cavalry was fired upon from the windows of some houses on the south bank. Exasperated by the difficulties met with, and their heavy casualties, the invaders forthwith drove out the inhabitants and fired the town. Many of the men, as they came out of the houses, were indiscriminately shot. The women and children were driven before the German troops with marked barbarity. Visé was reduced to ruins.

On the same day, the village of Argenteau, two miles up the river on the same bank, was similarly destroyed and its population decimated. There can be little doubt that this was an act of terrorism intended at once to conceal the attempt to bridge the river at that point, and to dispirit any defence of Liége.

To the Belgians the three days' struggle for the passage of the Meuse was of the utmost consequence. It gave General Leman the time necessary to prepare Liége for that resistance which has become, and will remain, one of the most famous episodes in European history.

Intrepid and resourceful, General Leman had thrown himself into Liége with the 3rd division of the Belgian Army, and a mixed brigade of such troops as could be hastily got together. This force, of not more than 25,000 men, was reinforced by the civic guard, of the city and district, but it was still far short of the 50,000 troops needed to make up a complete garrison.

Thousands of the civilian inhabitants were willingly employed along the south and south-eastern suburbs in hastily digging trenches, across the sectors between the forts. The troops blew up buildings likely to afford cover for an attack; tore up and blocked the roads; laid wire entanglements; mined the bridges across the Meuse, the Vesdre, and the Ourthe; prepared landmines; placed quick-firing guns at points of vantage, and installed searchlights and field telephones.

All this had to be done with the greatest possible expedition. The completeness and rapidity with which the work was carried out formed a surprising feat of skilful organisation.

When the advanced posts of the 7th German army corps came into touch with the outworks of the defence they found that nothing short of an assault in force would suffice. The prompt and effective fire of the forts within range proved that Liége was ready and on the alert.

The German plan provided for a simultaneous attack from the north, the south-east and the south-west, and if it had been carried out it is difficult to see how the fortress could have resisted even the first onset. The plan, however, miscarried.

In view of the time lost by the 9th corps in forcing a way across the Meuse General von Emmich was obliged to hold off the intended attack by the 7th corps. These troops unsupported were too weak to risk such an operation. The advance, besides, of the 10th corps by way of Verviers had not been so rapid as had been intended. Their march through a stretch of country, hilly and for the most part well wooded, had been actively harassed by a mobile force of Belgians intimately acquainted with the defensive possibilities of the region.

In the meantime, the preparations for resistance were pushed forward night and day, and General von Emmich knew that his task became tougher with every hour that was lost.

He was well aware of the weak spots of the fortress. Of its surrounding ring of twelve forts, six only were large and powerfully armed; the remainder were smaller works. The latter, however, were not regularly alternated with the larger forts. Two of the smaller works, Chaudfontaine and Embourg, were placed close together on the south-west; two others, Lantin and Liers, filled a gap of more than 10 miles across on the north-east; a fifth, Evegnée, was midway between the larger forts of Barchon and Fleron on the south-east. These were the three points selected for the assault. Fort Evegnée covered by the fire of both Barchon and Fleron was the most difficult point of the three.

Needless to say, General Leman, equally well aware of the strong and weak points, had taken his measures accordingly.

Evidently feeling that he could not afford delay, the German commander on August 5 launched the 7th army corps against Fort Evegnée with the object of taking it by storm. The bombardment had begun the day before, following a demand for surrender which had been refused, but the German howitzers were outranged by the heavy ordnance of the larger forts. The fire of the latter, skilfully directed, had proved unexpectedly destructive.

Taking advantage of such cover as had been left by partly demolished buildings, walls, and felled trees, the German infantry at the distance for the final rush closed up into columns of attack and, with the support of their artillery, endeavoured to carry the trenches on both sides of Evegnée with the bayonet. Not only, however, were they enfiladed by the guns of Barchon and Fleron, but they suffered huge losses from land mines.

The tactics adopted by the Belgians were well advised. The troops in the trenches held their fire until the attack fell into difficulties with the entanglements, and then withered the assault by well-aimed volleys.

The onset, nevertheless, was too determined to be shaken. Despite their heavy losses, the Germans negotiated the ditches, and though they were mowed down in hundreds by the machine guns now turned upon them, some gained the crest of the trenches. The earthworks were filled with dying and dead, but the storming parties still advanced over the bodies of their fallen comrades.

It was at this juncture that the Belgian troops received the order for a counterassault. Rushing from the trenches *en masse* and in good order, they drove back the storming columns by an irresistible onset. In the pursuit, the German losses were enormous. The first attack had failed. Eight hundred prisoners fell into the hands of the victors, and were sent to Brussels as the first evidence of the national valour.

While that night the 7th army corps, withdrawn beyond the range of the forts, was licking its wounds, the 9th corps, having won the passage of the river below Visé , had advanced to the positions before the forts on the north-east, and on August 6 a second attempt was made to carry the fortress by storm.

The attack was, of course, made from the south-east and from the north-east simultaneously. The sectors between the forts on the north-east had been not less carefully entrenched, and although the attack against Fort Evegnée was again repulsed with losses to the storming columns equal to, if not greater than, those inflicted on the preceding day, some troops, apparently of the 9th corps, managed, despite a fierce resistance, to break through the north-east defences. Furious street fighting, however, forced them to retire. It was while covering this perilous retreat that Prince William of Lippe fell at the head of his regiment. The assault from the north-east, though carried out with the greatest determination, broke before an appalling rifle and machine-gun fire, and was turned into defeat by a counter-attack made at the decisive moment.

A critical period in the fighting on this day was when a body of German troops had penetrated as far as the bridge at Wandre. The bridge had been mined, and before the invaders could obtain possession of it, it was blown up. A superior force of Belgians regained the position.

The defence remained intact, and the terrible scenes in the trenches bore testimony at once to its intrepidity and to the resolution of the assault. German dead and wounded lay thick upon the ground up to the very glacis of the forts. An evidence of the boldness of the enemy is that exploit of eight *uhlans*, two officers, and six privates, who, mistaken for Englishmen, rode during the fighting to the headquarters of General Leman with the object of taking him prisoner. They were killed or captured after a hand to hand struggle in the headquarters' building with members of the Belgian staff aided by *gendarmes*.

But though two assaults had failed with heavy loss of life, a third, even more desperate, was made the same night. This time it was delivered from the south-east against fort Evegnée, and from the south-west against Forts Chaudfontaine and Embourg. The attack from the latter quarter was carried out by the 10th corps, which had at length come into position. The third assault against fort Evegnée was open and supported by a heavy bombardment. That against Chaudfontaine and Embourg was intended as a surprise. The troops of the 10th corps advanced as silently as possible, hoping to steal up to the trenches under cover of darkness. They waited until the attack upon Evegnée had been going on for more than three hours.

The events of this anxious night in Liége have been admirably described in the vivid narrative of Mr. Gerald Fortescue, the special correspondent of the *Daily Telegraph*, who was an eye-witness of them.

There was a bright moonlight, and the Belgians took advantage of it to strengthen still further their defensive preparations, more especially to the south of the city. They were relieved from the necessity of using lights which would have exposed them to the guns of the enemy. Liége is undoubtedly most open to attack on the southeast and south, and most of all by the flat approach between the Vesdre and the Ourthe. This forms the industrial suburb. The great ironworks, the small-arms and gun factory, the electric lighting works, and the railway depots in this quarter would make the seizure of it particularly valuable. On the other hand the difficulties of preparing an effective defence were serious. Forts Embourg and Chaudfontaine are here placed close together in view of that fact. A practically complete line of entrenchments, however, closed the enceinte between Forts Fleron and Boncelles. It was, for the defenders, all to the good that these entrenchments and the obstacles in advance of them had been so recently completed that the Germans could have no reliable knowledge of their details.

The city lay without a light, its ancient citadel rising from amid the sombrely moonlit forest of buildings like a great shadow. Only the searchlights playing from the forts gave signs of life and watchfulness. They travelled across the positions where the enemy had placed his artillery; and swept fitfully over the intervals of trampled country, where round ruined buildings and broken walls, in ditches, and amid entanglements multitudes of dead remained unburied.

Of course, the German commander knew that great activity must be going on in the fortress. That activity, if continued, meant ruin to the chance of taking the place by storm.

Half-an-hour before midnight, a furious bombardment against the south-east forts opened. High explosive shells burst with brilliant flashes and sharp uproar on the very glacis of the forts; a storm of shrapnel broke upon the trenches. The forts replied with energy. The city shook under the thunder of the combat.

With little delay, heavy forces of German infantry advanced. The night was favourable to such an attack. It was light enough for the troops to see their way, and yet dark enough to give such cover as greatly to diminish the risk. This was intended to be a bayonet fight. Though the grey-green of the German uniforms was barely distinguishable in such a light, the masses betrayed themselves by their movement. They could be seen from the trenches creeping up for the last rush.

When it was made their columns flung themselves across the intervening ground, and into the ditches with reckless resolution. But the fire of the defenders was as steady as it was destructive. Notwithstanding that the deadly lightning of the machine guns swept away whole ranks, men fought their way to the parapet of the entrenchments. It was brave, but it was vain.

Repeatedly the onslaught was renewed and repulsed. This, however, was not the main attack. At 3 a.m., just before daybreak and when the night was darkest, the assault suddenly opened, against forts Chaudfontaine and Embourg. No artillery announced it. So far as they could, the columns of the 10th army corps crept up silently, feeling their way. They found the defence on the alert. In spite of the rifle fire from the trenches supported by the guns of the forts, they rushed on in close formation. Searchlights of the forts picked them out. They fell by hundreds, but time and again scaled the slope of the entrenchments. There were intervals of furious bayonet fighting. The brunt of the struggle was borne by the 9th and 14th Belgian regiments. The 9th, says Mr. Fortescue, fought like demons. Gun fire alone could not stop such rushes. Only the unshakable bravery of the defending infantry saved the situation, and not until the ditches were filled with their dead and wounded did the Germans break and run.

The fury of the assault may be judged from the fact that the rushes were continued for five successive hours. More than once, as assailants and defenders mingled in fierce hand to hand combats and the trenches at intervals became covered with masses of struggling men, the attack seemed on the point of success. But as daylight broadened the weight of the onset had spent itself. As the beaten foe sullenly withdrew, a vigorous counter-attack from Wandre threw their shaken columns into confusion. The pursuit was energetically pressed. Numbers of fugitives sought safety over the Dutch border.

On the same day, General von Emmich asked for an armistice of twenty-four hours to bury the German dead. It was refused. Liége had won a brief respite.

Refusal of the armistice may seem a harsh measure, but the Belgians doubtless remembered that it was by breach of the conditions of such an armistice that the Prussians in 1866 had overpowered Hanover. Such enemies were beyond the pale of confidence.

CHAPTER 3

The Moral and Military Effect

When, on August 4, King Albert read his speech to the joint meeting of the Belgian Chamber and Senate, it might well have been thought that the darkest hour had come in Belgium's long and troubled history. But the king spoke with unfaltering resolve. Come what might, the Belgian people would maintain the freedom which was their birthright. In the moment for action they would not shrink from sacrifices. King Albert concluded:

> I have faith in our destinies. A country which defends itself wins respect, and cannot perish.

The speech echoed the feelings of a united nation. In the face of peril, party was no longer known. M. Emile Vandervelde, leader of the Socialists, accepted a post in the ministry. Without hesitation, the two Houses voted the measures of emergency proposed by the government. The announcement by M. de Broqueville, the prime minister, that German troops were already on Belgian soil caused deep emotion, but the emotion was not born of fear. It was the realisation of how priceless is the heritage of liberty.

On that stirring day in Brussels, which witnessed the departure of the king to join his troops at the front, the sentiment uppermost was in truth "faith in the nation's destinies." Great Britain had sent her ultimatum to Berlin in defence of Belgian rights. Not merely reservists called to the colours, but volunteers in multitudes were anxious to take up arms. Crowds besieged the recruiting offices. The public feeling in the Belgian capital reflected the public feeling everywhere.

The mobilisation of the defensive forces of the country had proceeded smoothly and swiftly. Though it was common knowledge that in no part of Europe had the espionage system worked from Berlin become more elaborate, the national spirit was but intensified. Then came news of the fighting, and of the dauntless resistance offered by the garrison at Liége. Later came the first of many German prisoners of war.

Mistakes and miscalculations undoubtedly entered into the German disaster at Liége, and above all the mistake of grossly underestimating the quality and efficiency of the Belgian forces. That mistake was persisted in during all the attempts to storm the fortress. It cost thousands of German lives. Not certainly until this war is over will the extent of the disaster be really known. But that it was a disaster of the greatest magnitude is beyond any question.

From the merely military standpoint, the shattering of three army corps is a huge price to pay even for victory. But the shattering of General von Emmich's army accomplished nothing. It had merely proved that to hurl men in massed formation against positions defended by modern guns and rifles is folly. Elementary common sense, however, would enforce the same conclusion. As the assaults upon Liége showed, elementary common sense is not a strong point of Prussian militarism. Because massed formations were used with effect by Frederick the Great, massed formations were the one idea of some of his would-be venerators.

The moral effect was greater than the military. It brought down in three days all that edifice of prestige which Prussian diplomacy, Prussian espionage, and Prussianised philosophy had been labouring for a generation, to build up. To say that Europe gasped with surprise is to state the effect mildly. The peoples opposed to German ambitions woke as from a spell. The aspect of the war had changed.

Here was an army, part of the great Fighting Machine in which war was presumed to be practically embodied as an exact science, beginning a campaign with the blunder of assuming that men fighting for their country were no better than half-trained mercenaries. The resistance to the passage of the Meuse; the resistance offered to the troops sent to seize the country south of Liége was treated as negligible. A general of resource and experience would have reckoned on that resistance as a certainty.

Neither Prussian strategy then, nor Prussian tactics, were the perfection they had been taken to be. Both had broken at the first test. Nowhere was the gravity of the moral effect better appreciated than at Berlin. Henceforward the effort of Berlin was to efface it. In that fact will be found the key to all the succeeding "severities" in Belgium.

That in Berlin, at all events in official and informed quarters, the surprise was as profound as elsewhere is proved by the fact that on August 9, through the neutral channel of the Dutch Minister of Foreign Affairs, the German Government made a second offer. The offer was in these terms:—

> The fortress of Liége has been taken by assault after a courageous defence. The German Government regrets that as a consequence of the attitude of the Belgian Government against Germany such bloody encounters should have occurred. Germany does not want an enemy in Belgium. It is only by the force of events that she has been forced, by reason of the military measures of France, to take the grave determination of entering Belgium and occupying Liége as a base for her further military operations. Now that the Belgian Army has, in a heroic resistance against a great superiority, maintained the honour of its arms in the most brilliant fashion, the German Government prays his Majesty the King and the Belgian Government to avert from Belgium the further horrors of war. The German Government is ready for any agreement with Belgium which could be reconciled in any conceivable way with its conflict with France. Once more Germany offers her solemn assurance that she has not been actuated by any intention to appropriate Belgian territory, and that that intention is far from her. Germany is always ready to evacuate Belgium as soon as the state of war will permit her.

Of course, the fortress of Liége had not been taken by assault, though perhaps the government of Berlin had been led to believe it had. Coming from such a quarter the tribute to Belgian valour is significant. Germany had fallen into a pit, and her "solemn assurance" was not good enough to lift her out of it. The reply of the Belgian Government was, a second time, an unhesitating refusal. Berlin must take the consequences, and those consequences were serious.

The first necessity was to clear up the mess, and if possible to conceal it; above all to conceal it from the troops who had to pass over this same route. They must hear of nothing but victories. Necessity for clearing up and concealment had a greater result in delaying the German advance than even the successful resistance of the Liége garrison.

Why, it may be asked, was the garrison withdrawn from Liége, leaving only a force sufficient to man the fortifications? For that step there were imperative reasons. To begin with, the defence of the city, as distinct from the defence of the forts, had served its purpose. It had not only delayed the German advance; it had inflicted grave disorganisation. It was certain, however, that at the earliest moment heavy German reinforcements would be brought up, and the defence outside the forts overpowered by sheer weight of numbers.

In the violent fighting the garrison holding the trenches had suffered severe losses, though these were light in comparison with the crushing punishment they had inflicted. They formed, nevertheless, a body of excellent troops still more than 20,000 strong. To have risked the loss of these troops meant a reduction of the Belgian army in the field which must seriously cripple its effective. The need of the moment was a concentration of forces. Though the defence of Liége to the last was important, still more important was the purpose which the Belgian army was intended to serve throughout the campaign, and most important of all the successful defence of Antwerp. Upon the defence of Antwerp hung the nation's independence.

While, therefore, the way was still open for retreat, Generals Bertrand and Vermeulen, who had rendered conspicuous services and had proved, like General Leman, that the Military School at Brussels is a nursery of able and distinguished men, withdrew their forces and rejoined the main army.

This measure was carried out with so much promptitude and secrecy that the enemy, well-served as he was by spies, and in close observation of the movements of the garrison, was not able to interfere. General Leman remained to continue the defence of the permanent works. These had been provisioned for a siege of at least two months.

Before evacuating the city the troops blew up all save two of the many bridges which within the circle of fortifications cross the Meuse, the Ourthe, and the Vesdre. At Liége, the Meuse divides. A considerable district of the city is built on the island between the branches of the river. The bridges left intact were a concession to public necessity, but were those least likely to be of service to the enemy.

Destruction of the bridges greatly reduced the value of a hostile occupation. The importance of Liége to the Germans as part of their line of communications lay in command of the railways. These, however, were dominated by the forts. So long, then, as the latter held out, Liége, in any real military sense, was to the Germans valueless. In view of the position of the Belgians it was therefore a well-advised step to concentrate the strength of the defence on the works.

On August 8 and 9, the Germans before Liége were apparently quiescent. But this seeming respite covered an unceasing activity. Masses of wreckage mingled with dead bodies floating down stream bore testimony to the severity of the struggle for the passage of the Meuse. As rapidly as possible German engineers threw across the waterway beyond the range of the Liége forts five floating bridges. The passage secured, the enemy covered the country to the north with a screen of cavalry, obstructing observation by the Belgian outposts and guarding their bridge works against a surprise in force.

Evidently they were not certain that the departure of troops from Liége might not be a ruse. Their severe handling had taught them caution. Small bodies of *uhlans* stole into the city from the east on August 9. These, as usual, were men who had specially volunteered for the service. Though they might never return, the ambition for the Iron Cross is strong. They found the city and the entrenchments evidently evacuated. No hostilities were offered.

Reports to the German headquarters of this state of things led to a second demand for surrender. To secure protection for the defenceless population a deputation of seventeen leading citizens sought an interview with the German general. The deputation were seized as hostages.

On August 10, German troops marched in without resistance. The city was put under martial law and a "fine" of £2,000,000 imposed upon it. But the occupation was a hollow triumph. Liége, as a military possession, was a husk from which the kernel had been carefully withdrawn.

The defence, followed by the continued resistance of the forts, had created a formidable tangle of difficulties. As the forts, by the use of reinforced concrete, had been adapted to resist modern artillery the shells, even of the 5.9 howitzers, made no impression upon them. It was necessary to bring up from Essen the 28 centimetre howitzers, and even the still heavier guns, 42 centimetre, specially made for the prospective siege of Paris.

Needless to say, with the strategical railways to Aix already working at full pressure, the transport of these heavy pieces played havoc with the cut and dried time-table. There was the necessity, too, not calculated for at this stage, of sending wounded to the rear, and of replacing by fresh troops the battalions broken in the attempted assault. To hurry troops to the front, lest the Belgians should move in force upon the Meuse, was urgent. The sending forward of supplies was, in consequence, badly hung up. The commissariat became for the time almost a chaos.

If we sum up their situation at the end of the first fortnight of the war we find that the Germans had accomplished little or nothing. They had expected by that time to be close upon Paris. All they had, in fact, gained was a passage across the Meuse. It is impossible to over-rate the military importance of this delay. During that fortnight the mobilisation of the French had been completed without interruption. At the end of it the British Expeditionary Force had been landed at Boulogne. The calculated advantages of secret preparation which had inspired the ultimata launched from Berlin were nullified. The first principle of German strategy had failed.

Important as a subsidiary means of communication, the floating bridges across the Meuse were in no sense adequate for the supply of such a force as it was intended to send through Belgium to defeat the armies of France and Great Britain and to seize Paris. Command of the railways was indispensable. But without a reduction of the forts at Liége that was out of the question.

The forts at Liége held out until August 19. The larger works were each triangular in formation, armed with both heavy and quick-firing guns mounted in steel revolving turrets. Three of these turrets were of the disappearing type. On the discharge of the guns a turret of this type falls out of sight automatically. By means of telescopic and reflector sights, the guns can be "laid" for the next shot while the turret is hidden from outside view.

To storm the forts, as had been proved, was not practicable. They had to be broken up by the shells of the huge ordnance brought along for the purpose, and mounted on massive concrete beds.

One by one the forts were broken up. They offered, however, an unyielding resistance. Their garrisons knew that they were called upon to sell their lives for the Belgian fatherland. None deserted their posts of duty. There have been many acts of heroism in this war. The defenders of the forts at Liége deserve an honoured place in the memories of an emancipated Europe.

General Leman, who had taken up his quarters in Fort Loncin, was in the fort when it was blown up by a German shell, which had found its way into the magazine. He was saved by a signal act of bravery. He wrote in that affecting letter sent later from his place of confinement in Germany to the King of the Belgians:

That I did not lose my life is due to my escort, who drew me from a stronghold while I was being suffocated with gas from exploded powder. I was carried to a trench, where I fell.

Most of the garrison were buried under the ruins, but the few survivors risked themselves in this act of devotion. No better evidence could be offered of the spirit of Belgian defence.

A German captain found the intrepid commander helpless and after giving him liquid refreshment carried him as a prisoner into the city. The defence of Liége, however, had fulfilled its purpose.

CHAPTER 4

The Belgian Army and Its Work

Independently of delay, there was yet another reason for the defence of the forts at Liége which compelled the enemy to break them up. Their destruction meant that Liége *as a fortress* had ceased for the time to exist. For Belgium this was a heavy sacrifice. Its possible bearing, however, in the later stages of the war on a German defence of the Lower Rhine is manifest. As time goes by the trend of events makes it clear that the strategy of the Allied Powers was from the outset inspired by long views.

In consonance with those views the plan of the Belgian campaign was consistently carried out. From the first it was never part of that plan that the German inroad should be opposed in Belgium, where, close upon its base, its strength would have been greatest, and that of the Allies least. The purpose was to draw the German forces as far from their base and to lengthen out their line of communications as much as possible, and then, when they were at their weakest, and the Allies, in point of position, at their strongest, to face and defeat them.

But manifestly that purpose had by every device to be concealed. It was concealed. On the face of things all appearances lent colour to the conclusion that the Belgian Army meant to stand or to fall in an endeavour to cover Brussels. There were announcements of the arrival of strong French forces. In view of the sufferings entailed by the invasion the French were indeed ready to send forward five army corps. Those added to the six divisions of the Belgian army would have offered a powerful opposition. But it would have been inferior strategy. In the event of defeat, which has always to be reckoned with, the effective and designed part of the Belgian Army in the campaign must have been seriously crippled. The situation of the country would have been worsened.

Remembering that the object of the Belgians was to safeguard their independence, there was wisdom in the view, which weighed against present sufferings the vision of a long and peaceful future, and elected to act in co-operation with the larger scheme. It helps to appreciate the depth of the love of freedom and the steadfast fortitude which have justly won the admiration of liberal Europe.

Taking up his headquarters in Louvain, King Albert disposed his forces along a line from Diest to Wavre. Between Wavre and Namur, with headquarters at Gembloux, the country was watched by a division of French cavalry. This line, it will be noted, describes an arc some 45 miles in extent, covering both Brussels and Antwerp. At this stage of the hostilities the necessity was for a strong force of cavalry. That of the Belgian army was in numbers inadequate. The French reinforcement was consequently of the greatest value.

It has commonly been supposed that the Belgian Army was somewhat indifferent alike in discipline and in material. Such was the view then entertained at Berlin. Apparently it was not there realised that the time had long gone by when the Belgian as a soldier could justly be described as a bad copy of the Frenchman. Certainly the Belgian army was not trained upon the Prussian model. That, however, has proved to be all to its advantage.

Military efficiency is a relative term, but in every essential the Belgians were a highly efficient force. One of the best features of their system is that every regiment has its military school, where the men learn the elements of soldiering as an intelligent art. The essence of the Prussian system has been that the rank and file are taught to obey as machines. The Belgian recruit, on the other hand, had his interest enlisted in his work. He was taught the reason for things.

In Germany, the conscript spent much of his time learning to march in exact line at the parade step, every man with his rifle at the same angle. Even the length of the parade step was measured to an inch. Woe betide the *bursch* who fell short, or shouldered his rifle out of the correct slope. Points lost by officers at the inspection were passed on with interest. There is a value in this instruction, but in the Prussian system it was put before other things more valuable still.

The difference in essence between the Belgian Army and the German lay in the fact that the Belgian recruit was not politically suspect of his superiors. He was a freeman serving his country, not an inferior in training to support a dominant caste. He could without danger be made something more than mechanically efficient.

Again his military education in actual field work was distinctly practical. Belgium is a densely populated country, full of buildings, hedgerows, and plantations affording excellent cover. Its army anyhow would be called upon to face forces greatly superior in numbers. The practical work kept those points in view. It was addressed to successful ambuscades; to fighting in open order; to rapid changes of position akin to guerilla tactics; to the defence of trenches, canals, and bridges. The Belgian soldier was asked to be resourceful and alert. If on manoeuvres the army made none of the imposing show associated with mimic warfare in Germany, for the purposes it was designed to serve it was excellent. There could be no comparison, perhaps, between the parade smartness of a German and a Belgian regiment of infantry, but in essentials and for fighting on his own ground the Belgian was an easy first.

No better evidence of the business-like training of the Belgian Army need be offered than its making use of the admirable roads of the country by organising those corps of cyclist scouts whose co-operation with the cavalry proved invaluable.

These, then, were the forces the king had at his disposal. As to the artillery its only fault was that there was not enough of it. It was strong, however, in light field guns capable of being briskly manoeuvred, and forming a very serviceable and handy weapon of a recent type.

Hardly an expert is needed to reflect that with an army such as this the very last thing a capable general would do would be to offer a pitched battle against the ponderous legions of Germany, supported by an overwhelming mass of heavy guns. To do that would be asking for annihilation. The object of the Belgians was to harass, and wear down, and entrap.

It was a warfare in which instances of individual bravery and prowess and swift initiative established the value of the Belgian military training, and indicated that the Germans had no easier work before them than had Alva's Spaniards.

The country south of the Meuse the Belgians advisedly made no effort to defend. It is a country of deep valleys with rugged and precipitous sides; of ravines and streams falling between steep and rocky banks. The main mass of the Ardennes runs nearly south to north from Arlon to Namur. For the most part the hills are covered with dense forests alternating with marshy and wild plateaux and stretches of pastoral uplands. Little subsistence could be found by an invader in such a region.

Into Belgian Luxemburg the Germans poured the army of Saxons commanded by General von Hansen and the army commanded by Duke Albert of Wurtemburg. The former fixed his headquarters at Marche, and the latter at Neufchatel. At the same time the army of the Crown Prince of Prussia established an advanced base in the city of Luxemburg.

The first purpose of these movements was to seize the railways— the line from Verviers to Luxemburg, the line from Liége to Jemelle, and in particular the main line from Namur through Arlon.

In possession of the line from Verviers the invaders at Luxemburg were linked up with Aix, but until they were in command of Liége and the junctions there the rest of the railways were of no value to them. They were obliged to transport supplies at great labour and expense over roads with heavy gradients. A further forward movement across the French frontier was in such circumstances impossible. The defence of Liége consequently held up the advance both north and south of the Meuse, and imposed a huge and to all intents useless consumption of resources. It also caused a severe congestion at Aix, where no fewer than eight army corps were at that time massing for the advance north of the Meuse across the Belgian plain.

Meanwhile north of the Meuse the Belgians were not idle. They destroyed bridges, and tore up roads. The railway bridges over the Geer at Warenne and Tongres were blown up; the railway junction at Landen rendered useless. All the rolling stock was moved to behind their lines.

Partly to check these defensive measures, partly also to commandeer much needed supplies as well as to gather information of the Belgian dispositions and incidentally to overawe the population, the Germans covered the country immediately to the north-east of Liége with numerous parties of *uhlans*. These raiders speedily came into contact with Belgian cavalry and scouts supported by light artillery and mobile bodies of infantry expert as skirmishers.

The tactics adopted by the Belgians were skilful. Before a hostile squadron or flying column they fell back, until what the Germans thought to be a successful pursuit had been pushed far enough. Then when the enemy turned to retreat he realised that he had been led into a *cul-de-sac*, and was attacked in turn from both flanks and from the rear. From every bit of cover along roads and from plantations the retreating forces were shelled and sniped at. Their losses in these running fights were in the aggregate gruelling. Frequently a last remnant put up a desperate resistance to extermination from the nearest barn or other building into which they could fling themselves for refuge.

This unlooked-for experience was put down to the bitter hostility of the population whom the Belgian Government were assumed to have armed for the purposes of a guerilla warfare *à outrance*. It seems never to have entered the German mind that there could be military tactics different from their own. They still persisted in the belief that the Belgians as a military force were contemptible. When the heavy losses were realised, when numbers of their *uhlans* never returned, or were found lying dead in woods and along roadsides; above all when, owing to the danger of it, the requisitioning failed to give the supplies expected, "reprisals" were resolved upon. The columns sent out were strengthened, and reinforced by guns and infantry, with orders to lay waste the villages and farms which had been the scenes of annihilations and defeats. The "beasts" of Belgium were to be taught a severe lesson. Very soon the country within sight of Liége was a blaze of devastation. Without distinction of age or sex, those of the population who could not escape were butchered. In this rapine, apparently, the German troops were allowed a free hand.

From now the fighting presented many characteristics of a warfare of savagery. On the one side, the Belgians were dealt with as "rebels," to be slain without mercy. On the other side, revenge inspired a resistance still more daring. No doubt the reports brought in to the German headquarters by survivors of the raids asserted that the losses were mostly due to civilians. Very naturally they would be reluctant to admit defeat by Belgian soldiery. Men flying for their lives are not usually exact observers. Evidently on the part of those responsible the belief prevailed that their men had not been lost in military operations but had been waylaid and murdered. A policy of systematic terrorism was entered upon.

At the back of this policy evidently was exasperation at the Belgian resistance, and its grave results. The policy, however, only aggravated matters. On the same day (August 10) on which they entered into occupation of Liége, the invaders began their operations north of the Meuse on a larger scale. They dispatched a flying column of 6,000 cavalry with artillery and infantry supports towards Limburg by way of Tongres and Hasselt. At the same time, they attacked the passage over the Meuse at Huy.

Tongres, held only by some Belgian outposts, was seized by the Limburg column with little difficulty, but at Hasselt they were opposed by a nearly equal force of Belgians. They were allowed to advance in apparent security. Suddenly barricades of stones and carts thrown up across the roads proved to be cleverly contrived concealments for machine guns. An unexpected attack developed. The column hastily deployed through woods and across fields. A strong body attempted to push on through the town in order to secure the bridge. The attempt was not successful. The supporting infantry were forced to retreat. In covering that movement the cavalry lost heavily. A number were made prisoners. Others dashed across the Dutch frontier into Maastricht. The retreat was harassed on both flanks and rear as far as Tongres.

At Huy, where there were some fortifications of an unimportant character, the Belgians held a bridge-head across the river giving access to the country between Liége and Dinant. The Germans attacked the works with heavy howitzers. The fort, however, held out until August 12. Before evacuating the place the Belgians blew up the bridge. The rearguard of the defenders rushed across under a rain of hostile shells, closely pursued. A squadron of German cavalry heading the chase were on the bridge when the part of the structure already mined crashed skyward in a mass of dust and flame.

Next day (August 11) a reconnaissance in force was undertaken as far as Tirlemont and Jodoigne by a flying German column some 2,000 strong. These troops, advancing through Orsnaael and Landen, laid the country waste in a methodical manner. Civilians arrested on charges of sniping were shot on the wayside without ceremony. The population fled in terror. The wake of the invasion was marked by the pall of smoke rising from burning ricks, and homesteads, and ruined villages. What had been a fruitful countryside was turned into a desolation. Even priests administering the last unction to dying victims were cut down or speared.[1]

At Dormael the incursion was opposed by a body of Belgian lancers, who fell back before it. The column pushed on as far as Bost, in sight of Tirlemont. There the Belgian infantry closed in. Fearing an ambuscade the Germans beat a retreat. They were chased through St. Trond and Warenne to their lines near Liége. In this pursuit of over twenty miles they lost a large proportion of their total force.

One effect of these checks was that in succeeding operations the enemy made a confession of the efficiency of the Belgians by employ-

---

1. This has been officially denied from Berlin; but the Belgians declare that priests seemed specially to be marked out for attack. It is certain that a number lost their lives.

ing their crack troops. In no modern army is the difference, and it may be added the distinction, between crack regiments and the rest more marked than in that of Germany. Out of the mass of the infantry the best shots and the smartest men are picked to form the regiments of *jaegers* (hunters) who are trained to fight in open as well as in close order. This is a coveted promotion, but it leaves the ordinary line regiments at a standard below modern ideas of real fighting efficiency. The total strength of the *jaegers* was, at the beginning of the war, about 70,000. They form the only element in the Germany infantry which can seriously compare with, say, British infantry. Taking the Belgian infantry as a whole they were well up to the same level, and still mustered close upon 90,000 men.

Admission to the German cavalry rests on a basis of class, but some of the regiments are close corporations of the Prussian and Hanoverian aristocracy. One of the most famous, and most exclusive, the Death's Head Hussars, a corps which gained its reputation during the Seven Years' War,[2] boasted that it had never yet retreated save under orders. Stories of its daring form part of the pabulum of every German schoolbook.

On August 12 began the biggest attempt so far made to find out the disposition and strength of the Belgian main force. The energetic measures taken by the Belgian Government to deal with the spy system had evidently disorganised the practice. Nothing was known for certain either of the Belgian main army's movements or of its intentions, a proof of the prudent ability of its command.

It was essential that the enemy should if possible obtain that information. The importance to the Germans of manoeuvring the Belgian main army into a position which would uncover Antwerp, and, by forcing it upon Brussels, exposing it to defeat in a situation which would either compel it to retire across the French frontier or to surrender, need not be insisted upon. If that could have been accomplished it would not only affect the whole campaign in the western theatre of war, but would restore the prestige already so badly damaged.

These considerations explain the attack made upon the Belgian lines on August 12 and 13. The attack was directed to two points—Eghezée, to the north of Namur, and Diest. The main German column was directed against Diest in an attempted turning movement.

---

2. *Frederick the Great & the Seven Years' War* by F. W. Longman is also published by Leonaur.

The attack at Eghezée was designed to assist that movement by compelling the Belgians to carry out a general retirement westward.

The troops sent against Diest were a division of cavalry; a brigade made up of *jaeger* regiments, and a strong force of artillery. The total strength was probably some 26,000 men, more than half of them mounted. Of the cavalry one of the corps was the Death's Head Hussars. The force thrown forward to Eghezée was apparently a division, with strong cavalry support, and a fleet of motorcars carrying machine guns.

Neither attack accomplished its purpose. That directed against Diest proved disastrous. With every inhabitant a scout for the defending troops, it was impossible that, swift as its movement was, the column could take the Belgians by surprise. Most of the country the enemy passed through had been wasted, and was apparently deserted. Appearances, however, are in that respect not to be relied upon. Timely intimation was received in spite of all the precautions of German scouts, and when the column reached the village of Zelck both its strength was known and its objective accurately surmised.

The force divided for a simultaneous attack upon Diest and upon the village of Haelen three miles to the south-east. The Belgians had hastily got Haelen ready for a stout defence. They had loop-holed the houses, and had masked a battery of guns in an ancient fort commanding the main street. Seven hundred men held the position.

German cavalry tried to rush it. Mr. Wm. Maxwell, the special correspondent of the *Daily Telegraph*, in a graphic account of the affair, speaks of the headlong dash made by the German 17th Dragoons along the main street, and up the glacis of the fort, which they tried to mount on horseback. They were shot down from the houses, and from the fort at the same time, and left the street encumbered with dead and dying men and horses. As they retired they found their retreat cut off and 300 of the survivors remained in the hands of the victors as prisoners of war.

At Diest the like headlong tactics met with a similar fate. Evidently the Germans thought they had worked a surprise, and that impression was strengthened by their finding the bridge over the deep and sluggish Dyle still intact. The bridge had been left standing as a ruse. It was covered by well-hidden machine guns. When German horsemen tried to race across they were shot down in masses.

In this attack upon Diest the Death's Head Hussars maintained their tradition, but at an appalling cost. Only a comparative remnant of the corps returned alive. They lost the colours of the regiment, which were afterwards for a time hung in the ancient church as a trophy.

Despite the disaster to the cavalry the attack was fiercely pressed. At the height of the bombardment Lieut. van Donon, heading the men of the town fire brigade, crept round to a ditch from which they were enabled to enfilade a German battery, and shoot down the gunners.

As usual, the heaviest losses were sustained by the invaders during their retreat. Along the roads and across the fields south of Diest Belgian peasants found and buried some 2,800 German dead.

In this battle the Belgian force engaged was a cavalry division reinforced by a brigade of all arms. It was mainly on both sides a cavalry action, with the Belgian skill and resource in skirmishing pitted against that of the enemy.

At Eghezée the German attack was intended to break through the French cavalry. There, too, timely information had been received. At the critical moment the Germans found themselves suddenly assailed on flank by Belgian troops from Namur. The result was a severe repulse. Many of the motorcars, held up on the roads by troops in retreat, defending themselves against dashing charges of the French horse, had to be abandoned.

CHAPTER 5

The German Tidal Wave

Whether or not the operations just described had in the estimation of the German commanders fulfilled their purpose cannot be decided, but is at least open to doubt. Not only in the more serious fighting but in the numerous smaller skirmishes and unceasing affairs of outposts the losses to the invaders, were it really known, would probably appear surprising. The losses fell mainly upon their cavalry, and most of all upon their *uhlans*. A perfect cloud of these raiders had swarmed over the country, and had made themselves hated by acts of cruelty and pillage. They were most of all the agents of the Terror. Of the nineteen regiments of them in the German Army, some fourteen seem to have been employed in Belgium.

At the end of ten or twelve days the larger part of this force were either killed, wounded, or prisoners. No doubt can be entertained that they were turned out to live upon the country. They lived badly; were entrapped right and left; revenged themselves by acts of outrage; but waged against an enraged and unjustly ruined people what was in fact an impossible contest. The policy of sending out roving bands in a country as populous as northern Belgium was an absurdity.

Up to the point now reached the German campaign in Belgium had been one consistency of gross mistakes. Almost incalculable damage had been done; murder and rapine were rampant; but anything like a firm conquest, or the first steps towards it, was as far off as ever. It is notable that after his exploits in Belgium the *uhlan* fills a very minor part. Eastern Belgium had to no small extent become his grave.

So far the operations had enabled the Belgian army to inflict heavy losses while remaining itself intact. And now appeared a new factor—the advance of the French into Belgian Luxemburg. The Belgians still held Namur and the two bridges over the Meuse at that point. It was possible, since the Germans had seized Huy, that they would move in force upon Dinant, and, crossing the river above that place, attempt a diversion in the rear of the Belgian positions, in conjunction with a second effort to cut the Belgian Army off from its base at Antwerp.

To prevent this the French crossed the Meuse and occupied Dinant. By the time they arrived the anticipated German movement had already begun. In part the French advance was directed to feeling the strength and disposition of the enemy in the Ardennes with a view to their own plans, but it was also directed to assist the Belgians in holding up the hostile march westward.

The result of these opposing movements was, on August 15, a sharp collision. An effort on the part of the Germans to cross the river above Dinant was thrown back by the French. With a greatly superior force the Germans advanced against the town prepared to carry it by assault.

In describing the assault Mr. Granville Fortescue states that the Germans moved up a strong body of light infantry supported by mountain batteries. The French had established themselves on the outlying hills and in the ancient citadel, a rocky mass on the south bank of the Meuse, commanding from its summit a view of the river for many miles in either direction. The attack was determined and some of the outlying positions were carried by assault. French reinforcements, however, were brought up and the positions retaken.

In the town, defended by a French regiment of the line, barricades had been thrown across the streets. The bridge was fortified by wire entanglements, and held by an infantry detachment with a *mitrailleuse*.

The picturesque old place, sheltering under the high limestone cliffs on one side of the river, and struggling up the wooded hillside on the other, was subjected to a hot bombardment. As the shells tore through roofs and walls the inhabitants sought refuge in their cellars.

Following an obstinate fight, the Germans had won the crest of the cliffs above the old town, and under cover of a heavy artillery fire had stormed the citadel. The town and bridge, however, were still held. Further French reinforcements, with guns, cleared the Germans off the cliffs. From that position the French gunners in turn bombarded the citadel. One of their first shots cut through the flagstaff and brought down the German colour hoisted upon it.

Thus the first assault upon Dinant was beaten off, though not without serious casualties to the defending force. Renewing the attack next day with larger forces the Germans succeeded in gaining the town on the east bank of the river which here runs nearly north and south. The part of Dinant on the opposite bank remained in the hands of the defenders, who commanded the passage across the waterway.

In possession of the old town a resolute attempt was made by the enemy to force the passage. Two divisions of cavalry, one of them the cavalry of the Prussian Guard, 8,000 strong, with several battalions of *jaegers*, and maxim companies engaged in this operation. While infantry lined the positions on the east bank, and artillery opened a bombardment from the citadel and cliffs, the cavalry dashed across the bridge *en masse*, opening a way for the *jaegers*. In the steep streets and from behind garden walls in the new town an obstinate battle raged. It was determined by the onset of a division of French *chasseurs*, who drove the Germans in flight down to the margin of the river. The bridge became a mass of struggling fugitives, stumbling over fallen horses and men. To save themselves, those cut off threw themselves into the water. Many in the confusion were drowned.

From Namur the French remained masters of the west bank, and at Namur the Belgians still possessed an important bridge-head. The Allied forces too held their positions from Namur across the country through Gembloux and Louvain to beyond Diest. But behind this dyke opposed by the Allies the grey-green flood of invasion was steadily rising making ready to burst through, and with apparently irresistible mass and momentum to cover with its devastation the rich fields of Belgium and the fair land of France.

On the face of things it looked as though the enemy had been taught caution. In front of the Allied lines stretched a No-man's Land 10 to 15 miles in breadth. No Germans were met with nearer than Ramillies. In the intervening desolation, amid the hideous squalor of war, occasional terrified peasants, old men or widowed women, fled into hiding places at the distant approach of strangers, friend or foe.

Brussels had begun to regain breath. Though theatres, picture-houses, and other places of public entertainment were closed, and the busy traffic of the boulevards had shrunk to a rare and occasional vehicle, the shops, closely shuttered during the first days of the Terror, had reopened, and *cafés* were thronged with crowds eagerly debating the latest news.

When, on Monday, August 17, the government removed from Brussels to Antwerp, it was realised that grave events were impending. All had been in readiness for removal for some days. At the Palais de Justice the courts and registries were closed and seals placed on the doors. Measures had been taken for the protection of the nation's priceless art treasures, and to meet all emergencies. The government issued a reassuring proclamation, exhorting the public to confidence, and expressing the resolve at all costs to safeguard the country's freedom. Despite the deep anxiety of the moment, the public spirit remained firm. There was no trace either of disorder or of panic.

It was known that so long as the forts at Liége continued to fight the German advance could not begin. Notwithstanding the efforts of the Germans to cover their preparations with the closest veil of secrecy, the Belgian Government was kept well informed. Liége had become for its remaining inhabitants a prison. As a precaution the invaders had divided up the city by street barricades. Every approach to the place was closely patrolled. At night the only sounds were the heavy footfall of Prussian patrols, along streets where ruined houses showed the gaps made by shell fire, or over quays past bridges whose *débris* was heaped in the rivers. Many houses were doorless, but all were dark and silent. Nevertheless, news leaked through the German lines, and when on August 18, having silenced all but two of the forts, the German advance began, neither the Belgian Government nor the Belgian commanders were left in any uncertainty. The spirit and resource which had baffled all the energy of Spain, still baffled all the power of Prussianised Germany.

A strange spectacle was presented by that seemingly countless and endless host as it defiled along every main road leading to the northwest. No words can adequately picture the movement of an army, or rather a combination of armies, totalling nearly three-quarters of a million of men. The effect is too vast, and it might well be asked what human power could withstand such a multitude welded by an enormous labour of organisation into a machine of destruction and death. Onward it flowed, like the tide sweeping through the channels of a shore, ready to burst upon obstacles in angry breakers, but breakers of fire. Lines of lances moved among its forest of bayonets. Endless trains of guns and automobiles, field kitchens, field bakeries, huge wagons bearing pontoons and drawn by long teams of horses, ponderous caissons, camp equipment, portable smithies, rumbled successively past. The dust rose from the hot roads and floated over the deserted and trampled fields. Sabres and bayonets flashed back the August sunlight. And for hour after hour the mass rolled on, seemingly without end.

Not since the days of Attila has Western Europe been offered such a spectacle; nor has it been paralleled since the Gothic hordes rolled through the Alps on to the plain of northern Italy. The Goths were barbarians. These, their descendants, had the resources of civilisation, but applied to the same hopes and aspirations—dominion and the vision of material riches; inspired by the same belief in their own unconquerable prowess; impelled by the same conviction of their inborn right as the earth's most valiant to possess and to rule the sunny lands held by cowards and degenerates. It is a profound mistake to assume that the philosophy of a Treitschke is anything new. It is as ancient as Germany. Ever since the wild swamps, and sandy plains and gloomy forests of central Europe became the home of a prolific people, who win from them a hard and penurious livelihood, that people have dreamed of the countries to the west and south where the beauties of art speak of the resources of the soil, and where no dark and frozen winter binds the year.

Twelve army corps traversed the Belgian plain. A corps of the German army is made up on a war footing to 63,000 men. The total of this vast host could not therefore have been far short of 700,000 even allowing for losses. Commonly, an army corps is spoken of as though it were inconsiderable. An army corps, however, is a complete army, and a huge body of men.

Though it might look complex, and was indeed a triumph of machinery, the plan of the advance was simple. The right flank was covered by an overwhelming mass of cavalry. It was estimated that there were 65,000 out of the 83,000 sabres of the German Army in that truly formidable column. The rest advanced in three main columns heading for the roads between Brussels and Namur. It was the intention to push right on to the French frontier before the French could assemble there in sufficient strength to stem the onset. A host of this magnitude would take two days and a night to pass any given point. The distance between the van and the rear was half the breadth of Belgium.

One reason, it is now evident, for the German incursion into Limburg was a clearing of the country between Liége and Maastricht in order unobserved to muster their troops and transport for the great trek. The military situation immediately following the general advance was interesting. Probably it has given rise to more misunderstanding than any other phase of the war.

In the declaration, already alluded to, issued by the Belgian Government on its removal to Antwerp the statement was made that "pursuit of the aim assigned to the Belgian troops in the general plan of campaign predominates over everything. . . . What is going on at our gates is not the only thing to be thought of. A strategic movement conceived with a well-defined object is not of necessity a retreat. . . . There is at the present time no necessity for letting ourselves be hung up. To do so would be to play into the hands of the Germans."

Why pursuit of the aim assigned to the Belgian troops predominated has been pointed out. What was the strategic movement with a well-defined object?

In their dispositions for the advance the Germans had placed their main force of cavalry, and a great strength of mobile guns on their right in order that that wing might execute a rapid flank attack on the Belgian Army, and if possible envelop it. So far as was known the Belgian lines still extended from Diest through Aerschot and Louvain to Wavre. They certainly did until the night of August 17. But during that night they were rapidly and secretly changed. The left was extended eastward beyond Diest, and the right withdrawn so that the army in its new situation occupied entrenched positions along and behind the Dyle. In these positions it was well prepared successfully to resist a force vastly superior in numbers, and in any event was within easy distance of the outer forts of Antwerp.

To mask this change of front, a slight covering force was left at Louvain, and some cavalry was thrown forward for purposes of observation as far as Tirlemont.

On August 18, this cavalry came into contact with the *uhlans* forming the advanced front of the German columns. They promptly fell back towards Louvain, and after a show of opposition before that place retired upon Malines.

The Germans believed that Louvain was still held in force, and opened a bombardment. After their experience of Belgian ruses, they did not venture to enter the city until some hours later.

To the Belgians this gain in time was essential. Since it had been necessary to occupy the old lines until the last possible moment, the change of front had not been altogether completed when the rapidly moving right wing of the vast invading host threatened in part to frustrate it. An army with its impedimenta and guns cannot be transferred from place to place in a moment and one part of the Belgian force had a distance to cover of nearly 20 miles.

At all costs, therefore, it was necessary to hold up the German movement. That was not easy because the *uhlans* and armed motors spread themselves out along all the roads and by-roads in a broad fan-shaped formation covering many miles of country. Nevertheless, the stratagem at Louvain proved successful. Three regiments of infantry, a corps of guides and the 3rd and 9th, with a cavalry division deceived the enemy into the belief that they were the covering troops of a much larger force, and he drew up to deploy for battle. As was inevitable, the Belgian force employed suffered somewhat severe losses. It was indeed a devoted piece of service, but it served its purpose. When the Germans advanced in battle order against the assumed Belgian lines they found them deserted, and must have experienced some of the feeling of treading on a missing stair.

Beginning with outpost operations on August 18, the Battle of Louvain, as it has been called, was continued during August 19 and 20. On the one hand, there was the fighting between the Belgian troops already referred to, detailed to hold up the right of the German advance; on the other, there was an attempt by the Germans along the front from Diest to Aerschot to turn the left of the new Belgian position. Along the centre, to aid the attempted turning movement, a formidable artillery duel developed. The troops before Louvain, some 20,000 strong, carried out with brilliant gallantry the tactics most effective in such a situation. Retiring under all the cover available whenever the pressure of numbers became too threatening, they seized every opening afforded for a counter-attack, and by these alternative advances and retreats reduced the forward progress of the enemy to a minimum.

The Germans found themselves obliged to search every position with their artillery, before throwing forward their skirmishers, and finally advancing masses of infantry. With an intimate knowledge of the country the Belgians enticed them into the most difficult places, and then suddenly swept back and dislodged them. By the time reinforcements had been brought up, the enemy found the position evacuated.

So from hour to hour the struggle went on, along roads, through woods, behind hedges and ditches, with furious rushes and counter-rushes of infantry, and dashes of cavalry; the air filled with the puffs and smoke of bursting shrapnel, the boom of battle travelling slowly over the countryside like a laggard thunderstorm with its lightnings chained to earth. To what an extent skilful troops may arrest the advance of a hostile force enormously greater in numbers has been many times exemplified in warfare. The Germans employed their overwhelming superiority in cavalry and machine guns with the greatest energy. They had to deal, however, with elusive yet bold and persistent enemies. In this part of Belgium, the country is perfectly flat. There are no hillocks to assist observation. Information by airmen was rendered unreliable by the rapid movements of the Belgian forces. Literally the invaders had to grope their way, imagining that the main army was in front of them. Beyond the narrow horizon the danger lurked, but exactly where, it was hard to say.

The most serious effort on the part of the invaders was to throw a large force towards Antwerp. Against the strong position held by the Belgians and their change of front the effort failed. The assumed Belgian left wing had become its centre. Strongly posted as that now was with a deep river in front and a great fortress in the rear the position made an attack too costly to be pressed. Half at least of the whole mighty German host would have been necessary to force it. That, however, would have thrown the programme into confusion. The artillery duel went on from daylight to darkness, but the Belgians showed themselves unshakable. All the efforts of the invaders to throw troops over the Dyle were beaten off with heavy loss. Finally, the Germans were compelled to pass on, leaving the Belgian main army a still unbeaten menace.

The military considerations which dictated the Belgian strategy may be readily made clear. Since the base of the army was Antwerp, where it had all its supplies and munitions, the first essential was not to be cut off from that base. An army defending its native country, and among its own people may, so far as foodstuffs are concerned, be said to be at home anywhere, but it cannot in modern warfare fight without shells and bullets, and when those it brings with it are exhausted its power as a present-day fighting force is at an end. No army can encumber itself in the field with more than the munitions it immediately needs. It has consequently to keep in touch with its reserve stocks, or, in military phrase, to keep its line of communications open.

That to a general in command is as important as victory. Indeed, a victory gained if it left the communications cut would be illusory.

A second consideration, not less essential, is that of not fighting in such a position that, in the event of being compelled to retire, the army, in order to save its communications, must pass across the front of the victorious force. Irreparable defeat would almost certainly be the result. Fighting in a situation of that kind is known as fighting with the front of the army turned to what should be its flank, or in military phraseology is a "front to a flank" position. It is one of the purposes of strategy to manoeuvre a hostile force into such a position whenever possible.

As the Belgian Army was disposed up to August 17, it stood "front to a flank," and if it had fought in that situation it must, owing to its inferior numbers, have been surrounded, or been compelled to fall back upon or beyond Brussels, so that its communications with Antwerp would have been cut off. It must consequently, whatever the bravery of its officers and men, have been compelled in a few days either to lay down its arms or to be annihilated.

Possibly the Germans thought that it meant to remain where it was for the purpose of covering Brussels, and that sentimental rather than military reasons influenced its movements. As a fact, this seeming incompetence was a ruse, designed to induce the Germans to throw their main force forward in the direction of Brussels rather than in the direction of Antwerp. The latter place, if they had been ably commanded, would have been made their first objective. Seizure of Antwerp would have settled the business. They fell, however, blindly into the trap laid for them, and blundered on towards Brussels only to discover, too late, that they had been left with the shadow, but had lost the substance.

In any event, for the Belgians, save in a position of complete security to have offered battle to an army more than six times as numerous, with a crushing superiority of some 2,000 guns would simply have been throwing the lives of brave men away to no purpose. Decidedly the King of the Belgians was not the man to "play into the hands of the Germans."

CHAPTER 6

The Germans in Brussels

From August 17 to August 21 were days of intense suspense in Brussels. Dr. E. J. Dillon has drawn a picture of them sober yet arresting and faithful. Naturally, after the removal of the government, there was a feeling that the city was on the eve of grave events. Amid the public anxiety the *burgomaster*, M. Adolphe Max, showed the evidences of that civic spirit and unfaltering firmness, worthy of the greatest years in the old struggle for freedom, which later made him the hero of his fellow-citizens.

Emotions changed from hour to hour, but when the Civic Guard left for the front, amid demonstrations of patriotic fervour, it was the common belief that the forces of Belgium might successfully keep off the enemy, at any rate until aid arrived. Barricades were built across the streets, and lines of trenches thrown up. Brussels resigned itself to the prospect of a siege.

Little did the crowds who discussed these events know of the real purpose of them. Under present-day conditions of warfare Brussels is wholly indefensible. It lies for the most part in a hollow commanded by hills from which long-range guns could destroy it without the possibility of effective reply.

The object of the apparent preparations for a siege was to mislead, not the citizens of Brussels, but the foe who had trampled on the nation's rights. The government and the authorities in Brussels were well aware of the enemy's swarm of spies in their midst. They were not ignorant that their every movement was forthwith betrayed. A wireless installation discovered on the building lately occupied by the German Ministry had been unearthed and dismantled, but there were still, doubtless, secret channels of communication open. Rightly concluding that German plans would be adjusted to this information, they met ruse with ruse. The enemy was to be led on to an empty and merely theatrical triumph.

Of course, the ordinary citizen, not in the secret, took the siege preparations at their face value. The German advance was evidenced, apart from reports and rumours, by the crowds of homeless fugitives, who like flotsam driven before a storm, tramped into the city footsore, weary, and miserable, their few belongings, hastily snatched together, carried on their backs, or piled on the light carts drawn by dogs. At first in bands, the inflow swelled until these pitiful processions filled every eastern and south-eastern road; and soon the railway stations were crowded by people struggling for trains to the coast.

Then came ambulances and trains of wounded. On the night of Thursday, August 20, Brussels did not go to bed. News arrived in the early hours that the Germans were close upon the city. From their posts in the Forest of Soignies, the Civic Guard marched in. It became known that they had been ordered to Ghent, and that the capital was to be surrendered without firing a shot.

The public at large were stunned, and their astonishment was without doubt shared, not in Belgium only, but abroad. Undaunted by the turn of events, the 20,000 men of the Civic Guard passed through the streets *en route* for Ghent intoning the "*Marseillaise*" in a thunderous chorus. Meanwhile those responsible wisely kept their counsel. The proclamation that the military evacuation was a measure necessary for the well-being of Brussels itself and of the country was, with judicious suppression as to reasons, the truth.

The public, of course, did not realise the military situation. All they for the moment grasped was the peril of an occupation by troops whose atrocities had been marked by a trail of burned-out villages and slaughtered peasantry. The crowds of fugitives from the country into Brussels were speedily swelled by yet even greater crowds out of the city. The roads to Ghent became thronged with refugees. Afoot and in every sort of vehicle, they fled from the on-coming Terror, the darkness relieved only by distant glares which told of villages in flames, and the fear sharpened by the sullen boom of far-off guns. Meanwhile, in Brussels, the effort of the large non-resident population to get out while the way was yet open assumed the aspect of a panic.

The first care of the authorities was, of necessity, to remove the wounded, who had been placed, not only in hospitals, but in large stores turned for the time being into hospitals. This, of course, taxed the railway accommodation. It was necessary, too, that no rolling stock should fall into the hands of the invaders. Trains available were therefore limited. Would-be passengers fought their way with cries and curses into the compartments until these were choked with people all in a state of excitement or dread. Every train, even the last, left hundreds of the terror-stricken behind.

It would be untrue, however, to assume that these refugees represented the spirit or feeling of the population of Brussels as a whole. The first shock passed, the population awaited developments without any marked signs of dismay.

German cavalry reached Teuveren, a suburb of Brussels, about six o'clock that morning. The street barricades were hastily removed by the city authorities. Those had served their turn and were no longer wanted. The invaders' formal entry took place at two in the afternoon. The clatter and jingle of heavy dragoons through deserted suburban streets, where the houses had been closely shuttered, announced that Brussels was in the power of the Prussians. The dragoons were the head of a column of infantry. These dauntless warriors had waited nearly eight hours in order to make sure that the "contemptible" Belgian military had in fact withdrawn.

Very soon the fact became evident that the entry had been carefully stage-managed in order to render it as "impressive" as possible. Some 50,000 of the smartest and freshest troops were paraded across the city. This display, which occupied some hours, was intended to convince the Bruxellois of the utter futility of Belgian resistance. With many of the population curiosity prevailed over repugnance, and they stood in throngs along the boulevards while the show went by. Seeing this impassive but orderly multitude, and doubtless convinced that the conquest of Belgium had already been accomplished as the first fruits of the war, the troops, by permission, struck up "*Deutschland über Alles*." In the fighting during the earlier days of the campaign the German troops, despite the plundering of the territory they had overrun, were in a half-famished state, and the horses of their cavalry, in particular, perishing of hunger and fatigue. Many prisoners were picked up in the last state of exhaustion. They might readily have been murdered by the enraged peasantry, but it is doubtful if there is even one clearly proved instance of a German having been assassinated under such circumstances.

The forces, however, now paraded bore few of the traces of warfare, a proof to the spectators that the Belgian operations were on paper! An incident recorded is that of several officers who rode in a motor-car. The group, apparently part of a divisional staff, called for a newspaper, and on reading the news broke out into ostentatious laughter. At selected points the troops, on a whistle being sounded, fell into the parade or "goose" step. Decidedly, the Bruxellois ought to be impressed. What resistance could avail against such instantaneous discipline?

In truth, the discipline was rather on the side of the spectators than of the performers. A proclamation by M. Max had enjoined a scrupulous avoidance of acts of insult or violence. The injunction was implicitly obeyed. Though, like every great city, Brussels had its irresponsible elements, such was the influence and authority of its burgomaster, and the esteem in which he was justly held, that his requisition was taken by every inhabitant as a personal obligation. The Germans imagined that this remarkable effect arose from their show of mechanical and material power. It was, on the contrary, a marvel of moral force.

The occupation, or more strictly the seizure, of the city was carried out methodically, and had manifestly, like the rest of the German arrangements, long been cut and dried. Detachments of troops took possession of the post and telephone offices of the railways stations; of the public buildings; and of the barracks. At the Palais de Justice the doors were broken open, and the building turned into a military quarters. Brussels was cut off from communication with the outside world, Germany excepted. Guards were placed along the roads leading from it, and no person was allowed to pass without a military permit. On the great open space in front of the Palais de Justice heavy guns were ranged so that they could command the greater part of the lower town. From this space, as everyone familiar with Brussels knows, the city, a picture of the multitudinous beauty of roofs and streets and towers, can be seen stretching away across the broad valley of the Senne.

One of the first measures taken by General von Arnim, the German commandant, was to summon the *burgomaster* and the members of the civic council, and to inform them that they must consider themselves hostages for the good behaviour of the citizens. A long list of the wealthiest citizens proved to be in the possession of the invaders, and opposite each name the approximate total of the person's fortune. Such was one of the effects of the spy system. Opposite each name, too, was the amount which it was proposed to exact.

The *burgomaster* was told that the city must pay a war "fine" of £8,000,000, and that he must see to it that the sum was forthcoming promptly and in cash. He was also told that he would be looked to for the German soldiery being treated by Brussels citizens with proper respect. The police of the city would be left under his direction, subject, of course, to orders from the new authorities.

M. Max replied that a payment of £8,000,000 as demanded was out of the question. All the cash from the banks had been removed. In any event, if the levy was fairly assessed it must take time to collect. Hence at best it could only be paid by instalments. He added that measures had already been taken for the maintenance of public order, and that the occupying troops would meet with no molestation if they on their part behaved properly to the public. If he and the city council were to be responsible the civic rights and the persons and property of citizens must be respected.

The reply was that all this must be dependent on the amount of the fine being found somehow.

While this interview was in progress at the offices lately evacuated by the government where the "conquerors" had installed themselves, arrangements were being made for billeting some thousands of officers, who promptly took possession of the hotels, where, with the arrogant air of superiority which marks off the Prussian military caste, they proceeded to regale themselves without payment, adding to these acts of petty brigandage in many cases gross insults if their demands could not be complied with. Others were quartered on private families. During the evening of the first day of the occupation they sat at open windows or outside *cafés* on the *boulevards*, and refreshed with food and liquor beyond the dreams of their own exiguous commissariat, indulged in mocking observations on the manners and ways of citizens, who in the qualities of dignity, courtesy, and restraint offered an example which *"kultur"* had left the Prussian intruders unable to copy.

As for the troops not needed for garrison duty, they had been marched to an encampment to the north-west of the city. The delights of conquest were reserved for the officers. It was enough for the men that they shared the honour of its fatigues.

Two days later arrived from Berlin General von der Goltz who, it was announced, had been appointed civil governor of Belgium. This superannuated worthy brought with him instructions for more "fines," including the *modest* requisition of £18,000,000 from the province of Brabant.

It may be doubted whether the world, outside Germany, did not receive the news of the levy upon Brussels with even greater laughter than indignation. The preposterous character of the demand was only exceeded by its impudence. But the new viceroy of Belgium, like his employers, took himself seriously. Having installed himself with due ceremony in the royal palace, he proceeded to tackle the knotty business of converting the phantom £10 a head for every man, woman, and child into solid sinews of war.

There was no sign of the money making its appearance. The *burgomaster* was sent for and carpeted for his remissness. He intimated with polite sarcasm that if the new "government" could discover a better way of collecting the fine they did not need his assistance. General von der Goltz agreed to accept payments by instalments. Hints were thrown out that if the instalments were not paid it would be the worse for Brussels. The "government" would not stand on ceremony.

Nevertheless, the instalments were not forthcoming. After huge worry and effort, all that could be extracted was £800,000. The policy of making Belgium pay for its own subjugation, brilliant in theory, threatened in practice to become a comedy.

This was not the only light touch. A colleague of von der Goltz, General von Luttwitz, had been appointed military governor of Belgium. He signalised his arrival by a pompous proclamation in which, after the manner of the 4,000 or more police by-laws of Berlin, he forbade the citizens to do a variety of things, and strictly enjoined them on pain of instant arrest and trial by court martial to do a variety of others.

The public read the proclamation with ridicule. Since it was both an interference with the rights of the civic council as the police authority, and likely to provoke mischief by its blundering foolishness, the *burgomaster*, in the interests of public order and security, issued a counter-proclamation reassuring citizens of the endeavours for their protection, and enjoining pacific conduct and restraint. The *burgomaster's* announcement, not having been submitted and passed in the first instance, was considered a defiance. German soldiers were sent out as billstickers with sheets of blank paper to cover it over. During the following night the blank paper was found to have been oiled, and made transparent. This produced a threat that if such a trick was repeated the police would be disbanded and replaced by the military.

As lacking in any sense of proportion was the hurry to Germanise the Press. The Brussels newspapers, laid under a strict censorship, were forbidden to publish any save Berlin-provided war news, and to publish it in German. Henceforth the Brussels public were to hear of nothing save German victories. The newspapers declined to comply and were suppressed. To supply the lack of news the authorities established an official organ printed in the now official language. There was no demand, and the government and garrison alone enjoyed the pleasure afforded by its cultured and exciting contents. The Brussels public preferred to remain in unofficial darkness.

Familiarity with the "conquerors" rapidly bred in the population of the city a general contempt. It was speedily found out that their political incapacity was only paralleled by their assumption. Despite the elaborate imported machinery of government their authority remained a shadow. The passive resistance of the public was "correct," but annoying. When processions of street boys, each in an old hat with the end of a carrot pushed through the crown, played at German soldiers and gave comic imitations of the goose step and the words of command—a diversion General von Luttwitz had somehow forgotten to catalogue as *"verboten"*—the military government of Belgium felt itself drifting into a false position.

It was decided that the soul of the opposition was the *burgomaster*. Inevitably in the situation there was much distress arising from unemployment. The commerce of the city was at a standstill. M. Max, aided by other public-spirited citizens, worked with energy to organise relief. Brussels was divided into a score or so of districts, so that the most necessitous could be dealt with. The citizens had realised that by following the *burgomaster's* wise counsels, refraining from provocation on their own part, ignoring it on the part of their oppressors, they were serving their country as effectively as if they were on the battlefield. Indeed Brussels had become a battlefield—a moral battlefield on which the defeat of the foe was complete. On that battlefield in the dark days of the past the citizens of Brussels had won signal victory. Dark days had come again, and they were drawn together under the man raised up in the hour of need.

Whatever the show of power made by the combined civil and military governments of Belgium, the real ruler was the *burgomaster*, and the civil and military governments knew it. They tolerated him partly because it assisted public order, but mostly because he was considered indispensable in collecting the expected war fine. The latter was dribbling in very slowly. Requisitions of supplies for the German troops were "paid for" in vouchers to be met out of the tribute—when received. Citizens shrewdly suspected, however, that, like other Prussian promises, these were of little value. This system of plunder of necessity aggravated the distress, and all the more because similar seizures were going on in the smaller towns. Every day in face of greater secrecy on the part of the population the collection of supplies became more difficult. General von Luttwitz was at his wits' end.

Bold measures were resolved upon. The troops in occupation showed signs of becoming demoralised. Quarrels broke out in barracks between contingents of Prussians and Bavarians. As co-religionists of the Belgians, the latter were suspected of being sympathetic to the Brussels people. The old standing hatred of the Bavarians towards Prussia, and the equally old-standing contempt of the Prussians for all other Germans in general and for Bavarians in particular, led to free fights in which bayonets were used. Some of the combatants lost their lives. The military government decidedly had its hands full.

It endeavoured to show its authority by insisting on the presence of a representative at the meetings of the City Council. There was a suspicion that these meetings were in fact occupied with proposals to subvert it, and evade payment of the fine. The indomitable *burgomaster* declared that if the new civil or the new military government intruded no more meetings would be held. The civil and military governments were obliged to give way.

By way of reprisal, they insisted that the £1,200,000 still owing out of the first £2,000,000 of the war fine should be paid up by a given date. The *burgomaster* and council replied that the demand was an impossible one. The new "authorities" were peremptory. The council met them with a flat refusal. On receipt of it the *burgomaster* was sent for by the military governor. He did not return, and in fact had been arrested. The council were informed that payment of the £1,200,000 was the condition of his release.

Forthwith on the walls and kiosks the public read over the signature of the military governor the following proclamation:—

To the people of Brussels!
I have the honour to make it known that I have found myself obliged to suspend Burgomaster Max from his office on account of his unserviceable behaviour. He is now in honourable custody in a fortress.
The German Government ordered the payment of all military requisition vouchers in the supposition that the town would pay the war tribute voluntarily. Only on this condition were

special terms conceded to Brussels, whereas in other towns requisition vouchers will be paid after the conclusion of peace. As the Brussels municipality refuses to pay the remainder of the tribute, no further requisition vouchers will be paid by the German Government.

The device which had been relied upon to cajole the public into the belief that the requisitions were being bought and not stolen had broken down, and the proclamation was nothing more than a confession of its failure. Henceforth the robbery must be crude and unashamed. As crude were the threats of outrage which the *competent* von Luttwitz indulged in. Summoning the aldermen into his presence and requiring them to elect another *burgomaster*, he found that the spirit of M. Adolphe Max, the ancient spirit of the Netherlands, was not to be destroyed by arrests. The aldermen firmly refused compliance. They were threatened with a German *burgomaster* and German military patrols in place of the police, and told that if riots broke out Brussels would be bombarded and burned. Riots, as the aldermen knew, might readily be provoked for that purpose. Tension in face of the *burgomaster's* arrest was already acute. In these circumstances M. Maurice Lemonnier undertook with his colleagues the maintenance of public order, but the flat for the election of a successor to M. Max remained unfulfilled.

Thus would-be conquerors of Europe in the face of unarmed citizens offered the world a proof of their inborn incapacity to rule, and themselves exposed the folly of their aspirations.

M. Max, it was afterwards learned, had been put under confinement in the fortress of Wesel in Germany.

CHAPTER 7

The Final Hack

From Brussels by road to Mons is less than 40 miles; from Liége to Charleroi in the valley of the Sambre little more than 50. It is clear now that while one part of the great invading host took the direct route from Liége towards the Sambre, the other made a detour by way of Brussels to meet the Belgian army. The object was to strike towards the three great international roads running to Paris from Belgium. The most westerly of these great routes passes from Brussels through Mons and Valenciennes; the next through Charleroi and the French frontier fortress of Maubeuge; the third along the valley of the Meuse through Namur, past Dinant, and away to Laon. These brief facts on the topography of the country will help to explain the military operations. Briefly, if we imagine the march by way of Brussels as a bow, and the march direct from Liége as its string, we shall have a rough but in mind only that even the parts of a host of this magnitude, though the rear would be nearly two days' march behind the van, would each be pouring at once along adjacent roads leading in the same direction.

In any event, and quite apart from any opposition offered by the Belgians, with the delay resulting from it, the detour by way of Brussels involved an additional two days at least. But the fighting with the Belgians caused a further three days' delay. Of those days, two, certainly, were occupied in the battle, and the third in resting the troops engaged and in burying the dead. It was not, therefore, until August 23, five days after the start from Liége, that the forces, in fact, concentrated at the opposite end of the bow in southern Belgium.

Only a small part of them, as we have seen, passed through Brussels. The main body, even of the northern division, marched through Tirlemont and on to Hal, round the south of the capital. At the same time, the enormous column of cavalry, acting as a screen, rode round by the north of the city and then struck south through Enghien.

All the military display at Brussels was relatively but an aside to the main performance, intended both for moral effect, such as it was, and to throw dust in the eyes of the enemy.

We have therefore to imagine between August 21 and August 23 these great, and, from their size, inevitably unwieldy, forces concentrating towards the southern frontier of Belgium by every road available.

Here another brief note on geography is necessary. Eastern Belgium, or that part of it between the Meuse and the sea, is nearly all perfectly flat, and almost purely agricultural, and the invaders had there marched through a country which, before they laid it waste, was a habitation of industry and peace rejoicing in the bounties of harvest.

But western Belgium is largely a manufacturing country, though still marked by rich rural beauty. Even the main Belgian coalfield extending through the provinces of Hainault and West Flanders presents outwardly few of those evidences of utilitarian squalor commonly associated with coal and iron. The centre of the coal and iron industries of Western Belgium is Mons, a quaint old place built upon a hill rising amid a country thickly intersected by canals and railways. Looking east from Mons, we are looking down the valley of the Sambre, on each side low rolling hills, the sides and crests of which are in part clothed with woods and plantations. These hills are, so to say, the outworks of the Ardennes, one of the natural show-places of Europe. Fifteen miles from Mons, and on the north bank of the Sambre, is the town of Charleroi. Fifteen miles farther, at the juncture of the Sambre with the Meuse, rises the rocky mass forming the ancient citadel of Namur. The Sambre is not a wide stream, but is swift, its course alternating between rapids and deep pools. It is most passable, in the military sense, about ten miles west of Namur. Just there the river follows a succession of sharp bends.

Of the huge land Armada now moving south through this busy and populous but beautiful country, most people think as being in every sense a modern European army. But it was not. There were surgeons with it, but no field hospitals. It had encumbered itself with no tents. There was all the grim apparatus of modern war, but only the least possible of modern war's humane apparatus. It was the intention of those who could to quarter themselves on the population of the country through which the host passed to supplement food supplies by eating up the country's resources. The mass of the invaders slept, where other shelter was not to be had, in the fields. These hardships sharpened the lust of conquest. At the rear of the host trudged battalions of gravediggers. But they were to dig the graves of those who would dare to stand against it.

The comparative poverty and the native parsimony of the Prussians was reflected in these arrangements. Their all had been invested in artillery and instruments of death because the leaders of the host were sure of victory. What else they needed when winter came would be provided from the spoil of the conquered. In appearance a modern army, it presented essential features in common with the migrations of Huns and Goths, which form in Europe the history of the early Middle Ages. Under a modern disguise, it was a similar horde. It is easy, therefore, to estimate the rage and surprise which thwarted hopes, wounded pride, and heavy losses had produced in Belgium, and why there was behind it a land of mourning and blood.

We now come to the military movements. The 5th French Army and two divisions had advanced and had occupied the angle of country between the Meuse and the Sambre, and held the passages over both rivers; the British line was taken up behind the canal which runs from Condé on the west of Mons to Binche on the east. Mons lay somewhat in advance of the position, and occupied by the British 3rd division commanded by General Hamilton, formed an outward angle, or, in military terms, a salient.

The 5th British cavalry division under General Sir Philip Chetwode had been sent forward to reconnoitre. Part of the force had, on August 22, advanced as far as the forest of Soignies, close to Brussels. In face of the cavalry covering the German advance they had fallen back. Similar reconnaissances were made by the French cavalry round Gembloux to the north of Namur. Hence during the German advance southward from Brussels and westward of Namur the hostile forces were in touch with each other.

An interesting episode, characteristic of the scouting tactics of the Germans, is related by Mr. A. Beaumont, the special correspondent of the *Daily Telegraph*, who was at the time in Charleroi:—

> On my return to Charleroi I learnt that a detachment of twenty Hussars of the Death's Head, led by an officer, had entered the upper town at seven in the morning. They proceeded towards the Sambre, and quietly said, "Good-morning" to the people at

the doors. *"Bon jour, bon jour,"* they said to the housewives, who were looking on in wonder, and who, mistaking their khaki uniform, took them for English soldiers.

People even enthusiastically raised cheers for England. The soldiers, also misled, allowed them to pass. An officer finally saw them from a window, and rushed down to a detachment on guard in the Rue Pont Neuf, and gave the alarm. A number of infantry soldiers at once opened fire on them. It was at the corner of the Rue De Montigny, where the tramway and railway lines pass.

Three of the intruders were shot down. The rest, with their officer, took to flight. It was not believed that such a thing would be possible, but it proved that the Germans are capable of anything. They did the same thing many a time in 1870.

Apart from cavalry skirmishes, the fighting began on August 22, when the Germans attacked the passages over the Sambre about 10 miles to the west of Namur, already alluded to. Here reference may be made to a ruse on their part which explains the peculiarity of their movement across Belgium. The southern contingent was hurried into action evidently in order to lead the Allies to believe that it formed the bulk of the German force. After the Allies had made their dispositions to resist on that footing, the northern contingent was unexpectedly to appear, and to finish and win the battle by the weight of its forces.

While the fighting was going on for the passages of the Sambre, another part of the southern contingent, which was formed by the army apparently of General von Bülow, moved on to attack Charleroi, and yet another part, an army corps and a cavalry division, appeared before Mons.

The opening attack upon Mons, however, was what, in common parlance, is called a "blind," intended to screen the advance behind it of the northern contingent, the army of General von Kluck, consisting of the pick of the Prussian troops.

For it is known now that that commander had marched south from Brussels having in his pocket an Army Order issued by the German emperor from headquarters at Aix-la-Chapelle, under date August 19, which contained the following passage:—

> It is my royal and imperial command that you concentrate your energies for the immediate present upon one single purpose, and that is that you address all your skill and all the valour of

my soldiers to exterminate first the treacherous English and to walk over General French's contemptible[1] army.

What happened, therefore, on the arrival of these troops on that Sunday, August 23, was, briefly told, this. While the British troops holding Mons were resisting the opening attack on that place, an attack they readily defeated, the onslaught suddenly developed in great weight and fury. In face of it, the necessity arose of withdrawing the troops forming the British salient into line with the rest of the army.

This, in the face of such an attack by overwhelming numbers, was a most difficult and dangerous operation. It was carried out, however, with remarkable coolness and courage. Though the British suffered heavy losses, the masses thrown up against them failed to break their formations.

The attack thereupon developed all along the British line. Throughout that day, and far into the succeeding night, the German officers and men did their utmost faithfully to carry out the royal and imperial orders, and it is not too much to say that German arrogance met with the sharpest shock it had until then experienced. In the front of the British positions German dead lay in masses, and, after their custom, they left their wounded for the most part to perish. The unerring marksmanship of the British infantry was as unexpected as it was deadly; unshaken by the terrific artillery fire, the British troops met the attacks thrown upon then in mass formation with a withering hail of lead. Where, with an intensity of contempt and hate the onslaught succeeded momentarily in getting close in, the British dashed into it with the bayonet, and "the valour of my soldiers" wilted under the slaughter. Again and again the German rank and file were led or driven by their officers upon the British positions, again and again to be ripped into bloody confusion. They had come up against the unconquerable.

While these events were in progress, word was received of a formidable German turning movement in the direction of Tournai, held by a body of French troops of the second line. This made advisable a retirement of the British to the rear. Thanks alike to the rock-like steadiness combined with the inbred tenacity of the infantry, the heavy hitting power of the artillery, and not least the dauntless devotion of the cavalry, who faced and broke the heavy odds of the German horse, the

---

1. *Contemptible* by Casualty-A personal recollection of the 'Retreat From Mons' by a British Infantry officer is also published by Leonaur.

movement was successfully accomplished.

It is not the purpose here to tell the story of the British retreat from Mons. That feat of arms is related in another volume of this series. All that comes within present scope is to glance briefly over the other happenings of these eventful days along that line of battle.

Although in the struggle for the passages of the Sambre the Germans on the night of August 22 had succeeded in throwing troops across, they were long and heavily punished by the French artillery, which now, for the first time, clearly demonstrated the superiority destined to have so marked an effect during the war. The French field gun was a new type of weapon, better than the German alike in rapidity and accuracy of fire. Its more perfect rifling gave a higher muzzle velocity and a flatter trajectory; the melinite shells used were of intense explosive force, and the French gunners handled their guns with skill. A larger proportion of the German artillery consisted of guns of, as it proved, a relatively out-of-date type, retained and "converted," apparently, from motives of economy.

Crossing a river in the face of an enemy so supported is a costly business, as the Germans soon discovered. With their heavy advantage in numbers, and with at least four points of simultaneous attack strongly in their favour, they should have been across in very little time. They were held at bay for many hours, and repeatedly driven back by French charges. Only at length under cover of darkness were they able to grain a footing on the south bank.

Meanwhile, the assault was being pressed against Charleroi, and here was the centre and decisive point. The French held the place against repeated attacks, until the regiments of the Prussian Guard, always held in reserve for critical operations, and reputed invincible, were brought up against it. There are 20 regiments of the guard, each 3,000 strong. The French were driven out. In turn they launched against the town the infantry of their African Army Corps, the not less famous Zouaves and Turcos; and that Sunday afternoon witnessed one of the most terrible bayonet fights in the history of Europe, a fight in which the little Belgian town and its environs became a hell. Amid a cannonade too appalling for description men fought through its streets until the ways were heaped with dying and dead. Charleroi was set on fire by shells, but the combat, which knew no truce, went on amid blazing buildings and collapsing walls. It was a combat of men turned devils.

The town was taken and retaken. At the finish it remained in the hands of the invaders, but thousands of the flower of their army lay amid and around its ruins.

The Battle of Mons and Charleroi was a Pyrrhic victory. One decisive advantage, however, on that day the invaders had won. They had captured the fortress of Namur.

After the heroic defence of Liége the rapid fall of Namur formed one of the surprises of the campaign. The fortress was held by a Belgian garrison of some 26,000 men, and well provisioned. Though so far as natural situation goes a strong place, surrounded by a ring of four larger and five smaller forts, in which the guns were protected by armoured turrets of a type similar to those at Liége, it had some serious weak spots.

As secretly as possible and during the night-time the Germans had transported from Liége batteries of their huge howitzers, and had planted these on already prepared beds of concrete in positions beyond the range of the fortress artillery. It had been decided to renew the ordnance of the forts, and the guns had been ordered, according to report, though this lacks authority, from Germany. At all events the newer and heavier ordnance was not there. It may here be explained that an attack is rarely or never made upon a hostile fortress without the general in command of the attack and his principal officers being put into possession of plans of the works. These plans, the result of espionage, show every detail, and afford every particular; disclose every trench, entanglement, and obstacle, every building, wireless instalment, or line of telegraph and telephone wire. The exact range and power of every gun is stated. Between the field of fire of the guns there are spaces, known technically as "dead points," left uncovered, or at all events, the facts being disclosed, such dispositions for attack as will create "dead points" are readily made by drawing the fire of the forts in particular directions.

Now the defence of Liége was successful because the entrenchments and obstacles in the sectors between the forts were made when their details could not be disclosed to the enemy. But Namur had been prepared about the same time, and there was ample opportunity to discover the particulars.

All the Germans therefore had to do was to wait for the first autumn mist among the hills to open fire from guns whose position the defence did not know. To the attack the "laying" of such guns to hit any desired object in the fortress was, with the plans in their possession, a mere matter of mathematical calculation. Under cover of such a mist, the forts being unable to reply, to knock some of them to pieces by a heavily concentrated fire, and after that to stalk the place was comparatively easy. The garrison were aware that the fortress was untenable, or only to be held by meeting the attack by a counter-attack. Following a terrific two days' bombardment, during which two of the forts were demolished, the assault was launched on the afternoon of August 23. The garrison after a short resistance against great odds were driven out. The mist which had favoured the attack equally favoured their escape. They found their way fortunately into the French lines. (See note following).

Note:—A story published at Berlin gives the account sent in a letter from Lieu. von der Linde, of the Potsdam Guards, of how he carried out the capture of Fort Malonne at Namur. The lieutenant states that he was ordered to advance on the fort with 500 men by a route where mines were suspected. He advanced with four men on the bridge across the moat of the fort, and called upon the commander to surrender immediately, threatening him that otherwise the artillery would at once begin to bombard the fort. The commander, taken by surprise, allowed the lieutenant and his four men to enter and surrendered his sword.

Besides the commander, five officers and twenty men were taken prisoners. The remainder of the garrison, consisting of 400 men, had escaped. Four heavy guns and considerable war material were captured. For this exploit Lieut. von der Linde received from the *Kaiser* the Order of Merit, and it is recorded that he was the youngest officer in the German service to receive that distinction. He was only twenty-two. No reference is made in this account to the mist and rain which alone could have made such an adventure possible, much less successful. The story illustrates the difficulty of defending, under the conditions described, a fortress situated among hills, and also the facilities offered for escape.

CHAPTER 8

The Crime of Louvain

On August 20, the day before the formal entry of the German forces into Brussels, the Belgians had evacuated Malines. It was deemed prudent, as in fact it was, to withdraw the forces to the line of the outer forts of Antwerp. Some of the most violent fighting on August 19 and 20 had taken place 16 miles to the south-east of Antwerp at Aerschot. There the Germans had made their determined, but unsuccessful, effort to cross the Dyle.

Once in occupation of Brussels, they turned Malines into the headquarters of the troops, an army corps some 60,000 strong, told off to "mask" Antwerp by keeping the Belgian army if possible cooped up within the fortress. Malines lies exactly halfway between Antwerp and Brussels, about 12 miles from either city. It is, however, not more than half a mile from the outer ring of the Antwerp fortifications. The value of such a watch-tower to the Germans is manifest. No movement could possibly be made by the Belgians from Antwerp without the invaders knowing of it.

No sooner, however, had the march of the German main forces southward from Brussels begun, than the Belgians sallied forth. They were well-informed of the enemy's movements, and were fully aware that, acting in conjunction with the contingent moving from Liége direct to the Sambre, that moving by way of Brussels could not in any event turn back.

This sortie, made so soon—it took place on August 23—took the German troops in Malines by surprise. They were just beginning to make themselves comfortable after their fatigues, when the Belgian army burst in upon them. No effectual resistance was possible. The invaders were driven, a battered rout, as far as Vilvorde, a northern suburb of Brussels. There most of the 10,000 German troops forming the garrison of Brussels were drawn up to cover the retreat. Malines remained in the hands of the Belgians.

Realising from this defeat that they had a tough proposition in front of them, the Germans hurried additional troops into the country. Meanwhile the Belgians had again seized Aerschot, Termonde and Alost. The German force threatening Ghent had to be withdrawn, and the invaders found themselves in danger of being cooped up in the capital.

This situation throws light on the atrocities which almost immediately followed, and on the question of whether these atrocities were accidents of hasty indiscipline or were, in fact, military measures carried out according to a settled plan.

A glance at the map of Belgium will show that the towns of Jodoigne, Louvain, Malines, Termonde, and Alost form round Brussels an arc, rather more than a semi-circle. The middle point of that arc is the point nearest to Antwerp, that is to say, Malines.

Now these towns as well as Aerschot were destroyed with the exceptions of Malines and Alost. Though Malines was three times severely bombarded by the Germans, and in the succeeding struggles changed hands as many times over, it was, while deplorably damaged, not destroyed. Neither was Alost. Why? Because Malines was needed as a *point d'appui* against Antwerp, and Alost as a halfway position on the road to Ghent. Alost was also the scene of repeated struggles. It is beyond argument to suggest that this destruction of some places and not of others can have been haphazard.

When we look further into the military situation the question passes beyond all doubt. Entrenched at Antwerp the as yet undefeated Belgian main army remained a serious menace. In fact, the Germans both at Berlin and at Brussels were well aware that, so long as that state of things continued, their hold upon the country was, not only precarious, but, in the event of a reverse in France, to the last degree dangerous. For, in possession of Antwerp and the seaboard provinces, the Belgians might, in conjunction with the Allies, at once close the only door of escape, and force at Aix-la-Chapelle what is, in effect, the main door to Germany.

From the invaders' point of view, therefore, it was essential both to restrict the operations of the Belgian forces and to affirm their own grip on Brussels. And this explains why the threats indulged in to bombard and burn Brussels were merely threats. In a city of 800,000 people, numbers of whom, doubtless, secretly possessed arms, a rising on the part of the population, with a native army of nearly 100,000 men only a few miles away, meant a risk of the garrison of Brussels and even of the occupying troops altogether having to defend themselves against extermination, for the hatred they had inspired was unspeakable.

The plan resolved upon, it was carried out without mercy. Owing to its ancient renown, and the worldwide interest of its buildings and monuments, the destruction of Louvain has most shocked civilised peoples. The loss is a loss to the world, but as regards its utter inhumanity, the razing of the other towns, not to speak of the villages surrounding them, was equally pitiless and savage. In these murders the German soldiery spared neither age nor sex, and wreaked upon the most helpless their most indescribable and debased barbarities. It has been said that for every Belgian soldier killed in action, they slew three unarmed men, women, or children.

In the devastated districts the bodies of murdered peasants lay unburied in ditches by the roadside. The corpses of children, stiff in death, clung in their last attitude of terror to the corpses of their mutilated mothers. Others lay amid the roofless ruins of their homes. There were instances in which women were stripped, outraged by brutal soldiery, hanged from the branches of trees, and disembowelled in mockery of their final agony. Those who could escaped into the woods, where they hid without food or shelter. Numbers died of starvation and exposure. To destroy the last chance of life for these fugitives, and to avoid the trouble of hunting them out, corpses of murdered people were thrown into wells in order to poison the water.[2]

As might be expected, troops capable of such enormities were, as combatants, of little value. Well disciplined soldiers could not be driven to such excesses. Though their greater numbers, when reinforced, enabled the invaders to make headway against the native troops, yet in every encounter between anything like equal forces they were always decisively defeated, and without exception suffered losses out of all proportion to those they were able to inflict.

It was after an encounter having these results that, on August 25, a body of these demoralised ruffians burned Louvain. They sallied out of that place with the object of driving the Belgians from Aerschot and beyond the Dyle. They were repulsed, and chased back almost to the outskirts of Louvain, sustaining on the way, as usual, a galling fire

---

2. See, among other evidence, the details collected by and given in the Fifth Report of the Belgian Official Commission of Inquiry.

on both flanks. It has been suggested that the officer in command,[3] whose competence is sufficiently measured by the adventure, gave the order to sack and destroy the town in order to disguise the indiscipline of his troops. The motive assigned is not easy to accept. According to the statement for which the Belgian Government made itself responsible—a statement based on evidence which inquiry has not left open to doubt:—

> The German armed guard at the entrance to the town mistook the nature of this incursion, and fired on their routed fellow-countrymen, taking them for Belgians. In spite of all denials from the authorities, the Germans, in order to cover their mistake, pretended that it was the inhabitants who had fired on them, whereas the inhabitants, including the police, had all been disarmed more than a week before.
> Without inquiry and without listening to any protest, the German commander announced that the town would immediately be destroyed. The inhabitants were ordered to leave their dwellings; part of the men were made prisoners; the women and children put into trains of which the destination is unknown. Soldiers, furnished with bombs, set fire to all parts of the town. The splendid church of St. Pierre, the university buildings, the library, and the scientific establishments were delivered to the flames. Several notable citizens were shot.
> The town of 45,000 inhabitants, the intellectual metropolis of the Low Countries since the fifteenth century, is now no more than a heap of ashes.

Such is the brief official statement. It was, however, but the palest reflection of the facts. How scrupulously restrained the Belgian Government were in framing it, is shown from the accounts given by eye-witnesses of the tragedy.

One of these, a Dutchman who owed his escape to the possession of papers proving his nationality, and afterwards reached Breda, told his experiences:—

> On Tuesday, the 25th, many troops left the town. We had a few soldiers in our house. At six o'clock, when everything was ready for dinner, alarm signals sounded, and the soldiers rushed

---

3. Alleged to be a Major von Manteuffel. In a German Official Inquiry afterwards held at Brussels an officer of that name was reported to have been cashiered for this affair; but it is doubtful if he was more than an official scapegoat.

through the streets, shots whistled through the air, cries and groans arose on all sides; but we did not dare leave our house, and took refuge in the cellar, where we stayed through long and fearful hours. Our shelter was lighted up by the reflection from the burning houses. The firing continued unceasingly, and we feared that at any moment our house would be burnt over our heads. At break of day I crawled from the cellar to the street door, and saw nothing but a raging sea of fire.

At nine o'clock the shooting diminished, and we resolved to make a dash to the station. Abandoning our home and all our goods except what we could carry, and taking all the money we had, we rushed out. What we saw on our way to the station is hardly describable. Everything was burning, the streets were covered with bodies shot dead and half-burnt. Everywhere proclamations had been posted, summoning every man to assist in quenching the flames, and the women and children to stay inside the houses. The station was crowded with fugitives, and I was just trying to show an officer my legitimation papers when the soldiers separated me from my wife and children.

All protests were useless, and a lot of us were marched off to a big shed in the goods yard, from where we could see the finest buildings of the city, the most beautiful historical monuments, being burned down.

Shortly afterwards German soldiers drove before them 300 men and lads to the corner of the Boulevard van Tienen and the Maria Theresa-street, opposite the Café Vermalen. There they were shot. The sight filled us with horror. The *burgomaster*, two magistrates, the rector of the university, and all police officials had been shot already.

With our hands bound behind our backs we were then marched off by the soldiers, still without having seen our wives or children. We went through the Juste de Litshstreet, along the Diester Boulevard, across the Vaart and up the hill.

From the Mont Cesar we had a full view of the burning town, St. Peter in flames, while the troops incessantly sent shot after shot into the unfortunate town. We came through the village of Herent—one single heap of ruins—where another troop of prisoners, including half-a-dozen priests, joined us. Suddenly, about ten o'clock, evidently as the result of some false alarm, we were ordered to kneel down, and the soldiers stood behind us with their rifles ready to fire, using us as a shield. But fortunately for us nothing happened..

After a delay of half an hour, our march was continued. No conversation was allowed, and the soldiers continually maltreated us. One soldier struck me with all his might with the heavy butt-end of his rifle. I could hardly walk any further, but I had to. We were choked with thirst, but the Germans wasted their drinking water without offering us a drop.

At seven o'clock we arrived at Camperhout, *en route* for Malines. We saw many half-burnt bodies—men, women, and children. Frightened to death and half-starved, we were locked up in the church, and then later joined by another troop of prisoners from the surrounding villages.

At ten o'clock the church was lighted up by burning houses. Again shots whistled through the air, followed by cries and groans.

At five o'clock next morning, all the priests were taken out by the soldiers and shot together with eight Belgian soldiers, six cyclists, and two gamekeepers. Then the officer told us that we could go back to Louvain. This we did, but only to be recaptured by other soldiers, who brought us back to Camperhout. From there we marched to Malines, not by the high road, but along the river. Some of the party fell into the water, but all were rescued. After thirty-six hours of ceaseless excitement and danger we arrived at Malines, where we were able to buy some food, and from there I escaped to Holland. I still do not know where my wife and children are.[4]

Another witness was Mr. Gerald Morgan an American resident at Brussels. His narrative, given after his eventual arrival in England by way of Louvain, was published in the *Daily Telegraph* on September 3. He made a tour over the German line of march, and found their wounded scattered through every town and village not yet destroyed. In the absence of any German field hospitals, these men were left in any buildings available to be removed as far as possible back to Germany in returning supply wagons, 'buses or motorcars. To calculate their number was very difficult. Mr. Morgan goes on to say:—

After this I returned to Brussels, and we Americans in Brussels then decided that it was time we shook the soil of the coun-

---

4. The narrative was given to *Reuter's* special correspondent at Rotterdam.

try from our feet. We found that we could return to England on a troop-train, via Louvain, Liége, and Aix-la-Chapelle, and thence over the Dutch border. A question arose as to how long the train would stop at Louvain, but on the following morning the German staff office at the railway station said, "You won't stop at Louvain, as Louvain was being destroyed." We left at three o'clock, the train stopping with abominable jerks every few minutes, like a German soldier saluting. We began to see signs of destruction in the outlying villages shortly before we reached Louvain. Houses in the villages were in flames.

An hour before sunset we entered Louvain, and found the city a smoking furnace. The railway station was crowded with troops, drunk with loot and liquor, and rapine as well. From house to house, acting under orders, groups of soldiers were carrying lighted straw, placing it in the basement, and then passing it on to the next. It was not one's idea of a general conflagration, for each house burnt separately—hundreds of individual bonfires—while the sparks shot up like thousands of shooting stars into the still night air. It was exactly like a display of fireworks or Bengal lights, and set pieces, at a grand display in Coney Island.

Meanwhile, through the station arch we saw German justice being administered. In a square outside, where the cabs stand, an officer stood, and the soldiers drove the citizens of Louvain into his presence, like so many unwilling cattle on a market day. Some of the men, after a few words between the officer and the escorts, were marched off under fixed bayonets behind the railway station. Then we heard volleys, and the soldiers returned. Then the train moved out, and the last we saw of the doomed city was an immense red glare in the gathering darkness. My impressions after Louvain were just as if I had read and dreamed of one of Zola's novels.

Weighing this evidence, it is not possible to resist the conclusion that the atrocity of Louvain was planned and carried out deliberately and in cold blood, and it is difficult to avoid the suspicion that the trivial conflict between the German armed guard and their retreating troops, a conflict which apparently hurt nobody on either side, was prearranged in order to afford a colourable excuse. It has been alleged that the troops forming the guard were drunk, and that they had just turned out on the alarm being sounded, after a debauch following the sack of a brewery. There is no present proof that the sack of the brewery had anything to do with the affair, or that the connection was anything more than an afterthought.

The inference of a plan is strengthened, not only by the method with which, as Mr. Morgan shows, the destruction and its accompanying "military executions" were completed, but by the provocation which had previously been offered to the inhabitants, but offered, as it proved, without the evidently expected effect.

On the latter point the statement of the escaped Dutch resident already quoted is circumstantial, and since this is not a Belgian witness, his relation may be accepted as unbiased. He says:—

> Before the Germans entered the town the Civic Guard had been disarmed, and all weapons in the possession of the population had to be given up. Even toy guns and toy pistols and precious collections of old weapons, bows and arrows, and other antique arms useless for any kind of modern warfare had to be surrendered, and all these things—sometimes of great personal value to the owner—have since been destroyed by the Germans. The value of one single private collection has been estimated at about £1,000. From the pulpits the priests urged the people to keep calm, as that was the only way to prevent harm being done to them.
>
> A few days after the entry of the German troops the military authority agreed to cease quartering their men in private houses, in return for a payment of 100,000 *francs* (£4,000) per day. On some houses between forty and fifty men had been billeted. After the first payment of the voluntary contribution the soldiers camped in the open or in the public buildings. The beautiful rooms in the Town Hall, where the civil marriages take place, were used as a stable for cavalry horses.
>
> At first everything the soldiers bought was paid for in cash or promissory notes, but later this was altered. Soldiers came and asked for change, and when this was handed to them they tendered in return for the hard cash a piece of paper—a kind of receipt.
>
> All the houses abandoned by their owners were ransacked, notwithstanding the warnings from the military authorities forbidding the troops to pillage. The Germans imprisoned as hostages

of war the *burgomaster*, two magistrates, and a number of influential citizens.

On Sunday, the 23rd, I and some other influential people in the town were roused from our beds. We were informed that an order had been given that 250 mattresses, 200 lb. of coffee, 250 loaves of bread, and 500 eggs must be on the market-place within an hour. On turning out we found the *burgomaster* standing on the market-place, and crowds of citizens, half naked, or in their night attire, carrying everything they could lay hands on to the market, that no harm might befall their *burgomaster*. After this had been done the German officer in command told us that his orders had been misinterpreted, and that he only wanted the mattresses.

On this, it is clear that the townspeople did everything possible to avoid giving offence to these brutal enemies. On the other hand, it is equally clear that the German military "authorities" issued orders against pillage by the troops, which were taken by the latter, and must have been well known to be, hypocritical.

The proofs as to the real responsibility for this foul deed are irresistible. The soldiers of Alva at their worst never perpetrated any horror so utterly cowardly. They were fired by the fury of religious zeal. Blindly mistaken and politically disastrous as it proved to be, it was a motive worthy of respect by the side of the stupid hate and the mean fear born of the grovelling and greedy materialism of these "conquerors."

The destroyers saved the incomparable town hall, because they destined it to be an ornament of a Germanised Belgium. The rest of the town, however, and more particularly the older part of it, was reduced to a blackened ruin, from which, as from other burning towns, arose a mighty cloud of smoke. Doubtless it was hoped that this spectacle, visible from Antwerp, as well as from Brussels, would strike terror into the people. What they could not gain by arms the Germans sought to gain by the devices of barbarity. But a Nemesis waits on this mode of "warfare." It is related by Lamartine that after their subjugation of Servia the Turks collected into a pyramid the skulls of the slain. This ghastly monument, situated in a desolate valley, the scene of a great battle, was intended as an everlasting warning. To the Serbs it became a remembrance of the price their fathers had been willing to pay for liberty: a revered national memorial which kept alive the spirit which

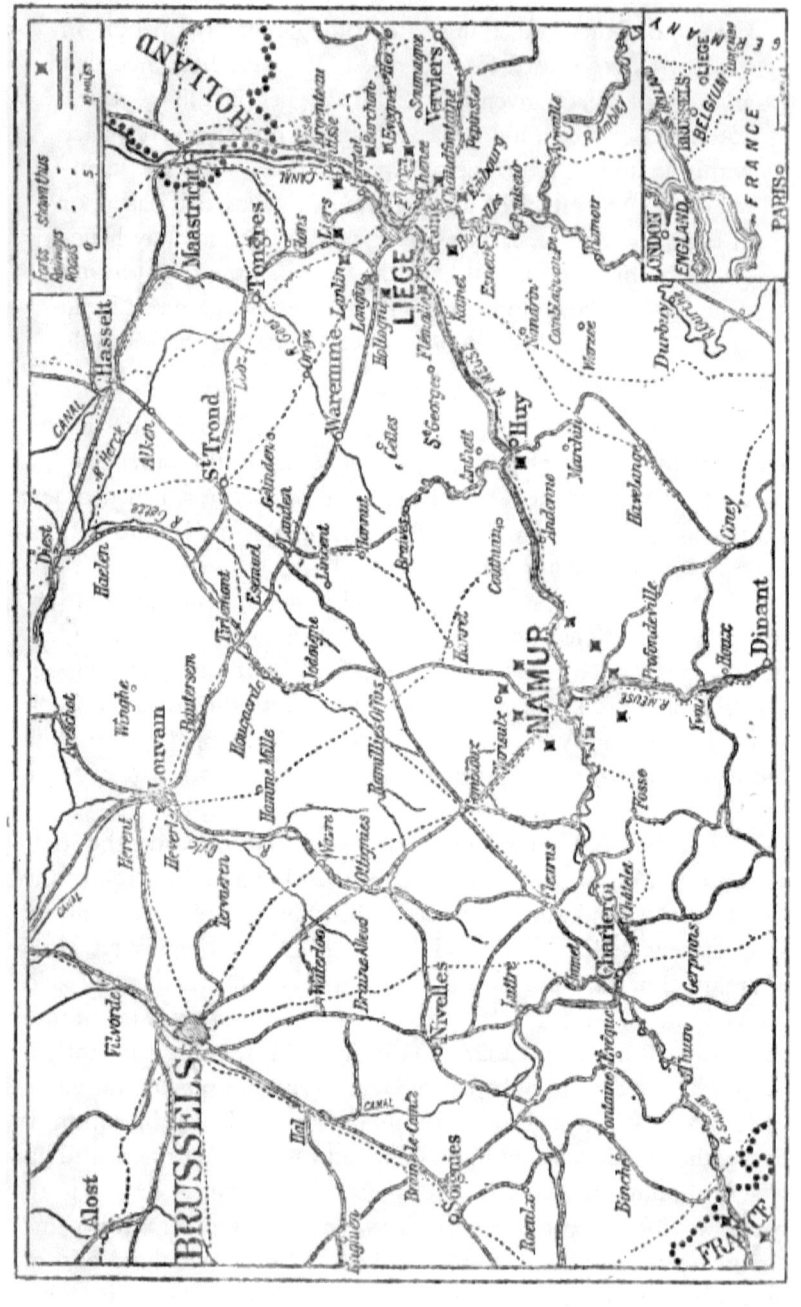

at last crushed their oppressors.

In the same way, the oppressors of Belgium fanned the fires of resistance. In the library of the University of Louvain they had destroyed ancient Greek, Hebrew, and Oriental texts and manuscripts of priceless value; they had not destroyed the valour of one Belgian heart. They had laid in ashes a place which had rightly been called by Lipsius the Belgian Athens, and had earned the praise and admiration of philosophers from Erasmus to Sir William Hamilton; they had but enhanced the glory of the town where, while Northern Europe was still covered by intellectual night, and *"kultur"* had not yet shed its radiance on Germany, nor contributed to produce a Prussian Army, a community of mere weavers had, first among the municipalities of Europe, founded out of their hard earnings, a seat of philosophy, science, and the arts, and in its twenty-eight colleges, the nurseries of many famous men, for centuries led the way in their cultivation. Its university buildings and its library; its art treasures; (see note following), its Academy of Painting; its School of Music; its Museum of National History had been committed to the flames at the hands of rabble soldiery, urged on by still more degraded officers, but the brand applied was applied to their own country, whose good name they had burned from among nations.

> Note:—Writing in the *Daily Telegraph* of the destroyed art treasures of Louvain, Sir Claude Phillips says:
>
> The chief treasures of the church of Saint-Pierre de Louvain were two famous paintings by Dierick (or Thierry) Bouts, who is as closely identified with the now, destroyed university city of Belgium as are the Van Eycks with Ghent and Bruges, and Roger van der Weyden with Tournay and Brussels. The earlier of these paintings is (or rather was) the remarkable triptych with the Martyrdom of St. Erasmus in the central panel, and the figures of St. Jerome and St. Bernard in the wings. This was seen at the Bruges retrospective exhibition of 1904. But perhaps the masterpiece of Dierick Bouts, and certainly one of the finest examples of Flemish fifteenth-century art, was the polyptych painted by him for the altar of the Holy Sacrament in the collegiate church of Saint-Pierre.
>
> The central panel of this work, whereupon was represented the Last Supper, was, until a few days ago, the

chief adornment of that church and of the ancient city. One of the most accomplished writers on modern Netherlandish art, M. Fiérens-Gevaert, has written thus of this 'Last Supper,' by Bouts: '*La Cène est une des oeuvres les plus profondes, les mieux peintes du XVme siècle, et si l'on dressait une liste des cinq ou six chefs-d'oeuvre de nos primitifs, il faudrait l'y comprendre.*'

And in committing this act of hideous, wanton violence, this crime for which posterity will refuse to find words of pardon or excuse, the Prussian commander has also been guilty of an act of incredible ignorance, of boundless stupidity. For, strange to say, the splendid wings which once completed this famous altarpiece, and would, if a reconstruction could have been effected, have caused Bouts's polyptych to stand forth one of the most important works of Flemish fifteenth-century art in existence—these wings are in Germany. In the *Alte Pinakothek* of Munich are preserved the 'Gathering of the Manna' and the 'Meeting of Abraham and Melchisedech.'

In the *Kaiser-Friedrich-Museum* of Berlin are to be found 'The Prophet Elijah in the Desert' and the 'Feast of Passover.' It would obviously have been far better to steal this ' Last Supper,' this central jewel of thq doomed city's pictorial adornment, to confide it either to Munich or to Berlin, than thus to blot it out for ever. It would have been cruel, iniquitous, to despoil heroic Belgium; it is infamous, and, above all, it is stupid to tear out the heart of a masterpiece, to rob the world, and in punishing Belgium to punish Germany, to punish Europe. Napoleon, the ruthless plunderer of museums and churches, was mild and humane in comparison.

If he stole, whether under forcibly imposed treaty or by sheer brute force, the accepted masterpieces of painting and sculpture belonging to the States which he overcame, he stole, with a certain reverence; much as the believer steals the most sacred treasures from the temple, or the most precious relics of the Passion and the saints from the church or the tomb. Robber though he was, he worshipped in awe-struck delight the masterpieces which he tore from the nations; and his triumphant fellow-countrymen, during the brief period of his supremacy, worshipped with him.

Not less than ourselves must the students, the gallery directors, the art historians of Germany suffer, compelled as they are to look on helpless at this incredible act of sacrilege. It is they, indeed, who have most contributed to place before the world in their right perspective, to estimate at their true value the greatest examples of Netherlandish art in its early prime. It is their galleries which contain the most complete collections of these early Netherlandish masters. We challenge them to defy in this, if in this only, the 'mailed fist'—to come forward and register their solemn protest against the greatest outrage upon civilisation, upon humanity, that the modern world has been called upon to witness.

CHAPTER 9

The Politics of Rapine

To follow in detail the operations from now of the Belgian forces from day to day would be less informing than to sum up their plan and their effect.

As it stood on August 25 the situation was that the Belgians held all the country to the north of the Scheldt and the Dyle, and the Germans all the country to the south of these rivers. From Turcoing on the French frontier to Antwerp, the Scheldt follows a course roughly parallel to the coast. At Antwerp its bed describes a sharp bend to seaward. Some ten miles south of this bend, the main waterway receives the Rupel, formed by the junction to the eastward of the Dyle and the Nethe. Taken together, the Scheldt and the Dyle, both deep, sluggish watercourses, offer a natural defence of the seaboard provinces.

From behind this natural line of defence the Belgians, ceaselessly on the watch, sallied forth at every chance offered, to harass and entrap the enemy. Sudden dashes were made upon his communications by armed motor-cars; attacks were made upon railway lines and bridges; his convoys were unexpectedly attacked and cut up by superior forces; in a word, he was kept in perpetual hot water.

The military effect of this was more important than may at first sight appear. In the first place, it was made necessary for the Germans, not only to keep heavy forces afoot in Belgium, but to disperse those forces. Hence though the forces, taken together, were large, the Belgians concentrated on Antwerp were in a position to deliver in superior strength a blow at any one of these bodies, and thus to worst the whole of them in detail.

In the second place, these Parthian tactics made the transport of munitions and supplies to the German armies in France by the line through Brussels a business calling for vigilance and caution. That greatly lessened the value of the line to the enemy. On this supply line the German right wing in France mainly depended. The Belgians, therefore, were not merely defending their own country, but indirectly were aiding the French and British operations on the farther side of the French frontier.

Now the weakness of the Belgian position was that, while they could hold the line of the Dyle and that of the Scheldt as far as Termonde, their force was too small to bar the passage of the Scheldt farther west. It was open to the Germans, by seizing Ghent, to turn the defensive position in a manner that would speedily have become dangerous. Well aware of this, the Germans advanced upon Ghent. Coincidently, however, the Belgian operations farther east became more active and threatening. To meet them, the Germans were obliged to withdraw most of the troops sent to Ghent. Just at that juncture (August 27) a body of British marines was landed at Ostend. From Ghent the enemy had hastily to withdraw. British troops advanced to Ghent, and the whole line of the Scheldt was secured.

The value of that move is clear. From behind the line of the Scheldt, the Allied forces were within easy striking distance of the main railways south of Brussels. Later on, and at a critical juncture for the German armies in France, the Belgians cut those railways. That these lines were not cut before was a part of the Allies' strategy.

What in these circumstances were the measures taken by the invaders? The main measure was, as far as possible, to depopulate the country between their lines and the Belgian defences. The measure had two objects—to prevent the Belgians receiving information of German movements, and more especially of the movement of reinforcements; and to embarrass the defence by driving into the seaboard districts crowds of homeless and starving refugees.

The measure, however, was carried out on such a scale as to suggest that yet another object was to prepare the way for a German immigration as a support of the contemplated conquest. The expropriation of native landowners on the frontier of Prussian Poland, and the granting of their lands to officers and non-commissioned officers of the German army reserves, is an example of the policy, accompanied in Prussian Poland by the prohibition of the native language in elementary schools.

European history affords happily few episodes equal to the depopulation of part of the valley of the Meuse, which was at this time entered upon. The towns of Dinant and Ardenne were totally destroyed, their male populations massacred, and the women and children carried off in defiance of every usage of civilised warfare. Indeed, to describe this devastation of Belgium as in any sense civilised warfare would be a travesty of the term. Its ferocity was possibly no more than a cloak to hide a calculated purpose.

In an official declaration issued from Berlin on August 27 it was stated that:—

> The distribution of arms and ammunition among the civil population of Belgium had been carried out on systematic lines, and the authorities enraged the public against Germany by assiduously circulating false reports.
>
> They were under the impression that with the aid of the French they would be able to drive the Germans out of Belgium in two days.
>
> The only means of preventing surprise attacks from the civil population has been to interfere with unrelenting severity and to create examples which, by their frightfulness, would be a warning to the whole country.

On that declaration, one or two observations are necessary. Part of the defensive force of Belgium was its Civic Guard, having a total strength of some 400,000. So far from arming the civil population, the Belgian Government called in the arms of this force. It was decided that, situated as the country was, the best course was to confide its defence to its regular troops and reserves, and so remove all excuse for military severities.

The reports circulated by the government of Belgium, as anybody who refers back to them may ascertain, were carefully drawn up and substantially true.

The statement that the Belgians were under the impression alleged in this declaration, is, in face of the now known facts of the Allied plan of the campaign, ludicrous.

Still more remarkable, however, is the calm assumption that neither Belgium nor its government had the smallest right to defend themselves, and that any attempt to exercise that right was, in effect, an act of rebellion against Germany. In fact, the presumption is that Belgium was already part of Germany; and this in face of the "solemn assurance" offered on August 9.

Last, but not least, has been the effort more recently made to suggest, despite this declaration, that the "unrelenting severity" and "examples of frightfulness" are hallucinations of Belgian excitement.[1].

These things speak for themselves. Nine towns in Belgium—Louvain, Aerschot, Tirlemont, Termonde, Jodoigne, Dinant, Ardenne, Visé, Charleroi, and Mons—had been reduced to ruins. Others, like Malines, Diest, and Alost, had been in great part wrecked. At Liége a whole quarter of the city had been surrounded, set on fire, and its terrified and unarmed inhabitants, as they fled from the burning houses, shot down wholesale by machine guns until the streets ran with blood.[2] Yet the world was solemnly assured that it was all no more than a bad dream.

So far from aiding, as intended, the military situation of the German forces, this policy of rapine tended to defeat itself. After the defeat of the German armies on the Marne, the government of Berlin made a second offer of accommodation to the Belgian Ministry. The reply was a sortie in full force from the Belgian lines, which obliged the enemy to employ against them three army corps of reserves they were just then sending through northern Belgium into France. In France, those reinforcements were urgently needed. It is evident that this second offer of accommodation merely had as its primary object the prompt arrival of those troops. They had to be recalled from the French frontier, and to join with the forces of occupation in a fiercely fought four days' battle.

In putting upon the renewed offer the interpretation here alluded to, the Belgian Government were well aware that, apart altogether from its worthlessness as a pledge, the Germans, in the political object

---

1. Several German medical men of eminence, among them Dr. Moll, were alleged to have offered this suggestion. On the other hand, Dr. Kaufman, of Aix-la-Chapelle, in a letter to the *Kölnische Volkszeitung*, says that tales of German soldiers mutilated by Belgians—tales the circulation of which was officially countenanced—spread like wildfire among the soldiers, and a single case of a man being mutilated by a shell was magnified into an outrage, and this was only one of a hundred similar instances. The soldiers, by auto-suggestion, got to believe their own wild fancies, and by propagating their stories caused a most dangerous state of anger and exasperation in the German Army. At Huy, a German non-commissioned officer and a private had been wounded by shots. On the assertion that the shots had been fired by inhabitants the German commander, Major von Baschuitch, ordered a number of houses to be burned. The *burgomaster*, however, persuaded him to hold an inquiry. This proved that the shots had been fired by German soldiers in a drunken panic.
2. Shortly before this atrocity, a proclamation had been issued at Liége ordering the citizens to raise their hats to German officers in the street, and to salute men of the rank and file. It was notified that if this command was not obeyed, the German soldiery were authorised to enforce "due respect."

which had plainly from the first dictated their treatment of the population, had signally failed. The invaders had relied as their chief instrument on terror. The instrument had broken in their hands. Neither had they as yet gained one real military success. On the contrary, they had suffered either heavy reverses, or had fought at great cost actions yielding no substantial fruits. It was in vain that half the country had been laid waste. So long as the Belgian Army, with a strongly fortified base, held the seaboard provinces, the situation of the invaders remained utterly secure.

To understand the true position of the Belgian resistance, it is advisable to realise the character of the defences of Antwerp. When, after a prolonged discussion, General Brialmont was, fifty years ago, authorised to modernise the defences of Antwerp and Namur, and to re-fortify Liége, he adopted, in the case of Antwerp, the resources afforded by its situation as a seaport. The older ramparts were demolished, and replaced, at a distance allowing for natural expansion of the city within them, by a new inner ring of massive earthworks between forts, of the form known as a blunted redan. The plan adopted by Brialmont was on the system described by military engineers as the polygonal trace, and his work has always been looked upon as one of the best examples of that system, considered best adapted to meet the range and accuracy of modern siege artillery.

But undoubtedly the distinctive feature was presented by the wet ditches, 150 feet broad with some 20 feet depth of water, which surround not only the inner works, but also the line of detached forts built on an average two miles in advance of those works. Brialmont was the first military engineer to carry out this idea, now followed in all present-day fortification. Each of his forts, with a front of 700 yards, mounted 15 howitzers and 120 guns. There were thus on the 9 forts, including Merxem, 1,080 pieces of ordnance.

Since Brialmont's time, however, his outer forts had been connected by an enceinte, now 15 miles or thereabouts in length, strengthened by 18 redoubts, and the second wet ditch. As a third line of defence, there were, at the same time, built the 25 large forts and 13 redoubts, enclosing round the city an area of some 200 square miles. Between the first and second line of defences, the space formed an entrenched camp of, roughly, 17,000 acres in extent.

To protect the navigation of the Scheldt, and to prevent the city from being deprived of supplies, six of these great outer forts were placed at commanding points along the river. By cutting the dykes on the Rupel and the Scheldt areas could be flooded which would limit an attack to the south and southeast, and not only enable a defending army to concentrate its strength in that direction, but enable it behind the outer third line of fortifications to dispute in force the passage of the Nethe.

There were thus on the various defences some 4,000 pieces of ordnance, and, looking at the rivers and wet ditches to be negotiated, it was evident that an attempt to take the fortress by storm could only hope to succeed after a very heavy bombardment followed by an attack with overwhelmingly superior forces.

Since at Liége, as proved by the identification tallies collected from the German dead, the attempt to storm that place, a far easier enterprise, had cost the attackers 16,000 lives, it is no matter for surprise that they intended to postpone an attack upon Antwerp until their enterprise against France had proved successful.

So acute, however, was the annoyance they experienced from the Belgian Army, and so manifest the political effects of its continued activity and being, that they resolved upon an attack with what was evidently an insufficient though, nevertheless, a large force. This force, more than twice as numerous as the Belgian army, succeeded in making its way round to the north of the fortress, where both the outer and the second line of defence were judged weakest. They had failed, however, to reckon upon the element of defence afforded by the dykes. These at Fort Oudendyk, and elsewhere along the Scheldt, the Belgians promptly cut, though not before they had allowed the besiegers to place their siege guns in position.

The result was that the Germans found themselves flooded out, and lost a considerable part of their artillery. Men struggling breast deep in water, or to save their guns, were shot down from the forts. Some climbed into trees; not a few were drowned. They were forced to beat a hasty and disastrous retreat, harassed by a sortie of the whole Belgian Army.

Not until the failure of their great expedition into France had become manifest, with the prospective loss, in consequence, of the possession of Belgium, the real and primary object of the war, did they address themselves, with all the resources available, to the reduction of the great fortress. Evidently the hope of being able, with Antwerp in their power, to defy efforts to turn them out, inspired this enterprise. After a bombardment with their huge 42-centimetre guns lasting some ten days they succeeded in making a breach in the outer ring of forts, and at the end of five days of heavy fighting drove the Belgians across the Nethe. These successes, however, were dearly bought.

CHAPTER 10

The Agony of Antwerp

In this drama of a gallant nation's sorrows, a spectacle which, the world over, must endear the name of freedom afresh to every heroic heart, no act has appealed more strongly than the gallant defence of Antwerp and its lurid close.

Once the commercial capital of the world, adorned, to quote the words of Motley, *"with some of the most splendid edifices in Christendom,"* Antwerp has the honour which no vicissitudes can dim of being one of the earliest seats in Europe of public spirit and liberty. Nor is it easy to accept the belief that such a city is destined to become merely the gateway of an ignoble Prussia.

As affairs stood at the beginning of October, the Germans were anxious to gain some decisive success. So far, the war had failed to yield any. They had met with heavy reverses. They were feeling sharply already the economic effects of the virtual closing of the Rhine. In the belief that, Belgium subjugated, no combination of powers would be able to tear it from their grasp, and urgent to complete that subjugation while time yet offered, they pushed the siege with all the energy they could command. This hurry, as at Liége, proved prodigal. An attempt to storm fort Waelhem alone cost nearly 8,000 men killed and wounded. As the reduction of the outer fortifications threatened to be slow, the 11- and 12-inch mortars at first employed were reinforced by the new 16-inch mortars throwing shells more than 800 lbs. in weight.

These ponderous engines, transported with immense labour into France, were, with equal labour, hauled back across Belgium, and on the foundations of demolished buildings, placed into position against the forts situated to the south of the Nethe. At the same time, in order to explode magazines and to fire buildings, shells were used filled with naphtha, designed to scatter a rain of blazing oil. The besiegers' loss of life in the attempt to storm Waelhem was avenged by destroying the city waterworks, situated close to that fort. This reduced the population of Antwerp to the supply afforded by such wells as were within the city limits and made it impossible to put out fires should they occur.

By October 5, Forts Waelhem, Wavre, Ste. Catherine, and Konighoyck had been overpowered, and the fort of Lierre silenced. All these forts lie south of the Nethe. The villages adjacent were burned to the ground. At Lierre, a mile to the rear of Fort Lierre, a German shell crashed through the roof of the Belgian military hospital. Some of the wounded men lost their lives. On October 7, after a furious concentrated bombardment, fort Broechem was a heap of ruins.

The way was thus open for a final attempt, under the weight of the German guns, to win the passage of the Nethe. Against great odds the Belgians offered a stubborn resistance. The action was one of the most bloody in the Belgian campaign. In it King Albert was wounded, though happily not seriously. This was the second injury he had met with. All through the war he had taken an active part with his troops, encouraging them in the trenches, braving every risk.

At the instance of the Belgian Government, the British sent to Antwerp on October 3, under the command of General Paris, of the Royal Marine Artillery, two naval brigades and one brigade of marines, a total of 8,000 men, with heavy naval guns and quick-firing naval ordnance mounted on armoured trains.

The Belgian command devolved upon General de Guise, military governor of Antwerp, one of the youngest, but also one of the ablest of the generals of the Belgian Army. On both sides, the passage of the Nethe was disputed with desperate determination. The German attack at this time was directed, not only against the Belgian position north of the Nethe, through Linth and Waerloos, but with particular energy against forts Lierre, Kessel, and Broechen. These forts still held out. They covered the left flank of the defence. The right flank, protected by the flooded area along the Rupel, was unassailable.

Regardless of losses, the Germans worked day and night to float into position and complete the parts of seven pontoon bridges they had put together on the reaches of the river beyond the range of the forts. It was evident that if they could turn the left of the Belgian defence by destroying Fort Broechen, and so breaching the outer defences at that point, just to the north of the Nethe, they could, having crossed in force farther up the stream, launch a formidable flank attack, which must compel the whole Belgian and British force to withdraw.

It was on the Belgian left, however, that the British naval brigades and marines had been posted. With the support of the naval guns, forts Lierre, Kessel, and Broechen defied all the efforts to reduce them. Very soon the fact became evident that this plan of turning the defence was impracticable. Hidden in bomb-proof entrenchments, the British suffered comparatively few losses, despite what seemed an appalling rain of shells. On the other hand, the naval guns, commanding the course of the river over a reach of ten miles, speedily made havoc of every attempt to cross.

In these circumstances, the Germans changed their tactics. They resolved upon a frontal attack through Duffel. Against the Belgian lines, a furious bombardment was concentrated. Under cover of this, and notwithstanding that, for a mile beyond the banks of the river, the country had been flooded, they advanced in masses to rush the passage. Simultaneously, and to prevent this attack being enfiladed by the naval guns, they made a feint of attempting to force their way over at Lierre.

Their losses were immense. Repeatedly their shattered columns were thrown back. For two days, at appalling sacrifice, they fought for the passage. On the British position the attack made no impression. But at daybreak on October 6, following an assault delivered in overwhelming force, the enemy succeeded at length in gaining a foothold on the north bank near Duffel, and in holding it despite all the efforts of the Belgians to dislodge them.

The Belgian Army was obliged to fall back, and with them the British contingent, but it is evidence enough of the character and vigour of the resistance that, heavily outnumbered though they were, the Belgians, in retiring upon the inner defences of the fortress, left the Germans unable immediately to follow up their advantage. The British force withdrew without the loss of any of its guns. Indeed, the naval guns and the armoured trains covered the retirement so effectually that it was impossible for the Germans, until they had transferred their heavy artillery to the north of the Nethe, to press the retreating forces.

Beyond the boom of the hostile guns away to the south, and the nearer crash of the fortress artillery in reply, those within the city had, during these days of stress, little idea of how affairs were really going.

A picture of the scene on the night of Tuesday, October 6, is given by the special correspondent of the *Daily Telegraph*:—

> The night was so impelling in its exquisite beauty that I found it impossible to sleep, or even to stay indoors.
>
> On the other side of the river the trees were silhouetted in the water, the slight haze giving a delicious mezzotint effect to a scene worthy of Venice. As I walked along the stone-paved landing piers the contrast between the beauty of the picture and the grim prospect of what the death-dealing machinery all along my path might make it at any moment was appealingly vivid

Within a few hours, however, the scene changed with what to most in the city seemed almost startling suddenness. Following a proclamation by the authorities warning all who could to leave Antwerp as soon as possible, began an exodus the like of which has not been witnessed since the days of "the Spanish Fury." The same eye-witness proceeds:—

> All day the streets have been clogged and jammed with panicky fugitives fleeing from a city which, in their terrified imagination, is foredoomed. Every avenue of approach to the pontoon bridge across the Scheldt leading to St. Nicolaes has been rendered impassable by a heterogeneous mass of vehicles of every size and kind, from the millionaire's motorcar to ramshackle gigs loaded up with the Lares and Penates of the unfortunate fugitives.
>
> Half a mile or so further on moored alongside each other were two of the Great Eastern Railway steamboats, which ply between Antwerp and Harwich, or, as at present, Tilbury. In view of the very great pressure of passengers, both were to be despatched. I walked through them. Each was filled to its utmost capacity with refugees who might have been sardines, so closely were they packed. In every chair round the saloon tables was a man or a woman asleep. Others were lying on the floors, on the deck, in chairs, or as they best could to seek a respite from their fatigues, a few, realising that theirs would be but a very short night—the boats were to sail at dawn so as to have as much daylight as possible with which to navigate safely the dangers of the mine-fields—preferred to walk about on the jetty discussing the while their hard fate.

The St. Antoine, the leading hotel of Antwerp, has for some weeks past been the temporary home of the various Foreign Ministers, but with their departure to-day has closed its doors. Last night it was the scene of an affecting leave-taking by the queen of the personnel of the British and Russian Legations, Her Majesty being visibly moved. I am informed that the king sent to the German commander yesterday by the hands of a neutral *attaché* a plan of Antwerp with the sites of the cathedral and other ancient monuments marked upon it, which he begged might be spared destruction.

In the meantime, the besiegers had made an attempt to carry the inner defences by storm. It was disastrous. Describing it, Mr. Granville Fortescue[1] says:—

In their advance to the inner line of forts the Germans literally filled the dykes with their own dead. Coming on in close formation, they were cut down by the machine guns as wheat before the scythe.

Realising that it was, to all intents, impossible to carry the inner defences by storm, and that the garrison must be forced to surrender by the destruction of the place, the Germans, who had by this brought their great guns within range of the city, opened from their new positions along the north side of the Nethe a bombardment which, for sustained fury, has rarely been equalled.

The bombardment began at midnight on October 7. From that time shells rained upon the place. The havoc, heightened by bombs thrown down from Zeppelins, speedily, and especially in the southern quarter, caused destructive fires. Viewed from afar—the fire was seen from the frontier of Holland—this great and beautiful seat of commerce, industry, and art, one of the glories of Europe, looked during those terrible hours like the crater of a volcano in eruption, with a shower of shooting stars falling into it. Silhouetted against the glare, its towers stood luminous amid the fiery light. Highest of all the incomparable spire of its cathedral pointed, as though a warning finger, into the dark sky.

For some time before midnight, the roar of the cannonade had ceased. The enemy's guns had for a spell become silent. To the deep

---

1. *At the Western Front* by Granville Fortescue-Two classic accounts of the First World War by an American correspondent—*At the Front With Three Armies & France Bears the Burden* is also published by Leonaur.

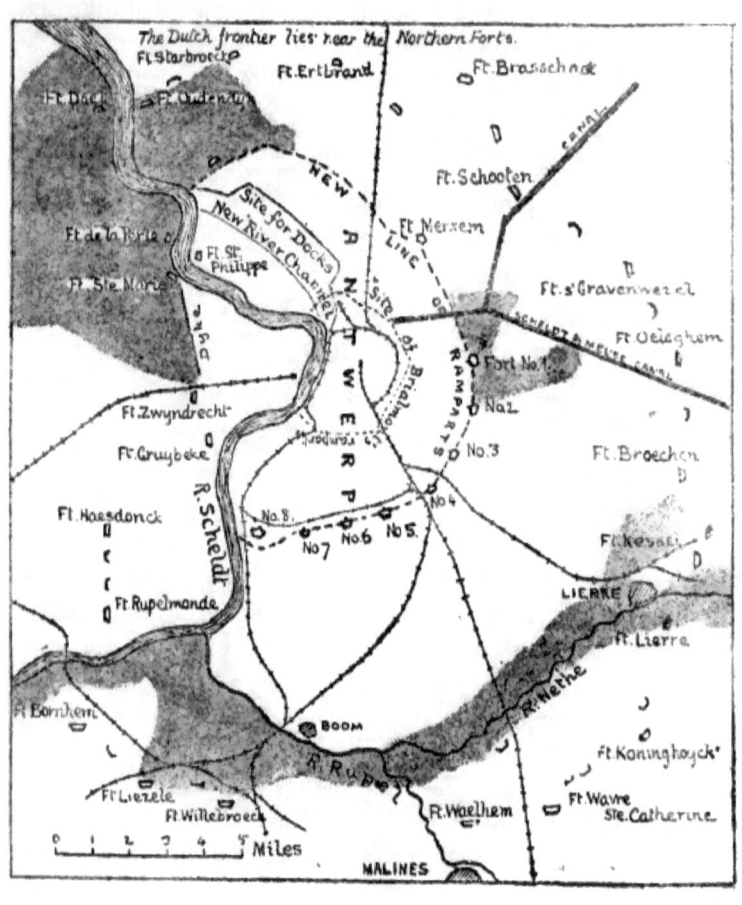

bay of the cannon on the defences there came no answering defiance. At last even the guns on the defences had suspended speech. Mr. B. J. Hudson, of the *Central News*, one of the last English correspondents to leave, says:—

> There was, uncannily enough, a grim calm before the midnight hour and the darkened city was like a town of the dead. The footsteps of a belated wayfarer echoed loudly.
> Then suddenly came the first shell, which brought numbers of women into the streets, their anxious object being to discover whether the bombardment had really begun. Very closely did the roar of the guns and the explosion and crash of the striking shells follow each other. All over the southern section of the city shells struck mansion, villa, and cottage indiscriminately. Then the fortress guns, the field batteries, and the armoured trains opened out in one loud chorus, and the din became terrific, while the reflection in the heavens was seemingly one huge, tossing flame.
> From the roof of my hotel the spectacle was an amazing one. The nerve-racking screech of the shells—the roof-tops of the city alternately dimmed, then illuminated by some sudden red light which left the darkness blacker than before—and then the tearing out of roof or wall by the explosion, made a picture which fell in no way short of Inferno. The assurance thus given to the population that the Germans were fulfilling their threat to bombard a helpless people, sent the citizens to their cellars, as they had been advised to go by the local papers of the day before.
> About nine o'clock in the morning the German fire once more became heavier, but the screaming of the projectiles and the thunder of falling masonry left the fugitive population quite unmoved.
> I noticed in one case a family of father, mother, and three small children who absolutely ignored the explosion of a shell some sixty yards in their rear, moving stolidly on.
> About ten o'clock one of the petrol storage tanks in the city was hit and fired, and one by one the others shared its fate.
> All along the River Scheldt quay barges and small steamers were taking on human freight as rapidly as they could, charging the wretched people 20 *francs* a head for the brief trip into

Dutch territory.

As soon as the flowing spirit from the petrol tanks began to come down the stream something like a panic at last broke out. Those on board the steamers yelled to the officers, pointing to the danger and crying, "Enough! Enough!" Those on the quay, unwilling to be left behind, made wild rushes to obtain a place on the boats.

I saw one woman drowned in one of these rushes, while her husband—rather more lucky—fell on the deck of a boat and escaped with an injured skull. Women handed down babies, young children, perambulators, and all manner of packages, and then themselves scrambled on to the decks, using any precarious foothold available. It was a wonder that many were not drowned or otherwise killed.

Eventually the captains of the river craft, having gained as many fares as could safely be taken, sheered off, leaving many thousands still on the quay-side.

Still the shells were falling all over the town. The smoke from the blazing petroleum and the burning houses rose in great columns and must have formed an appalling sight for the people as far north as the Dutch town of Roosendaal.

What the position is outside the city walls we do not know. We hear our guns crashing out loud defiance to the enemy in a persistent roar; we hear the enemy's reply almost as distinctly.

All that night and next day the stream of fugitives poured out—westward towards Ostend, northward towards Holland. Of the scene at Flushing, Mr. Fortescue wrote:—

> Hordes of refugees fill this town. Some come by train from Roosendaal, others have escaped from the city by boat. All sorts of river craft come ploughing through the muddy waters of the Scheldt, crowded to the gunwales with their human freight. Tugs tow long lines of grain-lighters filled with women, children, and old men.
>
> Their panic is pitiful. Since the first shell shrieked over the city a frightened, struggling mob has been pressing onward to escape the hail of fire and iron. Imagine the queue that shuffles forward at a championship football game increased a hundredfold in length and breadth, and you will see the crowd moving to the railway station. Another throng fought their way to the

quays. All the time German shells sang dismally overhead; for the most part they fell into the southern section of the city.

From the refugees I hear the same pitiful tales I have heard so often. A mother with two girls, one four and the other three, was torn from the arm of her husband and pushed on a departing boat. All through the panic of flight it has been "women and children first." Those who are here bear witness to the bravery of those who defend the city.

But if the besiegers had imagined that they were about to reap any solid military advantage, a disappointment was being prepared for them. For six days they had striven to cross the Scheldt at Termonde, and striven without success. The objective was to invest Antwerp from both sides of the Scheldt, and thus either for the remainder of the campaign to imprison the Belgian Army, or to destroy it, amid the ruins of Antwerp, by their shell fire. That would have been a military success of an important character. Not only would it have left Belgium for the time being at their mercy, but it must undoubtedly have a moral effect not to be ignored.

On October 8, however, the invaders had gained a passage over the Scheldt at Termonde, and had compelled the Belgian force opposing them, much inferior in point of numbers, to fall back upon Lokeren. That place is on the line of communication between Antwerp and Ostend. In view of this danger, the evacuation of Antwerp became a necessity. The danger had been foreseen. The Belgian authorities indeed had already arrived at their decision. It is now known that this had been reached on October 3, and that the object of the small British reinforcement was to enable the evacuation to be accomplished. That object they fulfilled. By the timely warning given to the population, nearly 150,000 had already been enabled to escape. All the available shipping in the port was used for transport purposes. The rest, including some 36 captured German merchant steamers, which could not be removed owing to the neutrality of Holland, was blown up and sunk in the docks. Objects of value were removed, and such stores as could not, and were likely to be of value to the enemy, were destroyed. The Belgian Government, on October 7, transferred itself to Ostend.

The Belgian Army followed. By the morning of Friday, October 9, the evacuation had been completed. All the guns on the abandoned defences were spiked. Under the command of General de Guise, however, the forts controlling the approaches on the Scheldt continued to hold out.

In the meantime, the Germans had been pressing their attack upon Lokeren. The main portion of the Belgian Army and 2nd British Naval Brigade, as well as the Marines, retired upon Ostend while the communications remained open. The first division of the Belgian Army, which had been the last to leave Antwerp, and had been engaged in rendering the place useless to the besiegers, retreated fighting with the Germans north of the Scheldt a succession of rearguard actions.

In the face of impossible odds, the 1st British Naval Brigade, now without the support of their heavy guns, were forced, fighting tenaciously, across the Dutch frontier at Huist. A division of the Belgian Army were also compelled to cross the boundary into Holland.

Just after noon on October 9, the besiegers entered Antwerp by a breach they had made near fort No. 3 on the south-east side of the inner line of works. By then, the burning and ruined city presented the appearance of a tomb. What remnant of the population remained were in hiding in their cellars. Every person of authority had fled. Amid this scene of wreck and desolation, the Germans made their entry and installed their "government." But the Belgian Army had once more eluded their grasp, and with the navigation of the Scheldt closed, the possession of Antwerp, gained at the sacrifice of so much blood had become a possession presenting no compensating military advantages.

At the time these lines were written, the record, as already said, remains incomplete. Enough, however, has been outlined in this brief sketch to prove that the struggle and the sufferings of Belgium form one of the bravest efforts ever made for a people's freedom, and a protest against the policy of rapine that can never fade from the memory of civilised nations, nor fail to command their admiration and their respect.

Chronology of Chief Events

July 31.—Germany declares war against Russia and sends 12 hours' ultimatum to France. Belgian Government orders partial mobilisation.

August 1—Germany formally announces mobilisation. France orders mobilisation.

August 2.—German troops invade Luxemburg. German ultimatum presented at Brussels, giving 12 hours for reply.

August 3.—Belgian Government refuse demand for German occupation of Belgium and "assisted passage" to German troops. German armies cross Belgian frontier.

August 4.—Combat opens at Visé and Argenteau for the passage of the Meuse. Bombardment of Liége begun.

August 5.—Special meeting of Belgian Parliament. Ministry of all parties formed. Emergency measures voted.
First attempt of Germans to storm Liége defeated.

August 6.—Germans win passage of the Meuse. Second attempt to storm Liége. King of the Belgians leaves Brussels for the front.

August 7.—Third attempt to storm Liége. General von Emmich asks for 24 hours' armistice. It is refused.

August 8.—Belgian troops evacuate trenches at Liége; 16,000 identification tallies collected from German dead.

August 9.—Germany offers accommodation with Belgium. Offer rejected. Railways and roads cut.

August 10.—German troops enter Liége.
Forts still hold out. Leading citizens of Liége seized as hostages.

"Fine" of £2,000,000 imposed on city and province of Liége.

German cavalry advance to Tongres and Ramillies. Attack upon Huy. French troops arrive in Belgium.

August 11.—German flying columns advance upon Diest and Eghezée. Country laid waste.

August 12.—Battle at Diest and Haelen. Combat of Eghezée. Germans repulsed, but capture Huy.

August 13.—Retreat of Germans from Diest. Pursuit by Belgians and French through St. Trond to Warenne.

August 14.—German expedition against Tirlemont defeated. French occupy Dinant.

August 15.—First attack upon Dinant.

August 16.—Second attack and battle of Dinant.

August 17.—Belgian Government removes from Brussels to Antwerp. British Expeditionary Force lands at Boulogne.

August 18.—General German advance across Belgium begins. Outpost fighting round Tirlemont and Gembloux.

August 19.—First day of battle of Louvain. Last of Liége forts destroyed.

August 20.—Second day of battle of Louvain. Germans occupy Malines.

August 21.—German entry into Brussels. "Fine" of £8,000,000 demanded.

August 22.—Germans advance upon Charleroi. Attack upon the passages of the Sambre.

August 23.—Battle of Mons and Charleroi. Fall of Namur. Belgians recapture Malines. Germans set up a new civil and military government for Belgium.

August 24.—Battle of Mons and Charleroi continued. Retirement of British and French forces. Germans occupy Ghent.

August 25.—Sack and destruction of Louvain.

August 26.—Destruction of Termonde and Dinant.

August 27.—British occupy Ostend. Germans driven out of Ghent. Bombardment of Malines.

August 28.—Sack and destruction of Aerschot. Belgian Government appoints Commission to inquire into atrocities.

August 29.—Efforts of German civil and military authorities at Brussels to collect the "fine." Resistance of Burgomaster and City Council.

August 30—September 6.—Belgian operations against German lines.

September 9.—Germany's second offer of an accommodation rejected. Belgian sortie in force from Antwerp.

September 10-11.—Heavy fighting. Belgians again recapture Malines and Termonde, and occupy Alost.

September 12.—German reinforcements recalled from French frontier.

September 13.—Belgians retire upon Antwerp.

September 15.—First German attack upon Antwerp. Belgians cut the dykes. Heavy loss of German guns. Invaders defeated in successful sortie.

September 25.—Opening of second attack upon Antwerp.

October 1-4.—Five days' battle along the Dyle.

October 3.—Antwerp garrison reinforced by British Naval Brigade and Marines.

October 4-6.—Battle on the Nethe. Germans cross the river.

October 7.—Belgian Government transferred to Ostend. Bombardment of city of Antwerp begun.

October 9.—Belgian Army evacuates Antwerp. Germans enter the city.

The Battle of the Rivers

Contents

Prefatory Note	111
The German Plans	113
Why the Plans Were Changed	124
General Joffre As a Strategist	134
The Battle of the Marne	141
The German Overthrow	151
How General Von Kluck Averted Ruin	166
The Operations On the Aisne	176
Warfare By Day and By Night	189
The Struggle Round Rheims	201
Review of Results	217
Appendix	224

Prefatory Note

On a scale before unknown in Western Europe, and save for the coincident operations in the Eastern theatre of war, unexampled in history, the succession of events named the "Battle of the Rivers" presents illustrations of strategy and tactics of absorbing interest. Apart even from the spectacular aspects of this lurid and grandiose drama, full as it is of strange and daring episodes, the problems it affords in the science of war must appeal to every intelligent mind.

An endeavour is here made to state these problems in outline. In the light they throw, events and episodes, which might otherwise appear confused, will be found to fit into a clear sequence of causes and consequences. The events and episodes themselves gain in grandeur as their import and relationship are unfolded.

Since the story of the retreat from Mons has been told in another volume of this series, it is only in the following pages dealt with so far as its military bearings elucidate succeeding phases of the campaign.

CHAPTER 1

The German Plans

Field Marshal Sir John French in his despatch dated a fortnight later[1] wrote:

About September 3, the enemy appears to have changed his plans, and to have determined to stop his advance south direct upon Paris, for on September 4 air reconnaissances showed that his main columns were moving in a south-easterly direction generally, east of a line drawn through Nanteuil and Lizy on the Ourcq.

In that passage the British commander summarises an event which changed the whole military aspect of the Great War and changed it not only in the Western, but in the Eastern theatre of hostilities.

What were the German plans and why were they changed?

In part the plans were military, and in part political. These two aspects, however, are so interwoven that it is necessary, in the first place, briefly to sketch the political aspect in order that the military aspect, which depended on the political, may be the better understood.

The political object was to reduce France to such powerlessness that she must not only agree to any terms imposed, but remain for the future in a state of vassalage to Germany. Further, the object was to extract from France a war fine so colossal [2] that, if paid, it would

---
1. Despatch from Sir John French to Earl Kitchener of September 17th, 1914. For the text of this see Appendix.
2. The contemplated fine has been alleged to be 4,000 millions sterling, coupled with the formal cession of all North Eastern France. This statement was circulated by *Reuter's* correspondent at Paris on what was asserted to be high diplomatic authority. Such a sum sounds incredible, though as a pretext it might possibly have been put forward.

furnish Germany with the means of carrying on the war against Great Britain and Russia, and, if not paid, or paid only in part, would offer a pretext for an occupation of a large part of France by German troops, indefinite in point of time, and, formalities apart, indistinguishable from annexation. By means of that occupation great resources for carrying on the war might, in any event, be drawn in kind from the French population and from their territory, or drawn in cash in the form of local war levies.

In a passage quoted by M. Edouard Simon,[3] the late Prince von Bismarck once spoke of the difficulty he met with at the end of the war with France in 1871, in restraining the cupidity of the then King of Prussia and in "mixing the water of reflection with the wine of victory." There was at the time, in Germany, much discussion as to the amount of the War Fine. The staggering total of 15,000 millions of *francs* (600 million pounds sterling) was freely asserted to be none too high. Fear of possible war with Great Britain mainly kept within bounds this desire of plunder, and led the Emperor William to accept, reluctantly, the 5,000 million *francs* afterwards paid.

There can be no doubt, however, that it became a settled opinion with the government, and also, even if to a less extent, a conviction with the public of Germany that, enormous as it was, the levy upon France in 1871 was insufficient. That opinion was sharpened by the promptitude, almost contemptuous, with which the French people discharged the demand, and brought the German military occupation to an end.

The opinion that the War Fine of 1871 had been too small inspired the political crisis of 1875, caused by a threatened renewal of the German attack. The pretext then was that France was forming, with Austria and Italy, a league designed to destroy the new German Empire. The true cause of hostility was that France had begun to reorganise her army. Intervention by the Cabinets of London and St. Petersburg averted the peril. The German Government found itself obliged to put off a further draft upon "opulent France"[4] until a more convenient season.

This discovery that neither Great Britain nor of Germany dictated the policy which led later to the Triple Alliance. Consistently from this time to the end of his life the Emperor William I. assumed the part of guardian of the peace of Europe. The Triple Alliance was *outwardly*

---

3. Simon: *The Emperor William and his Reign*.
4. This phrase is that of General F. von Bernhardi.

promoted by Germany with that object. (See note following).

Note:—After the Berlin Congress in 1878, Prince Gortschakov mooted the idea of an alliance between Russia and France. In 1879 Bismarck, in view of such a development, concluded the alliance between Germany and Austria. Italy joined this alliance in 1883, but on a purely defensive footing. The account given of the Triple Alliance by Prince Bernhard von Bülow, ex-Imperial Chancellor, is that it was designed to safeguard the Continental interests of the three Powers, leaving each free to pursue its extra-Continental interests. From 1815 to 1878 the three absolutist Powers, Russia, Prussia, and Austria, had aimed at dominating the politics of the Continent by their entente. For many years, however, German influence in Russia has been giving way before French influence.

This is one of the most important facts of modern European history. The Triple Alliance was undoubtedly designed to counteract its effect. Germany, with ambitions in Asia Minor, backed up Austria, with ambitions in the Balkans. Both sets of ambitions were opposed to the interests of Russia. Russia's desertion of the absolutist entente for the existing entente with the liberal Powers of the West has been due nevertheless as much to the growth of constitutionalism as to diplomacy. The *entente* with Great Britain and France is popular. On the other hand, the entente with Germany and Austria was unpopular. The view here taken that one of the real aims of the Triple Alliance was the furtherance of Prussia's designs against France is the view consistent with the course of Prussian policy. For Prince von Bülow's explanations, see his *Imperial Germany*.

Meanwhile, every opportunity was taken to strengthen the German military organisation. Only by possession of an invincible army could the German Empire, it was contended, fulfil its peace-keeping mission.

This growth of military armaments imposed on Germany a heavy burden. Was the burden borne merely for the sake of peace, or for the sake of the original inspiration and policy?

Few acquainted with the character of the Germans will credit them with a tendency to spend money out of sentiment. The answer, besides, has been given by General von Bernhardi.[5] He has not hesi-

---

5. F. von Bernhardi: *The Next War.* see Introduction.

tated to declare that the object of these preparations was to ensure victory in the offensive war made necessary by the growth of the German population, a growth calling for a proportionate "political expansion."

Outside Germany the so-called revelations of General von Bernhardi took many by surprise. That, however, was because, outside Germany, not many know much of German history, and fewer still the history of modern Prussia.

It was realised, when General von Bernhardi published his book, that the original inspiration and policy had never been changed. On the contrary, all the efforts and organisation of Prussia had been directed to the realisation of that policy, and the only alteration was that, as confidence in Prussia's offensive organisation grew, the policy had been enlarged by sundry added ambitions until at length it became that grotesque and Gothic political fabric known as Pan-Germanism.

M. Simon says:

> The military origin of the new German Empire is of vast importance; it gives that empire its fundamental character; it establishes its basis and its principle of existence. Empires derive their vitality from the principle to which they owe their birth.

The fact is of vast importance because, just as the British Empire had its origin in, and owes its character to, the embodiment of moral force in self-government, so the German Empire had its origin in, and owes its character to, the embodiment of material forces in armies, and existed, as General von Bernhardi says, for the employment of that force as and whenever favourable opportunity should present itself.

The political inspiration and purpose being clear, how was that purpose, as regards France, most readily and with fewest risks to be realised?

It was most readily to be realised by seizing Paris. As everybody is aware, the Government of France is more centralised than that of any other great State. Paris is the hub of the French roads and railways; Paris is also the hub of French finance; Paris is at once the brain and the heart of the country; the place to which all national taxes flow; the seat from which all national direction and control proceed. It was believed, therefore, that, Paris occupied, France would be stricken with political paralysis. Resistance might be offered by the provinces, for the area of France is roughly equal to the area of Germany, but the resistance could never be more than ineffectual.

Such was the plan on its political side. What were its military features?

A political plan of that character plainly called for a swift and, if possible, crushing military offensive. Rapidity was one of the first essentials. That affected materially the whole military side of the scheme. It meant that to facilitate mobility and transport, the equipment of the troops must be made as light as possible. Hence all the usual apparatus of field hospitals and impedimenta for encampment must be dispensed with. It meant that the force to be dispatched must be powerful enough to bear down the maximum of estimated opposition, and ensure the seizure of Paris, without delay. It meant again that the force must move by the shortest and most direct route.

If we bear in mind these three features—equipment cut down to give mobility, strength to ensure an uninterrupted sweep, shortest route—we shall find it the easier to grasp the nature of the operations which have since taken place. The point to be kept in mind is that what the military expedition contemplated was not only on an unusual scale, but was of an altogether unusual, and in many respects novel, character.

The most serious military problem in front of the German Government was the problem of route. The forces supposed to be strong enough Germany had at her disposal. Within her power, too, was it to make them, so far as meticulous preparation could do it, mobile. But command of the shortest and most direct route she did not possess.

That route we know passes in part through the plain of northern Belgium, and in part through the parallel valley of the Meuse to the points where, on the Belgium frontier, there begin the great international roads converging on Paris. All the way from Liége to Paris there are not only these great paved highways, but lines of main transcontinental railroads. The route, in short, presented every natural and artificial facility needed to keep a vast army fully supplied.

Here it should be recalled that two things govern the movements of armies. Hostile opposition is one; supplies are the other. In this instance, the possible hostile opposition was estimated for. It remained to ensure that neither the march of the great host, as a whole, nor the advance of any part of it should at any time be held up by waiting for the arrival of either foodstuffs, munitions, or reinforcements, but that the thousand and one necessaries for such an army, still a complex list even when everything omissible had been weeded out, should arrive, as, when, and where wanted.

Little imagination need be exercised to perceive that to work out a scheme like that on such a scale involves enormous labour. On the one side were the arrangements for gathering these necessaries and placing them in depots; on the other were the arrangements for issuing them, sending them forward, and distributing them. Nothing short of years of effort could connect such a mass of detail. If hopeless confusion was not almost from the outset to ensue, the greatest care was called for to make it certain that the mighty machination would move successfully.

A scheme of that kind suited the methodical genius of Germany, and there can be no doubt that the years spent upon it had brought it to perfection. It had been worked out to time table. Concurrently, arrangements for the mobilisation of reserve troops had become almost automatic. Every reservist in the German Army held instructions setting out minutely what to do and where and when to report himself as soon as the call came.

Now this elaborate plan had been drawn up on the assumption of an invasion of France by the route through Belgium. That assumption formed its basis. Not only so, but the extent to which the resources of Belgium and Northeast France might, by requisitioning, be drawn upon to relieve transport and so promote rapidity, had been exactly estimated.

It is evident, therefore, that the adoption of any other route must have upset the whole proposal. In any other country the fact of the Government devoting its energies over a long period of time to such a scheme on such a footing would appear extraordinary, and the more extraordinary since this, after all, was only part of a still larger plan, worked out with the same minuteness, for waging a war on both frontiers.

The fact, however, ceases to be extraordinary if we bear in mind that the modern German Empire is essentially military and aggressive.

Obviously, the weak point of plans so elaborate is that they cannot readily be changed. Neither even can they, save with difficulty, be modified. Even in face, therefore, of a declaration of war by Great Britain, the plan had to be adhered to. Unless it could be adhered to, the invasion of France must be given up.

Bearing in mind the labour and cost of preparation, the hopes built upon the success of the invasion, and the firm belief that the opposition to be expected by Belgium could at most be but trifling, it ceases to be surprising that, though there was every desire to put off that complication, a war with Great Britain proved no deterrent.

Further, the construction by the French just within their Eastern frontier of a chain of fortifications extremely difficult to force by means of a frontal attack, and quite impossible to break if defended by efficient field forces, manifestly suggested the plea of adopting the shorter and more advantageous route on the ground of necessity. In dealing with that plea it should not be forgotten that the State which elects to take the offensive in war needs resources superior to those of the State which elects to stand, to begin with, upon a policy of defence. Those superior resources, save in total population, Germany, as compared with France, did not possess. In adopting the offensive, therefore, on account of its initial military advantages, Germany was risking in this attack means needed for a prolonged struggle. It was necessary in consequence for the attack to be so designed that it could not only not fail, but should succeed rapidly enough to enable the attacking State to recoup itself—and, possibly, with a profit.

The conditions of first rapidity, and second certainty, formed the *political* aspects of the plan, and they affected its military aspects in regard to first numbers, secondly equipment, thirdly route.

But there were, if success was to be assured, still other conditions to be fulfilled, and these conditions were *purely* military. They were:—

(1) That in advancing the line of the invading armies must not expose a flank, and by so doing risk delay through local or partial defeat.

(2) That the invading armies must not lay bare their communications. Risk to their communications would also involve delay.

(3) That they must at no point incur the hazard of attacking a defended position save in superior force. To do so would again risk repulse and delay.

Did the plan drawn up by the German General Staff fulfil apparently all the conditions, both political and military, and did it promise swift success? It did.

The plan, in the first instance, covered the operations of eight armies, acting in combination. These were the armies of General von Emmich; General von Kluck; General von Bülow; General von Hausen; Albert, Duke of Wurtemberg; the Crown Prince of Germany; the Crown Prince of Bavaria; and General von Heeringen. Embodying first reserves, they comprised twenty-eight army corps out of the fortysix which Germany, on a war footing, could put immediately into the field.[6]

Having reached the French frontier from near the Belgian coast to Belfort, the eight armies were to have advanced across France in echelon. If you take a row of squares running across a chessboard from corner to corner you have such squares for what is known in military phraseology as echelon formation.

Almost invariably in a military scheme of that character the first body, or "formation" as it is called, of the echelon is reinforced and made stronger than the others, because, while such a line of formations is both supple and strong, it becomes liable to be badly disorganised if the leading body be broken. On the leading body is thrown the main work of initiating the thrust. That leading body, too, must be powerful enough to resist an attack in flank as well as in front.[7]

Advancing on this plan, these armies would present a line exposing, save as regarded the first of them, no flank open to attack. Indeed, the first object of the echelon is to render both a frontal and a flank attack upon it difficult.

Had the plan succeeded as designed, we should have had this position of affairs: the eight armies would have extended across France from Paris to Verdun by the valley of the Marne, the great natural highway running across France due east to the German frontier, and one having both first-rate road and railway facilities. It was hoped that by the time the first and strongest formation of this chain of armies

---

6. Of the remaining corps, five were posted along the frontier of East Prussia to watch the Russians. The rest were held chiefly at Mainz, Coblentz, and Breslau as an initial reserve.
The now definitely ascertained facts regarding the military strength of Germany appear to be these:—25 corps and one division of the active army mustering 1,530,000 men; and 21 corps of *Landwehr* mustering 1,260,000 men making a total 2,790,000 men In addition, there were raised 12 corps of Ersatz Reserve, and there were also the *Landsturm* and the Volunteers, whose numerical strength is uncertain. These troops, however, were not embodied until later in the campaign.
7. The leading army, that of General von Kluck, consisted of 6 corps; and the second army, that of General von Bülow, of 4 corps. The others were formed each of 3 corps, making an original total of 28 corps. Following the disaster at Liége, however, the army of General von Emmich was divided up, and the view here taken, which appears to be most consistent with the known facts, is that it was, after being reformed, employed to reinforce the armies of Generals von Kluck and von Bülow. That would make the strength of the German force, which marched through northern Belgium, 780,000 men.

had reached Paris and had fastened round it, the sixth, seventh, and eighth armies would, partly by attacking the fortified French frontier on the east, but chiefly by enveloping it on the west, have gained possession of the frontier defence works.

The main French Army must then have been driven westward from the valley of the Marne, across the Aube, brought to a decisive battle in the valley of the Seine, defeated, and, enclosed in a great arc by the German armies extending round from the north and by the east to the south of Paris, have been forced into surrender.

There is a common assumption that the German plan was designed to repeat the manoeuvres which in the preceding war led to Sedan, and almost with the same detail. That is rating the intelligence of the German General Staff far too low. They could not but know that the details of one campaign cannot be repeated in another against an opponent, who, aware of the repetition, would be ready in advance against every move.

Naturally, they fostered the notion of an intended repetition. That promoted their real design. The design itself, however, was based not merely on the war of 1870-1, but on the invasion of 1814, which led to the abdication of Napoleon, and the primary idea of it was to have *only one main line of advance*.

The reason was that if an assailant takes two main lines of advance simultaneously and has to advance along the valleys of rivers converging to a point, as the Oise, the Marne, and the Seine converge towards Paris, his advance may be effectively disputed by a much smaller defending force than if he adopts only one line of advance, provided always, of course, that he can safeguard his flanks and his communications.

Bear in mind the calculation that the main French Army would never in any event be strong enough successfully to resist an invasion so planned. Bear in mind, too, that an echelon formation is not only supple and difficult to attack along its length on either side, but that it can be stretched out or closed up like a concertina. To maintain a formation of that kind with smaller bodies of troops is fairly easy. To maintain it with the enormous masses forming the German armies would be difficult. But the Germans were so confident of being able to compel the French to conform to all the German movements, to stand, that is to say, as the weaker side, always on the defensive, leaving the invaders a practically unchallenged initiative, that they believed they could co-ordinate all their movements with exactitude. This was taking a risk, but they took it.

It is a mistake to suppose that they entered on the campaign with every movement mapped out from start to finish. No plan of any campaign was ever laid down on such lines, and none ever will be. The plan of a campaign has to be built on broad ideas. Those ideas, by taking all the essentials into consideration, the strategist seeks to convert into realised events. In this instance, there can be very little doubt that certain assumptions were treated as so probable as almost to be certainties. The first was that such forces as France could mobilise in the time would be mainly drafted to defend the fortified frontier. The next was that such forces as could be massed in time along the boundary of Belgium would be too weak seriously to impede the invasion. The third was that in any subsequent attempt to transfer forces from the fortified frontier to the Belgian boundary the French would be met and defeated by the advancing echelon of German masses. The fourth was that such an attempted transfer, followed by its defeat, would leave the fortified frontier so readily seizable, that German armies advancing swiftly into the valley of the Marne would fall upon these defeated French forces on the flank and rear. Besides, that attempted transfer would be the very thing that would promote the German design of envelopment.

If Paris could be reached by the strongest of the chain of armies in eight days, then the mobilisation of the French reserves would still be incomplete. Under the most favourable conditions, and even without the disturbance of invasion, that mobilisation takes a fortnight. Given a sudden and successful invasion with the resultant upset of communications and the mobilisation could never be completed. All, therefore, that the 1,680,000 men forming the invading hosts[8] would have to encounter would be the effectives of the French regular forces, less than half the number of the invaders.

When we speak of twenty-eight army corps moving in echelon, approximately like so many squares placed diagonally corner to corner, it is as well not to forget that such a chain of masses may assume quite sinuous and snake-like variations and yet remain perfectly intact and strong. For example, the head of the chain might be wound round and pivot upon Paris, and the rest of the chain extended across France in curves. This gigantic military boa-constrictor might therefore crush

---

8. A German Army corps is made up, with first reserves, embodied on mobilisation, to 60,000 men. Twenty-eight army corps, therefore, represent a total of 1,680,000 of all arms.

the heart out of France, while the defenders of the country remained helpless in its toils.

Such in brief was the daring and ambitious scheme conceived and worked out by the German General Headquarters Staff, and worked out in the most minute detail.

It will be seen from this summary that so far as its broad military features are concerned, the plan promised an almost certainly successful enterprise. There were concealed in its calculations, nevertheless, fatal flaws. What they were will appear in the course of the present narrative. Meanwhile it is necessary to add that possible opposition from Belgium had not been overlooked; nor the possibility, consequent upon that opposition, of intervention by Great Britain.

From the military standpoint, however, it was never calculated that any British military force would be able to land either in France or in Belgium promptly enough to save the French Army from disaster. In any event, such a force would be, from its limited numbers, comparatively unimportant.

CHAPTER 2

Why the Plans Were Changed

Let us now pass from designs to events, and, reviewing in their military bearing the operations between August 3, when the German troops crossed the Belgian frontier, to the day, exactly one month later, when the German plans were apparently changed, deal with the question: Why were the plans changed?

The Germans entered Liége on August 10. They had hoped by that time to be, if not at, at any rate close to, Paris. In part they were unable to begin their advance through Belgium until August 17 or August 18, because they had not, until that date, destroyed all the forts at Liége, but in part, also, these delays had played havoc with the details of their scheme.

Consider how the shock of such a delay would make itself felt. The mighty movement by this time going on throughout the length and breadth of Germany found itself suddenly jerked into stoppage. All its couplings clashed. Excellently designed as are the strategic railways of Germany they are no more than sufficient for the transport of troops, guns, munitions, foodstuffs, and other things necessary in such a case. If, owing to delays, troop trains got into the way of food trains, and *vice versa*, the resultant difficulties are readily conceivable. All this war transport is run on a military time table. The time table was there, and it was complete in every particular. But it had become unworkable. Gradually the tangle was straightened out, but the muddle, while it lasted, was gigantic, and we can well believe that masses of men, arriving from all parts of Germany at Aix-la-Chapelle, found no sufficient supplies awaiting them, and that sheer desperation drove the German Government to collect supplies by plundering all the districts of Belgium within reach.

As the Belgians were held to be wilfully responsible for the mess, the cruelty and ferocity shown in these raids ceases to be in any sense unbelievable.

Dislocation of the plan, however, was not all. In the attempts to carry the fortress of Liége by storm the Germans lost, out of the three corps forming the army of General von Emmich, 48,700 men killed and wounded.[1] These corps, troops from Hanover, Pomerania, and Brandenburg, formed the flower of the army. The work had to be carried out of burying the dead and evacuating the wounded. The shattered corps had to be reformed from reserves. All this of necessity meant additional complications.

Then there was the further fighting with the Belgians. What were the losses sustained by the Germans between the assaults on Liége and the occupation of Brussels is, outside of Germany, not known, nor is it known in Germany save to the government. To put that loss as at least equal to the losses at Liége is, however, a very conservative estimate.

Meanwhile, the French had advanced into Belgium along both banks of the Meuse and that further contributed to upset the great preparation.

We have, therefore, down to August 21, losses, including those in the fighting on the Meuse and in Belgian Luxemburg, probably equal to the destruction of two reinforced army corps.

Now we come to the Battle of Mons and Charleroi, when to the surprise of all non-German tacticians, the attacks in mass formation witnessed at Liége were repeated.

To describe that battle is beyond the scope of this narrative. But it is certain that the estimates so far formed of German losses are below, if not a long way below, the truth.

There is, however, a reliable comparative basis on which to arrive at a computation, and this has a most essential bearing on later events.

At Liége there were three heavy mass attacks against trenches defended by a total force of 20,000 Belgian riflemen with machine guns.[2] We have seen what the losses were. At Mons, against the British forces, there were mass attacks against lines held by five divisions of British infantry, a total roughly of 65,000 riflemen, with machine guns, and backed by over sixty batteries of artillery.

---

1. These figures are given on the authority of M. de Broqueville, Belgian Prime Minister and Minister of War, who has stated that the total here quoted was officially admitted by the German Government.
2. There are usually two machine guns to each section of infantry.

Now, taking them altogether, the British infantry reach, as marksmen, a level quite unknown in the armies of the Continent. Further, these mass attacks were made by the Germans with far greater numbers than at Liége, and there were far more of them. Indeed, they were pressed at frequent intervals during two days and part of the intervening night. The evidence as to the dense formations adopted in these attacks is conclusive.

What, from facts such as these, is the inference to be drawn as to losses incurred? The inference, and it is supported by the failure of any of these attacks to get home, is, and can only be, that the losses must have been proportionally on the same scale as those at Liége, for the attacks were, for the most part, as at Liége, launched frontally against entrenched positions. Though at first sight such figures may appear fantastic, to put the losses at three times the total of the losses at Liége is probably but a very slight exaggeration, even if it be any exaggeration at all.

There is, however, still another ground for such a conclusion. While the British front from Condé past and behind Mons to Binche allowed of the full and effective employment of the whole British force, even when holding in hand necessary reserves, it was obviously not a front wide enough to allow of the full and effective employment on the German side of a force four times as numerous. It must not be forgotten that troops cannot fight at their best without sufficient space to fight in.

But to employ in the same space a force no greater than the British, considering the advantage of position given with modern arms to an army acting on the defensive on well-chosen ground, would have meant the annihilation of the German Army section by section.

That in effect, apart from the turning movement undertaken through Tournai, and the attempt at Binche to enfilade the British position by an oblique line of attack, was the problem which General von Kluck had to face. His solution of it, in the belief that his artillery must have completely shaken the British resistance, was to follow up the bombardment by a succession of infantry attacks in close formation, one following immediately the other, so that each attack would, it was thought, start from a point nearer to the British trenches than that preceding it, until finally the rush could not possibly be stopped. In that way the whole weight of the German infantry might, despite the narrow front, be thrown against the British positions, and though the losses incurred must of necessity be severe, nevertheless, the British line would be entirely swept away, and the losses more than amply revenged in the rout that must ensue. Not only so, but the outcome should be the destruction of the British force

That this is as near the truth as any explanation which can be offered is hardly doubtful. The conclusion is consonant, besides, with what have been considered the newest German views on offensive tactics. To suppose that General von Kluck, or any other commander, would throw away the lives of his officers and men without some seemingly sufficient object is not reasonable.

Here we touch one of the hidden but fatal flaws in the German plan—the assumption that German troops, if not superior, must at any rate be equal in skill to any others. The German troops at Mons, admittedly, fought with great daring, but that they fought or were led with skill is disproved by all the testimony available. It is as clear as anything can be that not merely the coolness and the marksmanship of the British force was a surprise to the enemy, but the uniformity of its quality. Of the elements that go to make up military strength, uniformity of quality is among the most important. The cohesion of an army with no weak links is unbreakable. It is not only more supple than an army made up of troops of varying quality and skill, but it is more tenacious. Like a well-tempered sword, it is at once more flexible yet more unbreakable than an inferior weapon.

Against an inferior army the tactics of General von Kluck must infallibly have succeeded. Against such a military weapon as the British force at Mons they were foredoomed to failure. Assuming the British Army to be inferior, General von Kluck threw the full weight of his troops upon it before he had tried its temper.

Studying their bearing, the importance of these considerations becomes plain. Powerful as it was, the driving head of the great German chain had yet not proved powerful enough inevitably to sweep away resistance. That again disclosed a miscalculation. It is true that the British force had to retire, and it is equally true that that retirement exposed them to great danger, for the enemy, inflamed by his losses, was still in numbers far superior, and what, for troops obliged to adopt marching formations, was even more serious, he was times over superior in guns. Few armies in face of such superiority could have escaped annihilation; fewer still would not have fallen into complete demoralisation.

The British force, however, not only escaped annihilation, but came out both with losses *relatively* light, and wholly undemoralised.

This was no mere accident. Why, can be briefly told. Remember that quality of uniformity, remember the value of it in giving cohesion to the organic masses of the army. Remember further the hitting power of an army in which both gunners and riflemen are on the whole first-rate shots, and with a cavalry which the hostile horse had shown itself unable to contend against. On the other hand, bear in mind that the greater masses of the enemy were of necessity slower in movement, and that the larger an army is, the slower it *must* move.

Naturally the enemy used every effort to throw as large forces as he could upon the flanks of the retiring British divisions. He especially employed his weight of guns for that purpose. On the other hand, the British obviously and purposely occupied all the roads over as broad an extent of country as was advisable. They did so in order to impose wide detours on outflanking movements. While those forces were going round, the British were moving forward and so escaping them.

The difficulties the Germans had to contend against were first the difficulty of getting close in enough with bodies of troops large enough, and secondly that, in flowing up, their mass, while greater in depth from van to rear than the British, could not be much, if anything, greater in breadth. The numerical superiority, therefore, could not be made fully available.

Broadly, those were the conditions of this retirement; and when we come to examine them, comparing the effective force of the opponents, the *relatively* light losses of the British cease to be surprising. The retirement, of course, was full of exciting episodes. Sir John French began his movement with a vigorous counter-attack.[3] This wise tactic both misled the enemy and taught him caution.

It was by such tactics that the British general so far outpaced the enemy as to be able to form front for battle at Cambrai. Here again some brief notes are necessary in order to estimate the effect on later events.

On the right of the British position from Cambrai to Le Cateau, and somewhat in advance of it, the village of Landrecies was held by the 4th Brigade of Guards. Just to the north of Landrecies is the forest

---

3. "At daybreak on the 24th (Aug.) the Second Division from the neighbourhood of Harmignies made a powerful demonstration as if to retake Binche. This was supported by the artillery of the first and second divisions, while the First Division took up a supporting position in the neighbourhood of Peissant. Under cover of this demonstration the Second (Army) Corps retired on the line Dour—Quarouble—Frameries."—Despatch of Sir John French of September 7.

of Mormal. The forest is shaped like a triangle. Landrecies stands at the apex pointing south. Round the skirts of the forest both to the east and to the west are roads meeting at Landrecies. Along these roads the Germans were obliged to advance, although to obtain cover from the British guns enfilading these roads large bodies of them came through the forest.

The British right, the corps of General Sir Douglas Haig, held Marailles, and commanded the road to the west of the forest.

Towards the British centre a second slightly advanced position like that of Landrecies was held to the south of Solesmes by the 4th Division, commanded by General Snow.

The British left, formed of the corps of General Sir Horace Smith-Dorrien, was "refused" or drawn back, because in this quarter an attempted turning movement on the part of the enemy was looked for. In the position taken up, the front here was covered by a small river continued by a canal.

On the British left also, to the south of Cambrai, were posted the cavalry under General Allenby.

These dispositions commanded the roads and approaches along which the enemy must advance in order to obtain touch with the main body, and they were calculated both to break up the unity of his onset and to lay him open to effective attack while deploying for battle. They were, in fact, the same tactics which, in resisting the onset of a superior force, Wellington employed at Waterloo by holding in advance of his main line Hugomont and La Haye Sainte for a like purpose.

Sir John French had foreseen that, taught at Mons the cost of a frontal assault against British troops, General von Kluck would now seek to employ his greater numerical strength and weight of guns by throwing that strength as far as he could against the flanks of the British, hoping to crush the British line together and so destroy it.

That, in fact, was what General von Kluck did try to do. In this attack five German Army corps were engaged. The German general concentrated the main weight of his artillery, comprising some 112 batteries of field guns and howitzers, against the British left. The terrific bombardment was followed up by infantry attacks, in which mass formations were once more resorted to. Evidently it was thought that against such a strength in guns the British could not possibly hold their lines, and that the infantry, completely demoralised, must be so shaken as to fire wildly, rendering an onslaught by superior forces of the German infantry an assured and sweeping victory.

For a second time these calculations miscarried. As they rushed forward, expecting but feeble opposition, the hostile infantry masses were shot down by thousands. The spectacle of such masses was certainly designed to terrify. It failed to terrify. In this connection it is apposite to recall that the destruction of Baker Pasha's army at Suakim by a massed rush of Arab spearmen long formed with the newer school of German tacticians a classic example of the effect of such charges on British troops. No distinction seems to have been made between the half-trained Egyptian levies led by Baker Pasha and fully trained British infantry. The two are, in a military sense, worlds apart. Yet German theorists, their judgment influenced by natural bias, ignored the difference.

Nor was the fortune of the attacks upon the British right any better. The defence of Landrecies by the Guards Brigade forms one of the most heroic episodes of the war. Before it was evacuated the village had become a German charnel-house. Hard pressed as they were at both extremities of their line, the British during these two days fought to a standstill an army still nearly three times as large' as their own.

That simply upset all accepted computations. As Sir John French stated in his despatch of September 7, the fighting from the beginning of the action at Mons to the further British retirement from Cambrai formed in effect one continuous battle. The British withdrawal was materially helped by a timely attack upon the right flank of the German forces delivered by two French divisions which had advanced from Arras under the command of General d'Amade, and by the French cavalry under General Sordêt.

Now consider the effect upon the German plans. There is, to begin with, the losses. That those at Cambrai must have been extremely heavy is certain. The failure of such an attack pushed with such determination proves it.[4] We are fully justified in concluding that the attack did not cease until the power to continue it had come to an end. Losses on that scale meant, first, the collection of the wounded and the burial of the dead; and, secondly, the reforming of broken battalions from reserves. The latter had to be brought from the rear, and that, as well as their incorporation in the various corps, involved delay. Again, the vast expenditure of artillery munitions meant waiting

---

4. The reported extraordinary Army Order issued by the German emperor commanding "extermination" of the British force has since been officially disavowed as a fiction.

for replenishment; and though we may assume that arrangements for replenishment were as complete as possible, yet it would take time. For all these reasons the inability of General von Kluck to follow up becomes readily explicable.

Bear in mind that the whole German scheme of invasion hung for its success on his ability to follow up and on the continued power and solidity of his forces. It must not be supposed that that had not been fully foreseen and, as far as was thought necessary, provided for. There is ample evidence that, in view alike of the fighting in Belgium and of the landing of the British Expeditionary Force on August 17, this leading and largest formation of the German chain of armies had been made still larger than the original scheme had designed. Apparently at Mons it comprised eight instead of the originally proposed six army corps. After Cambrai, as later events will show, the force of General von Kluck included only five army corps of first line troops.

To account for that decrease, the suggestion has been made that at this time, consequent upon the defeat met with by the Germans at Gunbinnen in East Prussia and the advance of the Russians towards Königsberg, there was a heavy transfer of troops from the west front to the east. Not only would such a transfer have been in the circumstances the most manifest of military blunders, but no one acquainted with the methods of the German Government and of the German General Staff can accept the explanation. Whatever may be the shortcomings of the German Government, vacillation is not one of them. What evidently did take place was the transfer of the *débris* of army corps preparatory to their re-formation for service on the east front and their replacement by fresh reserves.

But though the mass was thus made up again, there is a wide difference between a great army consisting wholly of first line troops and an army, even of equal numbers, formed of troops of varying values. The driving head was no longer solid.

In the battle on the Somme when the British occupied positions from Ham to Peronne, and the French Army delivered a flank attack on the Germans along the line from St. Quentin to Guise, the invaders were again checked.

From St. Quentin to Peronne the course of the Somme, a deep and dangerous river, describes an irregular half-circle, sweeping first to the west, and then round to the north. General von Kluck had here to face the far from easy tactical problem of fighting on the inner line of that half-circle. He addressed himself to it with vigour. One part of his plan was a wide outflanking movement through Amiens; another was to throw a heavy force against St. Quentin; a third was to force the passage of the Somme both east and west of Ham.

These operations were undertaken, of course, in conjunction with the army of General von Bülow. Part of the troops of von Bülow, the 10th, and the Reserve Corps of the Prussian Guard were heavily defeated by the French at Guise. But while it was the object of the French and British to make the German operations as costly as possible, it formed, for reasons which will presently appear, no part of their strategy to follow up local advantages.

Why it formed no part of their strategy will become evident if at this point a glance is cast over the fortunes of the other German armies.

The army of General von Bülow had been engaged against the French in the battle at Charleroi and along the Sambre, and again in the battle at St. Quentin and Guise, and admittedly had in both encounters lost heavily.

The army of General von Hausen had been compelled to light its way across the Meuse in the face of fierce opposition. At Charleville, the centre of this great combat, its losses, too, were severe. Again, at Rethel, on the line of the Aisne, there was a furious six days' battle.

The army of Duke Albert of Wurtemberg had twice been driven back over the Meuse into Belgian Luxemburg.

The army of the Crown Prince of Germany, notwithstanding its initial success at Château Malins, had been defeated at Spincourt.

The army of the Crown Prince of Bavaria had been defeated with heavy loss at Luneville.

Divisions of the German Army operating in Alsace had been worsted, first at Altkirch, and again at Mulhausen.

Taking these events together, the fact stands out that the first aim in the strategy of General Joffre was, as far as possible, to defeat the German armies in detail, and thus to hinder and delay their co-operation. He was enabled to carry out that object because the French mobilisation had been completed without disturbance.

These two facts—completion of the French mobilisation and the throwing back of the German plan by the defeat of the several armies in detail—are facts of the first importance.

The aggregate losses sustained by the Germans were already huge. If, up to September 3, we put the total wastage of war from the outset at 500,000, remembering that the fatigues of a campaign conducted in a hurry mean a wastage from exhaustion equal at least to the losses in action, we shall, great as such a total may appear, still be within the truth.

But more serious even than the losses was the dislocation of the plan. The army of the Crown Prince of Germany, which was to have advanced by rapid marches through the defiles of the Argonne, to have invested Verdun, and to have taken the fortified frontier in the rear, found itself unable to effect that object. It was held up in the hills. That meant that the armies of the Crown Prince of Bavaria and the army of General von Heeringen were kept out of the main scheme of operations.

Consider what this meant. It meant that the freedom of movement of the whole chain of armies was for the time being gone. It meant further that, so long as that state of things continued, the primary condition on which the whole German scheme depended—a superiority of military strength—could not be realised. Not only were the German armies no longer, in a military sense, homogeneous, but a considerable part of the force, being on the wrong side of the fortified frontier, could not be brought to bear, and another considerable part of the force, the army of the Crown Prince of Germany, had fallen into an entanglement. Were the armies of von Kluck, von Bülow, von Hausen, and Duke Albert, the latter already badly mauled, sufficient to carry out the scheme laid down? Quite obviously not.

Obviously not, because on the one hand there was the completion of the French mobilisation, and the presence of a British Army; and on the other hand there were the losses met with, and the reductions in the *applicable* force.

Something must be done to pull affairs round. The something was to begin with the extraction of the Crown Prince of Germany from his predicament. If that could be effected and the fortified frontier turned, then the armies of the Crown Prince of Bavaria and of General von Heeringen could make their entry into the main arena; and the primary condition of superiority in strength restored.

Thus it is evident that the events preceding September 3, dictated the movement which, on September 3, changed for good the aspect of the campaign.

Chapter 3

General Joffre As a Strategist

From the strategy on the German side let us now turn to that on the side of the French. Between them a fundamental distinction at once appears.

Of both the aim was similar—to compel the other side to fight under a disadvantage. In that way strategy helps to ensure victory, or to lessen the consequences of defeat.

The strategy of the German General Staff, however, was from the outset obvious. The strategy of General Joffre was at the outset a mystery. Only as the campaign went on did the French scheme of operations become apparent. Even then the part of the scheme still to come remained unfathomable.

It has been assumed that with the employment of armies formed of millions of men the element of surprise must be banished. That was a German theory. The theory is unsound. Now, as ever, intellect is the ultimate commanding quality in war.

In truth, the factor of intellect was never more commanding than under conditions of war carried on with mass armies.

Reflect upon the difference between an opponent who, under such conditions, is able to fathom and to provide against hostile moves, and the opponent who has to take his measures in the dark as to hostile intentions.

The former can issue his orders with the reasonable certainty that they are what the situation will call for. Never were orders and instructions more complex than with modern armies numbering millions; never were there more contingencies to provide against and to foresee. To move and to manipulate these vast masses with effect, accurate *anticipation* is essential. Such complicated machines cannot be pushed about on the spur of the moment when a general suddenly wakes up to a discovery.

It follows that to conduct a campaign with mass armies there must either be a plan which you judge yourself strong enough in any event to realise or a plan which, because your opponent cannot fathom it, must throw him into complete confusion. The former was the German way; the latter the French.

That General Joffre would *try* in the first place to defeat the German armies in detail was not, of course, one of the surprises, because it is elementary, but that he should have so largely *succeeded* in defeating them was a surprise.

In these encounters, as during later battles of the campaign, the French troops discovered a cohesion and steadiness and a military habit of discipline assumed to be foreign to their temperament. But their units had been trained to act together in masses on practical lines. Of the value of that training General Joffre was well aware.

He knew also that success in the earlier encounters, which that training would go far to ensure, must give his troops an invaluable confidence in their own quality.

There were, however, two surprises even more marked. One of these was the quite unexpected use made of the fortified frontier; the other, associated with it, was that of allowing the Germans to advance upon Paris with an insufficient force, in the belief that French movements were being conformed to their own.

Undoubtedly as regards the fortified frontier the belief prevailed that the chief difficulty would be that of destroying its works with heavy guns. It had never been anticipated that the Germans might be prevented from getting near enough for the purpose. But in the French strategy Verdun, Toul, and Belfort were not employed as obstacles. They were employed as the fortified bases of armies. Being fortified, these bases were safe even if close to the scene of operations. Consequently the lines of communication could be correspondingly shortened, and the power and activity of the armies dependent on them correspondingly increased. So long as these armies remained afoot, the fortresses were unattackable. Used in that way, a fortress reaches its highest military value.

The strategy adopted by General Joffre in association with the German advance upon Paris is one of the most interesting phases of the war. His *tactics* were to delay and weaken the first and driving formation of the German chain of armies; his *strategy* was, while holding the tail of that chain of armies fast upon the fortified frontier, to attract the head of it southwest. In that way he at once weakened the chain and lengthened out the German communications. Not merely was the position of the first German Army the worse, and its effective strength the less, the further it advanced, thus ensuring its eventual defeat, but in the event of defeat retirement became proportionally more difficult. The means employed were the illusion that this army was driving before it, not a wing of the Allied forces engaged merely in operations of delay, but forces which, through defeat, were unable to withstand its march onward.

It cannot now be doubted that the Germans had believed themselves strong enough to undertake the investment of Paris concurrently with successful hostilities against the French forces in the field. But by the time General von Kluck's army arrived at Creil, the fact had become manifest that those two objectives could not be attempted concurrently. The necessity had therefore arisen of attempting them *successively*.

In face of that necessity the choice as to which of the two should be attempted first was not a choice which admitted of debate. Defeat of the French forces in the field must be first. Without it, the investment of Paris had clearly become an impossibility. How far it had become an impossibility will be realised by looking at the position of the German armies.

Five of them were echeloned across France from Creil, north-east of Paris, to near the southern point of the Argonne.

The army of von Kluck was between Creil and Soissons, with advanced posts extended to Meaux on the Marne.

The army of von Bülow was between Soissons and Rheims, with advanced posts pushed to Château-Thierry, also on the Marne.

The army of von Hausen held Rheims and the country between Rheims and Chalons, with advanced posts at Epernay.

The army of Duke Albert, with headquarters at Chalons, occupied the valley of the Marne as far as the Argonne.

The army of the Crown Prince of Prussia, with headquarters at St. Menehould, held the Argonne north of that place, with communications passing round Verdun to Metz.

If the line formed by these armies be traced on the map, it will be found to present from Creil to the southern part of the Argonne a great but somewhat flattened arc, its curvature northwards. Then from the southern part of the Argonne the line will present a sharp bend to the north-east.

Now these five armies, refortified by reserves, comprised nineteen army corps, plus divisions of cavalry—a vast force aggregating well over one million men, with more than 3,000 guns. Powerful as it appeared, however, this chain of armies was hampered by that capital disadvantage of being held fast by the tail. Held as it was, the chain could not be stretched to attempt an investment of Paris without peril of being broken, and the great project of defeating and enveloping the Allied forces was impossible.

No question was during the first weeks of the war more repeatedly asked than why, instead of drafting larger forces to the frontier of Belgium, General Joffre should have made what seemed to be a purposeless diversion into Upper Alsace, the Vosges, and Lorraine.

The operations of the French in those parts of the theatre of war were neither purposeless nor a diversion.

On the contrary, those operations formed the crux of the French General's counter-scheme.

Their object was, as shown, to prevent the Germans from making an effective attack on the fortified frontier. General Joffre well knew that in the absence of that effective attack, and so long as the German echelon of armies was pinned upon the frontier, Paris could not be invested. In short, the effect of General Joffre's strategy was to *rob the Germans of the advantages arising from their main body having taken the Belgian route.*

On September 3, then, the scale of advantage had begun to dip on the side of the defence. It remained to make that advantage decisive. The opportunity speedily offered. Since the opportunity had been looked for, General Joffre had made his dispositions accordingly, and was ready to seize it.

Let it be recalled that the most vulnerable and at the same time the most vital point of the German echelon was the outside or right flank of the leading formation, the force led by General von Kluck. Obviously that was the point against which the weight of the French and British attack was primarily directed.

To grasp clearly the operations which followed, it is necessary here to outline the natural features of the terrain and its roads and railways. For that purpose it will probably be best to start from the Vosges and take the country westward as far as Paris.

On their western side the Vosges are buttressed by a succession of wooded spurs divided by upland valleys, often narrowing into mere clefts called "*rupts.*" These valleys, as we move away from the Vosges, widen out and fall in level until they merge with the upper valley of the Moselle. If we think of this part of the valley of the Moselle as a main street, and these side valleys and "*rupts*" as *culs-de-sac* opening off it, we form a fairly accurate notion of the region.

From the valley of the upper Moselle the valley of the upper Meuse, roughly parallel to it farther west, is divided by a ridge of wooded country. Though not high, this ridge is continuous.

On the points of greatest natural strength commanding the roads and railways running across the ridge, and mostly on the east side of the valley of the Meuse, had been built the defence works of the fortified frontier.

Crossing the valley of the Meuse we come into a similar region of hills and woods, but this region is, on the whole, much wilder, the hills higher, and the forests more extensive and dense. The hills here, too, form a nearly continuous ridge, running north-north-west. The highlands east of the Meuse sink, as we go north, into the undulating country of Lorraine, but the ridge on the west side of the Meuse extends a good many miles farther. This ridge, with the Meuse flowing along the east side of it and the River Aire flowing along its west side, is the Argonne. It is divided by two main clefts. Through the more northerly runs the main road from Verdun to Chalons; through the more southerly the main road from St. Mihiel on the Meuse to Bar-le-Duc, on the Marne.

Thus from the Vosges to the Aire we have three nearly parallel rivers divided by two hilly ridges.

North of Verdun the undulating Lorraine country east of the Meuse again rises into a stretch of upland forest. This is the Woevre.

Now, westward of the Argonne and across the Aire there is a region in character very like the South Downs in England. It extends all the way from the upper reaches of the Marne north-west beyond the Aisne and the Oise to St. Quentin. In this open country, where the principal occupation is sheep grazing, the lonely main roads run across the downs for mile after mile straight as an arrow. Villages are far between. The few towns lie along the intersecting valleys.

But descending from the downs into the wide valley of the Marne we come into the region which has been not unaptly called the orchard of France, the land of vineyards and plantations, and flourishing, picturesque towns; in short, one of the most beautiful spots in Europe. The change from the wide horizons of the solitary downs to the populous and highly-cultivated lowlands is like coming into another world.

From the military point of view, however, the important features of all this part of France are its roads and rivers, and most of all its rivers.

The three main waterways, the Oise, the Marne, and the Seine, converge as they approach Paris. Between the Oise and the Marne flows the main tributary of the Oise, the Aisne. Also north of the Marne is its tributary, the Ourcq; south of the Marne flows its tributaries, the Petit Morin and the Grand Morin. All join the Marne in the lower part of the valley not far from Paris. Between the Marne and the Seine flows the Aube, a tributary of the Seine. The country between the Marne and the Seine forms a wide swell of land. It was along the plateaux forming the backbone of this broad ridge that the Battle of the Marne was, for the most part, fought.

That brings us to the question of the roads.

Eastward from Paris, along the valley of the Marne, run three great highways. The most northerly, passing through Meaux, La Ferté-sous-Jouarre, Château Thierry, and Epernay to Chalons, follows nearly the same course as the river, crossing it at several points to avoid bends. The next branches off at La Ferté-sous-Jouarre, and also runs to Chalons by way of Montmirail. The third, passing through La Ferté Gaucher, Sezanne, Fère Champenoise, and Sommesons to Vitry-le-François, follows the backbone of country already alluded to. All these great roads lead farther east into Germany, the northerly and the middle roads to Metz and the valley of the Moselle, the third road to Nancy and Strasburg.

Now, it must be manifest to anybody that command of these routes, with command of the railways corresponding with them, meant mastery of the communications between Paris and the French forces holding the fortified frontier all the way from Toul to Verdun.

If, consequently, the invading forces could seize and hold these routes and railways, and, as a result, which would to all intents follow, could seize and hold the great main routes and the railways running eastward through the valley of the Seine from Paris to Belfort, the fortified frontier—the key to the whole situation—would in military phrase, be completely "turned." Its defence consequently would have to be abandoned.

Not only must its defence have been abandoned, with the effect of giving freedom of movement to the German echelon, but, that barrier removed, the German armies would no longer be dependent for munitions and supplies on the route through Belgium. They could receive them just as conveniently by the route through Metz. Their facilities of supply would be doubled.

It will be seen, therefore, to what an extent the whole course of the war hung upon this great clash of arms on the Marne. German success must have affected the future of operations alike in the western theatre and in the eastern.

But there is another feature of the roads in the valley of the Marne which is of consequence. Great roads converge into it from the north. Sezanne has already been mentioned. It is halfway along the broad backbone dividing the valley of the Marne from the valley of the Seine. Five great roads meet there from La Ferté-sous-Jouarre, Soissons, Rheims, Chalons, Verdun, and Nancy. Hence the facility for massing at that place a huge body of troops.

It will be seen, therefore, that in making Sezanne the point at which they aimed their main blow at the whole French scheme of defence, the Germans had selected the spot where the blow would, in all probability, be at once decisive and possibly fatal. Clearly they had now grasped, at all events in its main intention, the strategy of the French general. *They saw that he was using the fortified frontier to checkmate their Belgian plan.*

Summing up the consequences, had success attended the stroke we find that it would have:

Opened to the invaders the valley of the Seine.

Turned the defence of the fortified frontier.

Released the whole of the German armies.

Given them additional, as well as safer, lines of supply from Germany.

Enabled the German armies to sweep westward along the valley of the Seine, enveloping or threatening to envelop the greater part of the French forces in the field.

CHAPTER 4

The Battle of the Marne

Why, then, if it was so necessary and the object of it so important, was the move begun by General von Kluck on September 3 a false move?

It was a false move because he ought to have stood against the forces opposed to him. The defeat of those forces was necessary before the attack against Sezanne could be successful. Conversely, his own defeat involved failure of the great enterprise.

Instead, however, of facing and continuing his offensive against the forces opposed to him, he turned towards Sezanne. By doing that he exposed his flank to the Allied counter-stroke.

This blunder can only be attributed to the combined influences of, firstly, hurry; secondly, bad information as to the strength and positions of the Allied forces; thirdly, the false impression formed from reports of victories unaccompanied by exact statements as to losses; and fourthly, and perhaps of most consequence, the failure of the Crown Prince of Germany in the Argonne.

General von Kluck doubtless acted upon imperative orders. His incomplete information and the false impression his advance had created probably also led him to accept those orders without protest. But it should not be forgotten that the commander primarily responsible for the blunder, and for the disasters it involved, was the Crown Prince of Germany.

Primarily the Crown Prince of Germany was responsible, but not wholly. In the responsibility General von Kluck had no small share. He was misled. When the British force arrived at Creil General Joffre resolved upon and carried out a masterly and remarkable piece of strategy. The British Army was withdrawn from the extreme left of the Allied line on the north-east of Paris, and transferred to the south-east, and its former place taken by the 6th French Army. This move, carried out with both secrecy and rapidity, was designed to give General von Kluck the impression that the British troops had been withdrawn from the front. That the ruse succeeded is now clear. So far from being withdrawn, the British Army was brought up by reinforcements to the strength of three army corps. Leaving out of account a force of that strength, the calculations of the German Commander were fatally wrong.

Let us now see what generally were the movements of the German and of the Allied forces between September 3 and September 6 when the Battle of the Marne began.

Leaving two army corps, the 2nd and the 4th Reserve corps, on the Ourcq to cover his flank and rear, General von Kluck struck southeast across the Marne with the 3rd, 4th, and 7th corps. The main body crossed the river at La Ferté-sous-Jouarre, and took the main route to Sezanne. Others crossed higher up between La Ferté-sous-Jouarre and Château-Thierry. For this purpose they threw bridges across the river. The Marne is deep and for 120 miles of its course navigable.

These movements were covered and screened by the 2nd division of cavalry, which advanced towards Coulommiers, and the 9th division, which pushed on to the west of Crecy. Both places are south of the Marne and east of Paris.

Writing of these events at the time, Mr. W. T. Massey, special correspondent of the *Daily Telegraph*, observed that:—

> The beginning of the alteration of German plans was noticeable at Creil. Hidden by a thick screen of troops from the army in the field, but observed by aerial squadrons, the enemy were seen to be on the move. Ground won at Senlis was given up, and the German troops, which at that point were nearer Paris than any other men of the *Kaiser's* army, were marched to the rear. Only the commandants in the field can say whether the movement was expected, but it is the fact that immediately the enemy began their strategic movement British and French dispositions were changed.

The movement *was* expected. Indeed, as we have seen, the whole strategy of the campaign on the French side had been designed to bring it about.

> The Germans must have observed that their new intentions had been noticed, but they steadily pursued their policy. Their

right was withdrawn from before Beauvais, and that pretty cathedral town has now been relieved of the danger of Teuton invasion. The shuttered houses are safe, temporarily at any rate. The ponderous machine did not turn at right angles with any rapidity. Its movements were slow, but they were not uncertain, and the change was made just where it was anticipated the driving wedge would meet with least resistance.

In the main the German right is a tired army. It is a great fighting force still. The advance has been rapid, and some big tasks have been accomplished. But the men have learnt many things which have surprised them. They thought they were invincible, that they could sweep away opposition like a tidal wave. Instead of a progress as easy as modern warfare would allow, their way has had to be fought step by step at a staggering sacrifice, and in place of an army which took the field full of confidence in the speedy ending of the war and taught that nothing could prevent a triumph for German arms, you have an army thoroughly disillusioned.

In this connection the service of the British Flying Corps proved invaluable. Covering though they did a vast area, and carefully as they were screened by ordinary military precautions, the movements of the Germans were watched and notified in detail. Upon this, as far as the dispositions of the Allied forces were concerned, everything depended, and no one knew that better than General Joffre. On September 9 he acknowledged it in a message to the British headquarters:—

> Please express most particularly to Marshal French my thanks for services rendered on every day by the English Flying Corps. The precision, exactitude, and regularity of the news brought in by its members are evidence of their perfect organisation, and also of the perfect training of pilots and observers.

Farther east the army of General von Bülow (the 9th, 10th, 10th Reserve corps, and the army corps of the Prussian Guard), advancing from Soissons through Château-Thierry, and crossing the Marne at that place as well as at points higher up towards Epernay, was following the main road to Montmirail on the Petit Morin.

The army of General von Hausen (the 11th, 12th, and 19th corps), advancing from Rheims, had crossed the Marne at Epernay and at other points towards Chalons, and was following the road towards Sezanne by way of Champaubert.

The army of Duke Albert, having passed the Marne above Chalons, was moving along the roads to Sommesous.

The army of the Crown Prince of Germany was endeavouring to move from St. Menehould to Vitry-le-François, also on the Marne.

On the side of the Allies, General Maunoury, with the 6th French Army, advanced from Paris upon the Ourcq. The right of this army rested on Meaux on the Marne. General French with the British Army, pivoting on its left, formed a new front extending south-east to north-west from Jouey, through Le Chatel and Faremoutiers, to Villeneuve-le-Comte.

General Conneau with the French cavalry was on the British right, between Coulommiers and La Ferté Gaucher.

General Desperey with the 5th French Army held the line from Courtagon to Esternay, barring the roads from La Ferté-sous-Jouarre and Montmirail to Sezanne.

General Foch, with headquarters at La Fère Champenoise, barred with his army the roads from Epernay and Chalons.

General de Langle, holding Vitry-le-François, barred the approaches to that place and to Sommesous.

General Serrail, with the French Army operating in the Argonne, held Revigny. His line extended north-east across the Argonne to Verdun, and was linked up with the positions held by the French Army base on that fortress.

General Pau held the line on the east of the fortified frontier.

Some observations on these dispositions of the Allies will elucidate their tactical intention.

The position of the Allied armies formed a great bow, with the western end of it bent sharply inwards.

The *weight* of the Allied forces was massed round that western bend against the now exposed flank of von Kluck's army. Here lay the most vulnerable point of the German line.

The tactical scheme of the Allied commander-in-chief was simple—a great military merit. He aimed first at defeating the German right led by Generals von Kluck and von Bülow. Having by that uncovered the flank of General von Hausen's army, his intention was to attack it also in both front and flank and defeat it. The same tactic was to be repeated with each of the other German armies in succession.

For that purpose the allied armies were not posted directly on the front of the German armies, but between them. Consequently the left of one German Army and the right of another was attacked by the same French Army. In that way two German generals would have to resist an attack directed by one French general, and every German general would have to resist two independent French attacks. Hence, too, if a German Army was forced back the French could at once double round the flank of the German Army next in the line if that army was still standing its ground.

Choice of the battle ground and command of the roads leading to it ensured that this would happen. As a fact, it did.

Finally, all the way behind the French line ran the great road leading across the plateaux from Paris to the fortified frontier. This, with railway communication, gave the needed facilities for the movement of reserves and the transport of munitions and food supplies.

Now let us glance at the tactical scheme on the German side.

The fact that General von Kluck had left two out of the five corps forming his army on the Ourcq, and was covering his movement to the south of the Marne with his cavalry, proves that he did not, as was supposed, intend to lose contact with Paris. His scheme was to establish an echelon of troops from the Ourcq to La Ferté Gaucher on the great eastern road, believing that to be meanwhile a quite sufficient defence.

With the rest of his force he was to join with von Bülow and von Hausen in smashing through the French position at Sezanne. Against that position there was to be the overwhelming concentration of ten army corps.

To assist the stroke against Sezanne there was a concurrent intention to break the French line at Vitry-le-François. The French line between Sezanne and Vitry-le-François would then be swept away.

Assuming the success of these operations, the German forces would be echeloned south-east from the Ourcq across the valley of the Marne and the plateau south of it to Troyes on the Aube. The Germans would then be in a position to attack in flank the French retreating from the frontier, and ready, when these French troops fell back, pursued by the armies of the Crown Princes of Germany and Bavaria and by von Heeringen's army of the Vosges, to join in the great sweep along the valley of the Seine and round to the south of Paris. By this time, remember, the long lines of communication through Belgium would have ceased to be vital.

It was a bold scheme.

There are, however, other factors to be taken into account besides tactical plans.

Not less a surprise than the apparently sudden change in the German movements had been, during the preceding week or more, the seemingly hardly less precipitate falling back of the French upon the Marne. All the world believed that the French were "on the run," and all the world thought they would keep on running. Day by day during that exciting time the inhabitants of the valley of the Marne witnessed column after column of their defenders apparently in full retreat. The marching qualities of the French are, as everybody knows, remarkable. They showed the enemy a clean pair of heels. Few could understand it.

Then came the Germans, hot on the scent, confident that the French could never withstand them. From over the highlands by every road they poured into the peaceful Marne valley like a destroying flood. In front of them swept a multitude of fugitives.

A special correspondent of the *Daily Telegraph* wrote:

> Champagne is now overrun with fugitive villagers from the neighbourhood of Rethel, Laon, and Soissons. It is painful to see these unfortunate people hurrying away with a few household goods on carts, or with bundles, and walking along the country roads in regular ragged processions, not knowing whither they are going. Château-Thierry and all the beautiful country of the Marne is by this time in the hands of the Germans. When I last drove through the place a few weeks ago, and lunched with a few amiable French officers at the best hotel in the place, "*L'Eléphant*," Château-Thierry was teeming with cattle and army horses requisitioned for the campaign. Four times I passed through it, and each time the great assemblage of horses, trucks, and army material had increased, although the horses and cattle were driven away each day, and fresh ones were led in from the great pastoral country round about. Little did I think then that the Germans would now be bivouacking on the great market place and stacking their rifles on the banks of the Marne.

It was by just this over-confidence in themselves that General Joffre had intended the enemy should be misled. He had foreseen that the Germans would come on in a hurry. On the other hand, the French retreat had apparently been precipitous because it was essential to make ready for the rebound. The retreat had rendered the French troops, still unbeaten, only the more dangerous. Describing the effect from his own observation, Mr. Massey wrote:—

The French eastern army has been on the move for days, and if the Germans were not in such strong force they would be in grave danger. The French have made such a strenuous effort to cope with the new condition of things that one of their infantry brigades marched continuously for three days, the men never resting for more than an hour at a time.

One who has seen only the Allied armies may be a bad judge, and less able to form an opinion than an armchair critic, who sums up the possibilities with the aid of maps and the knowledge of past achievements of German forces. But there is one guide which the stay-at-home strategist cannot possibly have, and that is the spirit of the Allied soldiery. I have seen far more of the French than of the English troops in this campaign, but anyone who has talked to the soldier must be infected with his cheery optimism.

His faith in his country and in the power of the army is stupendous, his patriotism is unquestionable, his confidence grows as the enemy approaches. With a smile he accepts the news of the German march southwards, and tells you nothing could be better; the further the line penetrates the more remote is the chance that it will continue unbroken. He will not believe that the German advance would have got so far if it had not been the plan of General Joffre to lure the enemy forwards, and so to weaken his line. The French soldier today, (as at time of first publication), is more confident of victory than ever.

These things, which a soldier can appreciate at their proper value, explain why the dash of the French troops has rivalled their attitude in the previous part of the campaign. Reinforced by great battalions, stiffened by reserves composed mainly of men with a stake in the country, and fighting for all they hold most dear—for France, for hearth, and home—they have offered a magnificent, resolute front to the machine-like advance.

General Joffre, therefore, had handled his machine with skill. He had used it for his design without impairing its spirit. On the contrary, he had stiffened its "form." And on the eve of the great encounter on which the fortunes of the campaign, and the future of France alike hung, he issued to the troops his now famous order:—

"At the moment, when a battle on which the welfare of the country depends is about to begin, I feel it incumbent upon me to remind you all that this is no longer the time to look behind. All our efforts must be directed towards attacking and driving back the enemy. An army which can no longer advance must at all costs keep the ground it has won and allow itself to be killed on the spot rather than give way. In the present circumstances no faltering can be tolerated."

That the Germans on their side equally realised how momentous was the impending battle is shown by their Army Order. A copy of it was, after the battle, found in a house at Vitry-le-François, which for a time had been used as a headquarters of the 8th German Army corps. In the haste of flight the document was left behind. Signed by Lieut.-General Tulff von Tscheppe und Wendenbach, commandant of the 8th corps, and dated September 7, it ran:—

> The object of our long and arduous marches has been achieved. The principal French troops have been forced to accept battle after having been continually forced back. The great decision is undoubtedly at hand.
> Tomorrow, therefore, the whole strength of the German Army, as well as of all that of our army corps, is bound to be engaged all along the line from Paris to Verdun.
> To save the welfare and honour of Germany I expect every officer and man, notwithstanding the hard and heroic fights of the last few days, to do his duty unswervingly, and to the last breath.
> Everything depends on the result of tomorrow.

This, then, was the spirit in which, on both sides, the mightiest clash of arms until then known to history was entered upon. Across France the battle front stretched for 150 miles. The fight raged, too, for another forty miles along the frontier, for coincidently with the main conflict from Paris to Verdun, the Germans made yet another great effort to break upon the frontier from the east. Fourteen great armies took part in the battle. They numbered altogether more than two millions of men. Taking the two great hosts each as a whole, the numbers were not very unequal. True, the Germans had but six armies as against the eight on the side of the Allies. The German armies, however, were larger. Their strength ranged from 160,000 to 180,000 men as against, on the side of the Allies, an average strength of 120,000. (See table following)

The following may be taken as the *approximate* strength of the armies engaged, allowing on the one hand for war wastage, and on the other for a filling up from reserves, which on the part of the Allies had been completed:—

GERMANS.

General von Kluck's Army (5 corps, Prussians)	245,000
2nd and 9th Cavalry Divisions	23,000
General von Bülow's Army (4 corps, Prussians)	180,000
Cavalry of the Prussian Guard	6,000
General von Hausen's Army (3 corps, Saxons)	165,000
Duke Albert's Army (3 corps, Wurtembergers)	150,000
Crown Prince of Germany's Army (3 corps, Prussians)	175,000
Crown Prince of Bavaria's Army (3 corps, Bavarians)	160,000
Approximate total	1,104,000

ALLIES.

General Maunoury's Army (3 corps and reserves)	140,000
General French's Army (3 corps)	110,000
British Cavalry Divisions	8,000
General Conneau's Cavalry	23,000
General Desperey's Army (3 corps and reserves)	150,000
General Foch's Army (3 corps)	120,000
General de Langle's Army (3 corps and reserves)	150,000
General Serrail's Army (3 corps)	120,000
General Pau's Army (3 corps and reserves)	140,000
Approximate total	961,000
Grand approximate total of combatants	2,065,000
Approximate guns and mortars, Germans	3,610
Approximate guns and mortars, Allies	3,680
Total	7,290

The Allies were superior in field-guns, but had fewer howitzers, especially of the heavy type, and the aggregate weight of the German artillery was on the whole greater. The estimate given of the number of combatants is rather below than above the actual.

During nearly six days there was, along that far extended battle line, the flash and thunder of more than 7,000 guns. Shells rose and burst like flights of warring meteorites. Masses of infantry moved to the attack. Incessant rifle fire accompanied the bolder bass of the artillery. In and through woods, across fields, in and round blazing villages and burning farms and *châteaux* they fought; an incessant movement to and fro, amid an unceasing roar—the rage of nations locked in deadly embrace. There were bayonet fights on a vast scale; there were charges by clouds of horsemen; there were furious and murderous combats for points of vantage; there was the capture and recapture of towns; the rush of fire-spitting automobiles below, and the flight of bomb-dropping aeroplanes above. There was the hurried movement of troops and the wild gallop of batteries of guns along the roads. There was, too, the ever-changing kaleidoscope of the masses of transport. Along the great road from Paris to Germany a spectator might have travelled from sunrise to sunset during the whole week of battle, and yet still have found himself in the midst of this seemingly unbounded fury of a world at war.

CHAPTER 5

The German Overthrow

Such were the spectacular aspects of the battle. It remains to sketch its phases as, first sullenly, then swiftly, the tide of conflict rolled backward across the miles of country between Sezanne and Rheims. These developments can best be followed day by day.

September 5.—General movement of the German armies across the Marne. The troops of von Kluck crossed at Trilport, Sommery, and La Ferté-sous-Jouarre; those of von Bülow at Château-Thierry; those of von Hansen at Epernay, and Duke Albert's at Chalons. Simultaneously columns of von Kluck's 2nd and 4th Reserve corps began to cross the Ourcq.

From the Marne the Germans pushed on without delay to the south. The 3rd, 4th, and 7th corps of von Kluck's army were on the march diagonally across the British near Coulommiers. They were making for La Ferté Gaucher. In face of this advance the 5th French army fell back on the latter place. This move lengthened the German flank and laid it more completely open to a British attack.

September 6.—General Joffre gave orders for a general advance. Before daybreak the 6th French, British, and 5th French armies began a combined offensive. While the 6th French Army advanced eastward towards the line of the Ourcq, the British advanced north-east to the line of the Grand Morin, and the 5th French Army north from east of La Ferté Gaucher upon Montmirail.

The 6th French Army, driving in the German advance posts, reached Nanteuil.

The British fell upon the flank of the divisions of von Kluck's army still crossing the Grand Morin, and drove them back upon the Petit Morin.

By this unexpected and swiftly delivered blow von Kluck's army, extending from the Marne to La Ferté Gaucher, was cut into two parts.

Coincidently with the British advance the 5th French Army had, in a night attack and at the point of the bayonet, driven the leading German divisions out of three villages near La Ferté Gaucher, where they had bivouacked.

In view of these attacks General von Kluck had no alternative save to retreat. To escape the British he fell back on the Petit Morin in the direction of Montmirail.

His retreat was assisted by the right of von Bülow's army, and covered by his divisions of cavalry, reinforced by von Bülow's cavalry of the Prussian Guard. The German cavalry, attacked by the French and British, was cut up with heavy loss. More than 60,000 horsemen were engaged in this gigantic combat.

September 7.—To assist the retreat, the centre divisions of von Kluck's army opposing the British made a stand upon the Petit Morin, and the army of von Bülow a stand from Montmirail to Le Petit Sompius. Along that line the 5th French Army was all day heavily engaged against the left wing of von Kluck's army and the right of von Bülow's.

On the Ourcq the Germans launched a general assault against the 6th French Army.

On the Petit Morin they occupied a strong position on the high north bank. This river flows during part of its course through marshes. A frontal attack on the position was out of the question, but the 1st British Army corps and the British cavalry found "a way round" higher up stream. Simultaneously the 3rd British corps crossed lower down. Threatened on both flanks, the Germans fled precipitately towards the Marne. Though they covered their retreat by a counter-attack, they lost many prisoners and some guns.

The armies of von Hausen and Duke Albert and the Crown Prince of Germany were now engaged against the armies of General Foch, General Langle, and General Serrail from the north of Sezanne to Sermaise-les-Bains in the south of the Argonne. The fighting north of Sezanne was obstinate, but the Wurtembergers at Vitry-le-François met with a repulse.

On this day the battle extended for more than 120 miles, from the line of the Ourcq across the country to Montmirail, from that place to Sezanne, and then along the plateaux into the Argonne. There was also a German attack upon Luneville designed to aid their operations west of the fortified frontier.

September 8.—Heavy fighting between the 6th French Army and the Germans on the Ourcq.

The British attacked the passages of the Marne. At La Ferté Gaucher, where the bridge had been destroyed, the Germans, supported by machine guns, obstinately disputed the passage against the British 3rd corps. The 1st and 2nd corps, however, succeeded in bridging the river higher up, and dislodged them. In their retreat the Germans again met with heavy losses.

At Montmirail the battle was continued with great severity. The French carried several of the German positions at the point of the bayonet. Von Bülow's troops began a general retirement, and were driven over the river.

Taking the offensive. General Foch's army attacked the troops of von Hausen in flank. The left of von Hausen's army north of Sezanne was forced back, but his right at Le Fère Champenoise made an obstinate stand.

To meet this, General Langle also began a general advance, and drove the Germans from Vitry-le-François.

A heavy German attack was directed against Clermont-en-Argonne. Beyond the fortified frontier there was a renewed effort to capture Nancy said to have been watched by the *Kaiser*.

September 9.—Reinforced, the Germans on the Ourcq made a great effort to break through the 6th French Army.

The British, having crossed the Marne, fell upon the Germans fighting on the Ourcq, and drove them northwards. Many guns, caissons, and large quantities of transport were captured.

The 5th French Army pursued the defeated troops of von Bülow from Montmirail to Château-Thierry. At that place the Germans are thrown across the Marne in disorder and with huge losses.

The German line had now been completely broken. Between the wreck of von Bülow's troops, north of the Marne, and von Hansen's positions, north of Sezanne, there was a gap of some fifteen miles.

From Sezanne eastward the battle from this time continued with more marked advantage to the Allies.

September 10.—The 6th French Army and the British continued the pursuit. On this day the British captured, besides further quantities of transport abandoned in the flight or surrounded, 13 guns, 19 machine guns, and 2,000 prisoners. German infantry, left behind in the hurried march of their army, were found hiding in the woods. There were evidences of general looting by the enemy and of his demoralisation.

In the pursuit of von Bülow's troops by the 5th French Army, the Prussian Guard were driven into the marshes of St. Gond.

Covered with tall reeds and rank grass, these marshes, drained by the Petit Morin, are a stretch of low-lying land lying between the Marne and a range of hills. They are probably the bed of an ancient lake. Safe in the dry season, they become in wet weather a dangerous swamp. They were at this time saturated with heavy rains. The Prussian Guards, who had borne the brunt of the recent fighting, had already suffered heavily. They now lost the greater part of their artillery, and a heavy proportion of the surviving force either perished in the quagmires or were killed by the French shells.

An effort nevertheless was made to retrieve the general disaster by a violent German attack from Sezanne to Vitry-le-François, accompanied by an energetic offensive in the Argonne, and by a renewed attempt against Nancy.

In the Argonne the Germans captured Revigny and Brabant-le-Roi, but west of Vitry were forced into retreat. The attack on Nancy was again unsuccessful.

September 11.—The 5th and 6th French armies and the British pursued the troops of von Kluck and von Bülow to the Aisne.

The armies of von Hansen and Duke Albert were now in full flight at Epernay and Chalons. Both incurred very heavy losses. The French captured 6,000 prisoners and 175 guns.

The Germans were driven by General Serrail's troops out of Revigny and Brabant-le-Roi. East of the frontier there was also a general falling back, notably from St. Die and round Luneville. The French seized Pont-a-Mousson, commanding one of the main passes across the Vosges.

Of the decisive character of the overthrow there could now be no doubt. On September 11, in an Order to the French armies, General Joffre, summing up the situation with soldierly brevity, said:—

> The battle which has been taking place for five days is finishing in an incontestable victory.
>
> The retreat of the 1st, 2nd, and 3rd German armies is being ac-

centuated before our left and our centre.

The enemy's 4th army, in its turn, is beginning to fall back to the north of Vitry and Sermaize.

Everywhere the enemy is leaving on the field numbers of wounded and quantities of munitions. On all hands prisoners are being taken.

Our troops, as they gain ground, are finding proofs of the intensity of the struggle and of the extent of the means employed by the Germans in attempting to resist our *élan*.

The vigorous resumption of the offensive has brought about success. Officers, non-commissioned officers, and men! you have all of you responded to my appeal, and all of you have deserved well of your country.—Joffre.

It had been no easy victory. The huge forces of Generals von Kluck, von Bülow, and von Hausen, comprising the flower of the German first line army, fought with stubborn and even reckless courage. During the opening days of the battle they contested the ground foot by foot. The character of the fighting in which the British taken part in it, was disclosed by the Paris correspondent of the *Daily Telegraph*:—

An officer who described to me some of the earlier phases said:

The more we killed the more they seemed to become. They swarmed like ants, coming on in masses, though rarely seeking close contact, for they have learned to respect our rifles and our bayonets.

On this point there is unprejudiced testimony, A non-commissioned officer of Hussars asked me to translate a letter found on a German officer killed while defending his battery. In the letter are these sentences:—

German infantry and cavalry will not attack English infantry and cavalry at close quarters. Their fire is murderous. The only way to attack them is with artillery.'

Upon this advice the enemy seem to act. They make the best use of their guns, and keep up an incessant fire, which is often well directed, though the effect is not nearly so deadly as they imagine. Their machine guns—of which they have great numbers—are also handled with skill, and make many gaps in our ranks. But the enemy rarely charge with the bayonet. Under cover of artillery they advance *en masse*, pour out volleys without taking aim, and retire when threatened. This is the general method of attack, and it is one in which numbers undoubtedly count. But numbers are not everything; spirit and dash count for more in the end, and these qualities our soldiers have beyond all others in this war. Every officer with whom I have spoken says the same thing. Nothing could be finer than the steadiness and the enterprise of our troops. They remember and obey the order given by Wellington at Waterloo—they stand fast—to the death. Before this insistent and vigorous offensive the enemy have fallen back every day, pressed hard on front and on flank.

Realising that the whole future of the campaign, if not of the war, hung upon the issue; the army of General von Hausen stood to the last. There was a hope that the German right might yet rally against the staggering attack thrown upon it. Mr. Massey wrote:—

The fighting on the line of the French centre has, from all accounts, been of a most terrific description. Neither side would give ground except under the heaviest pressure. Long-continued artillery duels paved the way for infantry attacks, and positions had to be carried at the point of the bayonet. Often when bayonet charges had cleared trenches the men driven out were rallied and reinforced, and retook the positions. Here was the most strenuous fighting of the campaign, and as the enemy's casualties are certain to have exceeded those of the French, the total of German killed, wounded, and prisoners must reach an enormous figure. The French losses were very heavy.

An infantryman wounded within sight of Vitryle-François told me that the French bayonet fighting was performed with an irresistible dash. The men were always eager—sometimes too eager—to get to close quarters. The weary waiting in trenches too hastily dug to give more than poor shelter from artillery fire caused many a murmur, and there was no attempt to move forward stealthily when the word to advance was given. Often a rushing line was severely torn by *mitrailleuse* fire, but the heart's desire to settle matters with cold steel could not be checked merely because comrades to the right and left were put out of action. The bayonet work of French infantry gave the enemy a terrible time.

Of the struggle on the left of von Hausen's army against the troops of General Langle, a graphic picture is given in the diary of a Saxon officer of infantry found later among the German dead. The army of von Hausen had arrived by forced marches, the left from Rethel, the right from Rheims:—

Sept. 1.—We marched to Rethel. Our battalion stayed there as escort to headquarters.

Sept. 2.—The French burnt half the town, probably to cut our lines of communications. It can't hurt us for long, of course, but it's a nuisance, as our field artillery is short of ammunition.

However, our division advanced. The burning of Rethel was dreadful. All the little houses with wooden beams in their roofs, and their stacks of furniture, fed the flames to the full. The Aisne was only a feeble protection; the sparks were soon carried over to the other side. Next day the town was nothing but a heap of ashes.

Sept. 3.—Still at Rethel, on guard over prisoners. The houses are charming inside. The middle-class in France has magnificent furniture. We found stylish pieces everywhere, and beautiful silk, but in what a state! ... Good God! ... Every bit of furniture broken, mirrors smashed. The vandals themselves could not have done more damage.

This place is a disgrace to our army. The inhabitants who fled could not have expected, of course, that all their goods would have been left in full after so many troops had passed. But the column commanders are responsible for the greater part of the damage, as they could have prevented the looting and destruction. The damage amounts to millions of *marks*; even the safes have been attacked.

In a solicitor's house, in which, as luck would have it, everything was in excellent taste, including a collection of old lace, and Eastern works of art, everything was smashed to bits.

I couldn't resist taking a little memento myself here and there. ... One house was particularly elegant, everything in the best taste. The hall was of light oak; near the staircase I found a splendid aquascutum and a camera by Felix.

The sappers have been ordered to march with the divisional bridging train. We shall start tomorrow. Yesterday at Chalons-sur-Marne a French aviator (officer) was taken prisoner. He imagined the village was held by French troops and so landed there. He was awfully disgusted at being taken prisoner.

Sept. 4.—To Tuniville, Pont-Fauerger, where we billeted.

Sept, 5.—Les Petites Loges, Tours-sur-Marne. I never want to make such marches again; simply tests of endurance. We crossed the Marne canal on Sept. 6. On our left the 19th corps marched straight on Chalons. On our right front the Guard corps was hotly engaged. When we reached Villeneuve we heard that the Guard corps had thrown the enemy back and that our division was to take up the pursuit. We were in a wood, which the enemy searched with shell fire.

Left and right it simply rained bullets, but the one I'm fated to stop was not among them. We could not advance any further, the enemy was too strong for us. On our left the 19th corps came up in time to give us a little breathing space. An infernal shell fire. We had a dreadful thirst, a glass of would have been a godsend.... A shell suddenly fell in the wood and killed six of my section; a second fell right in the middle of us; we couldn't hang on any longer, so we retired.

We made several attempts to reach the village of Lenharree, but the enemy's artillery swept the whole wood, so that we could not make any headway. And we never got a sight of the enemy's guns. We soon had the answer to the riddle as to why the enemy's shooting was so wonderfully accurate. We were actually on the enemy's practice range. Lenharree was the chief *point d'appui* on the right wing.

The situation was as follows: The Guard corps was on a ground which the enemy knew like the back of his hand, and so was in an extremely critical position. It was just like St. Privat, except that we were all in woods under a terrible shell fire. Our artillery could do nothing, as there was nothing to be seen.

We found an order from General Joffre to the commander of the 2nd French corps, telling him to hold the position at all costs, and saying that it was the last card. It was probably the best one, too. As we knew later, the artillery opposed to us had an immense reserve of ammunition.... Absolutely exhausted, we waited for the night. In front of us all was still.

Sept. 8.—We went forward again to the attack against an enemy perfectly entrenched. In spite of his artillery fire, which nothing could silence, we passed through the wood again. As soon as we reached the northern edge, a perfectly insane fire opened on us, infantry and shell fire with redoubled intensity.

A magnificent spectacle lay before us; in the far background Lenharree was in flames, and we saw the enemy retreating, beaten at last. The enemy withdrew from one wood to another, but shelled us furiously and scattered us with his machine guns. We got to the village at last, but were driven out of it again with heavy loss. Our losses were enormous. The 178th Regiment alone had 1,700 men wounded, besides those killed. It was hell itself. There were practically no officers left.

One word more about this artillery range; there were telephone wires everywhere. It is thought that French officers hidden in trees were telephoning our exact situation in the woods.

Sept. 9.—We marched to Oeuvry. The enemy was apparently two kilometres in front of us. Where was our intelligence branch? Our artillery arrived half an hour too late, unfortunately. The French are indefatigable in digging trenches. We passed through a wood and lost touch altogether. We saw companies retiring, and we ourselves received the order to withdraw.

We passed through Lenharree once more, where we found piles of bodies, and we billeted at Germinon. There was a rumour that the 1st army had had some disastrous fighting. Our sappers prepared the bridges for demolition. We passed through Chalons-sur-Marne. I am terribly depressed. Everybody thinks the situation is critical. The uncertainty is worst of all.

I think we advanced too quickly and were worn out by marching too rapidly and fighting incessantly. So we must wait for the other armies. We went on to Mourmelon-le-Petit, where we dug ourselves in thoroughly. Four of our aviators are said to have been brought down by the enemy.

Finally, when forced back to the Marne, after three days of incessant fighting—pounded by the French guns, broken by the fury of the French infantry, ripped by slashing onslaughts of the French horse—the Germans still made effort after effort to recover and to re-form. Of the struggle on the Marne, Mr. William Maxwell says:—

> I was fortunate enough to meet a non-commissioned officer who watched from an eminence the critical phase of the battle which routed the German centre. This is the substance of his story, which has since been corroborated by officers of my acquaintance. The enemy had been driven back fighting for three days, until they came to the river. There they made a desperate stand. Masses of them appeared on the flat and in the undulations of the ground—they seemed like the sands on the sea shore for numbers. They came on in masses and kept up a terrible fire from rifle and machine-gun. But our infantry were not

to be denied; they advanced in short rushes and in open order, while shells rained down upon the enemy, and rifles opened great gaps in their ranks.

"I began," said the sergeant, "to count the dead, but I soon found that impossible. Suddenly I heard a great shout, and turning to my left I saw a sight that made my heart stand still. Our cavalry were charging down on the enemy's cavalry."

In the bright sunshine their lances and sabres looked like a shower of falling stars. There was an avalanche of men and horses and cold steel. Huge gaps were torn in the enemy's ranks—and the whole thing was over in a few minutes. The German horsemen seemed to vanish into the earth.

Stubborn courage, however, was of no avail. In a brief six days that mighty host had been reduced to a military ruin. They had advanced in the confidence that they were irresistible. Down the valley of the Oise, over the highlands of Champagne they had streamed, in endless columns of men and guns. The earth had shaken beneath the rumble of their artillery and trembled under the hoofs of their horsemen; every road had re-echoed the united tread of their battalions; every horizon had bristled with the flash of their bayonets and sabres; every town and village had felt their arrogance as they "requisitioned" its foodstuffs, consumed its wines, slept in its beds, laid hands on whatever they fancied, and summoned mayors and officials before them to learn their will, and collect their "fines." On the substance of this country of the Marne they had revelled, imagining that the world was theirs.

And now they were a battered mass of fugitives, hiding in woods and orchards; littering the roads with the wrecks of their equipment; fagged and footsore; driven by hunger to tear up the crops from the fields, and devour roots and vegetables raw; their discipline replaced by brutal savagery. Not even the liveliest imagination can adequately picture the state of an army in flight after a heavy defeat. The bigger the army the worse that state becomes. The organisation of food supply is thrown out of gear. No man knows where the supplies may be, or whether they may not be lost. Guns become separated from their ammunition columns. Wagons break down or are disabled and have to be left behind. The horses drop from famine and overwork. Men grow sullen and intractable. The boom of guns bespeaking the pursuit alone gives the stimulus to cover the lengthening miles of weary road.

Without time to bury their dead, yet anxious to hide their losses from the enemy, the Germans, where they could, formed large pyres of timber, which they soaked with oil. On to these they threw the bodies of the slain. Across the country the smoke from such pyramids by day and the glare of flames by night added to the strangeness and tragedy of a scene removed even from what had been thought civilised war.

The sufferings of the beaten host were severe. Starving and depressed, or at the last point of exhaustion, men fell out or hid themselves in the thick woods which clothe the long undulating slopes on the northern side of the Marne valley.[1] Here they were found by the pursuing French and British. Most, when discovered, had been without food for two days. Partly to satisfy the pangs of hunger, partly out of mere senseless revenge, general and indiscriminate pillage was resorted to. *Châteaux*, country houses, and villages were ransacked, and pictures or pieces of furniture which could not be carried off destroyed. Though their military spirit had been broken, the ruthlessness of the invaders remained. They traversed the country like a horde of bandits.

Loss of horses forced them to leave behind whole batteries of heavy howitzers and trains of ammunition wagons, for these days of the retreat were days of heavy rain. To shorten the length of their columns, as well as to gain time, the hurrying troops plunged into by-roads. These, cut up by the weight of the guns, speedily became impassable. How hasty was the retreat is proved by the headquarters staff of the 2nd army leaving behind them at Montmirail maps, documents, and personal papers, as well as letters and parcels received by or waiting for the military post.

Following the track of General von Kluck's army, Mr. Gerald Morgan, another special correspondent of the *Daily Telegraph*, wrote:—

> At Vareddes horses and men littered the ground. Semi-permanent entrenchments had been suddenly abandoned. Alongside the German artillery positions I saw piles of unexploded shells which the Germans had abandoned in their hurry. These shells were in wicker baskets, three to a basket. The Germans had had there many batteries of field guns, both three-inch and five-

---

1. From the Oise to the Seine the general aspect of this part of France is a succession of broad ridges separated by valleys, some of them narrow and deep. One-fifth of the whole surface is covered by woods and forests of oak, beech and chestnut. Many of the forests are of great extent. The main ridge was the site of the battle in its first phases.

inch, and had meant evidently to make a determined resistance. But their artillery positions were plainly so badly placed that the French were able to blow them, literally to drench them, out. An avenue of large trees along the roadside, trees which the Germans hoped to use as a shelter, had been torn to pieces and flung to the ground by the French artillery as by strokes of lightning. The German dead had almost all been hit by shells or by shrapnel. A German aeroplane, brought down during the engagement, lay in the fields like a big dead bird.

I followed the line of the German retreat as far as a village called May. From the number of accoutrements thrown away along the road I judged the retreat was in bad order and greatly hurried.

The scene on the battlefield was rather terrible. There was no one to bury the dead, for the French Army had gone on in pursuit, and the villagers had almost all left the country some days before.

The German infantry position was in a valley. The entrenchments had undoubtedly been dug with a view to maintaining them permanently, but the fault lay in the artillery position. The German guns—evidently a large number—had been placed on a ridge behind the infantry position. This ridge was exposed to a fire from the French artillery on a ridge opposite, a fire which completely silenced the German guns, and left the German infantry to its fate. Few of the infantry escaped.

On the day after the Germans had been driven across the Marne, Mr. Wm. Maxwell, driving into the, at ordinary times, pleasant little town of Meaux, found it deserted:—

Its houses are standing; its churches and public buildings are untouched, yet its streets are silent, its windows shuttered, and its doors closed. It might be a plague-stricken city, forsaken by all except a few Red Cross nurses, who wait for the ambulances bringing the wounded from the battlefield.

Leaving the town with a feeling akin to awe, I came upon a new surprise. Walking calmly along the public road in broad day were men in Prussian uniform, and—more amazing still—women in the dark *gellab* or cloak of the Moors. This was certainly startling, but the explanation was waiting on the road to the east, and it was written in gruesome signs—dead men lying in the ditches—

Zouaves in their Oriental dress. Moors in their cloaks, French soldiers in their long blue coats, and Germans in their grey. Every hundred yards or so lay a disembowelled horse with a bloody saddle. This was the ragged edge of the battlefield of the Marne, and the men and women in Prussian and Moorish dress were harmless civilians who had gone to bury the dead and to succour the wounded. It was raining torrents; the wind was bitterly cold, and they had covered themselves with the garments of the dead. Passing along this road I came to a wood, where one of these civilian burial parties had dug a pit in which they laid the friend and foe side by side. Fresh mounds of earth that told their own story guided me to a path, where the battle had blazed, a trail of splintered shells, broken rifles, bullet-riddled helmets, bloodstained rags, with which the dying had stopped their wounds, tiny bags in which the German soldier had hoarded his crumbs of biscuit, letters with the crimson imprint of fingers, showing how in the hour of agony and death men's thoughts turn to the beloved ones they are leaving for ever.

Four miles east of Meaux the hills rise sharply to the north, and are covered with trees. Beyond this wood a broad undulating plain stretches northward over cultivated fields dotted with farmsteads. A hundred paces in front, on a gentle slope, the earth has been levelled in several places that are sown with brass cylinders, whose charge sent the shells on their deadly flight.

In these emplacements lie some gunners; their heads have been shattered by shells. Under an apple-tree, laden with green fruit, two livid faces turn to the pitiless sky; one man grasps a letter in his hand—it is a woman's writing. Dark huddled patches among the cabbages and the trampled wheat, brown stains on the path, fragments of blood-stained lint, broken rifles and bayonets, bullet-pierced helmets and rent cloaks—all the *débris* of battle show where the fight was fiercest.

On the crest of the rise are the trenches; they extend for nearly a mile parallel with the edge of the wood, and are thrown back on the west. They are deep trenches, protected with mounds of earth, and were not made hurriedly. About them lie the dead.

The position of the trenches and gun emplacements shows that here the enemy met a flanking attack from the west and north, and covered the retreat of their centre. It is not difficult to picture what happened.

Scenes like these, the aftermath of the storm of war, were repeated up the valley of the Marne from Meaux to beyond Chalons. Terrific in its intensity the whirlwind had passed as swiftly as it had come.

No estimate has been formed of the loss of life in this vast encounter. It is certain, however, that all the suppositions hitherto advanced have been far below reality. Equally is it certain that this was one of the most destructive battles even in a war of destructive battles. Since the losses on the side of the victorious troops in killed and wounded exceeded 80,000 men, the losses on the side of the vanquished must have been more than three times as great.

That at first sight may appear exaggerated. There exist, nevertheless, good grounds for concluding that such a figure is within the truth. The Germans made a series of grave tactical mistakes. When he discovered the error into which he had fallen. General von Kluck properly decided to withdraw. Had the rest of the German line in conformity with his movement fallen back upon the north bank of the Marne, their repulse, though serious, would not have been a disaster. But it is now manifest that, from a quarter in which the situation was not understood, imperative orders were received to press on.

These orders evidently led von Bülow to attempt a stand upon the Petit Morin. General von Kluck, in face of the attack by the British and by the 6th French Army on the Ourcq, realised that retirement on his part could not be delayed. But the retreat of his left from the Petit Morin exposed the army of von Bülow to an attack in flank. By that attack in flank, as well as in front, von Bülow's troops were forced at Château-Thierry to cross the Marne in full flight. Passing a deep and navigable river in such circumstances is, of all military operations, perhaps, the most destructive and dangerous, and this, from the German standpoint, formed one of the worst episodes of the battle.

Again, probably in obedience to the same imperative orders, the army of von Hausen remained before Sezanne until its decisive defeat was foregone, and its escape to the last degree jeopardised. In the retreat, consequently, the losses were terribly heavy. But even these were less than the losses which fell upon the army of Duke Albert. With almost inconceivable obstinacy and ill-judgment that army clung to its positions at Vitry until pressed by the French forces on both flanks. All the way across the valley of the Marne and over the highlands it had consequently to run a gauntlet of incessant attacks.

In the face of these facts, it is no exaggeration to say that the German losses must have been at least 250,000. To that has to be added nearly 70,000 prisoners. They lost also by capture or by abandonment about a tenth part of their artillery, besides masses of ammunition and transport.

CHAPTER 6

How General Von Kluck Averted Ruin

The German defeat had indeed been decisive. On the other hand, the defeat did not, in the immediate sequel, yield for the Allies all the results which might have been looked for. There have been misimpressions on both points.

Take the first misimpression. A victorious general, it has been well said, rarely knows the full damage he inflicts. Over the wide area covered by the Battle of the Marne and by the pursuit, it was not humanely possible to collect and to collate precise information without some delay. All the same, the French General Staff and the French War Ministry had by September 12 gathered facts enough to form a fairly accurate estimate of advantages won. Beyond vague indications of their nature, however, these facts were not made public. There was at the time a good reason. Situated as the German armies were, and with their intercommunication disorganised, they would take two or three days longer at least to discover on their part the full measure of their losses, and to judge of the effect. To the Allies, that difference in time was of the utmost moment. Certainly it would have been against their interest by publication of details to tell the German General Staff in effect what reinforcements they ought to send, and where they ought to send them. Why the difference in time was of moment will presently appear.

Again it has been repeatedly stated that the foremost effect of the Battle of the Marne was to confirm to the Allies the initiative which the strategy of General Joffre had so skilfully gained. That was one effect assuredly, and a vitally important effect. Another effect, however, hardly less important, was that, in point of military value and for effective operations, the German force in France was no longer the same. The blow had been too severe. Never again could that force be levelled up to those armies which had crossed the Marne in the confidence of prospective victory.

The effect was not moral merely, though *moral* had not a little to do with it. The effect was in the main material. War wastage arising from fatigue and privation must have reduced the effective strength of the German armies in nearly as great a degree as losses in killed and wounded. If on September 12 we put the armies which turned to hold the new line from Compiègne to Verdun at 600,000 men still fit for duty, we shall be adopting probably an outside figure.

Had this force, so reduced, not been able to make a stand along that new line, it must have been destroyed largely through exhaustion and famine. It was saved not, as imagined, chiefly by the defence works thrown up north of the Aisne and across the highlands to the Argonne. It was saved mainly by the tactics and by the energy of General von Kluck.

Rightly described by the British Official Bureau, doubtless on the authority of Sir John French himself, as "bold and skilful," those tactics form one of the outstanding features of the campaign, and they ought justly to be considered among the greatest feats in modern war. They are on the same plane indeed as the strategy and tactics of General Joffre, and these, beyond doubt, rank in point of mastery with the campaign of Napoleon in 1814. In this very area of Champagne on the eve of his fall the military genius of Napoleon was, like lightning in the gloom of tempest, displayed in its greatest splendour. For a thousand years this region of plateaux and rivers has been the arena of events which have shaped the history of Europe.[1] The features it offers for military defence are remarkable. Versed in the campaigns of Napoleon, aware of what have proved to be his mistakes, knowing the country in its every detail, knowing and judging rightly the qualities and capabilities of his troops, General Joffre drew the Germans on step by step to overthrow. The great feature of his plans was that this was meant to be an overthrow which would govern the fortune of the war. In great fact that aim was achieved, but in part also its fulfilment was postponed.

On the retreat of the German armies from the Marne there were,

---

1. The Italian historian, Signer Guglielmo Ferrero, has expressed the opinion that the Battle of the Marne has altered the face of European history. There is little doubt that time will prove this view to be fully justified.

in order to bring about the destruction of those armies as a fighting force, three things which the Allies had to accomplish, and accomplish, if possible, concurrently. The first was to cut the German communications with Luxemburg and Metz by barring the roads and railways across the eastern frontier; the second was to push forward and seize Rheims, and the outlet through the hills north of the Aisne at Berry-au-Bac; the third was to force the troops of von Kluck eastward off their lines of communication along the valley of the Oise, and to do that, if it could be done, south of the Aisne.

All three objectives were of great consequence. The third, however, was the most important of the three.

Of the three, the first, the closing of the eastern frontier, was accomplished in part; the second was so far successful that the French were able to seize Rheims without opposition; the third was not accomplished. Had it been the armies of von Kluck and von Bülow forming the German right must both have been severed from the German line to the east of Rheims, and, with their supplies of food and of munitions cut off, must have been compelled to surrender.

Appreciating the peril, and fully aware that the fate of the *whole* German force hung upon averting it. General von Kluck acted with resource and energy. Probably no commander ever extricated himself out of a more deadly predicament, and the achievement is all the more notable since he was opposed to skilful generals in command of skilful troops, directed by the greatest strategist of the age. The predicament in which General von Kluck found himself was this. If he opposed a front to the army of General Desperey, formed of the pick of the French regulars, he had on his flank both the British and the troops of General Maunoury. In that case, overwhelming defeat was certain. If on the other hand he formed a front against the troops of General French and General Maunoury, he presented a flank to the 5th French Army. Not only in such circumstances was a bad defeat almost equally foregone, but, forming front to a flank and fighting along the lines of his communications, he must, in the event of defeat, retire eastward, abandoning his lines of communication and obstructing the retreat of von Bülow.

As events prove, the measures he adopted were these. He recalled from Amiens the army corps sent to that place to undertake an outflanking movement against the Allied left, and to cut off communication between Paris and Boulogne and Calais. With all haste these troops fell back upon the Oise to secure the German right rear. Coincidently, his two army corps on the Ourcq were ordered to undertake against General Maunoury a vigorous offensive to the west of that river. With the remaining three army corps, which had crossed the Marne, General von Kluck fell back, presenting to the British and to the 5th French Army a line protected first by the Grand Morin, and then by the Petit Morin and the Marne. In order to carry out that movement he did not hesitate to sacrifice a considerable part of his cavalry.

The danger-point of this disposition was La Ferté-sous-Jouarre. Into that place, consequently, he threw a strong force with orders to hold it to the last moment. With the rest of his three corps he formed front partly against the British, partly against the left of the army of General Desperey. In these actions, as Mr. Maxwell has pointed out, his troops were swept by the flank attack of part of the 6th French Army. There is no doubt they fought, despite cruel losses, with the most stubborn courage. As the 6th French Army, who displayed equally unshakable resolution, strove, following the course of the Ourcq, to work round against the German line of retreat, and as their attacks had to be met as well as the attacks of the British, the expedient which the German general resorted to was, as he retired, to hurry divisions of troops successively from the south to the north of his flank defence, and, as the 6th French Army moved, to move his flank defence with it.

Not only was the object to do that, but there was, at the same time, an effort to press the 6th French Army towards the north-west. This, in fact, General von Kluck managed to do. He did it by extending his flank beyond the left of the French Army, and making a feint of envelopment. Imagine a row of coins, each coin a division, and a movement of the row by constantly shifting a coin from one end of the row to the other. That will give roughly an idea of what, on the events, appears to have been the expedient.

The success of such a series of movements depended, of course, on their rapidity, and, considering the severe and insistent pressure from the British on the rear of the line, forming an angle with the flank, the movements were carried out with surprising rapidity. The Ourcq, though not a long river, is, like the Marne, deep, and over more than half its length navigable. It flows between plateaux through a narrow valley with steep sides. The crossing of such a stream is no easy feat.

But General von Kluck did not mind the losses he incurred so long as he achieved his purpose. This was clearly his best policy. In the intervals of desperate fighting his men had to undertake long marches at a breakneck pace. For several days together they were without rest or sleep. To some extent they were aided by the entrenchments already dug to guard against an attack from the west. These positions, prepared to protect the head of the German chain of armies remaining in contact with Paris, now proved useful in covering the retirement. Nevertheless, the efforts of the Germans must have been exhausting to the last degree.[2]

Despite that, they were successful in reaching the Aisne in advance of the 6th French Army. The latter, it ought, however, to be said, had to operate through a difficult area. From the Ourcq to the Aisne there is a succession of forests. Of these the great forest of Villers-Cotterets extends northwards from the Ourcq to within six miles of Soissons. East of the stretch of forests the country is more open. Given these facts of topography, it is evident that on following the line of the Ourcq, with the object of barring its passage to the enemy, the French had in the forest belt a formidable obstacle. Perceiving that in this lay his chance, General von Kluck hurried as large a part of his force as possible across the Ourcq in order to bar the advance of the French by the forest roads through Villers, and by the comparatively narrow break in the forest belt between Crepy and Pierrefond. He was thus able, notwithstanding that the British were hanging on to and harrying his rear, to hold the outlets against the troops of General Maunoury until he slipped past them. (See note following).

> Note:—An interesting sidelight on the German movements is afforded by these particulars given on official authority:—
> At Villers-Cotterets, though supplies far in excess of the capabilities of the place were demanded, the town was not seriously damaged. The Germans evacuated the place on September 11th in such haste that they left behind a large amount of the bread requisitioned. It was stated by the inhabitants that the enemy destroyed and abandoned fifteen motor-lorries, seven guns, and ammunition wagons.
> At Crepy, on Sept. 3, various articles were requisitioned under

---

[2]. An official British note on this retreat stated: "Many isolated parties of Germans have been discovered hiding in the numerous woods a long way behind our line. As a rule they seem glad to surrender.

"An officer, who was proceeding along the road in charge of a number of led horses, received information that there were some of the enemy in the neighbourhood. Upon seeing them he gave the order to charge, whereupon three German officers and 106 men surrendered."

threat of a fine of 100,000*f.* for every day's delivery of the goods. The following list shows the amounts and natures of the supplies demanded, and also the actual quantities furnished:

	Requisitioned.	Supplied.
Flour	20,000 kilos.	20,000 kilos.
Dried vegetables …	5,000 ,,	800 ,,
Coffee … …	1,000 ,,	809 ,,
Salt …	1,000 ,,	2,000 ,,
Oats	100,000 ,,	55,000 ,,
Red wine	2,500 litres.	2,500 litres.

All smoked meats, ham, cloth, new boots, tobacco, biscuits, handkerchiefs, shirts, braces, stockings, horse shoes, bicycles, motorcars, petrol.
61 prs. boots
91 bicycles
15 motor tyres
6 inner tubes

And once on the Aisne and in touch with his Amiens rearguard, now on the Oise above Compiègne, he was in a position to initiate a complete change in tactics, and, his force being comparatively secure, the other German armies could again fall into line.

Before dealing with those new German tactics, it is advisable briefly to sketch the defence works thrown up by the Germans along their line, because both these defence works and the character of the country are intimately related to the tactics.

As already stated, the highlands of Champagne extend north-west nearly as far as Peronne. They are chalk hills and uplands cut by deep valleys. The most northerly of the valleys is that out of which flows the Somme. Then comes the much wider valley of the Oise. Still farther south is the valley of the Aisne. Between the Oise and the Aisne is a roughly triangular tract of country, its apex at the point where the Oise and the Aisne join. Across the broad end or base of this triangle run the open downs. Towards the narrower end of the area the country becomes broken and hilly, and is covered with great patches of wood and forest.

There is along the north of the Aisne a long wooded ridge, which on its northern edge slopes steeply. But the top of the ridge forms a gentle undulating slope to the south. It is not unlike the top of a rough, slightly tilted table. To a bird's-eye view this top would appear shaped rather like a very coarse-toothed comb, with the teeth jagged and broken. The top, that is to say, runs out on its south side into a succession of promontories, each ending in a round-ended bluff overlooking the Aisne valley. Some of these bluffs jut out close above the river. Others are much farther back. Between them are clefts and side valleys, in which the land slopes up from the bottom of the main valley to the top of the plateau. In the longer clefts, of course, the general gradient is much less stiff than in the shorter ones. Both the tops of the bluffs and most of the clefts are thickly wooded. The bluffs are on an average above 400 feet in height, that in fact being the general elevation of the plateau.

The aspect of the edge of the corresponding plateau on the south side of the valley of the Aisne is exactly similar. Since the bluffs on the opposite sides approach each other in some places and are farther apart in others, the valley varies in breadth from half a mile to two miles. The bottom of the valley is practically flat, and through this flat tract of meadow land the river winds, now near one side of the valley, now near the other. The stream is between fifty and sixty yards wide, but, like all the rivers in this part of France, deep. Where the valley opens out there are villages and small towns. The largest place is the picturesque old city of Soissons.

Now the ridge north of the Aisne extends west to east for some thirty-four miles. At Craonne, its eastern end, it rises to a summit about 500 feet high, and then falls abruptly. There is here, going from the Aisne northwards, a fairly level open gap some three miles wide. South of the Aisne, the same gap extends for about ten miles to Rheims. On each side of the gap rise hillsides clothed with woods. At the crossing of the Aisne is situated the village of Berry-au-Bac. This gap, it will be seen, forms an important feature in the Aisne battle.

Above and behind the hills to the east of the gap, and across the downs, the German entrenchments extended eastward for mile after mile right away to the Argonne. It is apposite here to note that near Rheims the traverse gap widens out and passes right and left round an isolated, hilly mass, lying like an island in a stream. Up the sides of this hilly mass climb the villages of Berru and Nogent-l'Abbesse.

Undoubtedly, one of the surprises of the war was the discovery that the Germans had prepared the positions just described. The preparation must have involved great labour. But it should not be forgotten that from time out of mind one of the chief industries in this part of France is represented by the chalk quarries, out of which is dug the material, known in its prepared state as plaster of Paris. All through Champagne there was, before the war, a considerable German population. Not a few of the plaster quarries had passed into the hands of Germans. The principal quarries are on the steep north slope of the ridge along the Aisne. Cut into the hillsides, these chalk pits present a labyrinth of galleries and chambers, where the quarrymen were accustomed to take their meals and even to sleep. These quarries, numbered by scores, might well form the refuge and stronghold of an army. The region is remarkable, also, for its many natural caves.

Even more important, however, from a military standpoint, is the southern side of this plateau. The only means of approaching the plateau from that side is either up the clefts or side valleys, or from the western end where the level gradually falls. But an attack made up one of the side valleys could be assailed from both sides. In possession of the plateau above, the defence, while keeping its force undivided, could move that force to any point where attack was threatened, having itself no clefts or fissures to deal with. It will be seen, therefore, that the ridge formed a sort of vast ready-made castle, big enough to stretch from London to beyond Oxford, or from Liverpool to Manchester, and that the quarries and galleries made it habitable, at all events on the *banditti* level of existence.

As Sir John French has pointed out,[3] owing to the patches of wood on the upper slopes and tops of the bluffs, only small areas of the plateau were open to view from the tops of bluffs on the south side of the river. Hence the movements of the defenders were, looked at from across the river, to no small extent concealed.

Two further *military* features of the ridge should be noted. One is the fact that its steep northern slope forms one side of the valley of the Lette, and that, therefore, it is bounded by a river on both sides; the other is, that some eight miles from its eastern end at Craonne the plateau narrows to a mere neck less than a mile wide, and that across this neck is carried the Oise and Aisne Canal.

Not relying, however, merely on the natural features of the place, the Germans dug along the plateau lines of entrenchments connected by galleries with other trenches in the rear where reserves, not in the firing line, were held. These back trenches formed living places. The mass of men was too large, for any save the smaller proportion, to find shelter in the quarries.

---

3. See Appendix, Despatch of Sir John French, Oct. 8, 1914.

It will be seen, therefore, that the business of turning the Germans out of such a fastness could be no easy matter.

On the choice of this position two questions suggest themselves. How was it that the Germans came to pitch upon this place—for there can be no doubt the choice was deliberate[4]—and what operations did they intend to undertake on the strength of its possession?

The answers to these questions are in no sense speculations in the secrets of War Offices. Those secrets it would be idle to profess to know. Like the observations made in preceding pages, the answers are deductions from admitted facts and events, perfectly plain to anyone who has knowledge enough of military operations to draw them. Only ignorance can assume that no true commentary can be written concerning a campaign save upon official confidences.

As to the German choice of this position, it should not be forgotten that the present war represents the fourth campaign which the Prussians have fought in this area of France. In forming their plans they had, we ought to presume, considered—bearing in mind the difference in military conditions—not only the war of 1870-1, but the campaign of Frederick William II., and the campaign of Blücher in 1814. A little earlier it was said that this arena offers great facilities for defence. The reason is that, since there is here a system of rivers flowing to a conjunction near Paris, it is always open to the defence to attack in superior force between any two of the rivers, while the assailant must, in advancing from east to west, have his forces divided by one or more of the streams. The whole German plan was intended to obviate and to overcome that difficulty, and yet the plan came to grief because, at the moment when their forces were divided by the Marne and by the Grand Morin, the defence were able to attack them in superior force on their extreme right—the vital point—and when the crossing of the rivers made it difficult to meet that attack. (See note following).

Note:—The late General Hamley, describing what he considered the most effective lines for an invasion of France from

---

4. The opinion on this point of the officers who took part in the Battle of the Aisne is embodied in the following official note published by the British Press Bureau:—"There is no doubt that the position on the Aisne was not hastily selected by the German Staff after the retreat had begun. From the choice of ground and the care with which the fields of fire have been arranged to cover all possible avenues of approach, and from the amount of work already carried out, it is clear that the contingency of having to act on the defensive was not overlooked when the details of the strategically offensive campaign were arranged."

Germany in opposition to the defensive adopted by Napoleon, points out that if the left of the defence threatens the invaders' communications, the invaders, leaving their right on the Ourcq and Marne, march through Sezanne to fight on the right bank of the Seine. Pushing the French right and centre to the Yères with their own centre and left, they fight then the decisive battle. It should be decisive, for the (Germans) on the two rivers, approaching each other in the narrowing angle can combine in a movement on Paris, holding the passages at Melun and Montereau on the one side, and at Meaux on the other.

In executing such a plan the weapons of the defender would be in some measure turned against himself.... But the assailants in taking these forward steps do so at the disadvantage of attacking a strongly posted enemy and under penalty of exposing a flank to him. This course demands a superiority in numbers of not less than 4 to 3, and probably greater than that.

The Germans had adopted this very plan, but they had not the superiority they imagined.

Foreseeing, however, the *possibility*, though not accepting the probability, of having to stand for a time on the defensive, the German General Staff, we cannot now doubt, had formed the subsidiary and provisional plan of concentrating, as far as possible and in case of necessity, between two of the rivers—the Oise and the Aisne—in positions which could be held with a minimum of numbers.

But this concentration was only preliminary. It was intended to aid the massing on their own right flank of an echelon of reserve formations to be thrown against the left of the Allied forces.

Concentration between two of the rivers was, as a defensive, beyond question the best measure in the situation. A mere defensive, however, would be tantamount to a confession that the whole expedition against France had proved a failure. Undoubtedly, therefore, as the later events show, the design was, at the earliest moment, to resume the offensive by means of masses of reserves. These, pivoting upon Noyon, at the western end of the fortified line, might sweep round and, by threatening to envelop the Allied armies compel their retirement.

Conversely, the Allied tactic was. plainly to envelop the Germans and to threaten their main communications through Belgium. The question now was: Which side could carry out its manoeuvre first?

CHAPTER 7

The Operations On the Aisne

The Battle of the Aisne, destined to develop into the longest conflict on record—it extended over two whole months—began on the afternoon of Sunday, September 13. To follow its complexities it is necessary clearly to grasp, not only the military purposes or objectives the two sides had immediately in view, but the respective situations of the opposing masses as regards fighting efficiency. When operations are on this gigantic scale a certain amount of imagination must be exercised to realise even the barest facts.

From Compiègne eastward to Rheims the Allied line was formed by the 6th French, the British, and the 5th French armies. To the first for the moment was assigned the duty of forcing the passages of the Aisne from below Soissons, clearing the enemy off the western end of the ridge, and pushing him up to Noyon on the Oise.

The business which fell to the British Army was that of delivering a frontal attack on this natural hill fortress from Soissons as far as Craonne.

The 6th French Army, which by a vigorous forward thrust had driven the enemy out of Rheims, was to push up through the transverse gap to Berry-au-Bac, and assault the hostile positions on the hillsides along the east side of the gap. Along these hills the Germans had settled themselves in force. Here, too, there were many chalk quarries and caves, which the Germans were using as shelters and stores.

At first sight it might well seem that the frontal attack undertaken by the British was not strictly a necessary operation. Clearly, the feasible way of driving the Germans out of their fastness was to turn the flanks of the position on the west through Lassigny and Noyon, and on the east through Berry-au-Bac. The main operation was, of course, that of turning the position from the west, for the right of the German position remained its vulnerable point. It was essential, however, to the success of that operation that General von Kluck should not be able to meet it in force until, at all events, the Allied troops had taken a firm grip.

Now, if the British Army had assumed a merely watching attitude on the south side of the Aisne, and had in consequence been able to extend their line from the south of Craonne down the river to, say, Attichy, some ten miles below Soissons, that, while leaving nearly the whole strength of the 6th French Army free to undertake the turning movement, would at the same time have left General von Kluck also free to throw his main strength against it.

A vigorous and pressing attack along his front was consequently essential, in order to keep his main force employed. Not only was the attack essential, but it had to be launched against him without delay, and before he could recover from the effects of his retreat.

Including the troops recalled from Amiens, Generals von Kluck and von Bülow had under their command, nominally at any rate, ten army corps. If, deducting losses and war wastages, we put their strength in effectives at not more than the equivalent of six corps—it could have been very little more—yet six corps was, *in the positions they held*, a force fully able to cope with the nine corps making up the three Allied armies pitted then against them. Bearing in mind, indeed, the natural defensive advantages of the ridges on which the Germans had established themselves, and their facility for moving troops either for the purposes of defence or of counterattack, their strongholds could have been held by three corps, leaving the remainder to be used on the flank for active operations.

Intended to frustrate that manoeuvre, the British attack compelled the German commanders to await, before they could make any such attempt, the arrival of reinforcements. On both sides there was now a race against time. French reinforcements and reserves had to be brought up and massed against the flank of the German position. Many of those troops had, however, to cover long distances afoot. The movements of mass armies are comparatively slow. After all, the roads and railways traversing a country have a capacity which is limited. Some idea of what such movement involves may be formed from the traffic on a popular bank holiday. In the case of armies there is, in addition to human numbers, the artillery, the munitions, the camp equipment, the foodstuffs, and all the rest of the transport. No one, therefore, can be surprised that by the time these masses could be concentrated on the German flank, there were German masses who, under the same conditions, had been hurried forward to meet them. From the very necessities of time and space the race resulted to a great extent in a draw.

The Battle of the Aisne is in every respect unique. A battle in the ordinary sense of field operations it was not. It was a siege. Nothing at all like it had ever occurred before in war. There have been many sieges of banditti in mountain retreats. There have been sieges in old times of fortified camps. There had never been the siege under such conditions of a great army.

The operations in this amazing and gigantic conflict, though interrelated, must for the purposes of clear narration be dealt with in sections. The story divides itself into:—

The attack upon the German positions north of the Aisne.
The struggle for and around Rheims.
The operations on and against the German right flank.

In this chapter it is proposed to deal with the attack upon the German positions north of the Aisne. The manner in which the British troops forced the passage of that river and secured a footing on the ridge, and held on to it, forms a particularly brilliant feat of arms.

As stated in the official account:—

The country across which the army has had to force its way is undulating and covered with patches of thick wood.
Within the area which faced the British before the advance commenced, right up to Laon, the chief feature of tactical importance is the fact that there are six rivers running right across the direction of advance, at all of which it was possible that the Germans might make a resistance.
These are, in order from the south, the Marne, the Ourcq, the Vesle, the Aisne, the Lette, and the Oise.

The Lette, it may here be stated, is a tributary of the Oise. Rising just to the north of Craonne and flowing westward through an upland valley, it is used in the lower part of its course as a section of the Oise and Aisne Canal.

On Friday, the 11th, the official account goes on to say, but little opposition was met with by us along any part of our front, and the direction of advance was, for the purpose of co-operating with our Allies, turned slightly to the northeast. The day was spent in pushing forward and in gathering in various hostile detachments, and by nightfall our forces had reached a line to the north of the Ourcq, extending from Oulchy Le Château to Long Pont.

On this day there was also a general advance on the part of the French along their whole line, which ended in substantial success, in one portion of the field Duke Albrecht of Würtemberg's fourth army being driven back across the Saulx; and elsewhere the whole of the corps artillery of a German corps being captured. Several German colours also were taken.

It was only on this day that the full extent of the victory gained by the Allies was appreciated by them. The moral effect of this success has been enormous.

When the British pushed forward on September 12 to the Aisne, they found that the Germans still held the heights to the south of the river above Soissons. German outposts also held the strip of hilly country between the Aisne and its tributary the Vesle.

The first step was to drive the Germans across the Aisne at Soissons. This was undertaken by the 3rd army corps. Pushing forward to Buzancy, south-east of Soissons, the troops won the heights overlooking the old city and the Aisne valley, which here opens to its greatest width. It was a stiff fight. Despite, however, a heavy bombardment from across the valley, the British, side by side with troops of General Maunoury, swept the Germans down into and through Soissons, and as the enemy crowded over the two bridges the artillery of the 3rd corps poured upon them a rain of shells. Immediately the Germans had crossed, the bridges, which had been mined, went up in two terrific explosions.

While this action was in progress, Sir John French had thrown the 1st army corps across the Vesle at Fismes. They advanced to Vaucere with but little opposition.

At Braisne on the Vesle, however, the Germans for a time made a resolute stand. They held the town in force, and covered the bridge with machine guns. They were strongly supported by artillery. Notwithstanding this, they were ousted out of the place by the 1st British Cavalry Division under General Allenby. While a brigade of British infantry cleared the enemy out of the town, which lies mainly on the south bank, the cavalry rushed the passage of the river under a galling fire and turned the hostile position. So rapidly did the Germans take to flight that they had to throw a large amount of their artillery ammunition into the river. There was no time to reload it into the caissons.[1] This feat of the British horse ranks among the finest bits of "derring do" in the campaign. The Queen's Bays have been mentioned in despatches as rendering distinguished service. Conspicuous gallantry was shown by the whole division. As a result of these operations from Braisne and Fismes, the British secured the country up to the Aisne.

Left and right, therefore, the advance had been completely successful. In the centre, however, the 2nd army corps had an exceptionally tough piece to negotiate. They advanced up to the Aisne between Soissons and Missy. The latter place lies on the north bank, just below the junction of the Aisne and the Vesle. Here there is a broad stretch of meadow flats, commanded north, east, and south by bluffs. On the south is the Sermoise bluff or spur; across the flats, directly opposite to the north, stands out the Chivre spur. The summit of the latter is crowned by an old defence work, the Fort de Condé. This the Germans held, and they made use of the spur, like a miniature Gibraltar, to sweep the flats of the valley with their guns. On this 12th September the 5th division found themselves unable to make headway. They advanced to the Aisne, which just here sweeps close under the Chivre spur, leaving between the cliff and the bank a narrow strip, occupied by the village of Condé-sur-Aisne. Across the river at Condé there was a road bridge, and the enemy had left the bridge intact, both because they held the houses of the village, which they had loop-holed, and because their guns above commanded the approach road. It may be stated that they held on to the Chivre spur and on to Condé all through the battle.

On the night of September 12 the British had possession of all the south bank of the Aisne from Soissons up to Maizy, immediately to the south of Craonne.

At daybreak on Sunday, September 13, Sir John French ordered a general advance across the river. Opposite the places where the waterway could most readily be crossed, the enemy had posted strong bodies of infantry with machine guns. Along the bluffs, and behind the side valleys above, they had disposed their artillery in a range of

---

1. A buried store of the enemy's munitions of war was also found not far from the Aisne, ten wagon-loads of live shell and two wagons of cable being dug up; and traces were discovered of large quantities of stores having been burnt, all tending to show that so far back as the Aisne the German retirement was hurried.

batteries upwards of fifteen miles in length.

The battle began with one of the most tremendous and concentrated artillery duels that has ever taken place, for the line was prolonged both east and west by the French artillery, until it stretched out to more than twice the length of the British front.

Of the nine bridges over this section of the Aisne, all save that at Condé had been blown up. Near a little place called Bourg on the north bank, some three miles below Maizy, the valley is crossed by an aqueduct carrying the Oise and Aisne canal. This canal passes in a series of locks over the ridge north-west. The canal is much used in connection with the chalk quarries.

Troops of the 1st British division, defying a fierce bombardment, advanced in rushes along the towing path, or crept along the parapets of the aqueduct. Every man deliberately took his life in his hands. Others crept breast high in the water along the canal sides. The German guns stormed at them, and many fell, but foot by foot and yard by yard they crawled on, while supporting riflemen from the ridges behind them picked off the Germans who strove to oppose their passage. The resistance was furious. They won, however, a footing on the north bank. Once there, no counter-assaults could dislodge them.

This bridgehead formed at the opposite end of the aqueduct, more troops rushed across, covered by a concentration of the British artillery. In this way, at length, the whole division got over, including the cavalry. Forthwith they advanced up the road leading across the ridge from Bourg, along the side valley, towards Chamouille.

While these events were taking place, troops of the 2nd division were, five miles farther down the river, near Vailly, carrying out a feat of equal daring. Just about Vailly, the Aisne is crossed obliquely by the railway line from Soissons. The railway bridge, a structure of iron, now lay in the stream. Most of the confusion of massive ribs and girders was under water, and the deep and smoothly sweeping current, swollen by recent rains, foamed and chafed against the obstacle. One of the long girders, however, still showed an edge above the flood. It was possible for men to cross upon this girder, but only in single file. Not more than two feet in breadth at the outside, not less than 250 feet in length, this path of iron resembled, if anything could, that bridge, narrow as the edge of a scimitar, over which the faithful Mussulman is fabled to pass into Paradise. It was swept by shot and shell. From the heights across the valley belched without ceasing the hail of death. Wounded or unnerved a man saw his end as surely in the grey-green swirl of waters.

But the soldiers who undertook this service did not hesitate. It may be doubted if there has ever been anything in ancient or in modern war more coolly heroic. Here was the spirit which has made Britain the mother of mighty nations. Not a few of these heroes fell, inevitably, but the spirit was in all, and if some fell, others won their way over, and having won it kept their footing against heavy odds.

In sight of this struggle, amid the unceasing roar of the batteries on either side, the 4th Guards Brigade were, a mile away at Chavonne, ferrying themselves over in boats. Notwithstanding the furious efforts to annihilate them, both as they crossed and as they sprang ashore, a whole battalion in this way got across and made good their foothold.

Halfway between Condé and Soissons, at the village of Venizel, at the same time, the 14th brigade were rafting themselves over on tree-trunks crossed with planks, derelict doors, and stairways.

These footholds won, the troops, like the 1st division, lost no time in pushing forward to seize points of vantage before the enemy could rally from his astonishment. The 2nd division advanced along the road from Vailly towards Courteçon; the 12th brigade made an attack in the direction of Chivres, situated in a small side valley to the west of the Chivres bluff. Slightly higher up this side valley, and on its opposite slope, the Germans held the hillside village of Vregny in force. The cleft at once became the scene of a furious combat.

Coincidently the work went on of throwing pontoon bridges across the river. Under persistent bombardment the Royal Engineers stuck to this business with grim resolve. The battle had gone on without a pause from daybreak. At half-past five in the evening, opposite Bucy-le-Long, three miles above Soissons, the first pontoon bridge had been completed, and the 10th brigade crossing by it drove the enemy out of Bucy. Working right through the night the Engineers completed eight pontoon bridges and one footbridge. On the following day they temporarily repaired the road bridges at Venizel, Missy, and Vailly, and the bridge at Villers. The army had thus twelve bridges connecting with the south bank, and was able to move across in force with a large part of his artillery.

Crossing the Aisne at Soissons, the main road running for about a mile and a half north-east to the little village of Crouy, there divides. On the right is a lower road eastward up the valley of the Aisne, past and under the bluffs on the north side to Berry-au-Bac. On the left is a road which climbs up hill, carried in some places through cuttings and tunnels, at others over short viaducts, until it reaches the summit of the ridge. There, parallel in direction with the lower road three miles away, it continues for some twelve miles to Craonne. From this summit road there is, between the patches of woods, a wide view of the country—to the north the valley of the Lette, and beyond it the height round which lies the town and fortress of Laon, to the south the rich woodland glimpses of the Aisne valley. This panoramic highway is the famous Chemin des Dames.

It is evident that command of the higher and of the lower roads meant command of all the part of the ridge between Soissons and Berry, and the operations were an effort on the one side to obtain, and on the other to retain, that command.

Already, with the exception of the break at Condé, the lower road, and the villages and the town of Vailly lying along its length, were, as the result of the fighting on September 13, in the hands of the British. The higher road remained in the possession of the Germans. Up the clefts and side valleys are a number of small villages and hamlets, inhabited for the most part by quarrymen and lime-burners, but with, here and there, a small factory. A sprinkling of these civilians were Germans. Most were known to the enemy, and were active spies, and one of the first measures taken by the Germans was to establish at various points secret telephones, forming an exchange of intercommunication with and along their positions. Where telephones could not be employed they arranged a system of ruses and signals. Among these devices was that of smoke from cottage chimneys.

On the morning of September 14, the 13th, 14th, and 15th Brigades, defeating a heavy counter-attack, seized the roads between Condé and Soissons. The object was to cut into the centre of the German defence.

During this day further bodies of British troops crossed the river. The forces already on the north side were heavily engaged. Towards nightfall the Germans attempted a counter-attack. It was beaten off after severe fighting, three hours later, about ten o'clock at night, they again descended in force against the positions and villages held by the British troops.

While the clefts and side valleys blazed with flashing fire of infantry, the valley of the Aisne was lit up for miles with the fluctuating and lurid flare from the heavy guns. Masses of German infantry tried to drive the British troops out of the villages they had seized. It was evidently hoped to prevail by weight of numbers. The onset fell back crippled by the losses sustained.

By this time the fact was becoming plain that the battle was no mere rearguard action. The enemy had manifestly resolved to make a stand. To ascertain the character and strength of his disposition, Sir John French ordered a general advance. It was timed to begin at daybreak.

The dawn broke amid rain and heavy mists, but this, if a disadvantage to the attack, was equally a disadvantage to the defence. One of the leading features of this offensive was what Sir John French has justly called the bold and decisive action of the 1st army corps, commanded by Sir Douglas Haig.

From Bourg, the scene of the crossing on the aqueduct, there runs northward climbing to the summit of the ridge a road to the village of Cerny, about half-way along the Chemin des Dames. The distance from Bourg to Cerny is rather more than three miles. It is, however, a stiff climb. Two-thirds of the way up, where the road bends sharply to the left round a spur, is the village of Vendresse-et-Troyon. The capture of this place was one of the immediate objectives, and the troops told off to accomplish it were the 1st infantry brigade and the 25th artillery brigade, under General Bulfin.[2] At Cerny there is a slight dip on the level of the ridge.

Vendresse is on the west slope of this side valley, and Troyon on the east slope just behind the spur. The Germans held in strong force both the spur and the houses on each slope. At Troyon they had fortified themselves in a factory.

Few operations could be more ticklish than the seizure of such a place. From the spur the Germans came down in a counter-attack like a human avalanche. After stemming this rush by a withering fire the Northamptons were ordered to carry the spur at the point of the bayonet. They did it. As they were chasing the survivors of the counter-attack up the slope there suddenly appeared on the skyline a second mass of German infantry, the reserves supporting the counter-attacking column. In a matter of seconds, however, the fugitives and the Northamptons were on them. Their ranks broken, they also turned and fled in rout across the plateau.

In the meantime the North Lancashires had stormed the factory and cleared the enemy out of Vendresse at the point of the bayonet. Other troops of the 1st army corps pushed on to Meulins, a mile to the south-east, and seized positions along the east end of the ridge.

---

2. This able and distinguished officer was later promoted for his services.

During the fighting the Germans lost 12 field guns and 600 prisoners. Many of the latter were found to belong to the *Landwehr*, proving that the enemy had already been compelled to fill up his formations from second reserves.

The fury of this fighting was intense. There could be no better evidence of its character than an unposted letter found later on an officer of the 7th German Army reserve corps. The letter runs:—

Cerny, S. of Laon, Sept. 17, 1914.

My dear Parents,—Our corps has the task of holding the heights south of Cerny in all circumstances till the 15th corps on our left flank can grip the enemy's flank. On our right are other corps. We are fighting with the English Guards, Highlanders, and Zouaves.[3] The losses on both sides have been enormous. For the most part this is due to the too brilliant French artillery. The English are marvellously trained in making use of the ground. One never sees them, and one is constantly under fire. Three days ago our division took possession of these heights, dug itself in, &c. Two days ago, early in the morning, we were attacked by immensely superior English forces (one brigade and two battalions), and were turned out of our positions; the fellows took five guns from us. It was a tremendous hand-to-hand fight. How I escaped myself I am not clear. I then had to bring up supports on foot (my horse was wounded and the others were too far in rear). Then came up the Guard Jager Battalion, 4th Jager, 65th Regiment, Reserve Regiment 13, Landwehr Regiments 13 and 16, and with the help of the artillery drove back the fellows out of the position again.

... During the first two days of the battle [4] I had only one piece of bread and no water, spent the night in the rain without my great coat. The rest of my kit was on the horses which have been left miles behind with the baggage, which cannot come up into the battle because as soon as you put your nose out from behind cover the bullets whistle.

Yesterday evening about six p.m., in the valley in which our reserves stood, there was such a terrible cannonade that we saw nothing of the sky but a cloud of smoke. We had few casual-

---

3. Part of the 5th French Army, which was operating on the right of the British from Rheims and Berry-au-Bac.
4. The reference is evidently to the fighting on Sept. 13 and 14.

ties.

Just to the west of Vendresse the 5th infantry brigade advanced against the part of the ridge where is situated the village of Courteçon. Simultaneously the 4th Guards Brigade, with the 36th brigade of artillery, debouched from Bourg along the Aisne and Oise canal, with the object of seizing Ostel. They had to fight their way, opposed foot by foot, through dense woods. The 6th brigade pressed up farther along the canal to Braye-en-Laonnois. It is immediately to the north of that place that the plateau is at the narrowest. Evidently to obtain possession of that neck would be a great advantage. The enemy held on to Braye at all costs.

Further west, again, the British advanced from Vailly to Aizy along another of the approaches to the plateau. The object was to hem in the Germans holding the Chivres bluff and Condé. On the farther side of the bluff from Aizy the division of Sir Charles Fergusson held on to Chivres village in the face of a succession of determined onslaughts.

As the outcome of this day's fighting, which had been very severe, the 1st army corps had won close up to the ridge by Craonne, and held positions extending along the plateau across the canal to Soupir, a distance of nearly nine miles. Concurrently the 2nd and 3rd corps had gained the plateau from Chavonne westward to Croucy, and with the exception of the Chivres bluff all the outer or southern edge of the plateau, as well as the intervening side valleys, were in the British hands, from Soissons to Craonne.

As soon as they had gained these positions the British troops set about digging themselves in, and although the rain fell all night in torrents, and the men had been through a long and fierce struggle since daybreak, they worked magnificently.

Next day (September 15) heavy rain blurred the view. Neither force could see the movements of the other, but when the mists lifted somewhat the Germans must have been surprised to discover that the foe were already in their stronghold.

On their side they had not been idle. They had brought along from Maubeuge the batteries of heavy howitzers used to destroy the forts at that place, and were putting them into well-concealed positions. Besides this they worked with energy to strengthen their entrenchments. These lines of trenches among and along the edges of the woods crowning the slopes of the ridge were elaborately made, and in general cleverly hidden. They were so placed as to sweep with rifle and machine gun fire the approaches to the plateau up the various clefts. Lengths of barbed-wire entanglements and rabbit fencing further defended the approaches, both in the woods and across open ground. Where behind or between the lines of trenches the land rose—the top of the plateau had been worn by ages of weather into sweeping undulations—there were batteries of field guns, so arranged that they laid approaches under a cross fire. Round and in front of these knobs of land the trenches swept like ditches round bastions. Everything, in fact, that resource could suggest had been done to make the positions impregnable.(See notes following)

Note:—The following descriptive notes on the German positions were made by the official "Eyewitness" with the British forces:—

> Owing to the concealment afforded to the Germans' fire trenches and gun emplacements by the woods and to the fact that nearly all the bridges and roads leading to them, as well as a great part of the southern slopes, are open to their fire, the position held by them is a very strong one. Except for these patches of wood, the terrain generally is not enclosed. No boundaries between the fields exist as in England. There are ditches here and there, but no hedges, wire fences, or walls, except round the enclosures in the villages. A large proportion of the woods, however, are enclosed by high rabbit netting, which is in some places supported by iron stanchions. The top of the plateau on the south of the river to some extent resembles Salisbury Plain, except that the latter is downland while the former is cultivated, being sown with lucerne, wheat, and beetroot.
>
> A feature of this part of the country, and one which is not confined to the neighbourhood of the Aisne, is the large number of caves, both natural and artificial, and of quarries. These are of great service to the forces on both sides, since they can often be used as sheltered accommodation for the troops in the second line. Other

points worthy of note are the excellence of the metalled roads, though the metalled portion is very narrow, and the comparative ease with which one can find one's way about, even without a map. This is due partly to the prevailing straightness of the roads and partly to the absence of hedges. There are signposts at all crossroads, whilst the name of each village is posted in a conspicuous place at the entry and exit of the main highway passing through it.

In addition to the absence of hedges, the tall, white ferro-concrete telegraph posts lining many of the main roads give a somewhat strange note to the landscape.

In addition to trenches, hamlets and villages were held by the two armies as advanced posts, and had been turned roughly into groups of block houses.

CHAPTER 8

Warfare By Day and By Night

In three days the British had not only gained the passages over the Aisne, but had won their way to the plateau. Both sides had fought with determination. The German commander knew that if he could not hold this position the whole contemplated strategy of throwing masses of reinforcements against the left flank of the Allied forces must collapse. He was well aware that if he failed, not only must his own force in al! probability be destroyed, but the whole German line as far as Verdun must in all probability be crumpled up.

Not less was Sir John French aware that the future success of the Allied campaign hung upon obtaining a purchase on the German position which would force General von Kluck to employ his whole strength in holding on. It is easy, therefore, to infer how fierce had been this three days' struggle.

The Germans had put forth the greatest effort of which they were capable. But despite the natural advantage given them, first by the river front, and next by the rugged and broken ground in the many side valleys, they had been beaten. Henceforward the struggle was on less uneven terms. The fact had become manifest that without a strenuous counter-offensive the Germans could not hope to hold on.

This counter-offensive was attempted without delay.

Since the top of the plateau sloped from north to south, the positions held by the British were in general on lower ground than the trenches cut by the Germans, and it must have been something of a disagreeable surprise to the latter when on the morning of September 15, the heavy mists having lifted, they saw miles of earthworks, which had literally sprung up in the night. The rain and mist during the hours of darkness had made a night attack impossible, even if, after the eighteen hours' furious battle in the mists on the preceding day, they had had the stomach for it.

They had their surprise ready, however, as well. From well-hidden positions behind the woods on the top of the plateau they opened a violent bombardment of the British lines with their huge 8-inch and 11-inch howitzers, throwing the enormous shells, which fell with such terrific force as to bury themselves in the ground. Giving off in exploding dense clouds of black smoke, these shells blew away the earth on all sides of them in a rain of fragments of rock, masses of soil and stones, leaving the surface filled with holes wide and deep enough to be the burial place of several horses. This heavy ordnance was kept well beyond the range of the British guns, and employed for high-angle fire. So far as life was concerned, the shells caused relatively little loss. Their flight being visible—they looked not unlike tree-trunks hurled from across the hills—they could be dodged. On realising how little they were to be feared, the British troops nicknamed them "Black Marias," "Coalboxes," and "Jack Johnsons," and shouted jocular warnings. The idea of using these shells was to knock the British defence works to pieces. Some of these works, hastily thrown up, proved to be too slight, and had to be replaced by diggings, which became regular underground barracks.

At this time the British lines were in general more than a mile distant, on the average, from those of the enemy. They followed no symmetrical plan, but, adapted to the defensive features of the ground, were cut where there were at once the best shelters from attack and the best jumping-off places for offence. Describing them, the British military correspondent wrote:—

> A striking feature of our line—to use the conventional term which so seldom expresses accurately the position taken up by an army—is that it consists really of a series of trenches not all placed alongside each other, but some more advanced than others, and many facing in different directions. At one place they run east and west, along one side of a valley; another, almost north and south, up some subsidiary valley; here they line the edge of wood, and there they are on the reverse slope of a hill, or possibly along a sunken road. And at different points both the German and British trenches jut out like promontories into what might be regarded as the opponent's territory.

While the British infantry had been entrenching, the artillery, with an equal energy, had hauled their guns up the steep roads, and in many cases up still steeper hillsides, and by the morning of September 15—another disagreeable surprise for the enemy—nearly 500 field pieces bristled from positions of vantage along the front. The reply to the German bombardment was a bombardment of the hostile trenches. The latter were crowded with men. If the German shells did a lot of injury to the landscape, the British shrapnel inflicted far heavier injury on the enemy's force. It swept the German trenches and field batteries with a regular hail of lead. Well-concealed though they to a great extent were, the German positions were not so well-concealed as the British positions. Both armies did their best to make themselves appear scarce, and beyond the deafening uproar of the guns belching from behind woods and undulations, there seemed at a distance few signs of life on either side. But, looked at from behind and within, the lines were very anthills of activity.

The bombardment went on until midnight. Then came a night battle of almost unexampled fury.

From the outline already given of the fighting on September 14 it will have been gathered that one of the most substantial advantages won had been the position seized by the 4th Guards Brigade along the Aisne and Oise Canal from Astel to Braye-en-Laonnois. At Braye and eastwards over the intervening spur of plateau to Vendresse the British positions were dangerously close to the narrow neck of the ridge. Across that neck, too, following the canal to its juncture with the Lette, and then up the short valley of the Ardon, was the easiest route to Laon, the main base of the 1st German Army. Obviously the British must, if possible, be ousted out of these villages.

Bombardment had failed to do it. Soon after midnight, therefore, a huge mass of German infantry moved down against the Guards' entrenchments by Braye. It was a murderous combat. Six times in succession the Germans were beaten off. But for every column of the enemy that went back, broken, decimated, and exhausted, there was another ready instantly to take its place. Advancing over the dying and the dead, the Germans faced the appalling and rapid volleys of the Guards with unflinching courage. They fell in hundreds, but still they rushed on. Machine guns on both sides spat sheets of bullets. At close grips, finally, men stabbed like demons. In and round houses, many set on fire, and throwing the scene of slaughter into lurid and Dantesque relief, there were fights to the death. No quarter was given or taken. The canal became choked with corpses. On the roads and hillsides dead and wounded lay in every posture of pain. Beyond the outer ring of the struggle, where shouts of fury mingled with cries of agony, the roaring choruses of the guns bayed across the valley with redoubled rage.

Great as it was, the effort proved vain. If the attack was heroic, the defence was super-heroic. When, for the last time, the lines of the Guards swept forward, withering the retreating and now disordered foe with their volleys, charging into them in what seemed a lightning-like energy, terrible alike in their forgetfulness of danger and in the irresistible impetus of victory, the Germans must have realised that their hopes of conquest were shattered.

This was but one out of similar scenes in that fierce night.[1] After it the cold, grey morning broke in strange silence. For a space the artillery had ceased to speak. Many and many a hero, unknown to fame, but faithful unto death, lay with face upturned on those hillsides. Never had duty been more valiantly done.

Sir John French realised the qualities of his soldiers. He had been compelled to demand from them a herculean energy. They had not failed him in any place nor in any particular. They had been in truth magnificent, and he could not but embody his admiration in a Special Order of the Day. That historic document ran:—

> Once more I have to express my deep appreciation of the splendid behaviour of officers, non-commissioned officers, and men of the army under my command throughout the great battle of the Aisne, which has been in progress since the evening of the 12th inst. The battle of the Marne, which lasted from the morning of the 6th to the evening of the 10th, had hardly ended in the precipitate flight of the enemy when we were brought face to face with a position of extraordinary strength, carefully entrenched and prepared for defence by an army and a staff which are thorough adepts in such work.
>
> Throughout the 13th and 14th that position was most gallantly attacked by the British forces, and the passage of the Aisne effected. This is the third day the troops have been gallantly holding the position they have gained against the most desperate counter-attacks and a hail of heavy artillery.
>
> I am unable to find adequate words in which to express the admiration I feel for their magnificent conduct.

---

1. The troops of the 5th Division under Sir Charles Fergusson repulsed with equal gallantry a furious attack against their position at Missy, on the west side of the Chivres bluff.

The self-sacrificing devotion and splendid spirit of the British Army in France will carry all before it.

(Signed)   J. D. P. French,
Field Marshal, Commanding-in-Chief
the British Army in the Field.

The enemy had been shaken. Of that there could be no doubt. Following his experiences in the battle of the Marne this fighting was beginning to prove too much for him.

> A considerable amount of information about the enemy has now been gleaned from prisoners (says the official record). It has been gathered that our bombardment on the 15th produced a great impression. The opinion is also recorded that our infantry make such good use of the ground that the German companies are decimated by our rifle fire before a British soldier can be seen.
>
> From an official diary captured by the First Army Corps it appears that one of the German corps contains an extraordinary mixture of units. If the composition of the other corps is at all similar, it may be assumed that the present efficiency of the enemy's forces is in no way comparable with what it was when war commenced. The losses in officers are noted as having been especially severe. A brigade is stated to be commanded by a major, and some companies of the Foot Guards to be commanded by one-year volunteers, while after the Battle of Montmirail one regiment lost fifty-five out of sixty officers.
>
> The prisoners recently captured appreciate the fact that the march on Paris has failed, and that their forces are retreating, but state that the object of this movement is explained by the officers as being to withdraw into closer touch with supports which have stayed too far in rear. The officers are also endeavouring to encourage the troops by telling them that they will be at home by Christmas. A large number of the men, however, believe that they are beaten. The following is an extract from one document:—
>
>> With the English troops we have great difficulties. They have a queer way of causing losses to the enemy. They make good trenches, in which they wait patiently. They carefully measure the ranges for their rifle fire, and they then open a truly hellish fire. This was the reason that we

had such heavy losses. . . .

From another source:—

The English are very brave, and fight to the last man. . . .
One of our companies has lost 130 men out of 240.

From this time the battle took on more and more the features of a regular siege. On the side of the Germans the operations resolved themselves into persistent bombardments by day alternated with infantry attacks by night. Infantry attacks in daylight they now knew to be foredoomed. It is questionable, indeed, if, with the lowered *moral* of their troops, such attacks were any longer possible. To assist their night attacks they rigged up searchlights, and when their infantry advanced played the beams upon the British lines in the hope of dazzling the defence and spoiling the rifle-fire they had learned to dread. These lights, however, served also as a warning. When that was found out the enemy went back to attacks in the darkness, but with no better results.

Sunday, September 20, was the date of another general night onslaught. Just before the attack developed military bands were heard playing in the German lines. After the manner of the natives of West Africa they were working themselves up to the fury pitch. It was to be a do-ordie business evidently. The enterprise, however, again failed to prosper. Against some of the British positions the attack was pushed with dogged bravery; and the scenes of five nights before were enacted again and again with the like results. Against one part of the line the onset wound up with an extraordinary disaster. Two German columns mistook each other in the darkness for British troops. They had apparently set out from different points to converge upon the same British position. In front of that position they fought a furious combat, and while no bullets reached the British trenches the men in them were afforded the unwonted spectacle of the enemy wiping themselves out.[2]

Between the two armies the country had now become a "no-

---

[2]. In the official account this singular episode is thus recorded:—"Since the last letter left General Headquarters evidence has been received which points to the fact that during the counter-attacks on the night of Sunday, the 20th, the German infantry fired into each other—the result of an attempt to carry out the dangerous expedient of a converging advance in the dark. Opposite one portion of our position a considerable massing of the hostile forces was observed before dark. Some hours later a furious fusillade was heard in front of our line, though no bullets came over our trenches."

man's land," deserted by both sides because, in the expressive phrase of the British soldier, it had turned "unhealthy." Over this tract the still unburied bodies of German infantry lay where they had fallen. Outside the village of Paissy, held by the British and near a ridge where there had been some of the severest fighting, the German dead lay in heaps. Lines of German trenches held at the beginning of the battle were by this time deserted.

Reconnoitring parties, says the authorised story, sent out during the night of the 21st-22nd, discovered some deserted trenches, and in them, or near them in the woods, over a hundred dead and wounded were picked up. A number of rifles, ammunition, and equipment were also found. There were various other signs that portions of the enemy's forces had withdrawn for some distance.

Unable to prevail in open fight, the Germans resorted to almost every variety of ruse. In the words of the official story:—

> The Germans, well trained, long-prepared, and brave, are carrying on the contest with skill and valour. Nevertheless, they are fighting to win anyhow, regardless of all the rules of fair play, and there is evidence that they do not hesitate at anything in order to gain victory.
>
> During a counter-attack by the German 53rd Regiment on portions of the Northampton and Queen's Regiments on Thursday, the 17th, a force of some 400 of the enemy were allowed to approach right up to the trench occupied by a platoon of the former regiment, owing to the fact that they had held up their hands and made gestures that were interpreted as signs that they wished to surrender. When they were actually on the parapet of the trench held by the Northamptons they opened fire on our men at point-blank range.
>
> Unluckily for the enemy, however, flanking them and only some 400 yards away, there happened to be a machine gun manned by a detachment of the "Queen's." This at once opened fire, cutting a lane through their mass, and they fell back to their own trench with great loss. Shortly afterwards they were driven further back with additional loss by a battalion of the Guards, which came up in support.
>
> During the fighting, also, some German ambulance wagons advanced in order to collect the wounded. An order to cease fire was consequently given to our guns, which were firing on this

particular section of ground. The German battery commanders at once took advantage of the lull in the action to climb up their observation ladders and on to haystacks to locate our guns, which soon afterwards came under a far more accurate fire than any to which they had been subjected up to that time.

A British officer who was captured by the Germans, and has since escaped, reports that while a prisoner he saw men who had been fighting subsequently put on Red Cross brassards. That the irregular use of the protection afforded by the Geneva Convention is not uncommon is confirmed by the fact that on one occasion men in the uniform of combatant units have been captured wearing the Red Cross brassard hastily slipped over the arm. The excuse given has been that they had been detailed after a fight to look after the wounded.

It is reported by a cavalry officer that the driver of a motor-car with a machine gun mounted on it, which he captured, was wearing the Red Cross.

A curious feature of this strange siege-battle was that villages and hamlets between the fighting lines still continued, where not destroyed, to be in part, at any rate, inhabited, and at intervals peasants worked in the intervening fields. The Germans took advantage of this to push their spy system.

The suspicions of some French troops (of the 5th army) were aroused by coming across a farm from which the horses had not been removed. After some search they discovered a telephone which was connected by an underground cable with the German lines, and the owner of the farm paid the penalty usual in war for his treachery. Some of the methods being employed for the collection or conveyance of intelligence were:—

> Men in plain clothes who signalled to the German lines from points in the hands of the enemy by means of coloured lights at night and puffs of smoke from chimneys by day.
>
> Pseudo-labourers working in the fields between the armies who conveyed information, and persons in plain clothes acting as advanced scouts.
>
> German officers and soldiers in plain clothes or in French or British uniforms remained in localities evacuated by the Germans in order to furnish them with intelligence.

One spy of this kind was found by the British troops hidden in a church tower. His presence was only discovered through the erratic movements of the hands of the church clock, which he was using to signal to his friends by means of an improvised semaphore code.

Women spies were also caught, and secret agents found observing entrainments and detrainments.

Amongst the precautions taken by the British to guard against spying was the publication of the following notice:—

(1) Motorcars and bicycles other than those carrying soldiers in uniform may not circulate on the roads.

(2) Inhabitants may not leave the localities in which they reside between six p.m. and six a.m.

(3) Inhabitants may not quit their homes after eight p.m.

(4) No person may on any pretext pass through the British lines without an authorisation countersigned by a British officer.

On October 23rd six batteries of heavy howitzers asked for by Sir John French reached the front, and were at once put into action. No effort was spared by the Germans to drive the British Army back across the Aisne. The quantity of heavy shells they fired was enormous, and they were probably under the impression that the effect was devastating.

> The object of the great proportion of artillery the Germans employ (observes the official record on this point) is to beat down the resistance of their enemy by a concentrated and prolonged fire, and to shatter their nerve with high explosives before the infantry attack is launched. They seem to have relied on doing this with us; but they have not done so, though it has taken them several costly experiments to discover this fact. From the statements of prisoners, indeed, it appears that they have been greatly disappointed by the moral effect produced by their heavy guns, which, despite the actual losses inflicted, has not been at all commensurate with the colossal expenditure of ammunition, which has really been wasted.
>
> By this it is not implied that their artillery fire is not good. It is more than good; it is excellent. But the British soldier is a difficult person to impress or depress, even by immense shells filled with high explosive which detonate with terrific violence and form craters large enough to act as graves for five horses.

How far the colossal expenditure of ammunition was thrown away is illustrated by this description of the effect in a given instance:—

At a certain point in our front our advanced trenches on the north of the Aisne are not far from a village on the hillside, and also within a short distance of the German works, being on the slope of a spur formed by a subsidiary valley running north and the main valley of the river. It was a calm, sunny afternoon, but hazy; and from a point of vantage south of the river it was difficult exactly to locate on the far bank the well-concealed trenches of either side. From far and near the sullen boom of guns echoed along the valley and at intervals, in different directions, the sky was flecked with the almost motionless smoke of anti-aircraft shrapnel. Suddenly, without any warning, for the reports of the distant howitzers from which they were fired could not be distinguished from other distant reports, three or four heavy shells fell into the village, sending up huge clouds of smoke and dust, which slowly ascended in a brownish-grey column. To this no reply was made by our side.

Shortly afterwards there was a quick succession of reports from a point some distance up the subsidiary valley on the side opposite our trenches, and therefore rather on their flank. It was not possible either by ear or by eye to locate the guns from which these sounds proceeded. Almost simultaneously, as it seemed, there was a corresponding succession of flashes and sharp detonations in a line on the hill side, along what appeared to be our trenches. There was then a pause, and several clouds of smoke rose slowly and remained stationary, spaced as regularly as a line of poplars. Again there was a succession of reports from the German quick-firers on the far side of the misty valley and—like echoes—the detonations of high explosive; and the row of expanding smoke clouds was prolonged by several new ones.

Another pause, and silence, except for the noise in the distance. After a few minutes there was a roar from our side of the main valley as our field guns opened one after another in a more deliberate fire upon the position of the German guns. After six reports there was again silence, save for the whirr of the shells as they sang up the small valley, and then followed the flashes and balls of smoke—one, two, three, four, five, six, as the shrapnel burst nicely over what in the haze looked like some ruined buildings at the edge of a wood.

Again, after a short interval, the enemy's gunners reopened with a burst, still further prolonging the smoke, which was by now merged into one solid screen above a considerable length of trench, and again did our guns reply. And so the duel went on for some time. Ignoring our guns, the German artillerymen, probably relying on concealment for immunity, were concentrating all their efforts in a particularly forceful effort to enfilade our trenches. For them it must have appeared to be the chance of a lifetime, and with their customary prodigality of ammunition they continued to pour bouquet after bouquet of high-explosive *Einheitsgeschoss*, or combined shrapnel and common shell, on to our works. Occasionally, with a roar, a high-angle projectile would sail over the hill and blast a gap in the village. In the hazy valleys bathed in sunlight not a man, not a horse, not a gun, nor even a trench was to be seen. There were only flashes, smoke, and noise. Above, against the blue sky, were several round white clouds hanging in the track of the only two visible human souls—represented by a glistening speck in the air. On high also were to be heard the more or less gentle reports of the bursts of the anti-aircraft projectiles.

Upon inquiry as to the losses sustained it was found that our men had dug themselves well in. In that collection of trenches were portions of four battalions of British soldiers—the Dorsets, the West Kents, the King's Own Yorkshire Light Infantry, and the King's Own Scottish Borderers. Over 300 projectiles were fired against them. The result was nine men wounded.

On the following day 109 shells were fired at the trenches occupied by the West Kent Regiment alone. Four officers were buried, but dug out unhurt. One man was scratched.

All through the second week of the battle, from September 20 to September 28, there was a succession of night attacks. Those delivered on the nights of September 21 and September 23 were especially violent. In the fierce bayonet fights—sometimes on the line of the trenches—the British infantry never failed to prove their superiority. The losses of the enemy were punishingly heavy, not merely in the fire-fights, but in the pursuit when the survivors turned to fly. The object of these tactics of bombardment throughout the day, and of infantry assaults at night, kept up without intermission, was plainly so to wear the British force down that in the end it must give way and be swept back to the Aisne in rout.

For such a victory the Germans were ready to pay a very high price. They paid it—but for defeat. What may be considered the culminating effort was launched against the trenches held by the 1st division on the extreme British right. The division's advanced position close under the ridge near Craonne had all through been a thorn. On the night of September 27 an apparently overwhelming force was flung upon it. Aided by the play of searchlights the German masses strove with might and main. The fight lasted for hours. To say that it was repulsed is evidence enough. The next night the attack was repeated with, if anything, greater violence. It was the fight of the Guards Brigade over again, but on a greater scale. Imagine such a struggle with 50,000 men involved; a fighting mass nearly three miles in extent; the fire of rifles and machine guns and artillery; the gleam of clashing bayonets; the searchlights throwing momentarily into view the fury of a *mêlée* and then shutting it off to light up another scene of struggle. Fortunately for the British, the columns of attack were ripped up before the trenches could be reached. Men fell in rows, held up by the wire entanglements and shot wholesale. This was the enemy's last great stroke.

From that time the British won forward until they gained the ridge, seized Craonne and all the hostile positions along the Chemin des Dames.

CHAPTER 9

The Struggle Round Rheims

It will have been gathered from the preceding pages that the tactics adopted by the Germans north of the Aisne were tactics designed to wear down the British force. No troops, it was supposed, could, even if they survived, withstand such an experience as that of the eight days from September 20 to September 28. Their lines pounded during all the hours of daylight by heavy shells, and assaulted during the hours of darkness by masses of infantry, the British force ought, upon every German hypothesis of modern warfare, to have been either driven back, or broken to pieces. The theory had proved unsound. To say nothing of the enormous monetary cost of the ammunition used, the attacks had turned out appallingly wasteful of life. The best troops of the Prussian Army had been engulfed.

In this savage struggle, between 13,000 and 14,000 British soldiers had been killed or wounded. What the losses were on the side of the Germans we do not know, for their casualties If, however, their losses were on anything like the same scale as those at Mons and at Cambrai, the casualties must have been severe in the extreme. That they were severe is certain. The tactics adopted on the Aisne were not yet substantially different from the tactics followed in the earlier battles. At this stage of the campaign, the Germans still held to the principle that for victory hardly any price was too high.

Remembering at the same time that neither lives nor money are sacrificed by Germany without what is considered good cause, it becomes necessary when there are heavy sacrifices to search for the most adequate and assignable reason. In this instance, the search need not go far. After the first week of the battle, the enemy were not merely defending their stronghold, they were attempting to carry out an offensive, and that offensive had two objects. One was tlie scheme of operations against the left of the Allied line. The other was the recapture of Rheims.

Consider how a defeat of the British force must have affected the situation. On the one hand, it would have enabled the Germans to push back the 6th French Army upon Paris; on the other, it would have compelled the French to evacuate Rheims.

Now Rheims was clearly at this time the key of the Allied position. The roads and railways converging upon the city made it an advanced base of the first importance. Driven out of Rheims, the Allies would have found their communications between Noyon and Verdun hopelessly confused. Neither reinforcements, nor munitions, nor supplies could have been brought up save by difficult and circuitous routes. A general retreat must have become imperative, and all the advantages arising from the recent victory on the Marne have been lost.

Why, then, it may be asked, did the Germans not keep Rheims when they had it? To that question there is but one answer. The Germans evacuated Rheims because they had no choice. Possession of Rheims means command of all the country between the Aisne and the Marne, because that possession also means command of the communications. From Roman times the military importance of the city has been recognised. Eight great roads converge into it from, as many points of the compass. These are military roads, made originally by the Romans, and mostly straight as arrows. They are now supplemented, but in time of war not superseded, by the railways.

The occupation of Rheims by the Germans, and their forced evacuation of the place twelve days later, are two of the most notable episodes of the campaign. If there was one position where it might have been expected the French would make a stand between Belgium and Paris, it was assuredly here. The Germans looked for that opposition. The city was plainly too valuable a prize, and too important a military possession to be yielded without a struggle. Yet when the invaders came within sight of it, there were no signs of resistance. As they debouched from the highlands the splendid picture which spread before their eyes to the south-west was touched with a strange peace.

Framed in its theatre of wooded hills, and dominated by the twin towers of its peerless cathedral, the lordly city, a seat of civilisation and the arts when ancient Germany was still a wilderness, seemed far removed from the scene of war. No cannon boomed from any of its surrounding forts; no trenches were anywhere visible; no troops could be seen along the distant roads. German officers swept the landscape with their field glasses. They found a military blank. Naturally, they suspected a ruse. Volunteers were called for, and a band of eighteen valiants enrolled themselves. The eighteen rode into the city. They were not molested. At the same time, another band crept cautiously up to the nearest of the outlying forts. They entered it without challenge. It was empty. Both bands came back to headquarters with the same surprising report. The French troops had fled to the last man. What better proof could there be of total demoralisation?

Now, there was a ruse, and if anything could illustrate the combined boldness and depth of the French strategy it was this. Let us see what the ruse was. To begin with, Rheims was supposed to be a fortress, but the forts, situated on the surrounding hills, and constructed after the war of 1870-71, were mere earthworks. They were not adapted to withstand modern artillery. It was part of the French plan that they should not be adapted. On the contrary, just before the German advance, the forts had been dismantled and abandoned. That measure had been postponed to the last moment, and though the invaders had their spies at Rheims, as elsewhere, they remained unaware of it.

Clearly the effect of the abandonment was a belief that the French were already, to all intents, beaten. In the Berlin papers there appeared glowing accounts of the triumph. Conversely, at all events in England among those who did not know, the French evacuation came as a shock. This was all part of the foreseen result. It not only heightened the confidence of the German armies, but it had no small influence on that fatal change of plan on their part which we may now say was decided upon at this very time. General Joffre purposely misled the enemy, both as to the power at his command, and as to his disposition of that power.

Thus it was that the Germans, unopposed, made their triumphal entry. They swept through the famous Gate of Mars, the triumphal arch built by the then townsmen of Rheims in honour of Julius Caesar and Augustus and to mark the completion of the scheme of military roads by Agrippa. They parked their cannon along the noble Public Promenade which stretches beyond this great monument. In the square before the Cathedral, about which at that time German war correspondents went into ecstasies of admiration, the statue of Joan of Arc was ringed by stacks of German lances. Ranks of men in *pickelhauben*, headed by bands playing "*Deutschland über Alles*," were in movement along the great Boulevard Victor Hugo. The very name now seemed a mockery. Rheims appeared helpless.

Taking possession of the town hall, the invaders seized the Mayor, Dr. Langlet, and compelled him to remain up all through the succeeding night issuing the orders which they dictated at the muzzle of a revolver.[1] Nearly one hundred of the leading citizens found themselves placed under arrest as hostages. This was alleged to be a guarantee for the preservation of order. As a fact, it was intended to assist collection, both of the heavy "fine" imposed on the city, and of the extortionate requisitions demanded in kind. With the stocks of champagne contained in the labyrinth of vast cellars hollowed out beneath Rheims in the chalk rock, the German officers made themselves unrestrainedly free. The occupation degenerated into an orgy. Much wine that could not be consumed was, on the advance being resumed, taken to the front, loaded on ambulance wagons.[2] It is alleged that nearly 2,000,000 bottles of wine were either consumed, plundered, or wasted.

Every house, too, had its complement of soldiers billeted on the occupants. When they marched south to the Marne, the Germans had been refreshed with unwonted good cheer and by rest in comfortable beds.

But three days later there began to come in, both by road and by railway, convoys of wounded, and these swelled in number day by day, until every hotel and many houses had been filled with human wrecks of battle. The cathedral, its floor strewn with straw, was turned into a great hospital. All this, however, was but a presage. Rarely has there been in so brief a time a contrast more startling than that between the outward march of the German troops and their return.

Just ten days had gone by when Rheims witnessed the influx of haggard, hungry, and dog-tired men; many bare-headed or bootless; not a few wearing uniforms which were in rags; numbers injured. The bands had ceased to play. Instead of the steady march and the imperious word of command, there was the tramp of a sullen, beaten, and battered army; a tramp mingled with shouts and curses of exasperation; and the rumble of guns dragged by exhausted horses, mercilessly lashed in order to get the last ounce of pace out of them. All day, on September 12, the tide of defeat rolled into Rheims from the south, and surged out of it by the north; but above the clash and confusion

1. This incident was narrated by the special correspondent of the *Berliner Tageblatt*.
2. Letters from the front published in the Berlin newspapers leave no doubt on this point. One such account described how a French shell in the Battle of the Marne wrecked an ambulance wagon loaded with bottles of wine—an instance of French contempt for civilised warfare! In 1870-71 the Germans impoverished Rheims by heavy requisitions.

was borne the boom of cannon, growing steadily louder and nearer. Knowing that the population of Rheims had been driven to exasperation, the Germans feared they might be entrapped in the city by street fighting. An evidence of their panic is found in the proclamation which, on the morning of September 12, they compelled the mayor to issue. The document speaks for itself. It ran:—

> In the event of an action being fought either today or in the immediate future in the neighbourhood of Rheims, or in the city itself, the inhabitants are warned that they must remain absolutely calm and must in no way try to take part in the fighting. They must not attempt to attack either isolated soldiers or detachments of the German Army. The erection of barricades, the taking up of paving stones in the streets in a way to hinder the movements of troops, or, in a word, any action that may embarrass the German Army, is formally forbidden.
>
> With a view to securing adequately the safety of the troops and to instil calm into the population of Rheims, the persons named below have been seized as hostages by the commander-in-chief of the German Army. These hostages will be hanged at the slightest attempt at disorder. Also, the city will be totally or partly burnt and the inhabitants will be hanged for any infraction of the above.
>
> By order of the German Authorities.
>
> The Mayor (Dr. Langlet).
>
> Rheims, Sept. 12, 1914.

Then followed the names of 81 of the principal inhabitants, with their addresses, including four priests, the list ending with the words, "and some others."

There was good reason for this German panic. These troops of the army of von Bülow had been completely defeated. Of that no better evidence can be offered than a letter found on a soldier of the 74th German Regiment of infantry, part of the 10th army corps. The letter is of vivid human interest.

> My Dear Wife,—I have just been living through days that defy imagination. I should never have thought that men could stand it. Not a second has passed but my life has been in danger, and yet not a hair of my head has been hurt. It was horrible, it was ghastly. But I have been saved for you and for our happiness, and I take heart again, although I am still terribly unnerved.

God grant that I may see you again soon, and that this horror may soon be over. None of us can do any more; human strength is at an end.

I will try to tell you about it.

On Sept. 5 the enemy were reported to be taking up a position near St. Prix (north-east of Paris). The 10th corps, which had made an astonishingly rapid advance, of course attacked on the Sunday.

Steep slopes led up to heights which were held in considerable force. With our weak detachments of the 74th and 91st Regiments we reached the crest and came under a terrible artillery fire that mowed us down. However, we entered St. Prix. Hardly had we done so than we were met with shell fire and a violent fusillade from the enemy's infantry. Our colonel was badly wounded—he is the third we have had. Fourteen men were killed round me.... We got away in a lull without being hit.

The 7th, 8th, and 9th of Sept. we were constantly under shell and shrapnel fire, and suffered terrible losses. I was in a house which was hit several times. The fear of a death of agony which is in every man's heart, and naturally so, is a terrible feeling.

How often I thought of you, my darling, and what I suffered in that terrifying battle, which extended along a front of many miles near Montmirail, you cannot possibly imagine. Our heavy artillery was being used for the siege of Maubeuge; we wanted it badly, as the enemy had theirs in force, and kept up a furious bombardment. For four days I was under artillery fire; it is like hell, but a thousand times worse.

On the night of the 9th the order was given to retreat, as it would have been madness to attempt to hold our position with our few men, and we should have risked a terrible defeat the next day. The first and third armies had not been able to attack with us, as we had advanced too rapidly. Our *moral* was absolutely broken.

In spite of unheard-of sacrifices we had achieved nothing. I cannot understand how our army, after fighting three great battles and being terribly weakened, was sent against a position which the enemy had prepared for three weeks, but naturally I know nothing of the intentions of our chiefs.... They say nothing has been lost. In a word, we retired towards Cormontreuil and Rheims by forced marches by day and night.

We hear that three armies are going to get into line, entrench, rest, and then start afresh our victorious march on Paris. It was not a defeat, but only a strategic retreat. I have confidence in our chiefs that everything will be successful. Our first battalion, which has fought with unparalleled bravery, is reduced from 1,200 to 194 men. These numbers speak for themselves. . . .

If the defeat had been complete, the pursuit had been relentless. The 5th French Army had excelled itself. It comprised the Algerian army corps, and had been reinforced by the Moroccan and Senegalese regiments. Not only along the main roads, but along all the by-roads, and in and among the vineyards and woods, there had been ceaseless fighting. If one side is reflected by the letter of the dead German soldier, that revelation is completed by the Order issued to his troops by General Desperey when they had broken the enemy at Montmirail on September 9.

> Soldiers,—Upon the memorable fields of Montmirail, of Vauchamps, and of Champaubert, which a century ago witnessed the victories of our ancestors over Blücher's Prussians, your vigorous offensive has triumphed over the resistance of the Germans.
> Held on his flanks, his centre broken, the enemy is now retreating towards east and north by forced marches. The most renowned army corps of Old Prussia, the contingents of Westphalia, of Hanover, of Brandenburg, have retired in haste before you.
> This first success is no more than a prelude. The enemy is shaken, but not yet decisively beaten.
> You have still to undergo severe hardships, to make long marches, to fight hard battles.
> May the image of our country, soiled by barbarians, always remain before your eyes. Never was it more necessary to sacrifice all for her.
> Saluting the heroes who have fallen in the fighting of the last few days, my thoughts turn towards you—the victors in the next battle.
>   Forward, soldiers, for France!

Forward for France they had gone. Thus it was that, shut in their houses throughout the night of September 12, the people of Rheims heard above the uproar of the German retreat the always swelling thunder of the French guns. When morning broke the only German military still left in Rheims were the abandoned wounded, and the main streets echoed to the welcome tread of the war-worn but triumphant defenders of the fatherland.

Through the transverse gap from Rheims to Berry-au-Bac on the Aisne there is one of those wonderful old Roman roads, now a great modern highway. The road runs nearly straight as a ruler north-west to Laon. The first step taken by General Desperey was to secure this road, as well as the railway which on the western side of the gap winds curiously in and out along the foot of the hills. From Berry-au-Bac north of the Aisne the French lent most material aid to the British attack upon Craonne. South-east of Rheims they were occupied in securing the railway to Chalons, which for some twenty miles runs through the valley of the Vesle. Above Rheims this valley, in character not unlike the valley of the Aisne, but wilder, may be compared to a great crack in the plateau of the highlands. On each side are chalk cliffs, and side valleys of gravel soil covered with woods. Between the cliffs the river winds through flat meadows. Towards Rheims the valley opens out into that theatre of wooded hills in the midst of which the city is situated.

The operations of this part of the great battle resolved themselves partly into a struggle for the transverse gap; next into a gigantic combat waged from opposite sides of the theatre of hills; and lastly, into a fight for command of the upper valley of the Vesle.

Sheltered among the caves and quarries on the north-east side of the gap and of the theatre of hills, the Germans had contrived a scheme of defence works not less elaborate than those along the ridge north of the Aisne, and these defence works extended round the theatre of hills to the outlet from the narrow part of the Vesle valley, blockading both the main military road from Rheims to Chalons, and also the railway.

At the outset their reduced strength limited them to merely defensive tactics, and, as on the north of the Aisne, they steadily, and day by day, lost ground. But they then began steadily and day by day to receive reinforcements, both of men and of heavy artillery. The reinforcements of men included a reconstitution of the Prussian Guard drawn from its reserves at Berlin.

Before the end of September an immense body 4 additional troops had arrived at this part of the front. On the side of the French, also, strong reserves were hurried forward.

It will assist to understand the description of the operations to state first their plan and purpose both on the one side and the other, since this formed strategically the critical section of the battle.

At Condé-sur-Aisne, it will be recalled, the Germans held a position right on the river, and that position formed a wedge or salient jutting into the British lines east and west of it.

The fact is recalled here because it illustrates what in this campaign has proved a well-marked feature of German strategy. It has been proved, that is to say, that whenever the Germans found it necessary to resist very heavy pressure they seized some point capable of obstinate defence, and, even if pushed back to right and left, kept their grip as long as possible, using the position as a general hold-up along that section of the front.

Thus their grip on Condé and the Chivres bluff was essential to their retention of the Aisne ridge.

They had a similar position at Prunay on the railway between Rheims and Chalons. The village of Prunay is at the point where the theatre of hills narrows into the upper valley of the Vesle. The position jutted out like an angle from the German line, and it commanded the valley.

Figuratively taking these positions of Condé-sur-Aisne on the one side and Prunay on the other, we may imagine the German Army like a man clinging to a couple of posts or railings and so defying the effort to move him.

That is the aspect of the matter so far as defensive tactics go. For offensive tactics grip on such positions is obviously a great aid to pressure on a hostile line lying between them. A military salient serves exactly the same purpose as a wedge. It is a device for splitting the opposition. Here, then, were two wedges in the Allied front, and the object was manifestly to break off the part of the front intervening. On that part of the front with Rheims as its main advanced base the Allied line, all the way round from beyond Noyon to Verdun, structurally depended.

Such was the German scheme. But the Allies on their part had a wedge or salient driven into the German front at Craonne, and as they were there two-thirds of the way along the road from Rheims to Laon, the main advanced base and communication centre of the German line, that salient was extremely awkward. They were intent, on their part, in hammering in their wedge, because it meant a collapse of the whole German right flank from the Aisne ridge to the

Belgian frontier.

It is not difficult, therefore, to understand the fury of the resulting struggle. The best troops on both sides were engaged. In point of magnitude the fighting round Rheims was hardly less than the fighting which occurred later round Ypres.

The struggle in its acute phase lasted for fifteen days and nights without the slightest pause or intermission. In the tracks of the German retreat from the Marne great gaps among the vineyards, where rose mounds of earth, marked the common graves of the slain. Along the boundaries of woods appeared the blackened sites of the hecatombs. Nevertheless, many of the fallen still lay in the woods or among the vines, unburied and infecting the air. Through this country and these scenes marched the reinforcements of the 5th French Army. In the opposite direction flowed a ceaseless stream of civilian fugitives—poor people carrying their few personal belongings strapped on their backs, or pushing them along in wheelbarrows; women carrying children in their arms, and with other children trailing at their skirts; a procession on foot and in vehicles of every sort.

Against Rheims the Germans employed much of the artillery and material and apparatus they had intended for the siege of Paris. On the eastern side of the theatre of hills behind the advanced island mass where stand the villages of Berru and Nogent l'Abbesse, they had mounted their huge mortars. From these positions and from others to the north-east they threw into Rheims an incessant crash of monster shells. Viewed from any of the villages of its circumference, this theatre of hills ten miles across presented during these days a spectacle at once grandiose and awful. The battle spread out round and below like a panorama of fire. Out of advanced positions among the woods on the south-west, across by Rheims, and to the north, hundreds of the French field guns searched the German positions with their terrible high explosive shells.

At brief regular intervals amid the angry roar arose a deep resounding boom—the note of the enemy's great howitzers. The earth shook beneath the salvoes, for the French had also massed here their heaviest artillery. Amid the flash of bursting shells appeared here a village, there a mill a mass of flames, with the smoke drifting above it in a dense cloud. The roar was that of hurricane and earthquake rolled into one. And the uproar went on without ceasing through all the hours of daylight, and far into the night.

Furious and destructive as it was, however, the artillery duel was not the deadliest part. The great slaughter occurred when the armies came to grips. The Germans launched an attack upon Rheims from the north and an attack at the same time from the south-east. Of the first attack the immediate objective was the suburb of La Neuvillette. That place is on the great road from Rheims to Berry-au-Bac, and if it could be seized the French positions along the transverse gap would be endangered, and their position at Craonne made untenable. The immediate objective of the second attack was the fort of La Pompelle, commanding the great road to Chalons. To the French both communications were vital.

In the attack upon La Neuvillette the troops employed were the re-formed Prussian Guard. Over 40,000 strong, men for the most part in the prime of life, and men who, though reservists, had received the highest military training, they formed probably as formidable a body of troops as any in Europe. Against them were pitted the finest of French regular infantry, including a division 20,000 strong of the Zouaves. Both sides fought with the fury of mutual hate. It was a contest in which race passion had been stirred to its depths. The Guard advanced south along the great road from Neuchatel; descended into the transverse gap; and crossed the Aisne and Marne canal at Loivre. They braved the deadly hail of the French 75-millimetre guns, than which there is nothing more deadly; they fought through the gap against charges of the Zouaves in which there was no quarter; they reached St. Thierry; they reached, after fourteen hours' continuous fighting, La Neuvillette itself—that is to say, a remnant reached it.

It was a splendid feat of courage; for more than half the force had fallen. At Neuvillette, however, they were overpowered. The French troops who held that place could not be dislodged. The scenes in the streets were terrible. Meanwhile, the French had shattered the succeeding and supporting German columns, and had closed in on the rear. The Guards, finding themselves entrapped, had to cut their way out. How many again reached the German lines we do not know. It must have been very few.

At Fort La Pompelle the garrison heroically held out against a vastly superior force. The fort was stormed. Then it was retaken by the French. The order to the officer commanding was, "Fight to the last man." He fought. When the position became desperate he appealed for reinforcements. As he was sending off the message he was killed by a shell. The command devolved upon a sergeant. Relief came while the survivors of the garrison were still resisting.

To throw the relief into La Pompelle it was necessary to attack the tiers of trenches cut by the Germans along the hills as far as Prunay. The French had to cross the Aisne and Oise canal, which after passing through Rheims is joined up with the Vesle. This, in face of the German infantry fire and in face of well-concealed batteries of guns, was a desperate business. It was done not only through the dauntless courage of the French foot, but by the terrible effect of their artillery. The Germans, notwithstanding, advanced from their trenches to dispute the passage. There was a hand-to-hand battle in the canal itself—a battle to the death. The French won over; they carried the first line of German trenches; supports, regiment after regiment, were thrown across; they carried the second line; then the third; at each it was bayonet work, thrust and parry.

But the Germans still clung to Prunay. That place was the real centre of this part of the struggle. The village lies between the Rheims-Chalons railway line and the Vesle. Out of the place the enemy had to be cleared, cost what it might. It was one of those episodes in which an army puts forth its whole strength of nerve. From the wooded heights above the valley a massing of German batteries sought to wither the attack. A massing of French batteries on the nearer side strove to put the German guns out of action. The duel was gigantic. Reports of the guns became no longer distinguishable. They were merged into what seemed one continued solid and unbroken explosion.

The French infantry advanced to the assault. Their losses were heavy. Prunay was set alight by shells. Still the attack was pressed. Then the ring of fire round the distant woods which marked the line of German batteries became ragged, and died down. The French guns had proved their superiority. At the point of the bayonet the Germans were driven out of Prunay and across the railway. Here they made a last stand. It was in vain. French gunners were now racing their pieces forward and opening in new positions; German batteries, on the other hand, were seen limbering up and in flight. At last, as night fell, the Germans broke in rout along the road to Beine. Prunay they had lost for good.

These were leading but only typical episodes of those fifteen days. The fighting went on, too, through the night. As daylight faded, masses of Algerian and Moroccan troops, held in reserve, crept forward, and gathered stealthily in chalk-pits or among the woods. They moved with an almost catlike tread. In these secret rendezvous they waited until the dead of night. Then in file after file, thousands of them, they stole up, invisible, to the German trenches; and in the first faint shimmer of dawn launched themselves with a savage yell upon the foe. There was terrible work among those hills.

Do these episodes throw no light on the damage done to Rheims Cathedral? Here round Rheims and north of the Aisne had been the mightiest effort the German armies had yet made. Here was concentrated the full force of their most disciplined and most valiant troops. Those troops had been sacrificed and with no result. Many storms of war had passed by the cathedral at Rheims since it was completed in 1231, and from the time when nearly a hundred more years of patient labour had put the last touches on its marvellous sculptures, and it had stood forth a thing of wonder and of beauty, no hand of violence had been laid on its consecrated stones. At the news that Prussian cannon had been turned upon it to destroy it, and had reduced it to a burned-out skeleton, from which Prussian wounded had to be carried out lest they should be roasted alive, the whole civilised world gasped.

Mr. E. Ashmead-Bartlett, who visited the cathedral while the bombardment was going on, sent to the *Daily Telegraph* a remarkable account of his experiences:

> Round the cathedral hardly a house had escaped damage, and even before we reached the open square in which it stands it became evident that the Germans had concentrated their fire on the building. The pavement of the square had been torn up by the bursting of these 6-in. shells and was covered with fragments of steel, cracked masonry, glass, and loose stones. In front of the *façade* of the cathedral stands the well-known statue of Jeanne d'Arc. Someone had placed a Tricolour in her outstretched arm. The great shells had burst all round her, leaving the Maid of Orleans and her flag unscathed, but her horse's belly and legs were chipped and seared with fragments of flying steel.
>
> At the first view the exterior of the cathedral did not appear to have suffered much damage, although the masonry was chipped and scarred white by countless shrapnel bullets or pieces of steel, and many of the carved figures and gargoyles on the western *façade* were broken and chipped.
>
> We found no one in the square; in fact, this part of the town appeared to be deserted, but as we approached the main entrance to try to obtain admittance a curious sight met our eyes. We saw the recumbent figure of a man lying against the door. He had long since lost both his legs, which had been replaced by wood-

en stumps. He lay covered with dust, small stones, and broken glass, which had been thrown over him by bursting shells, but by some chance his remaining limbs had escaped all injury. This old veteran of the war of 1870, as he described himself, has accosted all and sundry at the gate of the cathedral for generations past, and even in the midst of the bombardment he had crawled once more to his accustomed post. As we knocked on the great wooden door, from this shapeless and filthy wreck of what had once been a man there came the feeble cry: '*Monsieur, un petit sou. Monsieur, un petit sou.*'

Our knock was answered by a priest, who, on seeing that we were English, at once allowed us to enter. The father then told us, in language that was not altogether priestly, when speaking of the vandals whose guns were still thundering outside, of how the Germans had bombarded the cathedral for two hours that morning, landing over fifty shells in its immediate neighbourhood, but, luckily, the range being very great, over eight kilometres, the solid stonework of the building had resisted the successive shocks of these six-inch howitzers, and how it was that ancient and priceless glass which had suffered the most.[3]

'*Monsieur*, they respect nothing. We placed 125 of them inside and hoisted the red cross on the spire in order to protect the cathedral, and yet they fire at it all the same, and have killed their own soldiers. Pray, *monsieur*, make these facts known all over Europe and America.'

With these words he unlocked a wicket and conducted us toward the altar, close to which stands a small painted statue of Jeanne d'Arc. The east end of Notre Dame had up to this period suffered but little, and although some of the windows were damaged they were not lost beyond repair. The light still shone through in rays of dark blue and red, broken here and there by streaks of pure light.

Then our guide conducted us to the great cold stone body of the cathedral, where the Gothic pillars rise in sombre majesty, relieved by no ornamentation[4] until they hold aloft the blue

---

3. The windows of Rheims Cathedral were filled with stained Venetian glass dating from the 12th century and impossible to replace.

4. The Interior of Rheims Cathedral was furnished with sixty-six large pieces of priceless old tapestry, representing scenes in the life of Christ, the story of the Virgin, and scenes from the life of St. Paul, the latter after designs by Raphael. These tapestries had been removed to a place of safety.

masterpieces of the unknown artist. Here one of the strangest of spectacles met the eye. The whole of this vast vault was covered with dust half an inch thick, with chipped-off masonry, pieces of lead piping from the shattered windows, and with countless fragments of varied coloured glass. In the centre lay an ancient candelabrum which had hung for centuries from the roof suspended by a steel chain. That morning a fragment of shell had cut the chain in half and dropped its ancient burden to the hard stone floor beneath, where it lay bent and crumpled.

A great wave of sunshine lit up a sombre picture of carnage and suffering at the western end near the main entrance. Here on piles of straw lay the wounded Germans in all stages of suffering—their round shaven heads, thin cheeks, and bluish-grey uniforms contrasting strangely with the sombre black of the silent priests attending them, while in the background the red trousers of the French soldiers were just visible on the steps outside. Most of the wounded had dragged their straw behind the great Gothic pillars as if seeking shelter from their own shells. The priest conducted us to one of the aisles beneath the window where the shell had entered that morning. A great pool of blood lay there, staining the column just as the blood of Thomas à Becket must have stained the altar of Canterbury seven centuries before.

'That, *Monsieur*, is the blood of the French *gendarme* who was killed at eleven this morning, but he did not go alone.' The priest pointed to two more recumbent figures clad in the bluish-grey of the *Kaiser's* legions. There they lay stiff and cold as the effigies around them. All three had perished by the same shell. Civilian doctors of Rheims moved amongst the wounded, who for the most part maintained an attitude of stoical indifference to everything around them. We moved around collecting fragments of the precious glass which the *Kaiser* had so unexpectedly thrown within our reach. We were brought back to realities by hearing the unmistakable whistle of an approaching shell, followed by a deafening explosion, and more fragments of glass came tumbling from aloft. The weary war-worn Teutons instinctively huddled closer to the Gothic arches. A dying officer, his eyes already fixed in a glassy stare on the sunlight above, gave an involuntary groan. We heard outside the crash of falling masonry. The shell was followed by another, and more breaking glass. Our chauffeur came hastening in with the Virgin's broken arm in his hands. A fragment of shell had broken it off outside. We lingered long gazing at this strange scene.

Outside the guns were thundering all round Rheims.

It was after this that the cathedral was set on fire by the shells.

CHAPTER 10

Review of Results

Had the fighting round Rheims and the fighting north of the Aisne no result? Were these combats, vast as they were, merely drawn combats? By no means. North of the Aisne the British gained the eastern end of the ridge; round Rheims the French won all the eastern side of the theatre of hills, with the exception of Nogent l'Abbesse, and also the eastern side of the transverse gap. Those results were both decisive and important.

They were decisive and important because they achieved strategical purposes vital to the Allied campaign. Let us try to make that clear.

When after the defeat on the Marne the Germans took up their new line from the north of the Aisne to the Argonne, their utmost energy and resource were put forth to send into the fighting line from Germany fresh reserve formations which would give their forces not only a numerical but a military superiority.

But the effect and value of those fresh masses clearly depended on their being employed at the decisive points. Where were those decisive points?

The decisive points were first the extreme left of the Allied line, where it turned round from the north of the Aisne to the Oise, and secondly Verdun and along the eastern frontier.

Consider the effect had the Germans been able promptly to throw *decisively* superior forces against the Allies at those points. They would have turned both flanks of the Allied line, they would have forced a general retreat, and they would have been able once more to resume the offensive, but this time probably with the fortified frontier in their hands.

There can be no doubt that, broadly, that was their intention; and it was plainly seen by General Joffre to be their intention, because eastward from Rheims to the Argonne in their fortified line across the highlands *the Germans remained from first to last upon the defensive.*

This, however, was the situation the Germans had to meet: between the Aisne and the Oise a new and powerful French Army under the command of General de Castlenau; on the Aisne and round Rheims, a tremendous and sustained onset by the 6th French, the British, and the 5th French Army; between Rheims and the Argonne, an offensive which pushed them successively out of Suippes, and Souain, and therefore off the great cross-roads; in the Argonne, an offensive which forced them back from St. Menehould and beyond Varennes, and closed the defiles; round Verdun, and in the Woevre, an onset which threatened to cut communications with Metz.

Now the effect of these operations was, among other things, to restrict the German means of movement and supply; and it was a consequence of that restriction that even though there might be two or more millions of men then ready in Germany to be sent forward, there were neither roads nor railways enough to send them forward save after delay, nor roads or railways enough to keep them supplied when they had been sent.

With the means at their disposal—those means were still great, though not great enough—the German Government had to choose between various alternatives. As to the choice they made, later events leave no doubt. They sent forward troops enough to *defend* their flank between the Aisne and the Oise—it was all at the moment they could do; and they employed the best and heaviest of their masses of reserves partly to resist the British attack, but mainly to resist the 5th French Army. At this time they had to let the position in the Argonne, round Verdun, and on the eastern frontier go; that is to say, they had there to remain for the time being on the defensive.

The fighting north of the Aisne and round Rheims therefore crippled their operations at what were, in truth, the decisive points—the Allied flanks; and that was unavoidable, because unless the centre of their line remained secure, operations on the flanks would be impracticable. But these operations in the centre *used up their best troops.*

Conversely, of course, the same operations left General Joffre the more free both to pursue his envelopment of the Germans on their flank northwards from the Aisne towards the Belgian frontier, and to go on with his seizures of positions round Verdun and on the eastern frontier, seizures which pressed upon and embarrassed the German communications, and consequently limited the total strength they could put into the field.

It will be seen, therefore, that the fighting north of the Aisne and round Rheims was important and *was* decisive.

The fact must not be lost sight of that the aim of the Germans was at this time, if they could, to re-seize the initiative. Again the fact ought to be kept in mind that the aim of the Allied strategy was not to drive the German armies from France, but both to prevent them from getting out of France and to destroy them as a military force. If we know the governing motive on each side, we hold the key to the strategy adopted. Here the governing motive of neither was a secret.

To show the effect of governing motive, let us in the first instance follow the course of German strategy. We shall find that from the middle of September, during the succeeding nine weeks—that is, until about November 20—they made six great efforts, any one of which, had it succeeded, would once more have given them the initiative in this western campaign. The first was the effort to break the Allied line at Rheims.

Foiled in their outflanking scheme by the inherent difficulties of the situation, but not less by the powerful Allied attack north of the Aisne and round Rheims, there can be no question that the German Headquarters Staff decided that their best, most direct, and most decisive stroke would be a counter-offensive made against Rheims with their utmost force, and as the situation stood at the end of September, there can be no question that they were right.

Had the effort succeeded both parts of the Allies' line must have been forced into retreat and their communications severed. This success must have changed the entire aspect of the western operations. For the Allies it would have been a disaster of the first magnitude. If in this effort the Germans sacrificed their best troops, it affords only another illustration of the statement that they do not make such sacrifices without what they consider good cause.

But the effort failed, and the German Headquarters Staff, at any rate, must have realised that the failure and the cost of it had imperilled the whole position of their armies in France. Matters of this kind have not to be judged only by ground lost or won. The success or failure to achieve objectives is the true test.

Meanwhile heavy forces of the Allies had been massed against the German right flank. The next effort of the Germans consequently was to push back those forces. They met the outflanking movement in the way such movements can best be met—by trying to outflank the outflankers.

At this time the Allied forces on the flank extended from near Noyon on the Oise northward to the Somme. The Germans promptly pushed westward in force north of the Somme and across the outside edge of the Allied line to the town of Albert and the heights commanding it.

With notable promptitude, however, the Allied line was extended across the Somme to the north, and by the west of Arras, and the German movement was held. Gradually, after days of obstinate fighting, the enemy were battled out of Albert and then out of Arras; and the Allied outflanking line was stretched up to Bethune and La Bassée.

Night and day, day and night, by railway, by motor-omnibus, on motorcars,[1] French troops during three whole weeks were rushed up from the south and west of France. This movement towards the fighting line had begun with the pursuit after the Battle of the Marne. It never ceased. First the army of General de Castlenau appeared on the front. Next came the army of General de Maudhuy. Territorials and marines from the fleet were hurried into the service; divisions of cavalry spaced out the line, and defended communications. In Germany as in France no effort was spared. The issue was momentous. During these first weeks of October the German Government put forth its supreme effort to stem and to turn the adverse tide of war. Hitherto they had found their measures baffled. Two new and powerful French armies had fastened on to the flank of their position. Their own forces had come up just too late. The peril was menacing and it was growing. They redoubled their energies.

Their decision was another supreme effort to outflank the outflankers. With fresh masses of Reservists, sent westward at all possible speed, they pushed behind a heavy screen of cavalry across the Aa and across the Lys at Estaires and threatened the rear of the French troops holding Bethune.

It is probably not realised that this was strategically the most important offensive movement the Germans had made in the western theatre of war since their advance upon Paris.

Yet that undoubtedly was the fact. Had the movement succeeded it must not only have given them control of the north-east coast of France as far probably as Havre, but it must have rolled up the Allied line as far as Noyon. The whole original scheme of turning the Allies'

---

1. Some 70,000 motorcars and motor-omnibuses are said to have been employed.

left flank would have been within realisation.

The movement did not succeed. It was met by a counter-move probably as unexpected by the Germans as it was bold. The counter-move was the transfer of the British Army from the Aisne.

Recognising the decisive character of these operations, General Joffre had entrusted the control of affairs on this part of the front to General Foch, not only one of the ablest among the able soldiers whom this war has shown the French Army to possess, but one of the most brilliant authorities on the science of modern military tactics. As he had met the situation magnificently at Sezanne, so now he met it with equal resource under circumstances hardly less critical.

There were now three French armies on the German flank, and they fought as they were led with a skill equal to their valour. Yet the necessity remained for a great counter-stroke. In view of that necessity the idea occurred to Sir John French to transfer the British Army, a proposal to which General Joffre at once agreed.

It is beyond the scope of this volume to enter into details of the new great battle which, beginning with the arrival of the British troops, culminated in the heroic defence of Ypres. Justice could not be done to that great and memorable feat of arms in a brief summary.

Suffice it to say that here, on the great coalfield of northern France, in a labyrinth of railway sidings and canals, villages and lanes, pit heaps, and factories, the British troops, helped by the French cavalry, after furious fighting, drove back the Germans from the Aa and the Lys and took up a line continuing the outflanking positions from La Bassée to Ypres in Belgium.

A third effort of the Germans to outflank the outflanking line was directed across the Yser. This was the last attempt of the kind that could be made. Its success was consequently vital, and its failure equally disastrous. Again it illustrates the fact that the Germans sacrifice neither money nor lives without good cause. The fighting on the Yser was as deadly for the enemy as the fighting round Rheims.

Coincidently, however, with these movements were others of a different kind. The official *communiqués*, covering the two kinds of movements as the evidences of them appeared day by day, have naturally led to a certain amount of mystification—not intentional, but inevitable from the brevity and caution of these statements and the fact that they cover separately only the operations of a few hours.

The movements of a different kind were those designed at one point or another to drive a wedge or salient into the Allied front.

In the operations on the German flank between the Aisne and the Belgian coast there have been two main efforts of that character. The first was the attempt to split the Allied front at Roye and at Arras, and to break up the line between those places; the second was the effort on an even larger scale, and pursued with still greater determination, to split the front at La Bassée and at Ypres, and to break up the line intervening.

It is no mere accident that this latter attempt followed immediately on the failure to cross the Yser. *The attempt arose out of the necessity of the situation.*

On the Upper Meuse, by another great effort, the Germans had driven a wedge into the French fortified frontier at St. Mihiel, and that wedge appeared to some the prelude of a mysterious scheme. In fact, the intention and the effect of it was to hold off the French advance along the frontier of Lorraine and across the Vosges. Again it is the case of a desperate man clinging to a railing.

We have, therefore, three great efforts to break the Allied front by their wedge tactics, and three to outflank the Allied outflanking development. None of these efforts succeeded.

What was the consequence? The consequence was that the German armies in France and Belgium could neither advance nor retreat. They could not advance because they are not strong enough. They could not retreat, because retreat would mean their destruction.

The retreat of any army—and most of all the retreat of a huge mass army—is not a simple matter. On the contrary, it is a most difficult and complex operation in the most favourable circumstances. Here, however, was not one mass army, but a line of mass armies, occupying a front forming a right angle, and opposed on each arm of that right angle by forces which had proved stronger than they. So situated, they could only retreat with any chance of safety by falling directly back; but either arm of the angle if it fell directly back must obstruct the retreat of the other; and if they fell directly back each at the same time, their movements must become exactly like those of the blades of a pair of scissors as they are being closed. *A retreat under such conditions is a military impossibility.*

Not a few fantastic motives have been attributed to the Germans, more particularly as regards the terrible struggle in West Flanders, but the plain truth of the matter is that here stated.

Now if we turn to the strategy of the Allies, bearing their governing motive in mind, we shall find that it rested primarily on the attack launched against the German positions north of the Aisne and round Rheims.

That attack wrecked the German scheme for resuming the offensive, and was the most effective means of assuring that end. It is impossible indeed not to recognise that the feat which reduced a force like the German armies to immobility is a masterpiece of strategy wholly without parallel in the annals of war. Whether we look at the breadth and boldness of its conception, at the patience and command of organisation with which it was carried out, at the grasp it displayed of the real conditions governing the operations of modern mass armies, or at the clear purpose and unswerving resolution with which it was followed, the plan equally calls forth surprise and admiration.

From the military standpoint, victory or defeat is the answer to the question: Which side has accomplished the purpose it had in view?

The German purpose of re-seizing the initiative was not accomplished. The German scheme of turning either one or both flanks of the Allied line was not accomplished. That is military failure.

From the beginning of October, when the struggle round Rheims was at its height, the feature of the campaign broadly was that the weight of the fighting passed progressively from the centre of the fighting front to the wings—to West Flanders on the one side, and to the Argonne and the Upper Meuse on the other. Progressively the Allied forces were placed where it was intended they should be placed. They accomplished the purpose which it was intended they should accomplish—that of keeping the main military strength of Germany helpless while they wasted that strength. That is military success.

To sum up. The Germans entered France with a force of more than a million and a half of men. The like of such a military expedition the world till then had never seen. The plan of it had been studied and worked out in detail for years. On the preparations for it had been bestowed a colossal labour. It appeared certain of success. It was defeated by an exercise of military skill and resource which, however regarded, must stand as one of the greatest records of mastery in the art of war.

Appendix

Despatches of Field-Marshal Sir John French on the Battles of the Marne and the Aisne, addressed to Lord Kitchener, Secretary of State for War.

1.

Sept. 17, 1914.

My Lord—

In continuation of my despatch of Sept. 7, I have the honour to report the further progress of the operations of the forces under my command from Aug. 28.

On that evening the retirement of the force was followed closely by two of the enemy's cavalry columns, moving south-east from St. Quentin.

The retreat in this part of the field was being covered by the 3rd and 5th Cavalry Brigades. South of the Somme General Gough, with the 3rd Cavalry Brigade, threw back the *Uhlans* of the Guard with considerable loss.

General Chetwode, with the 5th Cavalry Brigade, encountered the eastern column near Cérizy, moving south. The Brigade attacked and routed the column, the leading German regiment suffering very severe casualties and being almost broken up.

The 7th French Army Corps was now in course of being railed up from the south to the east of Amiens. On the 29th it nearly completed its detrainment, and the French 6th Army got into position on my left, its right resting on Roye.

The 5th French Army was behind the line of the Oise between La Fère and Guise.

The pursuit of the enemy was very vigorous; some five or six German corps were on the Somme, facing the 5th Army on the Oise. At least two corps were advancing towards my front, and were crossing the Somme east and west of Ham. Three or four more German corps were opposing the 6th French Army on my left.

This was the situation at one o'clock on the 29th, when I received a visit from General Joffre at my headquarters.

I strongly represented my position to the French commander-in-chief, who was most kind, cordial, and sympathetic, as he has always been. He told me that he had directed the 5th French Army on the Oise to move forward and attack the Germans on the Somme, with a view to checking pursuit. He also told me of the formation of the 6th French Army on my left flank, composed of the 7th Army Corps, four reserve divisions, and Sordêt's corps of cavalry.

I finally arranged with General Joffre to effect a further short retirement towards the line Compiègne-Soissons, promising him, however, to do my utmost to keep always within a day's march of him.

In pursuance of this arrangement the British forces retired to a position a few miles north of the line Compiègne-Soissons on the 29th.

The right flank of the German Army was now reaching a point which appeared seriously to endanger my line of communications with Havre. I had already evacuated Amiens, into which place a German reserve division was reported to have moved.

Orders were given to change the base to St. Nazaire, and establish an advance base at Le Mans. This operation was well carried out by the Inspector-General of Communications.

In spite of a severe defeat inflicted upon the Guard 10th and Guard Reserve Corps of the German Army by the 1st and 3rd French Corps on the right of the 5th Army, it was not part of General Joffre's plan to pursue this advantage, and a general retirement on to the line of the Marne was ordered, to which the French forces in the more eastern theatre were directed to conform.

A new army (the 9th) has been formed from three corps in the south by General Joffre, and moved into the space between the right of the 5th and left of the 4th Armies.

Whilst closely adhering to his strategic conception to draw the enemy on at all points until a favourable situation was created from which to assume the offensive, General Joffre found it necessary to modify from day to day the methods by which he sought to attain this object, owing to the development of the enemy's plans and changes in the general situation.

In conformity with the movements of the French forces, my retirement continued practically from day to day. Although we were not severely pressed by the enemy, rearguard actions took place continually.

On Sept. 1, when retiring from the thickly-wooded country to the south of Compiègne, the 1st Cavalry Brigade was overtaken by some German cavalry. They momentarily lost a horse artillery battery, and several officers and men were killed and wounded. With the help, however, of some detachments from the 3rd Corps operating on their left, they not only recovered their own guns, but succeeded in capturing twelve of the enemy's.

Similarly, to the eastward, the 1st Corps, retiring south, also got into some very difficult forest country, and a somewhat severe rearguard action ensued at Villers-Cotterets, in which the 4th Guards Brigade suffered considerably.

On Sept. 3 the British forces were in position south of the Marne between Lagny and Signy-Signets. Up to this time I had been requested by General Joffre to defend the passages of the river as long as possible, and to blow up the bridges in my front. After I had made the necessary dispositions, and the destruction of the bridges had been effected, I was asked by the French commander-in-chief to continue my retirement to a point some twelve miles in rear of the position I then occupied, with a view to taking up a second position behind the Seine. This retirement was duly carried out. In the meantime the enemy had thrown bridges and crossed the Marne in considerable force, and was threatening the Allies all along the line of the British forces and the 5th and 9th French armies. Consequently several small outpost actions took place.

On Saturday, Sept. 5, I met the French commander-in-chief at his request, and he informed me of his intention to take the offensive forthwith, as he considered conditions were very favourable to success.

General Joffre announced to me his intention of wheeling up the left flank of the 6th Army, pivoting on the Marne, and directing it to move on the Ourcq; cross and attack the flank of the 1st German Army, which was then moving in a southeasterly direction east of that river.

He requested me to effect a change of front to my right—my left resting on the Marne and my right on the 5th Army—to fill the gap between that army and the 6th. I was then to advance against the enemy in my front and join in the general offensive movement.

These combined movements practically commenced on Sunday, Sept. 6, at sunrise; and on that day it may be said that a great battle opened on a front extending from Ermenonville, which was just in front of the left flank of the 6th French Army, through Lizy on the Marne, Mauperthuis, which was about the British centre, Courteçon, which was the left of the 5th French Army, to Esternay and Charleville, the left of the 9th Army under General Foch, and so along the front of the 9th, 4th, and 3rd French Armies to a point north of the fortress of Verdun.

This battle, in so far as the 6th French Army, the British Army, the 5th French Army, and the 9th French Army were concerned, may be said to have concluded on the evening of Sept. 10, by which time the Germans had been driven back to the line Soissons-Rheims, with a loss of thousands of prisoners, many guns, and enormous masses of transport.

About Sept. 3 the enemy appears to have changed his plans and to have determined to stop his advance south direct upon Paris, for on Sept. 4 air reconnaissances showed that his main columns were moving in a south-easterly direction generally east of a line drawn through Nanteuil and Lizy on the Ourcq.

On Sept. 5 several of these columns were observed to have crossed the Marne; whilst German troops, which were observed moving south-east up the left bank of the Ourcq on the 4th, were now reported to be halted and facing that river. Heads of the enemy's columns were seen crossing at Changis, La Ferté, Nogent, Château-Thierry, and Mezy.

Considerable German columns of all arms were seen to be converging on Montmirail, whilst before sunset large bivouacs of the enemy were located in the neighbourhood of Coulommiers, south of Rebais, La Ferté Gaucher and Dagny.

I should conceive it to have been about noon on Sept. 6, after the British forces had changed their front to the right and occupied the line Jouy-Le Chatel-Faremoutiers-Villeneuve Le

Comte, and the advance of the 6th French Army north of the Marne towards the Ourcq became apparent, that the enemy realised the powerful threat that was being made against the flank of his columns moving south-east, and began the great retreat which opened the battle above referred to.

On the evening of Sept. 6, therefore, the fronts and positions of the opposing armies were, roughly, as follows:

Allies.

6th French Army.—Right on the Marne at Meux, left towards Betz.
British Forces.—On the line Dagny-Coulommiers-Maison.
5th French Army.—At Courtagon, right on Esternay.
Conneau's Cavalry Corps.—Between the right of the British and the left of the French 5th Army.

Germans.

4th Reserve and 2nd Corps.— East of the Ourcq and facing that river.
9th Cavalry Division,—West of Crecy.
2nd Cavalry Division. North of Coulommiers.
4th Corps.—Rebais.
3rd and 7th Corps.—South-west of Montmirail.

All these troops constituted the 1st German Army, which was directed against the French 6th Army on the Ourcq, and the British forces, and the left of the 5th French Army south of the Marne.

The 2nd German Army (IX., X., X.R. and Guard) was moving against the centre and right of the 5th French Army and the 9th French Army.

On Sept. 7 both the 5th and 6th French Armies were heavily engaged on our flank. The 2nd and 4th Reserve German Corps on the Ourcq vigorously opposed the advance of the French towards that river, but did not prevent the 6th Army from gaining some headway, the Germans themselves suffering serious losses. The French 5th Army threw the enemy back to the line of the Petit Morin River, after inflicting severe losses upon them, especially about Montceaux, which was carried at the point of the bayonet.

The enemy retreated before our advance, covered by his 2nd and 9th and Guard Cavalry Divisions, which suffered severely.

Our cavalry acted with great vigour, especially General De Lisle's Brigade, with the 9th Lancers and 18th Hussars.

On Sept. 8 the enemy continued his retreat northward, and our army was successfully engaged during the day with strong rearguards of all arms on the Petit Morin River, thereby materially assisting the progress of the French armies on our right and left, against whom the enemy was making his greatest efforts. On both sides the enemy was thrown back with very heavy loss. The First Army Corps encountered stubborn resistance at La Trétoire (north of Rebais). The enemy occupied a strong position with infantry and guns on the northern bank of the Petit Morin River; they were dislodged with considerable loss. Several machine guns and many prisoners were captured, and upwards of 200 German dead were left on the ground.

The forcing of the Petit Morin at this point was much assisted by the cavalry and the 1st Division, which crossed higher up the stream.

Later in the day a counter attack by the enemy was well repulsed by the First Army Corps, a great many prisoners and some guns again falling into our hands.

On this day (Sept. 8) the Second Army Corps encountered considerable opposition, but drove back the enemy at all points with great loss, making considerable captures.

The Third Army Corps also drove back considerable bodies of the enemy's infantry and made some captures.

On Sept. 9 the First and Second Army Corps forced the passage of the Marne and advanced some miles to the north of it. The Third Corps encountered considerable opposition, as the bridge at La Ferté was destroyed and the enemy held the town on the opposite bank in some strength, and thence persistently obstructed the construction of a bridge; so the passage was not effected until after nightfall.

During the day's pursuit the enemy suffered heavy loss in killed and wounded, some hundreds of prisoners fell into our hands, and a battery of eight machine guns was captured by the 2nd Division.

On this day the 6th French Army was heavily engaged west of the River Ourcq. The enemy had largely increased his force opposing them, and very heavy fighting ensued, in which the French were successful throughout.

The left of the 5th French Army reached the neighbourhood of Château-Thierry after the most severe fighting, having driven the enemy completely north of the river with great loss.

The fighting of this army in the neighbourhood of Montmirail was very severe.

The advance was resumed at daybreak on the 10th up to the line of the Ourcq, opposed by strong rearguards of all arms. The 1st and 2nd Corps, assisted by the Cavalry Division on the right, the 3rd and 5th Cavalry Brigades on the left, drove the enemy northwards. Thirteen guns, seven machine guns, about 2,000 prisoners, and quantities of transport fell into our hands. The enemy left many dead on the field. On this day the French 5th and 6th Armies had little opposition.

As the 1st and 2nd German Armies were now in full retreat, this evening marks the end of the battle which practically commenced on the morning of the 6th instant, and it is at this point in the operations that I am concluding the present despatch.

Although I deeply regret to have had to report heavy losses in killed and wounded throughout these operations, I do not think they have been excessive in view of the magnitude of the great fight, the outlines of which I have only been able very briefly to describe, and the demoralisation and loss in killed and wounded which are known to have been caused to the enemy by the vigour and severity of the pursuit.

In concluding this despatch I must call your lordship's special attention to the fact that from Sunday, Aug. 23, up to the present date (Sept. 17), from Mons back almost to the Seine, and from the Seine to the Aisne, the army under my command has been ceaselessly engaged without one single day's halt or rest of any kind.

Since the date to which in this dispatch I have limited my report of the operations, a great battle on the Aisne has been proceeding. A full report of this battle will be made in an early further despatch.

It will, however, be of interest to say here that, in spite of a very determined resistance on the part of the enemy, who is holding in strength and great tenacity a position peculiarly favourable to defence, the battle which commenced on the evening of the 12th Inst, has, so far, forced the enemy back from his first position, secured the passage of the river, and inflicted great loss upon him, including the capture of over 2,000 prisoners and several guns.—I have the honour to be, your lordship's most obedient servant,

   (Signed)   J. D. P. French,
    Field-Marshal, Commanding-in-Chief,
     the British Forces in the Field.

2.

Oct. 8, 1914.

My Lord—

I have the honour to report the operations in which the British forces in France have been engaged since the evening of Sept. 10.

1. In the early morning of the 11th the further pursuit of the enemy was commenced, and the three corps crossed the Ourcq practically unopposed, the cavalry reaching the line of the Aisne River; the 3rd and 5th Brigades south of Soissons, the 1st, 2nd, and 4th on the high ground at Couvrelles and Cerseuil.

On the afternoon of the 12th from the opposition encountered by the 6th French Army to the west of Soissons, by the 3rd Corps south-east of that place, by the 2nd Corps south of Missy and Vailly, and certain indications all along the line, I formed the opinion that the enemy had, for the moment at any rate, arrested his retreat, and was preparing to dispute the passage of the Aisne with some vigour.

South of Soissons the Germans were holding Mont de Paris against the attack of the right of the French 6th Army when the 3rd Corps reached the neighbourhood of Buzancy, south-east of that place. With the assistance of the artillery of the 3rd Corps the French drove them back across the river at Soissons, where they destroyed "the bridges.

The heavy artillery fire which was visible for several miles in a westerly direction in the valley of the Aisne showed that the 6th French Army was meeting with strong opposition all along the line.

On this day the cavalry under General Allenby reached the neighbourhood of Braine, and did good work in clearing the town and the high ground beyond it of strong hostile detachments. The Queen's Bays are particularly mentioned by the general as having assisted greatly in the success of this operation. They were well supported by the 3rd Division, which on this night bivouacked at Brenelle, south of the river.

The 5th Division approached Missy, but were unable to make headway.

The 1st Army Corps reached the neighbourhood of Vauxcéré without much opposition.

In this manner the Battle of the Aisne commenced.

2. The Aisne Valley runs generally east and west, and consists of a flat-bottomed depression of width varying from half a mile to two miles, down which the river follows a winding course to the west at some points near the southern slopes of the valley and at others near the northern. The high ground both on the north and south of the river is approximately 400 ft. above the bottom of the valley, and is very similar in character, as are both slopes of the valley itself, which are broken into numerous rounded spurs and re-entrants. The most prominent of the former are the Chivre spur on the right bank and Sermoise spur on the left. Near the latter place the general plateau on the south is divided by a subsidiary valley of much the same character, down which the small River Vesle flows to the main stream near Sermoise. The slopes of the plateau overlooking the Aisne on the north and south are of varying steepness, and are covered with numerous patches of wood, which also stretch upwards and backwards over the edge on to the top of the high ground. There are several villages and small towns dotted about in the valley itself and along its sides, the chief of which is the town of Soissons.

The Aisne is a sluggish stream of some 170 ft. in breadth, but, being 15 ft. deep in the centre, it is unfordable. Between Soissons on the west and Villers on the east (the part of the river attacked and secured by the British forces) there are eleven road bridges across it. On the north bank a narrow-gauge railway runs from Soissons to Vailly, where it crosses the river and continues eastward along the south bank. From Soissons to Sermoise a double line of railway runs along the south bank, turning at the latter place up the Vesle Valley towards Bazoches.

The position held by the enemy is a very strong one, either for a delaying action or for a defensive battle. One of its chief military characteristics is that from the high ground on neither side can the top of the plateau on the other side be seen except for small stretches. This is chiefly due to the woods on the edges of the slopes. Another important point is that all the bridges are under either direct or high-angle artillery fire.

The tract of country above described, which lies north of the Aisne, is well adapted to concealment, and was so skilfully turned to account by the enemy as to render it impossible to judge the real nature of his opposition to our passage of the river, or to accurately gauge his strength; but I have every reason to conclude that strong rearguards of at least three army corps were holding the passages on the early morning of the 13th.

3. On that morning I ordered the British Forces to advance and make good the Aisne.

The 1st Corps and the cavalry advanced on the river. The First Division was directed on Chanouille, *via* the canal bridge at Bourg, and the Second Division on Courteçon and Presles, *via* Pont-Arcy and on the canal to the north of Braye, *via* Chavonne. On the right the cavalry and First Division met with slight opposition, and found a passage by means of the canal which crosses the river by an aqueduct. The division was, therefore, able to press on, supported by the Cavalry Division on its outer flank, driving back the enemy in front of it.

On the left the leading troops of the Second Division reached the river by nine o'clock. The Fifth Infantry Brigade were only enabled to cross, in single file and under considerable shell fire, by means of the broken girder of the bridge which was not entirely submerged in the river. The construction of a pontoon bridge was at once undertaken, and was completed by five o'clock in the afternoon.

On the extreme left the 4th Guards Brigade met with severe opposition at Chavonne, and it was only late in the afternoon that it was able to establish a foothold on the northern bank of the river by ferrying one battalion across in boats.

By nightfall the First Division occupied the area Moulins-Paissy-Geny, with posts in the village of Vendresse.

The Second Division bivouacked as a whole on the southern bank of the river, leaving only the Fifth Brigade on the north bank to establish a bridge head.

The Second Corps found all the bridges in front of them destroyed, except that of Condé, which was in possession of the enemy, and remained so until the end of the battle.

In the approach to Missy, where the 5th Division eventually crossed, there is some open ground which was swept by heavy fire from the opposite bank. The 13th Brigade was, therefore, unable to advance; but the 14th, which was directed to the east of Venizel at a less exposed point, was rafted across, and by night established itself with its left at St. Marguerite. They were followed by the 15th Brigade, and later on both the 14th and 15th supported the 4th Division on their left in repelling a heavy counter-attack on the Third Corps.

On the morning of the 13th the Third Corps found the enemy had established himself in strength on the Vregny Plateau. The road bridge at Venizel was repaired during the morning, and a reconnaissance was made with a view to throwing a pontoon bridge at Soissons.

The 12th Infantry Brigade crossed at Venizel, and was assembled at Bucy Le Long by one p.m., but the bridge was so far damaged that artillery could only be manhandled across it. Meanwhile the construction of a bridge was commenced close to the road bridge at Venizel.

At two p.m. the 12th Infantry Brigade attacked in the direction of Chivres and Vregny with the object of securing the high ground east of Chivres, as a necessary preliminary to a further advance northwards. This attack made good progress, but at 5.30 p.m. the enemy's artillery and machine-gun fire from the direction of Vregny became so severe that no further advance could be made. The positions reached were held till dark.

The pontoon bridge at Venizel was completed at 5.30 p.m., when the 10th Infantry Brigade crossed the river and moved to Bucy Le Long.

The 19th Infantry Brigade moved to Billy-sur-Aisne, and before dark all the artillery of the division had crossed the river, with the exception of the heavy battery and one brigade of field artillery.

During the night the positions gained by the 12th Infantry Brigade to the east of the stream running through Chivres were handed over to the 5th Division.

The section of the bridging train allotted to the Third Corps began to arrive in the neighbourhood of Soissons late in the afternoon, when an attempt to throw a heavy pontoon bridge at Soissons had to be abandoned, owing to the fire of the enemy's heavy howitzers.

In the evening the enemy retired at all points and entrenched himself on the high ground about two miles north of the river, along which runs the Chemin-des-Dames. Detachments of infantry, however, strongly entrenched in commanding points down slopes of the various spurs, were left in front of all three corps, with powerful artillery in support of them.

During the night of the 13th and on the 14th and following days the field companies were incessantly at work night and day. Eight pontoon bridges and one foot bridge were thrown across the river under generally very heavy artillery fire, which was incessantly kept up on to most of the crossings after completion. Three of the road bridges, *i.e.*, Venizel, Missy, and Vailly, and the railway bridge east of Vailly were temporarily repaired so as to take foot traffic, and the Villers Bridge made fit to carry weights up to six tons.

Preparations were also made for the repair of the Missy, Vailly, and Bourg Bridges, so as to take mechanical transport.

The weather was very wet and added to the difficulties by cutting up the already indifferent approaches, entailing a large amount of work to repair and improve.

The operations of the field companies during this most trying time are worthy of the best traditions of the Royal Engineers.

4. On the evening of the 14th it was still impossible to decide whether the enemy was only making a temporary halt, covered by rearguards, or whether he intended to stand and defend the position.

With a view to clearing up the situation, I ordered a general advance.

The action of the 1st Corps on this day under the direction and command of Sir Douglas Haig was of so skilful, bold, and decisive a character that he gained positions which alone have enabled me to maintain my position for more than three weeks of very severe fighting on the north bank of the river.

The corps was directed to cross the line Moulins-Moussy by seven a.m.

On the right the General Officer Commanding the 1st Division directed the 2nd Infantry Brigade (which was in billets and bivouacked about Moulins), and the 25th Artillery Brigade (less one battery), under General Bulfin, to move forward before daybreak, in order to protect the advance of the division sent up the valley to Vendresse. An officers' patrol sent out by this brigade reported a considerable force of the enemy near the factory north of Troyon, and the Brigadier accordingly directed two regiments (the King's Royal Rifles and the Royal Sussex Regiment) to move at three a.m. The Northamptonshire Regiment was ordered to move at four a.m. to occupy the spur east of Troyon. The remaining regiment of the brigade (the Loyal North Lancashire Regiment) moved at 5.30 a.m. to the village of Vendresse. The factory was found to be held in considerable strength by the enemy, and the brigadier ordered the Loyal North Lancashire Regiment to support the King's Royal Rifles and the Sussex Regiment. Even with this support the force was unable to make headway, and on the arrival of the 1st Brigade the Coldstream Guards were moved up to support the right of the leading brigade (the 2nd), while the remainder of the 1st Brigade supported its left.

About noon the situation was, roughly, that the whole of these two brigades were extended along a line running east and west, north of the line Troyon and south of the Chemin-des-Dames. A party of the Loyal North Lancashire Regiment had seized and were holding the factory. The enemy held a line of entrenchments north and east of the factory in considerable strength, and every effort to advance against this line was driven back by heavy shell and machine-gun fire. The morning was wet, and a heavy mist hung over the hills, so that the 25th Artillery Brigade and the Divisional Artillery were unable to render effective support to the advanced troops until about nine o'clock.

By ten o'clock the 3rd Infantry Brigade had reached a point one mile south of Vendresse, and from there it was ordered to continue the line of the 1st Brigade and to connect with and help the right of the 2nd Division. A strong hostile column was found to be advancing, and by a vigorous counter-stroke with two of his battalions the brigadier checked the advance of this column and relieved the pressure on the 2nd Division. From this period until late in the afternoon the fighting consisted of a series of attacks and counter-attacks. The counterstrokes by the enemy were delivered at first with great vigour, but later on they decreased in strength, and all were driven off with heavy loss.

On the left the 6th Infantry Brigade had been ordered to cross the river and to pass through the line held during the preceding night by the 5th Infantry Brigade and occupy the Courteçon Ridge, whilst a detached force, consisting of the 4th Guards Brigade and the 36th Brigade, Royal Field Artillery, under Brigadier-General Perceval, were ordered to proceed to a point east of the village of Ostel.

The 6th Infantry Brigade crossed the river at Pont-Arcy, moved up the valley towards Braye, and at nine a.m. had reached the line Tilleul—La Buvelle. On this line they came under heavy artillery and rifle fire, and were unable to advance until supported by the 34th Brigade, Royal Field Artillery, and the 44th Howitzer Brigade and the Heavy Artillery.

The 4th Guards Brigade crossed the river at ten a.m., and met with very heavy opposition. It had to pass through dense woods; field artillery support was difficult to obtain; but one section of the field battery pushed up to and within the firing line. At one p.m. the left of the brigade was south of the Ostel Ridge.

At this period of the action the enemy obtained a footing between the First and Second Corps, and threatened to cut the communications of the latter.

Sir Douglas Haig was very hardly pressed, and had no reserve in hand. I placed the cavalry division at his disposal, part of which he skilfully used to prolong and secure the left flank of the Guards Brigade. Some heavy fighting ensued, which resulted in the enemy being driven back with heavy loss.

About four o'clock the weakening of the counterattacks by the enemy and other indications tended to show that his resistance was decreasing, and a general advance was ordered by the Army Corps Commander. Although meeting with considerable opposition, and coming under very heavy artillery and rifle fire, the position of the corps at the end of the day's operations extended from the Chemin-des-Dames on the right, through Chivy, to Le Cour de Soupir, with the 1st Cavalry Brigade extending to the Chavonne—Soissons road.

On the right the corps was in close touch with the French Moroccan troops of the 18th Corps, which were entrenched in echelon to its right rear. During the night they entrenched this position.

Throughout the battle of the Aisne this advanced and commanding position was maintained, and I cannot speak too highly of the valuable services rendered by Sir Douglas Haig and the army corps under his command. Day after day and night after night the enemy's infantry has been hurled against him in violent counterattack, which has never on any one occasion succeeded, whilst the trenches all over his position have been under continuous heavy artillery fire.

The operations of the First Corps on this day resulted in the capture of several hundred prisoners, some field pieces, and machine guns.

The casualties were very severe, one brigade alone losing three of its four colonels.

The 3rd Division commenced a further advance, and had nearly reached the plateau of Aizy when they were driven back by a powerful counter-attack supported by heavy artillery. The division, however, fell back in the best order, and finally entrenched itself about a mile north of Vailly Bridge, effectively covering the passage.

The 4th and 5th Divisions were unable to do more than maintain their ground.

5. On the morning of the 15th, after close examination of the position, it became clear to me that the enemy was making a determined stand, and this view was confirmed by reports which reached me from the French armies fighting on my right and left, which clearly showed that a strongly entrenched line of defence was being taken up from the north of Compiègne, eastward and south-eastward, along the whole valley of the Aisne up to and beyond Rheims.

A few days previously the fortress of Maubeuge fell, and a considerable quantity of siege artillery was brought down from that place to strengthen the enemy's position in front of us.

During the 15th shells fell in our position which have been judged by experts to be thrown by eight-inch siege guns with a range of 10,000 yards. Throughout the whole course of the battle our troops have suffered very heavily from this fire, although its effect latterly was largely mitigated by more efficient and thorough entrenching, the necessity for which I impressed strongly upon army corps commanders. In order to assist them in this work all villages within the area of our occupation were searched for heavy entrenching tools, a large number of which were collected.

In view of the peculiar formation of the ground on the north side of the river between Missy and Soissons, and its extraordinary adaptability to a force on the defensive, the 5th Division found it impossible to maintain its position on the southern edge of the Chivres Plateau, as the enemy in possession of the village of Vregny to the west was able to bring a flank fire to bear upon it. The division had, therefore, to retire to a line the left of which was at the village of Marguerite, and thence ran by the north edge of Missy back to the river to the east of that place.

With great skill and tenacity Sir Charles Fergusson maintained this position throughout the whole battle, although his trenches were necessarily on lower ground than that occupied by the enemy on the southern edge of the plateau, which was only 400 yards away.

General Hamilton with the 3rd Division vigorously attacked to the north, and regained all the ground he had lost on the 15th, which throughout the battle had formed a most powerful and effective bridge head.

6. On the 16th the 6th Division came up into line.

It had been my intention to direct the First Corps to attack and seize the enemy's position on the Chemin-des-Dames, supporting it with this new reinforcement. I hoped from the position thus gained to bring effective fire to bear across the front of the 3rd Division which, by securing the advance of the latter, would also take the pressure off the 5th Division and the Third Corps.

But any further advance of the First Corps would have dangerously exposed my right flank. And, further, I learned from the French commander-in-chief that he was strongly reinforcing the 6th French Army on my left, with the intention of bringing up the Allied left to attack the enemy's flank, and thus compel his retirement. I therefore sent the 6th Division to join the Third Corps, with orders to keep it on the south side of the river, as it might be available in general reserve.

On the 17th, 18th, and 19th the whole of our line was heavily bombarded, and the First Corps was constantly and heavily engaged. On the afternoon of the 17th the right flank of the 1st Division was seriously threatened. A counter-attack was made by the Northamptonshire Regiment in combination with the Queen's, and one battalion of the Divisional Reserve was moved up in support. The Northamptonshire Regiment, under cover of mist, crept up to within a hundred yards of the enemy's trenches and charged with the bayonet, driving them out of the trenches and up the hill. A very strong force of hostile infantry was then disclosed on the crest line. This new line was enfiladed by part of the Queen's and the King's Royal Rifles, which wheeled to their left on the extreme right of our infantry line, and were supported by a squadron of cavalry on their outer flank. The enemy's attack was ultimately driven back with heavy loss.

On the 18th, during the night, the Gloucestershire Regiment advanced from their position near Chivy, filled in the enemy's trenches and captured two Maxim guns.

On the extreme right the Queen's were heavily attacked, but the enemy was repulsed with great loss. About midnight the attack was renewed on the 1st Division, supported by artillery fire, but was again repulsed.

Shortly after midnight an attack was made on the left of the 2nd Division with considerable force, which was also thrown back.

At about one p.m. on the 19th the 2nd Division drove back a heavy infantry attack strongly supported by artillery fire. At dusk the attack was renewed and again repulsed.

On the 18th I discussed with the general officer commanding the 2nd Army Corps and his divisional commanders the possibility of driving the enemy out of Condé, which lay between his two divisions, and seizing the bridge which has remained throughout in his possession.

As, however, I found that the bridge was closely commanded from all points on the south side and that satisfactory arrangements were made to prevent any issue from it by the enemy by day or night, I decided that it was not necessary to incur the losses which an attack would entail, as, in view of the position of the 2nd and 3rd Corps, the enemy could make no use of Condé, and would be automatically forced out of it by any advance which might become possible for us.

7. On this day information reached me from General Joffre that

he had found it necessary to make a new plan, and to attack and envelop the German right flank.

It was now evident to me that the battle in which we had been engaged since the 12th instant must last some days longer, until the effect of this new flank movement could be felt, and a way opened to drive the enemy from his positions.

It thus became essential to establish some system of regular relief in the trenches, and I have used the infantry of the 6th Division for this purpose with good results. The relieved brigades were brought back alternately south of the river, and, with the artillery of the 6th Division, formed a general reserve on which I could rely in case of necessity.

The cavalry has rendered most efficient and ready help in the trenches, and have done all they possibly could to lighten the arduous and trying task which has of necessity fallen to the lot of the infantry.

On the evening of the 19th, and throughout the 20th, the enemy again commenced to show considerable activity. On the former night a severe counter-attack on the 3rd Division was repulsed with considerable loss, and from early on Sunday morning various hostile attempts were made on the trenches of the 1st Division. During the day the enemy suffered another severe repulse in front of the 2nd Division, losing heavily in the attempt. In the course of the afternoon the enemy made desperate attempts against the trenches all along the front of the First Corps, but with similar results.

After dark the enemy again attacked the 2nd Division, only to be again driven back.

Our losses on these two days were considerable, but the number, as obtained, of the enemy's killed and wounded vastly exceeded them.

As the troops of the First Army Corps were much exhausted by this continual fighting, I reinforced Sir Douglas Haig with a brigade from the reserve, and called upon the 1st Cavalry Division to assist them.

On the night of the 21st another violent counterattack was repulsed by the 3rd Division, the enemy losing heavily.

On the 23rd the four six-inch howitzer batteries, which I had asked to be sent from home, arrived. Two batteries were handed over to the Second Corps and two to the First Corps. They were brought into action on the 24th with very good results.

Our experiences in this campaign seem to point to the employment of more heavy guns of a larger calibre in great battles which last for several days, during which time powerful entrenching work on both sides can be carried out.

These batteries were used with considerable effect on the 24th and the following days.

8. On the 23rd the action of General de Castelnau's army on the Allied left developed considerably, and apparently withdrew considerable forces of the enemy away from the centre and east. I am not aware whether it was due to this cause or not, but until the 26th it appeared as though the enemy's opposition in our front was weakening. On that day, however, a very marked renewal of activity commenced. A constant and vigorous artillery bombardment was maintained all day, and the Germans in front of the 1st Division were observed to be "sapping" up to our lines and trying to establish new trenches. Renewed counter-attacks were delivered and beaten off during the course of the day, and in the afternoon a well-timed attack by the 1st Division stopped the enemy's entrenching work.

During the night of 27th–28th the enemy again made the most determined attempts to capture the trenches of the 1st Division, but without the slightest success.

Similar attacks were reported during these three days all along the line of the Allied front, and it is certain that the enemy then made one last great effort to establish ascendancy. He was, however, unsuccessful everywhere, and is reported to have suffered heavy losses. The same futile attempts were made all along our front up to the evening of the 28th, when they died away, and have not since been renewed.

On former occasions I have brought to your lordship's notice the valuable services performed during this campaign by the Royal Artillery.

Throughout the Battle of the Aisne they have displayed the same skill, endurance, and tenacity, and I deeply appreciate the work they have done.

Sir David Henderson and the Royal Flying Corps under his command have again proved their incalculable value. Great strides have been made in the development of the use of aircraft in the tactical sphere by establishing effective communication between aircraft and units in action.

It is difficult to describe adequately and accurately the great strain to which officers and men were subjected almost every hour of the day and night throughout this battle.

I have described above the severe character of the artillery fire which was directed from morning till night, not only upon the trenches, but over the whole surface of the ground occupied by our forces. It was not until a few days before the position was evacuated that the heavy guns were removed and the fire slackened. Attack and counter-attack occurred at all hours of the night and day throughout the whole position, demanding extreme vigilance, and permitting only a minimum of rest.

The fact that between Sept. 12 to the date of this despatch the total numbers of killed, wounded, and missing reached the figures amounting to 561 officers, 12,980 men, proves the severity of the struggle.

The tax on the endurance of the troops was further increased by the heavy rain and cold which prevailed for some ten or twelve days of this trying time.

The Battle of the Aisne has once more demonstrated the splendid spirit, gallantry, and devotion which animates the officers and men of his Majesty's Forces,

With reference to the last paragraph of my despatch of Sept. 7, I append the names of officers, non-commissioned officers, and men brought forward for special mention by Army Corps commanders and heads of departments for services rendered from the commencement of the campaign up to the present date.

I entirely agree with these recommendations and beg to submit them for your lordship's consideration.

I further wish to bring forward the names of the following officers who have rendered valuable service: General Sir Horace Smith-Dorrien and Lieutenant-General Sir Douglas Haig (commanding First and Second Corps respectively) I have already mentioned in the present and former despatches for particularly marked and distinguished service in critical situations. Since the commencement of the campaign they have carried out all my orders and instructions with the utmost ability.

Lieutenant-General W. P. Pulteney took over the command of the Third Corps just before the commencement of the Battle of the Marne. Throughout the subsequent operations he showed himself to be a most capable commander in the field, and has rendered very valuable services.

Major-General E. H. H. Allenby and Major-General H. de la P. Gough have proved themselves to be cavalry leaders of a high order, and I am deeply indebted to them. The undoubted moral superiority which our cavalry has obtained over that of the enemy has been due to the skill with which they have turned to the best account the qualities inherent in the splendid troops they command.

In my despatch of Sept. 7 I mentioned the name of Brigadier-General Sir David Henderson and his valuable work in command of the Royal Flying Corps, and I have once more to express my deep appreciation of the help he has since rendered me.

Lieutenant-General Sir Archibald Murray has continued to render me invaluable help as Chief of the Staff, and in his arduous and responsible duties he has been ably assisted by Major-General Henry Wilson, Sub-Chief.

Lieutenant-General Sir Nevil Macready and Lieutenant-General Sir William Robertson have continued to perform excellent service as Adjutant-General and Quartermaster-General respectively.

The Director of Army Signals, Lieutenant-Colonel J. S. Fowler, has materially assisted the operations by the skill and energy which he has displayed in the working of the important department over which he presides.

My Military Secretary, Brigadier-General the Hon. W. Lambton, has performed his arduous and difficult duties with much zeal and great efficiency.

I am anxious also to bring to your lordship's notice the following names of officers of my Personal Staff, who throughout these arduous operations have shown untiring zeal and energy in the performance of their duties:—

Aides-de-Camp.

Lieut.-Colonel Stanley Barry.
Lieut.-Colonel Lord Brooke.
Major Fitzgerald Watt.

Extra *Aide-de-Camp.*

Captain the Hon. F. E. Guest.

Private Secretary.
Lieut.-Colonel Brindsley Fitzgerald.

Major his Royal Highness Prince Arthur of Connaught, K.G., joined my staff as *Aide-de-Camp* on Sept. 14.

His Royal Highness's intimate knowledge of languages enabled me to employ him with great advantage on confidential missions of some importance, and his services have proved of considerable value.

I cannot close this despatch without informing your lordship of the valuable services rendered by the chief of the French Military Mission at my headquarters, Colonel Victor Huguet, of the French Artillery. He has displayed tact and judgment of a high order in many difficult situations, and has rendered conspicuous service to the Allied cause.—I have the honour to be, your lordship's most obedient servant,

  (Signed)   J. D. P. French, Field-Marshal,
Commanding-in-Chief,
the British Army in the Field.

The Battles in Flanders

Contents

Prefatory Note	251
The Crisis of October	253
How the Crisis Was Met	259
The Eve of Ypres	267
The Battle of Ypres—First Phase	273
The Battle of Ypres—Second Phase	282
The Battle of Ypres—The Crisis	295
The Battle of Ypres—Final Phase	308
The Battle on the Yser	318
The Winter Campaign	333
Neuve Chapelle	348

Prefatory Note

Ever since the middle of November last there has been on the West front in the present war what many have called and considered a "deadlock." In the account which follows of that part of the campaign represented by the battles in Flanders the true character of the great and brilliant military scheme by means of which, and against apparently impossible odds, the Allied commanders succeeded in reducing the main fighting forces of Germany to impotence, and in defeating the purposes of the invasion, will, I hope, become clear. The success or failure of that scheme depended upon the issue of the Battle of Ypres. Not only was that great battle the most prolonged, furious, and destructive clash of arms yet known, but upon it also, for reasons which in fact disclose the real history of this struggle, hung the issue of the war as a whole. No accident merely of a despot's desires caused the fury and the terror of Ypres. It was the big bid of Prussian Militarism for supremacy. Equally in the terrible and ghastly defeat it there sustained Prussian Militarism faced its doom.

CHAPTER 1

The Crisis of October

At the beginning of October there had arisen in the Western campaign a crisis with which it needed the utmost skill and resource of the Allied generals to grapple.

Both the nature of this crisis, and the necessity of reticence concerning it at the time, ought to be made clear if we are to appreciate either the momentous character of the Battle of Ypres, or the profound effect which that glorious feat of the Allied arms has had upon the fortunes of this war.

Into France at the beginning of the war the Germans threw their mighty Expeditionary Force of twenty-eight army corps, disposed into eight armies acting in co-operation. With the circumstances under which that line of armies, in part held on the French fortified frontier, was compelled to turn from Paris to the valley of the Marne and was there defeated, I have dealt in *The Battle of the Rivers*. For the reasons there set out the original objective, the seizure of Paris, was seen by the Germans when the army of General von Kluck reached Creil, to have become impossible until the French fortified frontier was in their hands. Their armies were directed upon the Marne with that aim. In the manoeuvre they exposed the vulnerable point of their line, its right flank, to the powerful onset, which General Joffre, who had foreseen the situation, at once launched against it.

Defeated on the Marne, the Germans lost the military initiative—the power to decide upon their movements and to compel the enemy to conform to them. To the soldier the initiative is the practical embodiment of military superiority. It is the first great step to victory. In every war the struggle has been to seize and to hold it. More than in any war has that been the motive in this. Campaigning with armies, not only vast in point of numbers, but dependent upon a huge, varied, and costly machinery of destruction, transport, and supply, has made victory more than ever hang upon this power to direct their complex organisation to the desired end.

All that the initiative implies. It can therefore be no matter of surprise that Germany's long preparations were without exception designed to seize the initiative at the outset, and to hold it if possible. In that event the whole force of the German Empire would with the least wastage and in the shortest possible time be applied to the accomplishment of its gGovernment's political aims. From the Great Main Headquarters Staff down to the strategical railways, the depots, the arsenals, and the military workshops, the German military system was planned to combine swiftness with complete co-operation, and provided the German commanders discovered the ability properly to control and direct the machine, not merely the seizure of the initiative, but the retention of it seemed assured. In that case, however long and bitter the conflict, the outcome could never have been in doubt. Applied, in accordance with the plans of the German staff, first on the West, and then on the East, the initiative, seized at the beginning and held to the end, must have given the armies of Germany the victory.

The Battle of the Marne was of vital importance in two respects. In depriving the Germans of the initiative, it snatched from them the chief advantage of their preparations. From that time their organisation had to be adapted not to fulfil their own designs but to meet the designs of their opponents. The difficulties in detail consequent upon this change need not be exaggerated. They were great. From the German point of view the whole problem of carrying on the war was altered, and for the worse.

Again, the defeat on the Marne brought the Germans face to face with a contingency which most of all they had hoped to avoid. Their plans had been drawn on the assumption of being able to employ practically their total active force, first on the West front and then on the East. They had never calculated on the necessity of having to divide that force, and to employ one half of it on the West, and the other half of it on the East *at the same time.*

With the defeat of the Marne, however, that necessity came into view. It meant, unless by some means the necessity could while time yet allowed be overcome, elimination of the condition mainly essential to success in the war—unity of the active force of the Empire.

These two changes, loss of the initiative, and necessity for a division of forces, were changes which the Germans had, if they could, at all costs to wipe out, and it is but stating truly and without exaggeration the problem which during the later weeks of September confronted the German Staff, to say that it was the problem of bringing the last man and the last gun then available to bear on the West for the purpose of regaining the lost power of the offensive. If such a strength could be brought to bear in time, then the initiative might be restored, division of force avoided, and the probable course of the war shifted once more on to its original lines.

It was because considerations such as these lay at the back of it, that the Germans, quite contrary to their traditions and training, went to the almost incredible labour of constructing across France from the Aisne ridge to Lorraine, that phenomenal line of more than 150 miles of deliberate fortifications and entrenchments. The risk involved in the Marne operations had, we now know, not been unforeseen. Nor were the consequences of failure, if it proved a grave failure, miscalculated. Indeed, the very precautions taken to prepare this line from the Aisne to Lorraine prove that they were not. That line, and that line alone, offered the probability of restoring the lost advantages, and of parrying the effects of the disaster.

Enabling the Germans to hold their front and to bar the advance of the Allies with the minimum of force, that line at the same time was to have aided them—and this was its chief design—to throw the largest possible masses westward from their flank, pivoting on Noyon. By that movement they might cut the main Allied armies off from Paris.

The scheme had the merit at once of boldness and of simplicity. For success it depended on bringing their fresh masses forward with the utmost rapidity. To that end the German military machine was worked to its fullest capacity. Thus began the new and enormous movement of *Landwehr* army corps into France.

In part the German scheme was frustrated by the attack carried out by the British Army in the Battle of the Aisne, and in part by the delays due to the very magnitude of the preparations. Unless attempted on a great scale a scheme of this character had better not be attempted at all. Since the success or failure of Germany in the war plainly hung upon it, the effort *had* to be on a great scale. Of Germany's corps of *Landwehr*, by far the greater number were embodied during these weeks of September. It may seem to the uninitiated a simple matter to call up, embody, and make ready for the field a million and a half of men, or thereabouts. But even with a military mechanism like that of the German Empire, it is a complicated business. That all this was done in fact in rather less than three weeks is nothing short of marvellous.

Because it was done, however, was the reason of the crisis at the beginning of October.

Within the same later weeks of September General Joffre had been able to throw against the German flank from Noyon to the Somme the powerful French Army commanded by General Castleneau. He was thus in a position to forestall the German design. On the other side German army corps had by extraordinary forced marches arrived from Belgium just in time to ward off the thrust of this French Army against Laon, a thrust which would have crippled the whole German defence and a thrust which the Battle of the Aisne was fought to assist. The fighting from Noyon to the Somme was deadly. On the German side losses were not regarded. The purpose of these troops was, cost what it might, to hold the ground until the main reinforcements came up. They suffered appalling losses. Nevertheless, though at a heavy sacrifice of life, the immediate objective, that of preventing a French advance along the valley of the Oise, was accomplished. The German resistance was undoubtedly very brave. To begin with, thanks alike to the superiority of their artillery, and to the *élan* of their recent victory, the French advanced with some rapidity. The Germans were driven out of Compiegne. Their hastily thrown-up trenches were found filled with dead, many slain by the terrible concussion of the French high explosive shells. As the French advanced these trenches were filled in.

Meanwhile, packed into every available train and by every available railway, the masses of the new German formations were being rushed westward. Immediately they detrained they were hurried into the fighting line. In the face of these increasing numbers the French advance along the valley of the Oise was held.

From the defensive the Germans passed at once to the counter-offensive. In great strength they launched an attack from Noyon and towards Roye. The front swayed. In the end, however, the French line from the Oise to the Somme remained firm.

It must then have been seen that the German outflanking scheme, thus anticipated, had become, on the lines first laid down, impracticable. The result was the great attack on Rheims.

It is clear now that when the attack was decided upon, the Germans believed the army of General Castleneau to consist not of fresh troops, but of the reserve of the main French army. Acting upon that belief they concluded that a vigorous assault upon Rheims ought to be successful. If successful the assault would accomplish all that the outflanking scheme promised. In any event it would prevent the French from massing further forces to the north of the Somme. With the German reinforcements still coming forward, the outflanking scheme could be tried again at the point where the French line at that time ended.

The attack upon Rheims failed because the German hypothesis upon which the attack had been founded was in fact false. The army of General Castleneau *did* consist of fresh troops, and *not* of the reserves of the main French Army.

After the attack upon Rheims came the attempted German turning movement north of the Somme through Albert. Here, however, the Germans found themselves unexpectedly confronted by yet two other French armies under the command of Generals D'Armade and Maudhuy. Their great plan for re-seizing the initiative consequently still hung fire. General Joffre had been at work to good purpose. The result was to extend the fighting front from the Oise to the great northern coalfield.

All this while the Russian pressure on the East front had been growing and that prospective but fatal division of German forces was threatening to become more inevitable.

All this while, too, in order eventually to avoid that division more German reinforcements were pouring west.

As it stood at the beginning of October the position was thus : at Antwerp there was the Belgian Army; at Ghent, under the command of Sir Henry Rawlinson there was the 7th British division of infantry, and the 3rd brigade of cavalry; there were some, though not many, British troops at Dunkerque; there were a few French troops at Bethune. Practically, however, between Ghent and the terminus of the French front west of Lens there were no Allied forces. Here was a gap of nearly 60 miles. If through that gap the Germans could push their way in strength, they could:

(1) Separate the Belgian Army and the British troops in Belgium from the rest of the Allied armies;

(2) Reach the coast and cut the most direct communications with England;

(3) Pursue their outflanking scheme by turning the right of the French line.

For the Germans the necessity for carrying out that scheme had day by day become more urgent. The opportunity at last seemed to lie to their hand. They proceeded to seize it.

Now let us turn to the other side. If General Joffre could close this gap and extend his line directly northwards to the coast, he would:

(1) Save a considerable slice of territory and coast from German occupation;

(2) Keep open the most direct communication with England;

(3) Both defeat the German outflanking scheme, and himself outflank the enemy;

(4) Impose on the Germans the necessity, arising from such a position, of constant counter attacks, and so waste their strength;

(5) Hold them ineffective on the West whatever might happen on the East;

(6) Compel them to meet Russian pressure on the East out of their further reserves, and thus ensure at once the division of their forces, their more rapid exhaustion, and the victory of the Allies in the war.

Such were broadly the issues which at the beginning of October last hung in the balance. Every appearance seemed to favour the German chances. General Joffre was then raising yet another (the tenth) French army. Even, however, at the utmost speed it could not be organised and equipped under a further fortnight. The Germans, however, had on their side begun their movement. Through the wide gap between Ghent and Bethune they were already pouring a great mass of cavalry, screening the oncoming of their main masses. They had launched their final assault upon Antwerp. It looked as if for them the moment had arrived.

CHAPTER 2

How the Crisis Was Met

General Joffre is a great man. So much is known now to all the world. But this war was not a month old before every military man was aware that the head of the French Staff, a galaxy of brilliant men, was a star of the first magnitude.

The greatness of Joffre as a general lies not so much in his simplicity, about which many stories are told, nor yet in his strength of character, his incorruptible honesty, or his unshakable fortitude. It lies in the force of his intellect which, joined to his character, makes his judgment unerring. He is marked off because he foresees, and foresees truly. It has been stated that his plans for the Battle of the Marne were drawn up and completed on August 27. Quite possibly they were. The movement which then substituted the Sixth French Army, that of General D'Armade, for the British on the extreme left of the Allied line, argues a clearly settled purpose and plan.

All the movements just stated in the briefest outline were parts of a settled purpose and plan. Is it likely that, the situation being what it was at the beginning of October, General Joffre was at a loss to meet it? He was not at a loss. At least he was not at a loss for ideas. The difficulty was the means.

Three French armies were already fastened on the flank of the German position. To fill the gap between Bethune and the coast it was essential to find three others, and at once. He had only one.

Time here was everything. Ever since the Germans had grasped the necessity of re-seizing the initiative at all costs, it had been a race against time. Their military railways and their organisation, carefully elaborated through years to meet just such a contingency as this, was pitted against the resources of a great military genius. It was the brain of one man against a system.

And the man won and the system lost.

To any ordinary mind it might have appeared that the situation of the Allies in that first week of October was well-nigh hopeless. To a great mind, however, difficulty is the measure of opportunity. General Joffre visited Sir John French at the British headquarters. The result of that interview is stated by Sir John French in his dispatch of November 20:

> Early in October a study of the general situation strongly impressed me with the necessity of bringing the greatest possible force to bear in support of the northern flank of the Allies, in order effectively to outflank the enemy and compel him to evacuate his positions.
>
> At the same time the position on the Aisne, as described in the concluding paragraphs of my last despatch, appeared to me to warrant a withdrawal of the British Forces from the positions they then held.
>
> The enemy had been weakened by continual abortive and futile attacks, while the fortification of the position had been much improved.
>
> I represented these views to General Joffre, who fully agreed.
>
> Arrangements for withdrawal and relief having been made by the French General Staff, the operation commenced on October 3, and the 2nd Cavalry Division, under General Gough, marched for Compiègne *en route* for the new theatre.
>
> The army corps followed in succession at intervals of a few days, and the move was completed on October 19, when the First Corps, under Sir Douglas Haig, completed its detrainment at St. Omer.
>
> That this delicate operation was carried out so successfully is in great measure due to the excellent feeling which exists between the French and British Armies; and I am deeply indebted to the commander-in-chief and the French General Staff for their cordial and most effective co-operation.

In a word, the British commander-in-chief, seizing the nature of the difficulty, knowing its causes, and realising how much turned upon it, stepped forthwith into the breach. With Sir John French, as with General Joffre, to decide was to act. "Early in October" the decision was taken. On October 3 began the carrying of it out. What difference in time is there between "early in October" and October 3? No difference.

Thus while the Germans still imagined themselves opposed on the Aisne ridge to those British troops who, dug into their almost invisible entrenchments, had for nearly a month successfully withstood the repeated and furious attacks of the flower of the Prussian Army twice or more than twice as numerous as themselves, the British had silently ebbed away. Their places were taken by French troops of the reserve, and the Germans remained no wiser for the change. And the British travelled through Paris, and by roundabout routes, as it seemed to them, through north-west France, and very few remained wiser for their journey. Nor after long successive hours in crowded railway carriages followed by detrainment at a place altogether strange did any but a very few of the British even know where they were going to or for what purpose. All they knew was that they were going somewhere to meet the Germans.

No move in the campaign was more unexpected or more daring than this. It affords but one more proof of how false is the assumption that the element of surprise has been banished from modern war.

The secrecy of it was only less remarkable than its boldness. With an Intelligence Service supposed to be second to none, the German Staff were left without even a suspicion of it until it had been accomplished.

The importance of the move was that it made General Joffre's scheme for the military envelopment of the Germans immediately feasible. There was now but one more thing to do, and that was to withdraw the Belgian Army from Antwerp in order that they should complete the Allied line.

That it is true involved the evacuation of Antwerp. Quite apart from the fact that the Belgian Army, reduced by the casualties and the hardships of their heroic campaign, were no longer sufficient in numbers properly to garrison that great fortress, their withdrawal served a purpose more valuable even than its defence. Many no doubt are much more readily impressed by the evacuation for the time of a great fortified city than by what they consider a mere military scheme, the value of which is a matter of opinion. In this instance, however, the carrying out of the scheme meant the assurance of victory in the war. The evacuation of Antwerp was advisable on the principle that the greater comprehends the less.

After the transfer of the British forces from the Aisne, and the removal on October 8 and 9 of the Belgian troops from Antwerp to the

Yser, there were on the German flank from Noyon to the sea six Allied armies. Taking them in the order of position from south to north they were : the army of General Castleneau; the army of General D'Armade; the army of General D'Urbal; the army of Sir J. French; the army of General Maudhuy; and the army of King Albert.

Let it be remembered that in addition to the twenty-eight army corps of the German Expeditionary force as at first constituted, there were at this time either in or on their way to France twenty-one Reserve and Volunteer Corps, making the enormous total of forty-nine. That, independently of casualties and wastage, gives, on the German war footing, an aggregate of 2,940,000 of all arms. Undoubtedly the casualties and wastage had even up to this time been very heavy. It is reasonable and moderate to put it roundly at nearly 900,000 men, two-thirds of those losses being casualties in battle. Even that, however, left approximately 2,000,000 combatants. Besides, the casualties and wastages had been largely made good by fresh drafts.

When we bear in mind the vital consequence to Germany of the plan for re-seizing the initiative which the German Staff were endeavouring to carry out, there is nothing in the least surprising in their hurrying into France reinforcements and drafts of such magnitude.

The position in brief was that the total German force in France had been brought up to at least a million men above the immense, and as it was supposed crushing, strength of the initial Expeditionary Force, and that, too, despite the losses incurred.

Many of the facts relating to this war are so wholly without parallel that not a few people, unaware of the true vastness and menace of the military system of modern Germany, find it hard to give them credence. As nearly as possible, however, the figures of the forces sent from Germany into Belgium and France will be found to be these:

Original Expeditionary Force (25 Active and 3 Reserve Corps)	1,680,000
Fresh drafts to supply losses (approximately)	450,000
Additional Reserve Corps	1,260,000
Total	3,390,000

The problem of dealing with such a force, and of dealing with it when the total strength that could on the side of the Allies then be put into the field against it was in round figures a million less, is a problem quite unlike anything in war since in 1814 Napoleon fought the memorable campaign which preceded his abdication and exile to Elba.[1]

Nobody will venture to say that, having such a superiority in numbers at their command, and occupying besides a strongly fortified line of front, enabling them further to economise their strength in one direction while they threw it with greater weight in another, the Germans were not fully warranted in thinking that the success of their scheme was assured, and that if it was assured, the French having shot their bolt in the Battle of the Marne, and shot it in vain, there was an end to all intents of the struggle on the West.

How was General Joffre to grapple with this vast enigma? By meeting the Germans on traditional lines of tactics? It was impossible. Besides, in the face of modern arms traditional tactics are out of date. They survive only in popular tradition, and in the criticism based upon it.

The only way on the Allied side at once to secure and eventually and fully to reap the advantages won at the Battle of the Marne was to complete and to solidify the military envelopment which would render the whole of this gigantic force of invaders for all the purposes of the invasion impotent. It was plain, too, that the immediate purpose of the Germans was now to straighten out their front across France. If the reader looks at a map he will see that the fortified line held by the enemy from the Argonne to the Aisne, would, if continued to the northwest, touch the French coast near to Havre. With such a straight-

---

[1] This statement is based on the following facts which at this date (the beginning of October) summarises the then immediately prospective situation as regards numbers:—

Total German forces sent into or about to be sent into France and Belgium		3,390,000
Less casualties and wastage approximately		900,000
Net German forces		2,490,000
Allies:—		
Nine French armies, reinforced to full strength	1,080,000	
10th French army (in formation)	120,000	
British (including forces at Ghent)	145,000	
Belgians	40,000	
		1,385,000
		1,105,000

The disparity of course was afterwards redressed. It took, as it proved, some twenty days before all the additional German forces could be sent West, and on the other hand the embodiment of French Reservists was proceeding at the same time, but the possibility, not to say the probability, that the Germans would get in first, constituted the crisis.

ened front not only would the Germans have the Channel ports in their possession, but they would be free either to advance, if they had the power, or to retreat if they chose. What is more, they would then be able to advance or to retreat as a whole. In such a position it is clear their advance would have enormously greater momentum, and their retreat be an operation of far greater safety. Moreover, their front would be shorter, and in consequence stronger.

When, therefore, I speak of General Joffre's scheme of military envelopment, I mean by it the difference, and it is a vast difference, between the position of the Germans were their front straightened out and their position in an angle. Placed in an angle their armies were for all the purposes of their campaign paralysed, and except to counter-attack, which after all is no more than a defensive tactic, they could do nothing. Besides, in such a situation counter-attack is a necessity. It is an axiom confirmed by all experience that troops in such a situation cannot maintain their position merely by a passive defence.

If from this situation there was for the Germans but one outlet, that of wheeling round their flank until it came into line with the rest of their front, it followed that their pressure would inevitably be greatest on the extremity of the radius, that is on the part of it nearest the coast, and it was manifest that no effort possible would be spared by them to apply that pressure before the line of the Allies here could be formed, or at all events before it could be made firm.

To the British army therefore in this scheme was assigned a post which was at once a post of honour and of danger. Strangely enough some of the greatest and most striking facts in this war appear to have been overlooked. Among them is the fact that this military envelopment, or outflankment, meant to the Germans, if they could not prevent it, both the ruin of their hopes of victory in France, and the certain loss of the war. Clearly then it was to be expected that every ounce of strength and of energy they could command would be put into the struggle.

We can well understand, though the public, perhaps happily, remained in ignorance for the time, the anxiety that prevailed, except it would seem at the headquarters of the French Staff. There the characteristic calm does not appear to have been disturbed. Following his custom, the French commander-in-chief went usually to bed at nine o'clock, and rose at 5.30, save when duty took him, as it did take him at times, to places in the fighting line. He gave his instructions, knowing that if carried out, as they would be if possible, the result would be right. A mighty worker and the very personification of the commanding quality of decision, he never swerved by a hair's breath from his plan, foreseeing all its consequences and judging justly of its effects.

He judged justly of its effects because he relied upon essentials. On the one hand the Germans had a huge superiority in numbers. They had also at this time a superiority in heavy guns. On the other hand the Allies held the superior position. Further, they had a decisive superiority in field guns; not a numerical superiority, but one based on the greater power and accuracy of the "75" gun as compared with the German converted "77" gun. In 1899 just after the German Government had completed rearmament of its artillery with the "77," the French brought out the "75," the first really practicable quick-firing field gun until then known.

This invention revolutionised modern gunnery. To meet it the Germans were forced to "convert" their '"77" into a quick-firer. Their gun, however, remained distinctly inferior and out-classed. Neither in muzzle energy, muzzle velocity, nor consequently in range was it any match for the French weapon. Leading the way as they always have done in artillery improvements, the French had evolved, besides, a novel system of "fire discipline," for using this gun scientifically and with the maximum of effect. That system had already justified itself by striking results. In no small degree it was the "75" gun which had crushed the German resistance on the Marne. In no small degree, too, it was the "75" which had ruined the German attack upon Rheims. The "75" had withered the attempted turning movements from Noyon, and north of the Somme with the breath of death. Clearly, apart altogether from its strategical conception, sound and great at once as that conception was.

General Joffre's plan of military envelopment was inspired by the aim of giving the widest effect to this superiority in gun-power. Here again is one of the facts of the war which has not been estimated at its right value, and has misled many critics of the Western "deadlock." Now the German Higher Command well knew that in field artillery they were out-classed. The "75" has a muzzle energy of 333 foot-tons as compared with the 241.7 foot-tons of the German "77." The French artillerists also had solved the problem of the "universal shell," that is of a projectile combining the effects of a high explosive shell with those of a shrapnel shell. With the Germans this problem was still in the stage of experiment. In order to off-set such marked disadvantages the German Government had gone in largely for heavy howitzers. When the war broke out they had undoubtedly a superiority in that class of weapon. The French scheme of rearmament with howitzers had only begun. This was perhaps one reason for the German precipitancy. Upon their superiority in heavy howitzers they now largely relied for their second contemplated "drive."

Artillery, however, is not the final word. Nor was this placing of the British Force on the northern wing of the German armies in any sense an accidental choice of location. It was certain that the German attack, initiated with their heavy cannon, would be driven home, if it could be driven home, by assaults in mass formation from their infantry. The necessity then was for a force which could be relied upon in any event to stop such rushes. That force was pre-eminently the British army. The British army were a body of expert riflemen. They were more. They, and they alone, were armed with a rifle capable of firing 15 rounds "rapid." Delivered by troops who can keep cool under the experience, 15 rounds "rapid" will stop the densest rush ever organised. The British Army had shown themselves able to do it. They formed the element of the Allied forces which in a case like this could, if it were humanly possible, save the situation.

It will be seen, therefore, that the scheme of the Allied generals though it seemed to lack spectacular magnificence, was business, and was in every sense and emphatically *war*.

CHAPTER 3

The Eve of Ypres

The plan of the Allied commanders, at once original and bold, was decided upon at that conference at the British headquarters on the Aisne. From the first in this war the French Intelligence Service has shown itself excellent. The French Headquarters Staff has not only been well and reliably informed of the enemy's preparations and movements, but promptly informed. In this instance the prospective movements were a matter of almost certain inference. Given the motives of the German Government, and the military principles favoured by the German Staff, both quite well known, and what they would do and how they would try to do it, was a conclusion that a general much less sagacious than Joffre might safely draw. The exact extent and character, however, of the German preparations, and the degree to which those preparations had been advanced was definite information of a valuable kind.

It is apposite here to note its effect. On September 9 the Belgians made a sortie in force from Antwerp, and on the following day recaptured Malines and Termonde. In consequence of this part of the German reinforcements, three army corps, which were on the march from Liège and had already reached the French frontier, had to be recalled. That army became engaged in the first attack upon Antwerp. The object, their diversion, had been gained. When, after discovering that an attack upon Antwerp was hopeless without heavy siege guns, they finally reached the front in France, the purpose for which they had been dispatched, that of attempting to outflank the Allies to the west of Noyon, had become impracticable.

We know now that the German Government had determined to avenge this disappointment by the capture of Antwerp. That, however, for the reasons already stated was fully expected. The siege employed another German army from September 25 to October 9. True, the Germans had the satisfaction of occupying the city, and of such political effects and impressions as that occupation produced. On the other hand there can be no sort of doubt that had those troops, thrown through the gap which then existed between Ghent and Bethune, seized Calais, and been able hold to the line from the coast to Bethune, the military effect would have been twenty times more serious. Instead of doing that the German Government swallowed the bait of Antwerp, only to discover when too late, and when they had let the critical days pass, that the hook was the British army at Ypres, which during a month's furious fighting in the effort to retrieve their error cost the Germans over 300,000 casualties, and what was worse, the wreckage of their Western campaign.

Before entering on a description of the operations which, in fact, during the later weeks of October and the first two weeks of November decided the future course of the war, it is advisable to have in mind a clear picture of the terrain of this mighty and memorable conflict.

If the reader looks at a map of France he will see that from the outlet of the Somme, the coast of the English Channel takes a sudden bend to the north, and that not far from Calais it swerves sharply round again to the east. If from near the mouth of the Somme we draw a line running north-east, that line, roughly parallel to the line of the coast from the point at which the shore bends round near Calais, will mark approximately the boundary of a difference in the height of the country above sea level. South-east of this line the country is considerably higher. North-west of it the country is as a whole low-lying and flat. In fact the line may be called an inland coast divided from the sea by a stretch of flats having an average breadth of some twenty-five miles. The eastern area of these flats is the Pas de Calais; the western area Flanders.

This inland coast line, geographically the northern edge of the plateau whose central and highest part is the chalk downs of Champagne, presents numerous sinuosities. Its course, that is to say, is a succession of capes and bays. In far-off times when in fact it was the sea coast, it must have presented a contour not unlike that of the present coast of Devonshire.

Formed of alluvial deposits and reclaimed little by little, the flats lying between this inland coastline and the sea are a very fertile tract. They gradually became the seat of a numerous population; and then, owing alike to proximity to the sea and to the number of the navigable waterways, the earliest and most important seat of industry and commerce on the Continent of Europe. The ancient capital of this country, the centre of its trade and the seat of its government when it formed an independent dukedom, was Ypres. In the eighteenth century was made the discovery that underlying or contiguous to this area was one of the largest of the European coalfields. That discovery changed large parts of the flats by degrees into modern industrial districts.

The point to be kept in mind for present purposes is that geographically Flanders is one area, though now situated politically partly in France and partly in Belgium. Its two chief centres of population and industry are Ghent and Lille, both seats of the cotton trade, for like Lancashire in England, this Lancashire of the Continent is engaged mainly in the textile industry and in coal-mining. Lille is close to and in fact situated in one of the larger bays of the inland coastline already spoken of.

Nearly midway between Lille and the coast at Dunkirk there is a feature it is important to notice. The otherwise uniform flatness of the country is here broken by a range of low hills shaped like a crescent moon. This range of hills lies to the south of Ypres. From Kleine Zillebeke on the east to the Mont de Cats on the west the ridge is not more than ten miles in length. Ypres is situated within the crescent.

The feature is important to notice because of the streams which here take their rise. From the higher level of inland country there flow north-east the Scheldt, and north-west the Somme, and the lower courses of those rivers mark what may be called the natural outer boundaries of this flat area. From the hills south of Ypres again rise the Aa, the Yser, and the Lys. The first two flow outward towards the coast; the Lys bending first round to the south and then to the east, falls into the Scheldt at Ghent.

From Dunkirk eastward the country is protected against inroads of the sea by dykes. This part of it is below sea level. At Nieuport, the outlet of the Yser, there are locks which permit the outflow of the river at low tide, but bar the inflow of the sea at high tide. For a thousand years Flanders, owing to its natural fertility, has been the scene of a developed agriculture. Characteristic of it are the great substantial old farmhouses usually built round a square courtyard, places marked by the proverbial Flemish cleanliness and by the equally proverbial Flemish plenty. Practically every acre of the country was under cultivation. The only exceptions were the woods situated round the old *châteaux* and country houses, evidences of the general wealth. In addition to these there existed one or two not very extensive tracts of ancient forest.

Round Ypres, more especially to the east and north, these woods and *pleasaunces* formed an almost continuous ring. In the fourteenth century Ypres was a great industrial city with something like 200,000 inhabitants. During the struggles against first Spanish and then Austrian domination, and in the destructive wars of the seventeenth and eighteenth centuries, it steadily lost its importance. The population dwindled. At the outbreak of the present war the number of inhabitants was not more than 20,000. The old city offered nevertheless many evidences of its former consequence and wealth.

There was the monumental and famous Cloth Hall, one of the finest Gothic buildings in Europe. Erected by Baldwin, Count of Flanders, and adorned with statues of the forty-four counts, it had a *façade* 462 feet in length, noble alike in design and in proportions. A conspicuous feature of the building was its central and massive square tower. In the Middle Ages Ypres was a fortress. From the top of the tower the view extended on every side over a wide extent of country. The sea and the coastline to the north, and the higher land across the Lys to the south came equally within the prospect. Conversely from outside Ypres the tower formed a notable landmark, seen rising above the horizon many miles away.

In old days the Cloth Hall was a great mart where, to merchants from every part of Europe, Flemish manufacturers displayed their fabrics, the then unrivalled wonders of the loom. In modern times, trade having departed save for an almost local industry in lace and linen, the Cloth Hall had become a museum and gallery of art. Under the public-spirited and careful government of the present Royal Family of Belgium, the building, one of the cherished monuments of the country, was in 1860 lovingly restored.[1]

---

1. Mr. N. E. Monckton Jones, formerly tutor in Modern History in the University of Liverpool, in a letter to the *Observer*, thus describes the impression made by the first sight of the building: "Turning perforce with the street at right angles, we passed into a narrower, more winding, one with more old gabled houses, and here and there a fine sculptured moulding or portal. Then of a sudden we were at the Place, and the Cloth Hall in all its full glory before us. It was not the size of the building nor its richness that halted us so abruptly and made us all eyes for the moment. It was, I think, the arresting dignity of it, a dignity built up of fine and simple lines and the mellow contentment of age. (Continued next page.)

Besides the Cloth Hall, however, and the fine cathedral dedicated to St. Martin, the former importance of Ypres was shown in its wide and elegant streets, bordered by antique Flemish mansions, abodes of an old world tranquillity, and with interiors like pictures. The most pleasantly situated perhaps of all the Flemish cities, Ypres was a favourite place of residence, an urban cameo set amid woods and hills of broad and sweeping yet softened outline, round about it a ring of peaceful villages, and the private seats of old-time and settled wealth.

If this was the ancient capital of Flanders, the scene on the farther side of the crescent of hills across the valley of the Lys presented the most striking of contrasts. In that direction the background of the picture was a forest of tall chimneys—the great city of Lille overhung by its cloud of smoke. The foreground was an apparent tangle of railways, roads, canals, brickworks, industrial villages, mills, dyeworks, machine shops, the multitudinous aspects in short of industry as it exists today, superposed upon the ancient Flemish features of the countryside—its spacious farms, its sluggish rivers, and its everlasting flatness.

For with the growth of commerce the rivers had been linked up with a network of canals, and over these, with joints represented by scores of bridges, had been spun a webwork of railways branching in all directions into sidings. Lille itself is but the centre of half a hundred industrial villages and smaller towns, the heart of a huge ganglion of commerce and manufacture.

Farther south we come to the coalfield. Of the discovery of the coalfield all this modern activity is the outcome. There the industry changes in character. Cotton mills give place to ironworks and blast furnaces. The face of the country is dotted with great mounds of "spoil." Its general aspect is grimier. In all directions it is cut up by narrow, badly-paved and rutty lanes, tracks leading mostly from the pits and works to the villages of the pitmen and ironworkers. To the tangle of canals and railways and railway sidings there is added this third tangle of foot and cart tracks, made for the most part at haphazard and as convenience directed. Through this maze of ways and byways the only guiding lines are the usually straight and excellent

---

Many buildings in other towns were statelier, more ornate, more imposing, but from the pointed arcade below to the long line of the great roof the Hall told of a fine sense of proportion, of reserve. Its builders did not aim at outdoing other men, but they knew what they needed, and would have it seemly, and by sheer reiteration of a simple plan well conceived they made homely simplicity glorious. The Cloth Hall expressed the self-respect of *burghers* who had won their rights two centuries before Magna Carta."

French main roads which sweep across the country from town to town with an imperial disregard of local obstacles. The plan and purpose of the main roads is largely military, and has come down from the days of the Roman occupation.

Such in brief are the main features of the country. As will be seen in the following pages, their bearing upon the operations of the war is of the first importance

CHAPTER 4

The Battle of Ypres—First Phase

The main body of the British forces arrived in French Flanders on October 11. It will be recalled that in his dispatch Sir John French states that the movement from the Aisne began on October 3. Why, it may be asked, were eight days taken to complete this transfer if it was so urgent?[1]

Well, in the first place the withdrawal of the British forces from the Aisne had to be carried out in detail. To have effected the withdrawal in mass would at once have aroused the observation and suspicion of the enemy. Next the forces thus withdrawn in detail, and in detail replaced by French troops, had to be massed at a convenient place secure from hostile intelligence hunters. Finally this main body of the British army had to be sent forward to the new line of front as a whole. Thus it was that the 2nd Army Corps, under the command of General Sir H. Smith-Dorrien, detrained at Bethune on the same day, October 11, that the 3rd Army Corps under the command of General Pulteney detrained at St. Omer. These towns are some twenty miles apart. Co-incidently with the detrainment of the infantry and the guns, the 2nd and 3rd Divisions of the British cavalry advanced under the command of General Allenby and occupied the little town of Aire, which lies

---

1. In the French official review of the first six months of the war it is stated that: "Field-Marshal Sir John French had, as early as the end of September, expressed the wish to see his army resume its initial place on the left of the Allied armies. He explained this wish on the ground of the greater facility of which his communications would have the advantage in this new position, and also of the impending arrival of reinforcements from Great Britain and from India, which would be able to deploy more easily on that terrain. "In spite of the difficulties which such a removal involved owing to the intensive use of the railways by our own units. General Joffre decided, at the beginning of October, to meet the marshal's wishes, and to have the British Army removed from the Aisne."

nearly half-way between them. By this move a front was formed from near Lens, where the French line ended across the country north-westward to the coast. The gap, so far as outflanking the Allied forces was concerned, was closed.

In the latter part of September, as a prelude to their scheme, the Germans had occupied Lille. An occupying force which they had left there on their advance towards Paris had been driven out by the British. They now detached for the seizure of the city the 19th Active Corps and the 7th Reserve Corps. In the face of this overwhelming strength the British troops in Lille, part only of a division from Dunkirk, had no alternative but to retire. It was a bitter day for the inhabitants of Lille which witnessed the departure of these defenders, welcomed only a little while before with every demonstration of public joy.

Besides these two German army corps who, based on Lille, began at once to drive westward towards Boulogne, a powerful mobile column, consisting of four divisions of cavalry, supported by horse artillery and three brigades of *jaegers*, crossed the Lys, and passing to the south of Ypres, made a dash through Bailleul for Hazebrouck, covering at once the flank of the main advance from a possible attack from Dunkirk, and carrying out a turning movement against such French forces as were then supposed to be holding Bethune. These German troops, the two army corps and the flying column, though mustering in all more than 150,000 men, were only the vanguard of the mass intended to be thrown forward. It is clear that their expectation was that of attack from Dunkirk on the one side and from Bethune on the other. The flying column advanced to Hazebrouck, and the cavalry occupied the Forest of Nieppe to the south of that town without opposition.

Meanwhile the Belgian Army, which had evacuated Antwerp two days before on October 9, was on its way westward along the coast covered by the British troops under the command of General Sir Henry Rawlinson. All the probabilities appeared to be that both the Belgian Army and these British troops would be cut off.

We may judge then of the surprise of these German forces when, along the line of the Aa, they came suddenly up against this massive wall of the British Army supposed to be on the Aisne. Sir John French, however, had not transferred his army to Northern France in order to stand on the defensive. The wall of British troops was in rapid movement. On this same day, October 11, the British cavalry dashed across the Aa, swept the German horse through and out of the Forest of

Nieppe, and drove them as far as the Mont des Cats. There the Germans attempted, at the end of a flight of some fourteen miles, to make a stand. In the attack upon the Forest of Nieppe the British cavalry of the 6th Division had carried out to the north a movement which threatened the German force from the rear. When this was discovered the German retreat became a flight. Reaching the Mont des Cats their horses were blown, but they were compelled to defend that position if possible because the *Jaegers*, evacuating Hazebrouck under cover of their cavalry, had thrown themselves into Meteren and Bailleul.

This cavalry fight, in which on both sides more than 20,000 men took part, though relatively, perhaps, but one of the minor episodes of the war, was, in fact, of its kind colossal. It was a clash of sabre against sabre, man to man. In numbers ought to have been decisive, but apart from the fact that their mounts hard ridden across country, were winded, the superiority of the British was so marked that they had not hesitated earlier in the campaign, and with success, to attack the German horse when the enemy had a proportion of two to one. In cavalry fighting skill, spirit and cohesion count for more than numbers.

The defeat of the German cavalry in this action was decisive. It was not that they did not fight with bravery. They did. Broken in one charge they were rallied by their officers for another. Some four times in succession in the battle among the hills they attempted to recover.

While the British cavalry were carrying out their brilliant drive, the 3rd Army Corps advanced east from St. Omer to Hazebrouck. In the meantime also the 2nd Corps had taken up a line of positions along the canal from Bethune to Aire. Next day (October 12) the 2nd Corps moved forward to Merville, a little town southeast of the Forest of Nieppe.

The plan of the British operations may be briefly stated. Taking Givenchy, a village two miles west of La Bassée, as the pivoting point, it was intended to swing the line round until it reached the Lys. In this movement the British front would swing through a quarter circle, that is, from north-west to north-east. The British cavalry would be on the outer, or left wing; the inner, or right wing, at Givenchy would be hinged on to the French positions. In this way the country between the Lys and the sea would be cleared of the enemy, and the Allies envelopment carried from Givenchy past Lille, so that that important place could no longer be used by the Germans as a base for overrunning the country to the coast.

There was a further aim. This was to seize, if possible, the railway junction at Menin, ten miles north of Lille. The move would both embarrass the German occupation of Lille, and hamper the enemy in any attempt to throw troops in force over the Lys.

On the other hand, the immediate purpose of the Germans is equally clear. Not strong enough, as they judged, to risk a pitched battle; their right wing exposed by the defeat of their cavalry; and the probability owing to this unexpected appearance of the British army now being that the Belgians from Antwerp and the British troops from Ghent would get through, they determined to obstruct the British movement by guerilla tactics, and until their main forces came up to defend in detachments the numerous and almost contiguous villages of the country, taking advantage of its network of canals and railways, and of its tangle of roads and cross roads. It is difficult to imagine what is in military language called a "close" country more difficult to operate in than this, one of the most densely populated areas of the world. The German scheme was to treat the civilian inhabitants with ruthlessness, wasting and plundering as they retired.

Manifestly, the success of the British movement would depend upon its energy. The Germans were fighting to gain time. Not stopping, therefore, at Merville, the 2nd Corps fought forward directly towards Lille by way of Laventie, in the valley of the Lys. Laventie, about ten miles west of Lille, is the centre of a dense semi-urban industrial district. Concurrently the 3rd Corps advanced eastward from Hazebrouck towards Bailleul. Seven miles to the south-west of Ypres, that place lies on the southern slope of the crescent of hills already referred to. Some scattered advance posts of the enemy were met with in intermediate villages, and were driven in. The Germans had taken up a position along the ridge from Berthen, between the Mont des Cats and Mont Noir on the north through St. Jans Cappel and Bailleul, and on the main road to Armentières. About two miles in advance of this line they held in force the villages of Fletre and Meteren, which they had fortified and barricaded.

The British attack began at daybreak on October 13. It was a day of rain and fog, one of those fogs which, in autumn, cover these flats with an almost impenetrable mist. Such conditions rendered movement over the low-lying sodden country slow. On the other hand, as against the British troops moving to the attack the conditions put the German guns out of action, and, what was not less material, they concealed the movements of the Allied cavalry. For by this time the

French horse, under the command of General Conneau had arrived, and the plan of battle was that the French cavalry should assault and turn the left of the German position at Nieppe, on the main road from Bailleul to Armentières, thus cutting off the enemy from Lille, while the British cavalry attacked Berthen, In the meantime, the main assault would be delivered by the infantry against Bailleul, the centre of the hostile position.

Throughout the 13th the fighting raged round Fletre and Meteren. Both places were taken. Meteren was stormed in an onset which at nightfall drove the Germans who were holding it in a ragged rout to Bailleul. General Pulteney decided at once to follow up this advantage. An advance on Bailleul was immediately begun. All this while the cavalry on both wings had been active. At daybreak on October 14 the British horse broke into Berthen, and despite a bitter resistance drove the Germans out, and began to roll up their flank on that side. The French cavalry had got astride of the Armentières road. Realising that their whole force was in danger of being rounded up, the Germans took the chance offered by darkness, intensified by heavy rain, to beat a precipitate retreat. When the British infantry reached Bailleul, they found the town evacuated.

These operations opened up the way to Lys, and the 3rd Corps advanced on October 15 to the line of that river extending from Armentières to near Laventie. They thus came into line with the 2nd Corps, which, driving the Germans off the main road from La Bassée to Estaires, an important road junction on the Lys two miles above Sailly, had pushed on to Fournes. At that place, four miles east of Neuve Chapelle, and not more than seven from the centre of Lille, they cut the German communications between Lille and La Bassée.

Thus, at the end of four days, the British were both at Armentières and at Fournes, within seven miles of Lille, and formed with Laventie as the base of it, a front of almost a right angle, the apex pointing westward. At the same time the cavalry had received orders to continue their drive from Berthen across the country and down the valley of the Lys towards Menin. (See note following). In those four days the Germans had been driven back some twenty miles. Decidedly the surprise provided for them by the British army had been anything but agreeable.

Note:—On reaching Warneton, on the Lys, ten miles above Menin, the cavalry found the place strongly held by the Germans, who at the entrance to the town had constructed a high barricade loopholed at the bottom so that men could fire through it from a lying position. This formidable obstacle was encountered by a squadron of our cavalry. Nothing daunted, they obtained help from the artillery, who man-handled a gun into position and blew the barricade to pieces, scattering the defenders. They then advanced some three-quarters of a mile into the centre of the town, where they found themselves in a large "place." They had hardly reached the farther end when one of the buildings suddenly appeared to leap skywards in a sheet of flame, a shower of star shells at the same time making the place as light as day and enabling the enemy—who were ensconced in the surrounding houses—to pour in a devastating fire from rifles and machine guns.

Our cavalry managed to extricate themselves from this trap with a loss of only one officer—the squadron leader—wounded and nine men killed and wounded; but, determining that none of their number should fall into the enemy's hands, a party of volunteers went back and, taking off their boots in order to make no noise on the pavement, re-entered the inferno they had just left, and succeeded in carrying off their wounded comrades.

In these four days the British line had been pivoted round from St. Omer to Armentières. However looked at, the feat ahke in its swiftness and its energy is remarkable. The numbers engaged on each side, roundly some 150,000 men, had been about equal. Reinforced on the way from the Aisne by fresh drafts from England, the British Army had the support of that French cavalry which in combination with our own had rendered such brilliant service at the Battle of the Marne. The German troops were among the best of the enemy's forces, and the operations had shown that, even with the defensive advantages offered by this exceptionally "close" country, they were, on a footing of equality in numbers, no match for the Allies.

> Note:—On the 15th the 3rd Division fought splendidly, crossing the dykes with which this country is intersected with planks, and driving the enemy from one entrenched position to another in loopholed villages, till at night they pushed the Germans off the Estaires-La Bassée road, and establishing themselves on the line Pont de Ham-Croix Barbée.—*Dispatch of Sir John French of November 20,* 1914.

An episode of the fighting is thus described in an officer's letter published in the *Daily Telegraph*:

> The enemy are no match for us in this kind of fighting, and we enjoyed thoroughly the work of hunting up the Germans, whom we shot down like rabbits. When we reached the outskirts of the wood we came under a terrible artillery fire from the enemy's guns, which were only 800 yards away. I withdrew my men under the cover of a ditch.
>
> I took eight men and again moved to the outskirts of the wood, where I found a perfectly flat turnip field stretching away towards the enemy. About 300 yards out I saw a line of our infantry lying flat on the ground, and made my way towards them. No sooner did we leave the cover of the wood when the enemy's guns opened up on us.
>
> It seemed impossible that my little party could escape. Three were almost immediately hit, but we others kept on and reached the line lying in the open. Half a platoon were extended at five paces. To my horror I found all were dead or wounded except about three, who were keeping perfectly still. I found the Subaltern Lieutenant B on one knee, with one hand resting on the ground just in the attitude of a runner who is waiting the signal for the start of a race. He was stone dead. A shrapnel bullet had pierced his head.
>
> The man next him, who was badly wounded in the thigh, told me they were ordered to support the firing line, which was 200 yards ahead, and had only advanced 300 yards from the wood when the entire line was struck down as if by lightning.

As the Belgians had during the opening weeks of the campaign followed out a system of tactics admirably and skilfully adapted to the populous and settled character of the terrain over which the fighting then took place, so the Germans now attempted to resort to similar tactics. They tried to contest the ground foot by foot. They endeavoured to turn every farmhouse into a stronghold; to barricade with the debris of buildings every road; they threw garrisons into every works; they loopholed the houses of and placed hidden machine guns in every village; they gathered for a rally behind every canal. The country was swept by fire and devastation.

None of these efforts availed. Nor are the reasons why they did not avail far to seek. Such tactics were wholly at variance with modem German military training. The training aimed at a crushing movement in masses; the tactics to be successful, demanded alertness and initiative. So sudden a change in method and so complete a break with tradition meant, at any rate, that the mass of these German forces were but indifferent practitioners; they might know much of the abstract science but they knew little of the practical art of war. In one thing only were they thorough. They made up for their defects in practical military skill by their energy in plunder and destruction.[2]

They were opposed besides in the British army to troops with whom alertness and initiative were valued as among the highest of military qualities. Those troops also were expert riflemen. Though standing on the defence under such conditions the Germans ought, like the Belgians at the outset of the war, to have inflicted far heavier losses than they themselves sustained, in fact, owing to the sweeping energy of the attack, their losses were out of all proportion the heavier. Through the defeat at Meteren and the drive of the Allied cavalry towards the Lys, their right flank had been turned, and the result was that they had been "bunched up" by the British in the tangled industrial district to the west of Lille.

Bodies of them still held out at Aubers and at Herlies, two contiguous villages to the southeast of Laventie, but both those places were on October 16 attacked by the troops of the British 2nd Army Corps. This fighting went on amid streets obstructed by barricades, followed by hand to hand combats in the houses. The Germans had now brought up a mass of fresh forces, including their 14th Army Corps, additional battalions of *jagers*, and four divisions of cavalry. Notwithstanding these reinforcements both Aubers and Herlies were on October 17 carried by storm. In the assault upon Herlies the Lincolns and the Royal Fusiliers, under the command of Brigadier-General Shaw, displayed an undaunted gallantry.

On October 16 the Belgian Army from Antwerp reached the Yser,

---

2. Dr. Ludwig Tasker, of the R.A.M.C, from the rear of the British line at this date wrote: "Some of the villages are nothing but masses of ruins. We are covering ground passed over by the Germans. They have not left a cupboard or a drawer alone. We respect all property, and when we go where the Germans have been we tidy the things up so that the place looks very much better by the time the people return. Day after day the same thing goes on here—fighting, fighting, fighting, collecting the wounded, and burying the dead."

and the British troops covering their retreat had arrived to the east of Ypres. Next day four divisions of the French cavalry drove out of the Forest of Hoethuist, north of Ypres, a German force which attempted to cut in between the Belgians and the British. Concurrently, the British line west of Lille was extended down the valley of the Lys as far as Le Ghier opposite to Freninghein, and the army fought forward through three miles of suburbs from Laventie to Bois Grenier and Radinghem, the latter place not more than five miles from the centre of the city.

Such broadly was the situation. The German attempt to overrun western Flanders had not failed merely; it had collapsed.

CHAPTER 5

The Battle of Ypres—Second Phase

It is true that no line of demarcation divides the operations which resulted in the advance of the British Army from St. Omer to Lille, and the operations which followed. Technically they are all one, for the fighting was continuous. At the same time it is advisable for the sake of clearness to consider those operations rather in the nature of a prelude, and the main Battle of Ypres as extending from October 17 to November 15, when the defeat of the Germans was complete.

On October 17 the Allied forces were: the Belgians, who occupied the line of the Yser from Nieuport to Dixmude; two divisions of French territorials, the 87th and the 89th, who had also arrived on October 16 and were at Vlamertynghe and Poperinghe; the French cavalry, who held the ten miles of country between Dixmude and Ypres; the British troops under the command of General Rawlinson, who held a line to the east of Ypres extending from Poelcappel through Gheluvelt to Zandvoorde; the British cavalry under the command of General Allenby, who had pushed down to the valley of the Lys towards Werwick, three miles above Menin; and finally, the main body of the British force, the 3rd and the 2nd Army Corps, holding a line to the west of Lille from Le Ghier to Herlies, and from there south-west, through the village of Violaines, just outside La Bassée, to Givenchy.

We may anticipate here by saying that on October 19 the detrainment of the 1st British Army Corps, under the command of General Sir Douglas Haig was completed at St. Omer; that on the same date the 10th French Army, under the command of General Maudhuy, reached the line between Ypres and Dixmude; and that on October 20 the first of the Indian troops, the Lahore Division, also arrived at the front.

There were now three armies, the Belgians, the French, and the British, the latter consisting, with the Indians, of four Corps. The 10th French army included a division of Marines from Brest, and a Corps of Moroccans and Senegalese. This was the force, equivalent, with the two bodies of British and French cavalry, to some 320,000 men, on which fell during the ensuing four weeks, the weight of an attack by eighteen German army corps mustering in the aggregate nearly 1,080,000 of all arms.

These German forces included:

The troops of General von Deimling liberated by the evacuation of Antwerp, among them a division of Marines.

The army of the Duke of Wurtemberg, comprising the 22nd, the 23rd, part of the 24th, the 26th, and the 27th Reserve (*Landwehr*) Corps.

The army of General von Fabeck, consisting of four corps and one division.

The army of the Crown Prince of Bavaria, comprising the Prussian Guards, the 4th, 7th, 13th, 14th and 19th Corps; the 18th Reserve Corps; and the 1st Bavarian Reserve Corps.[1]

The gathering together of this vast mass of combatants does not appear to have been completed until October 23 or 24. Such delay as occurred, though in fact the massing was carried out at remarkable speed, sprang not from the embodiment of fresh formations, nor from any difficulty in sending them westward from Germany. In order to make up this force which was intended to be another spear head, the Germans had creamed the whole of their fighting front in the West. Having before them the example of the transfer of the British Army from the Aisne, they had taken a leaf out of the book of the Allies. All save the best of their Reserve Corps had been distributed along their front. These new levies released the more reliable and seasoned men alike of the Active army and of the *Landwehr*, and the importance of the Battle of Ypres is, apart from other consequences, that it broke or destroyed the best of the remaining troops of Germany.

To begin with, the weight of the German counter-offensive was thrown, not against Ypres, but against the British positions to the west of Lille. Their objective was to secure La Bassée, the little mining town on the northern edge of the coalfield, some eight miles to the south-

---

1. Some of these German army corps were not complete. A French Army Bulletin issued in November last stated that north of the Lys, on October 30, the Germans had fourteen army corps and four corps of cavalry.

west of Lille. This point it is now clear they intended to make the immediate pivot on which to swing round their northern front. As the British positions at this time stood, communication between Lille and La Bassée by the main road was cut. There is another point it is insistent to notice. La Bassée lies at the end of one of the promontories of the inland "coastline." It was already held by the Germans and the spur had been strongly entrenched.

Yet another reason dictated the plan. One of the evident objects of the British operations was to push down the Lys and seize the crossing and railway junction at Menin. That would not only have gravely embarrassed the German occupation of Lille, but would equally have embarrassed a development of their attack between the Lys and the coast.

Menin, of course, could only be seized and held before the main mass of the German forces came up. Accordingly, Sir John French on October 17 directed Sir Henry Rawlinson to move from his position east of Ypres and attack the place. The distance from the British line then at Gheluvelt to Menin was not more than five miles. No doubt the move would have left the country to the east of Ypres for the time being open. The importance, however, of occupying Menin appeared fully to justify the taking of such a risk. Sir Henry Rawlinson moved forward to the attack, but it was not pressed. Concerning this matter Sir John French says in his dispatch:

> Instructions for a vigorous attempt to establish the British Forces east of the Lys were given on the night of the 17th to the Second, Third, and Cavalry Corps.
> I considered, however, that the possession of Menin constituted a very important point of passage, and would much facilitate the advance of the rest of the army. So I directed the general officer commanding the Fourth Corps to advance the 7th Division upon Menin, and endeavour to seize that crossing on the morning of the 18th,
> The left of the 7th Division was to be supported by the 3rd Cavalry Brigade, and further north by the French Cavalry in the neighbourhood of Roulers.
> Sir Henry Rawlinson represented to me that large hostile forces were advancing upon him from the east and north-east, and that his left flank was severely threatened.
> I was aware of the threats from that direction, but hoped that

at this particular time there was no greater force coming from the north-east than could be held off by the combined efforts of the French and British cavalry and the Territorial troops supporting them until the passage at Menin could be seized and the First Corps brought up in support.

Sir Henry Rawlinson probably exercised a wise judgment in not committing his troops to this attack in their somewhat weakened condition; but the result was that the enemy's continued possession of the passage at Menin certainly facilitated his rapid reinforcement of his troops and thus rendered any further advance impracticable.

On the morning of October 20 the 7th Division and 3rd Cavalry Division had retired to their old position extending from Zandvoorde through Kruiseik and Gheluvelt to Zonnebeke.

Proving abortive, this effort must have served to some extent at all events to disclose to the enemy the British general's intentions, and must in consequence have been of material assistance in deciding upon his dispositions. In justice to Sir Henry Rawlinson it is necessary to point out that his position was by no means an easy one to maintain. As Sir John French states:

> A very difficult task was allotted to Sir Henry Rawlinson and his command. Owing to the importance of keeping possession of all the ground towards the north which we already held, it was necessary for him to operate on a very wide front, and, until the arrival of the First Corps in the northern theatre—which I expected about the 20th—I had no troops available with which to support or reinforce him.
> Although on this extended front he had eventually to encounter very superior forces, his troops, both cavalry and infantry, fought with the utmost gallantry, and rendered very signal service.

The army of the Crown Prince of Bavaria was at this time opposed to the British between the line of the Lys and Lille, and it was along the ten miles between La Bassée and Freninghein, amid a mass of almost continuous industrial villages, that the clash of the great battle began. Outnumbered by nearly three to one, the British troops were subjected to an incessant series of desperate assaults. It was clear that the rapid success of the British operations during the preceding week, as well as the collapse of the German projects, had stung the enemy to fury. The attacks began against Herlies and Aubers, villages north of the La Bassée spur, and themselves built along the tops or straggling down the slopes of two minor promontories. Beaten off with heavy loss to the enemy, these attacks were, regardless of the punishment received, renewed both by day and by night. The villages were reduced by the German artillery to ruins. Amid these ruins, however, and in the trenches cut for the defence, the British troops held out.

In repulsing one of these attacks the Royal Irish, with magnificent dash, and burning to give the enemy a real taste of their quality, fought across the spur to Le Pilly, driving the Germans before them like as though their advance was that of a column of irresistible demons. In Le Pilly they entrenched themselves. They had gone so far forward, however, in the impetus of the pursuit that they were cut off from communication with the rest of the British force. They fought until their last cartridge was used up. For more than thirty hours they held out, surrounded by masses of Germans on all sides. Sheer famine at the finish compelled them, and their gallant commander. Major Daniell, to surrender.

Instead of diminishing, the German attacks increased in violence. Every successive repulse seemed only to add to the rage of their commanders. For four days and nights these onsets followed one upon another. To describe these but a little while before peaceful suburbs of Lille, now cut and blown into wreckage and swept by the fire and hurricane of war, as a hell is to put it mildly. The days and nights were days and nights of dismal darkness and rain. Foiled in the effort by a frontal attack to drive the British once more across the Lys, the Germans, now supported by the arrival of additional masses, developed their assault to the east and north of Ypres. On October 20 they captured Le Gheir, but were on the same day driven out of the place again with heavy loss. This important crossing of the Lys is the most direct route from Lille to Ypres.

In view of the heavy attack which by this time had been launched towards the flank position of the 3rd Army Corps at Le Gheir, the British cavalry were dismounted and put into the fighting line to fill the gap of some four miles still existing between Le Gheir and Zandvoorde to the south of Ypres. Throwing aside the sabre for the rifle and bayonet and the spade, the cavalry promptly dug themselves in, and proved as valiant in the trenches as they had time and again shown themselves in the saddle. They were a thin line of less than one man to the yard. Thin as it was, however, it turned out to be a line of steel.

On October 20 the 1st British Army Corps reached Ypres from St. Omer. They had covered the intervening twenty-five miles in one long day's tramp. It had been intended to send them in co-operation with the French cavalry forward to Thourout, and possibly on to Bruges. This scheme had to be abandoned.

On October 22 the battle became general from La Bassée to Dixmude. Following upon a terrific bombardment, a powerful column of the enemy, debouching from La Bassée, attempted in mass formation to rush the trenches held by the Wiltshires and the Manchester Regiment at Violaines. The attack never got home. The mass of the enemy, something like 6,000 strong, thrown into confusion by the deadly fire from the trenches, broke and fled. They were rallied and reformed from supports. A second time the assault was launched. It met with no better fortune.

In the meantime an attack in enormous force had been hurled against the positions held by the 3rd British Army Corps. This attack, one of the bloodiest episodes of the battle, also failed. The Germans, nevertheless, had got across the Lys at Warneton and at Comines, two miles farther down stream, and, forming behind the railway, which here runs on an embankment along the valley to the north of the river, advanced in overwhelming force upon Messines and Houthem. Though offering a desperate resistance, the British cavalry were forced to retire as far as Hollebeke and Wytscheate. Part of the Indian troops, the 7th Division, sent to their support, delivered a brilliant flank attack on the Germans from Wulverghem. The Germans held the ground they had gained, but their onset was paralysed.

The British front had now been dented in. In consequence it became necessary to reform it. The line was withdrawn. From Givenchy the positions extended to the high road running from Violaines through Neuve Chapelle to Armentières, and then through Armentières across the Lys to Wytscheate. This is, in fact, the main road from La Bassée to Ypres.

Disposed along a line from Bixschoote through Langemaark on the north of Ypres, the troops of the British 1st Army Corps were attacked by the whole strength of the army of General von Fabeck. The resistance opposed to these enormous odds was heroic. Time and again the attacks made in mass formation were beaten back. Upon the Prussian commanders the frightful losses suffered by their troops, who fell not man by man, but by ranks and companies, appeared to make no impression. A combined infantry and artillery attack drove the French cavalry across the Ypres and Nieuport canal. The British line had then to be retired. Under heavy fire the Cameron Highlanders dug themselves in at Pilkem on the canal two miles to the north of Ypres. At the end of a day of awful carnage the Germans at this point made a last desperate effort. They got at length up to the line of the trenches, hastily made to meet the exigencies of the moment.

It came to the bayonet, with this comparative handful of British heroes against a mass of foes maddened by their losses. The Highlanders fought like lions. At the cold steel the Germans were no match for them. Nothing but their dauntless courage and their military superiority saved them from being totally wiped out. Out of that terrible fray the remnant of them retired, bloodstained and with bloodstained arms, but fierce and unconquerable, opposing a sullen front still to the enemy who, having at a fearful price won the position, had been too punished to follow up the advantage.

These trenches at Pilkem, it is interesting to note, were the nearest point at which during any part of the battle the Germans approached to Ypres. The enemy, however, did not enjoy his dearly-bought advantage long. At daybreak an attack upon the Germans was made by the Queens, the Northamptons, and the King's Own Rifles. The enemy had occupied the night clearing the trenches of the dead, mostly their own dead, with which they were choked. For so prompt a counter-attack they were evidently not prepared. In the cold grey of this October dawn they suddenly saw these lines of khaki detach themselves from the mist. It was like a bad dream, but it turned in a flash into a fiery reality. The British infantry were into them with the bayonet. Led by General Bulfin, who had proved on the Aisne that he was the man for a tight corner, the British brigade were out to retake those trenches.

Of British bayonet work these German troops had already seen enough. There was a scene, as they endeavoured to rally, of mad rage and confusion; the shouts and curses of their officers mingling with the roar of conflict, and the clash of steel on steel in the savage work of thrust and parry. German reinforcements were hurried up. The line of fighting men, their own troops in retreat, the British pressing on the rear, met the reinforcements as they advanced. With this fresh mass to deal with, the British troops in turn were forced backwards. They fought with a bulldog tenacity, and once more the Germans gave way. By the end of the day, despite repeated attacks upon them, the British were masters of the position.

Even now the weight of such a battle as this was severe, and yet it was to go on for another twenty-six days. On October 22 General Joffre visited the British Headquarters. The result was the arrival on this, the 23rd of October, of the 9th French Army Corps. This reinforcement was sorely needed. On the east of Ypres the line was drawn perilously thin. From Zandvoorde round to Peolcappel it was held only by the 7th Division of infantry under Major-General Capper, and by the 3rd Cavalry Division, commanded by Major-General Byng. The cavalry, like the rest of the British mounted force, had gone into the trenches, or, rather, into hastily-made lines of fire-cover. Somewhat remarkably, the Germans had not been quick to discover the Relative weakness of this part of the front. So far they had thrown the weight and fury of their attack against the north and south. Their mistake undoubtedly arose from the bold tactics adopted by the British commander-in-chief.

On the east of Ypres he had kept up a show of counter-attack. The 7th Division had, on the 21st, made a bound forward to Passchendeale. on the way to Roulers. This, following upon the movement towards Menin, had evidently led the enemy to suppose that here was the strongest part of the British line. In plain language, the enemy had been most successfully "bluffed." As a consequence, the Germans opposite the 7th Division remained on the defensive, and there was gained a respite, if a bitter and incessant bombardment can so be called, of nearly two days. The interval was beyond estimate valuable. It enabled the 9th French Army Corps to take up part of the vastly too extended position held by these British forces, who had been spaced out over some six miles of country at the rate of considerably less than one man to the yard—a single line without reserves of any kind.

Following upon their arduous march from Ghent, during which, covering the retreat of the Belgian Army, they had fought a rearguard action for the greater part of the way, the 7th Division had, since October 17, been almost incessantly engaged. Even the toughest of British troops—and these were among the toughest toughs in the army—would feel the worse for wear after such an experience. It had indeed approached "the limit"—as the limit was understood before the Battle of Ypres.

Picture the situation. These British and French troops in their hastily made trenches had not only masses of the enemy in front of them—masses thrown forward in dense columns of attack, which at all hazards they had to break—but the roar of battle in their rear, and from minute to minute they could not tell how the fortune of battle in their rear was going. They could only hope that their comrades, too, were "sticking it." Overhead was the almost incessant flight and ear-splitting explosions of shells, an indescribable din. To right and left flared the burning ruins of houses and villages. An acrid smoke rolled over the awful scene, darkening the grey sky with its lowering pall. In this pallid hght and amid the contending thunders of the cannon, a monstrous chorus from hundreds of iron throats, the grey-green ranks of the enemy would suddenly swarm out of their trenches, and their savage yells mingling with their volleys, would try to dash across the intervening space, 200, sometimes not more than 100 yards.

To reach the British trenches was a matter not of minutes; it was a matter of seconds. How were such rushes to be stopped? The only way was for these British infantrymen to sit tight and give them fifteen rounds "rapid"—fifteen rounds in less than as many seconds, rounds in which every bullet found its billet. The hostile mass came on trampling over its dying and its dead, but it was ragged and it grew more ragged with every one of those successive blasts of death. Then it became a mere torn remnant, then it wavered. Its fury was gone; its courage was gone; the driving power of its ruthless officers was gone; the fear of disciplinary punishment was gone; all were swallowed up in the instinctive love of life. A lightning rush back to cover to avoid that devastating hail of lead swept every protester off his feet. From first to last such an episode would be measured in time by minutes. Into those minutes, however, seemed crowded an eternity of experience. In circumstances like these the sole thought of the soldier is his individual duty. He feels with an absorbing intensity that the issue depends upon him doing it even to the death. In that feeling lies the glorious "joy of battle."

All round Ypres was ringed with these contending fires. The heaviest pressure of the German attack, however, was still on the sector of the front between Armentières and La Bassée. It was plainly hoped that if success attended this onset, the retirement of the whole of the British, French and Belgian forces to the north of it must follow, and strategically that must have been the result, for if the 2nd British Army Corps had given way, neither Ypres nor the line of the Yser could have been held. In the accounts which have been given hitherto of the battle, attention has mostly been directed to its later stages when the attack developed against Ypres from the east, but the vital combat which went far to secure the eventual victory was the death grapple between the 2nd Army Corps and the masses of Prince Ruprecht's Army thrown against them west of Lille. These troops of the 2nd British Army Corps had been fighting almost day and night since October ii, that is up to this time for twelve days, and it had been impossible to afford them any relief.

Along this sector of the front the 2nd and 3rd Corps of the British Army were opposed to eight corps of Germans. That immense superiority in numbers enabled the enemy to keep up an unbroken succession of assaults by a system of reliefs. Costly in life to the enemy though such tactics were, he was evidently convinced that under this strain the British must inevitably break. The fighting raged through this now desolated area of ruined houses and wrecked roads. Roofless, with great gaps torn in their walls by shells, the smashed remains of furniture mixed up with fallen and broken beams, splintered doors, and battered stairways, often the scenes of bitter hand-to-hand duels, the houses bordering the streets littered and obstructed by window-shutters shot-riddled and blown off their hinges, piles and fragments of bricks, slates and glass, the shapeless remains of chimneys and other flotsam of ruin. In face of the hostile pressure the British line had had to be drawn back on to the lower ground of the valley. This withdrawal, however, had tightened up and strengthened it, and the whole position was without question saved through General Smith-Dorrien making that necessary and prudent move in the right time.[1]

How the Devons at a decisive point of the line covered this retirement and beat off a furious German attack is told by one of the officers of the corps. He says:

> On the night of October 22, we advanced a bit and dug ourselves more or less in by dawn, and soon after light we saw great masses of German infantry emerge from woods and hedges

---

1. The German attack against the Lincolns in the village of Herlies and the retirement of that corps is described in a letter from Corporal E. Clark to Major Haggard, Chairman of the Veterans' Club. Corporal Clark says: "...We found ourselves surrounded in the shape of a horseshoe, the enemy .firing at us from all angles. We just got the order to retire when a shell struck the trench in front, a piece catching me on the nose and burying me, but I managed to crawl out nearly blind, and started to retire under a murderous rifle fire. No one could realise what it was like unless actually there. Men were crawling about like ants trying to reach safety, but it was only luck for those that did. I managed to get to a wood, where I found a number of wounded, and waited until the firing cooled down, when we chanced it over the river, getting there as best we could, the Germans shelling the bridge the whole time, also a railway cutting, in which we got for shelter."

some 1,000 yards to our front, and advance to attack us. We opened fire on them, and killed dozens.

This was answered by the Germans with a tremendous shell fire from their heavy guns. The Devons were perfectly wonderful; not a man left his trench. All day long the battle raged, and you never saw such an inferno. By night the place was a mass of fire, smoke, dead, and dying. All night they attacked us. Sometimes they got right up to our trenches, only to be hurled back by the Devons' bayonets. Dawn broke on the 24th with the same struggle still going on, and it continued all day and night, and all through the 25th. We never slept a wink, and by night we were absolutely done. No humans could have done more.

The men were perfectly splendid, and repulsed every attack, with great loss to the enemy. We were relieved at 1 a.m. on October 26, and as we marched back a mile into billets all the troops cheered us frantically. General Smith-Dorrien sent a wire congratulating us on our splendid fight. We heard officially from Divisional Headquarters that there were 1,000 dead Germans in front of our trenches. The whole place was littered with their dead.

On October 24 the Indian troops under the command of General Watkis were sent to Lacon, three miles in the rear of the front, as a reserve. In the evening of that day, a day like those preceding it of dismal rain, the Germans made an exceptional effort. With the advantage of the bad and failing light, which it was probably hoped would confuse the British rifle fire, a thing they had now learned to dread, they delivered a massed assault in enormous force. The attack was made simultaneously by three columns directed one against the trenches held by the Wiltshires above Givenchy; the second against the trenches held by the Royal West Kents; and the third against the position of the Gordons at the farther end of the line near Fauquissart. The first two attacks failed completely. The third had a temporary success.

The Gordons, with odds which no skill with the rifle could overcome, were driven from their trenches. This was undoubtedly the chief point of the German onset. While the struggle was going on the Middlesex regiment had been ordered up to support. They arrived nearly as soon as the Germans had seized the position. Darkness had now come on. Shaken by their heavy losses, the Germans were not prepared for this practically instantaneous counter-attack. They did not know what was behind it. The Middlesex regiment appeared to spring at them out of the ground. Though elated at their victory they were exhausted. For aught they could tell other forces were at the back of these. The fight was fierce but brief. The end of it saw the enemy flying back into the night to escape the deadly bayonets wielded with what seemed almost superhuman energy. The attack added another blank to Prince Ruprecht's record.

In the meantime persistent attacks had been kept up on the position of the 3rd Corps along the railway from Laventie to Armentières, as well as on the line held by the Cavalry Corps along the hills from Wytscheate to Zandvoorde. It was the evident intention of the Germans to seize this ridge as dominating the British position in Ypres. Along this sector they were massed in great strength. Shortened, however, as it now was the front held. The struggle round the village of Hollebeke was to the last degree desperate. The line, however, of the Indian troops along the high road from Armentières to Wytscheate still menaced this German attack in flank, and materially helped the Cavalry Corps to hold its ground.

In view of this failure of the onslaught from the south, the enemy on October 25 renewed his attack in strength against the line of the 1st British Army Corps to the north of Ypres, and combined it with yet another onset south of Ypres against the trenches held by the Cavalry Corps. It was deemed prudent to reinforce part of the line here from the Reserve of French Territorials. Those of the cavalry whom they replaced were withdrawn and concentrated at Zillebeke to the north of the Zandvoorde ridge.

Apparently the losses and the confusion arising from the defeat of the great assault of the evening before (October 24) made it impossible for the Germans to renew their efforts on this day (October 25) against the front from Armentières to La Bassée. Their only success in the fighting of the 25th was the capture of the trenches held by the Leicestershire Regiment whom they had managed to overwhelm.

We now come to a lull in the battle. It had gone on along the southern sector of the front since October 17, and along the whole front since October 22. During the last three days more especially the Germans had exerted their total strength. They had incurred a terrible sacrifice of life, and so far the only result, a miserable result for such a price, had been the slight retirement of the British line to the west of Lille, and a foothold across the Lys to the south of Ypres.

It is not surprising therefore that for the time being they ceased their attacks while they moved up additional forces. These were not merely to repair losses but to add to the mass and momentum of the onset. None of the objects sought by this battle had been gained, nor did any one of them appear to any nearer of attainment.

The position from the German side is reflected in the army order which on October 26 Prince Ruprecht issued to his troops. Copies of it were afterwards found on dead German officers of his army:

"You have been fighting under very difficult conditions. It is our business now not to let the struggle with our most detested enemy drag on longer. The decisive blow has still to be struck."

The *Kaiser* at this time came to Courtrai and Thielt to supervise the massing of his legions, and went round their billets and cantonments making a succession of speeches. Everything was done to fortify their determination, and heighten their ardour. A general army order was issued reminding them that "the thrust against Ypres" was of decisive importance. On October 29 the mighty mass of a front extending from Lille to the coast was judged to have been refitted and in every respect ready for the final and irresistible blow.

On his side Sir John French had made use of the interval to reform and tighten his line. The comparatively weak spot to the east of Ypres was stiffened, and if this lull was necessary to the enemy it proved of equal advantage to the Allies, and opposed to the enemy's intended final blow a new set of difficulties.

CHAPTER 6

The Battle of Ypres—The Crisis

The critical phase of the great battle began on October 29. Its feature is that not only was the mass of the German force now at its maximum, but that the weight of the attack shifted from the part of the British front between La Bassée and Armentières to the centre of the British line to the south and east of Ypres. It is this phase which has been commonly called the Battle of Ypres. Except, however, as a phase, it is in no sense distinguished from the earlier fighting.

On the third day (October 31) the struggle to the east and south of Ypres reached its crisis. From that date, notwithstanding that efforts and desperate efforts continued to be made by the enemy, his defeat was in truth assured. He had shot his bolt, and shot it in vain.

To the strategical reasons which induced the Germans to throw the chief force of their attack in the first place against the right of the British line to the west of Lille, reference has already been made, and those reasons are sufficiently clear. The reasons which induced the Germans to shift it to the south and south-east of Ypres are not so obvious. Indeed, the only acceptable explanation is that their severe defeat on October 24 caused such discouragement that the plan of forcing the right of the British position was given up as impracticable.

In order to reach Ypres from the south it was necessary to win the ridge, while to reach Ypres from the east it was necessary to penetrate the almost continuous belt of woods. These woods presented an obstacle which made the organisation of the huge mass attacks, in favour with the reigning school of German tacticians, almost out of the question. Sir John French as we have seen took advantage of these features of the country skilfully to economise his force, and at the same time to conceal that fact and mislead the enemy. The Germans it is evident had by October 26 found out their mistake. They discovered that west of Lille they had been running their heads against a stone wall, and deceived by the aspects and features of the country, had been neglecting what they now considered had been a comparatively easy entrance.

When they changed their plans, however, they made yet another mistake—that of thinking or rather of presuming that the British dispositions would remain unaltered.

Through the woods to the east of Ypres there is one great main road. Beginning at Menin—that town is just on the Belgian side of the French frontier—this broad, well-paved highway runs nearly straight as an avenue into Ypres.[1] The distance is ten miles. From Ypres the great road is continued towards the coast until at Furnes it joins on to the great road which runs along the coast from Ostend through Nieuport, Dunkirk, and Gravelines to Calais.

The importance of Menin lay in the fact that not only do several lines of railway branch out from that place southwards into France, including the railways to Lille, which is not more than ten miles away, but that it was the starting-point of this great road. Ypres again is the starting-point of a converging great road to Dunkirk. It may be remarked generally that the great main roads of Flanders run across the country from inland to the sea, and not along the country parallel with the sea. There are certain nodal points in this road system. In West Flanders, Ypres is the chief of those points. If we study the disposition of the Allied forces at this time with reference to the lines of communication, it will be seen both that they barred access to Ypres, and that west of Lille they were astride of, and therefore rendered useless to the enemy, the main line of railway from Lille to Calais. On that line Bailleul, Hazebrouck, and St. Omer are alike situated. The German advance, checked and thrown back by the unexpected appearance of the British from the Aisne, was an advance intended both to master the main line of railway, and the road system.

For a distance of some three miles the avenue from Menin to Ypres runs through the belt of woods. Six miles from Menin and four from Ypres it passes through the village of Gheluvelt, cresting there the ridge of hills. A mile to the east of Gheluvelt, and five miles from Menin, a road branches off the main avenue to Werwick on the Lys, and, on the opposite side of the avenue here there is a cross road of no great consequence, save that it serpentines northward through the belt

---

1. There is only one slight bend in this road, that at the hamlet of Hooge, a mile and a half out of Ypres, but this bend proved, as will be seen, of considerable tactical importance.

of woodland until it joins the main road from Ypres to Bruges. Trivial, therefore, as a public way, this cross-road was of considerable military value, since it gave access to some five miles or more of the woods.

It may be added that just by these cross-roads, east of Gheluvelt, there is a small outer ridge or rise called the hill of Kruyseik, after the village of that name lying in the hollow, and that over the main crest at Gheluvelt, and between that point and Ypres there is another rise or ridge. Behind this, on the side towards Ypres, lies the village of Zillebeke. Across the hills, again, to the south of Ypres and between that city and the Lys, there are two somewhat zigzag minor roads. The first of these passes through the village of Zandvoorde, and the second through the village of Hollebeke. Then further west we come to the main road running due south from Ypres to Armentières. Along this road, some two and a half miles out of Ypres, is St. Eloi, and two miles farther on Wytscheate.

These topographical details may appear minute, but they have to be understood because they show that, to get into Ypres from the south and south-east, the Germans had as lines of attack these four routes : the main avenue from Menin; the road through Zandvoorde; the road through Hollebeke; and the road through Wytscheate and St. Eloi; and it will be found that in fact their attacks were made along those lines.

Shrewdly foreseeing such a development of the battle. Sir John French, on October 27, unified the immediate command of the troops on his eastern front by adding them to the 1st Army Corps. They were redistributed in order to meet the probable weight of the coming assault which was almost certainly to be looked for along the main avenue from Menin. The line, in fact, was tightened up.

The 7th Division was disposed along a line some two miles in length from Zandvoorde to the Menin avenue, and held the Hill of Kruyseik.

The 1st Division continued the line from this point northwards and along the outer or eastern fringe of the belt of woods to near the village of Reytel.

The 2nd Division continued the line, also along the outer fringe of the woods, to Zonnebeke.

Altogether these troops, some 50,000 strong, occupied a front of about six miles. It was an exceptionally strong position, affording among other things first-rate shelter for the guns. Bearing in mind, however, that they were preparing to meet an assault from nearly ten times their own number, supported by an enormously superior strength in artillery, no precaution could be neglected.

The dispositions just outlined were made only just in time. At daybreak, on October 29, the attack began. The three divisions, all of them seasoned veterans, had hardly dug themselves in when a terrific bombardment opened. Since their trenches were practically invisible, this bombardment proved more noisy than harmful. It was the prelude to the advance along the Menin road of an enormous German column. Flank and supporting columns advanced at the same time along the road to Zandvoorde, and the minor roads north of the main avenue to Reytel and Zonnebeke. The attack was pressed along almost the whole front with the greatest determination. Its principal object was to secure the Kruyseik Hill, and with it the road junction east of Gheluvelt. By weight of numbers, and despite heavy losses—the terms used with regard to German losses in this battle may appear to be exaggeration, but in fact they are not—the enemy succeeded in capturing the Kruyseik Hill. That was about two in the afternoon, after a struggle lasting nearly eight hours.

With the capture of the hill, they were able to assault the British line north of the Menin road in flank, and at this point they broke it. Elsewhere, however, along the front their onset had been disastrous. When close to the British lines they wavered under the almost unbroken fire from the trenches. General Sir Douglas Haig gave the order for a general counter-attack. Looking only for a "passive resistance," the Germans were taken wholly by surprise. They tried to rally, but in vain. The shock threw their columns into confusion, and their whole front gave way. In the impetus the British troops rushed and retook the Kruyseik Hill by storm. In the captured trenches across the main road to the north of it a body of the enemy, though raked by fire in front and in flank, held out until nightfall, when nearly the whole of them had been killed or wounded. The trenches were recovered, and the survivors taken prisoners.

Beaten in the attempt to advance from Menin, the enemy the same night renewed the battle in an endeavour to retake Le Gheir on the Lys and to break the front at that point. The attack proved a total failure, though the British position was here astride of the river, and consequently from the tactical standpoint weak. At midnight a huge column of 12,000 men was hurled against the trenches held at Croix Marechal by the Middlesex Regiment. They came on with the greatest determination. Part of the trenches fell into their hands. The Middlesex, however, with the Argyll and Sutherland Highlanders who had been hurried forward to their support, began a counter-attack. This fight, one of the bitterest episodes of the battle, went on through the night. The scene lighted up luridly and fitfully by star shell and flares, by the flashing volleys of the rifles, and by the explosions from minute to minute of shrapnel, was at once weird and awful. The Germans were raked by a destructive fire from both flanks.

As fast, however, as they fell others rushed into the trench line from their rear. So for nearly four hours the slaughter and the combat went on. At any price the enemy appeared resolved to hold this advantage. But towards daybreak the British infantry, having steadily closed in, rushed forward. The line of trenches, now choked with German dying and dead, was recaptured at the point of the bayonet. Fighting to the last gasp, not more than forty uninjured Germans were taken prisoners. The rout of the great column was driven back upon the hostile lines beyond the railway.

While this struggle to the death was taking place at Croix Marechal, the enemy was gathering his forces for another onslaught of unparalleled magnitude. It began at dawn on October 30, and was an effort to fight across the hills by way of Zandvoorde and Hollebeke. In this there were employed five German army corps, aggregating nearly 300,000 men. Opposed to them along this line were the British troops of the 7th Division and the Cavalry Division, less than a tenth of their number. The advance along the Menin road and through the woods having turned out to be too difficult, the Germans were now at last trying this way. Once more the onset was supported by a mighty bombardment, and once more the bombardment did comparatively little damage. What told was the weight of numbers. The attack came forward in two enormous masses. That thrown against Zandvoorde comprised three army corps, the 13th and 15th Prussians, and the 2nd Bavarians. That thrown against Hollebeke comprised two corps. A special Army Order had been issued telling the troops that the *Kaiser* considered the success of this attack to be of vital importance to the issue of the war, and, indeed, for the reasons already shown, it was. Of course and conversely its failure affected the issue of the war not less vitally.

Forward and up the southern slopes of the ridge these masses, fortified by the Imperial order, swarmed in numbers that appeared to be countless, for to the eye even 100,000 men looks a multitude innumerable. The British gunners, pushing their guns forward daringly for greater effect, lashed them with a storm of shrapnel; the thin line in the British trenches shot them until the rifles were red hot. They went down not in hundreds, but in thousands. Still they came on, crushing under their boots dead and dying indifferently. It was the supreme manifestation of the will to power; the climax of the War-lord's method of making war. Such numbers could not be finished in the time. When those in front wavered under the swishing lash of leaden death, those behind pushed them on. They surged onwards like the waves of a rising tide. Doubtless this sounds mere imagination.

It is, however, but the feeblest reflection of the truth. There was nothing for it except, while time yet allowed, for the 3rd Cavalry Division, who were holding the trenches on the ridge east of Zandvoorde, to decamp, and to decamp in a hurry. Likely enough, the Germans were astonished to discover the comparatively contemptible handful who had offered such a daring defence. The woods just to the rear of the British trenches aided the escape of these heroes. Relatively their casualties had been few. With the nimbleness of Redskins they disappeared among the tree trunks as the grey-green flood of the enemy, seeing their retreat, surged forward in a last rush and with a roar of triumph, sending after them a hail of in the main futile bullets. Through the woods of the mile of intervening valley to the Kleine Zillebeke ridge, the British raced from one cover to another, keeping up a lively fire from every point from which the enemy on the main ridge were in view. This seems to have given the impression that the little valley was crowded with skirmishers, a gentry for whom the Germans had by now imbibed a wholesome respect. They halted accordingly on the Zandvoorde ridge to reform.

This pause was fatal, and it is not too much to say that at that moment the issue of the battle lay upon the knees of the gods. The pause enabled Sir Douglas Haig to re-establish his line. The fateful moment had passed, and the grey-faced emperor waiting anxiously in Courtrai for the news that was to make him master of Europe was little conscious that the scale of fate had gone down against him.

Yet it had. The British line was re-formed from Gheluvelt along the Kleine Zillebeke ridge to the Ypres and Lille canal at the point where alongside the Ypres and Lille railway it enters the deep cutting in which both canal and railway are carried across the main ridge of hills. The strength of this position lay in the fact that behind it was an area of woodland nearly two miles in depth. Along the bottom of the valley or depression separating these woods from those on the opposite slope lay a space of cleared land. This afforded a good field of fire. On the other hand, the woods on the opposite slope made it impossible to organise an attack in the immense mass in which the Germans had swarmed over the cleared top of the ridge they now held.

The position now taken up by the British troops was, therefore, strong, and had been chosen with a good judgment and a practical eye. Besides that, the line was stiffened. It was intended to hold this position "at all costs." In the front trenches were the troops of the 1st Division and the 4th Brigade. The 2nd Brigade formed an immediately supporting line. A battalion was placed in the woods as a reserve.

The Germans, however, did not forthwith press their advance, but contented themselves, for the time being, with making good their position on the main ridge. This, as already pointed out, was a fatal mistake. To render the British line more secure, and to strengthen its weak point—that nearest the canal—three infantry battalions and a cavalry brigade were transferred from the 9th French Army Corps.

We now come to the concurrent German attack against Hollebeke. The British trenches at Hollebeke were held by the 2nd Cavalry Division; those on the right to the south-west and towards Messines by the 1st Cavalry Division. This comparative handful of men had had to be spaced out over four miles of country They were but a single line, less than a man, on the average, to every two yards, and yet they had to face the onset of two army corps of the best troops of Germany!

Since the front towards Hollebeke was too narrow for the employment of such a mass of the enemy with effect, and since, too, this attack was in fact a turning movement destined to assist the chief thrust through Zandvoorde, the onset here forked, one tremendous column pressing north towards Hollebeke and the other west towards Wytscheate.

It might well be supposed that with their weight of numbers .the Germans would have walked, or rather have romped, over the barrier. Instead of that the cavalry of the 2nd Division held on to their trenches, defeating assault after assault from daybreak until afternoon. They were at last, spent with the conflict, forced to give way. Meanwhile Sir John French had reached the front. At a glance he took in the crisis of the position. Two regiments of the 3rd Cavalry Division were rushed along the line to the 2nd Division's support. Two battalions of the 7th Indian Division were also held to meet the emergency. At the same time the London Scottish Territorials and four battalions of the 2nd British Army Corps were ordered forward to Neuve Eglise for the like purpose. During the lull in the battle already referred to, from October 27 to October 29, Sir John French had placed the Indian Army Corps in the positions on the right of his line to the west of Lille, then occupied by his 2nd Army Corps. The latter were exhausted by fourteen days of continuous hard fighting. They were now available as a general reserve. The value and the necessity of this precaution is too manifest to need emphasis.

Re-formed as the line now was a little beyond Hollebeke, it continued the front across the ridge from the Ypres and Lille canal to near Messines. This section of the front was important for two reasons. In the first place it barred the Germans off the main road from Lille to Ypres. In the second place it prevented the enemy from turning the position of the troops commanded by Sir Douglas Haig by cutting their communications with Ypres. That, of course, formed one of the objectives of this attack. Another was to obtain the command both of the main road and of the Ypres and Lille railway. At Hollebeke and even now just beyond it the British were astride the railway line.

With objects like these in view it is easy to infer that the onset was pressed with all the vigour at the enemy's command. He had on this section alone nearly 500 guns. These, both supporting and in the intervals between his massed infantry attacks, poured upon the trenches and behind them in order to keep reinforcements at bay, constant squalls of shrapnel. Because less than 5,000 men were here resisting more than 100,000, and continued to resist them all that day and all through the succeeding night, and all through the next day and all through the following night also, and because at the end of that, in truth, indescribable time, though the storm of the hostile guns never ceased, and infantry attack after infantry attack drove forward, only to melt into bloody confusion and wreck before the terrible power of the magazine rifle handled by resolute and veteran soldiers, it must not be supposed that the energy and the ferocity of the enemy were less than both had often before proved to be.

The Germans had never fought with greater determination. Their defeat arose from the attempt to ride rough-shod over this apparently feeble line of defence by sheer weight of numbers. The British fought not merely with skill, but with the skill of masters. The Germans, confident in their seemingly crushing strength, fought without patience, and with the clumsiness of amateurs. They aimed at a speedy and a showy triumph. In spite of all their military apparatus and machinery, and of their precision in drill, they fought, in fact, like a mob, and like a mob in such circumstances their losses were frightful. Not only the defects of their military system—its exaltation of the machine, and its depression of the man—were here exposed, but the still worse and superimposed defects of their latest ideas of tactics. Ignoring the realities as distinguished from the mere appearances of modern war, these ideas were the ideas of fantasy. To train men as an army, to employ them in battle as a mob, and, as a result, to look for victory, is of all notions the nearest akin to dementia.

A conflict with these odds, and with this outcome has never before occurred in modern war. Nothing like it, indeed, has occurred in war since Leonidas and his Spartans defended the Pass of Thermopylae. This fight was the Thermopylae of modern times. It is no fanciful comparison. There was the same heroic devotion and military brilliance on the one side; there was the same use of a vast army as a mob on the other. In spirit and in method the military systems of ancient Persia and of modern Prussia are by no means as far apart as the distance in time might lead us to suppose. The story of these heroes of the British cavalry ought to be remembered as long as in any part of the world there is a man of British stock who cherishes a love for the islands of his origin, and can thrill to the splendours of their story.

Of the onset made by the Bavarian Army Corps against Wytscheate a correspondent of the *Daily Telegraph* contributed an admirable record. This witness states:

> The perilous stroke smote the British line just south of Ypres, and, as luck would have it, was adequately lit up by a silver moonlight. The dense masses of Bavarian infantry sprang up with one accord. Their pale uniforms and bayonets were lit up by the ghostly light, and formed a strange and terrifying picture, for the attacking line stretched far, and was supported by numerous small columns in reserve. The sight of this concerted advance in the night was highly picturesque and impressive, but it failed to shake the nerves of our stalwart cavalry.
>
> Exposing their flank to sheets of fire from the neighbourhood of Ypres, the Bavarians pressed bravely forward, but all the while the steady rattle of the defenders' rifles from the trenches swept one rank away after the other. As fast as the German soldiers fell fresh groups pressed into the gap, and forced the line onward, but the toll of death shattered the constancy and corporate existence of an army corps.

At one point or more our line was pierced by the surging mass of the assailants, and a partial retirement took place for a mile or more in the dark. But the enemy's strength was sapped, and a comparatively weak counter-attack made in the grey of the morning by fragments of regiments and fragments of squadrons, collected hastily by the firmness of surviving officers, and backed by some infantry supports hastily thrust forward, was successful in recovering the greater part of the lost ground. As reinforcements arrived on the scene next day, and as our artillery concentrated its bombardment on the spot, the whole position was restored, and the attack of an army corps was definitely foiled by about one-fifth of its numbers.

October 31 was the crisis of the battle. During the night of October 30 the German flood, lashing in vain against the trenches held by the cavalry across the ridge, swirled in ponderous weight against those held by the nth Division Infantry at St. Yves, near the point where the British front crossed the Lys. The front here broke under the pressure. The breach, however, was only momentary. With a heroism beyond praise. Major Prowse instantly led the Somersets in a counter-attack. That intrepid corps, despite the enemy's ferociously tenacious resistance, drove him out. It was a bayonet fight, and a bayonet fight at its worst. The sturdy west countrymen, however, proved more than a match for any Prussians. They swept into the combat with the smash of a sledge-hammer added to the keenness of a high-speed tool, and wrought havoc. Against such a spirit and prowess numbers were unavailing.

All through that night, while the thunder of the conflict was heard and its flare seen fifty miles away, the enemy smashed at this section of the front. But it was a front of iron. Weighing his words. Sir John French says in his dispatch:

> I am anxious to bring to special notice the excellent work done throughout this battle by the Third Corps under General Pulteney's command. Their position in the right central part of my line was of the utmost importance to the general success of the operations. Besides the very undue length of front which the corps was called upon to cover (some twelve or thirteen miles), the position presented many weak spots, and was also astride of the River Lys, the right bank of which from Frelinghein downwards was strongly held by the enemy.

It was impossible to provide adequate reserves, and the constant work in the trenches tried the endurance of officers and men to the utmost. That the corps was invariably successful in repulsing the constant attacks, sometimes in great strength, made against them by day and by night is due entirely to the skilful manner in which the corps was disposed by its commander, who has told me of the able assistance he has received throughout from his staff, and the ability and resource displayed by Divisional, Brigade, and Regimental leaders in using the ground and the means of defence at their disposal to the very best advantage. The courage, tenacity, endurance, and cheerfulness of the men in such unparalleled circumstances are beyond all praise.

So far, then, we have this result : that neither the attack through Zandvoorde, the turning movement against Hollebeke and Wytscheate, nor the supporting attack against St. Yves had achieved its object.

Stopped in their advance through Zandvoorde, alike by the strength of the Allied position on the Kleine Zillebeke ridge, and by the reinforcement of the line, which, after this experience made them judge a frontal assault totally impracticable, the Germans determined to turn this barrier by reverting, on October 31, to their first scheme of an advance along the main avenue from Menin. This, indeed, was in this direction the only practicable way through the woodland belt.

When, at daybreak, their intention became evident, General Moussy, in command of the reinforcement sent the previous day from the 9th French Army Corps, tried to anticipate it by a counter-attack. He pushed forward to the south-east of Gheluvelt. There, however, in face of the great strength of the enemy he was brought to a standstill. Along the great road from Menin the Germans advanced in a mass of enormous depth, which was in truth a human battering ram. By this means they meant to smash through into Ypres despite any resistance that could be offered, and despite any losses. The battle developed at this point as a struggle at very short range. It swayed now this way and now that, as attack was followed by counter-attack. At length the pent-up mass of the enemy broke through, and swept along the road. The line of the 1st Division of Infantry at Gheluvelt was broken.

Gheluvelt was taken by the Germans; the flank of the 7th Division along the Kleine Zillebeke range was exposed; the Royal Scots Fusiliers, remaining in their trenches, were surrounded. The way open through Gheluvelt and the main road, the enemy rushed up a great force of guns and began shelling the British positions in enfilade right and left. Concurrently an attack was begun from Zandvoorde along the main road leading across the intervening valley, and through the woods past Kleine Zillebeke. The 7th Division were driven back through the woods towards Ypres. It looked this time as though the German thrust had gone home. The situation was assuredly critical. Sir John French earlier in the day had come to Hooge, on the Menin road. There, when the troops fell back, he found himself in the thick of the fighting. But he had taken his measures. Advancing along the Menin road the Germans exposed the flank of their huge column. This was their vulnerable point. The British general at once threw upon it all the force he had within striking distance to the north of the avenue.

The 1st and part of the 2nd Division of the 1st Army Corps, some 27,000 men, were swung against the German flank in a mighty counter-attack. The manoeuvre turned the tide of battle. It was one of those bold flashes of resource which mark off great commanders from mediocre commanders. The enemy's advance was immediately arrested. Thereupon the retiring British troops rallied. Thus held in front and attacked in flank, the German masses, crowded together in a space too small for their numbers, were destroyed wholesale. Their resistance, though fierce, was brief. The onset broke them. Into and through the woods south of the Menin road they fell back, confused and routed, upon Zandvoorde. Gheluvelt was retaken. Here, to cover the retreat, a large body of the enemy attempted, behind hastily thrown up barricades, to hold out. The gunners of the 42nd Brigade R.F.A. blew the barricades to pieces. Then the Worcestershires rushed the village with the bayonet.

The result of this signal success was that the front was restored nearly to the line it had occupied at the beginning of the day. Many of the enemy still remained in the woods. The 6th Cavalry Brigade was given the work of hunting them out. Sir John French says:

> They advanced with much dash, partly mounted and partly dismounted; and surprising the enemy, succeeded in killing large numbers and materially helped to restore the line.

If the chance of victory passed from the German arms with their fatal hesitancy on the preceding day, this crushing defeat of their main attack made efforts to retrieve their fortunes hopeless. The attacks against Hollebeke and round Messines continued all through this day, and as already said, through the following night. They were wasted. The hammering went on too against the front down to Givenchy. Though by one of their battering-ram assaults the enemy had driven the Indian troops out of and to the west of Neuve Chapelle, the hope of piercing the front was not realised. The Indians, probably thought an easy proposition by comparison, turned out also to be stuff too tough to be broken. The Gurkhas and the famous corps of Sappers and Miners were brilliant, and justly won the honourable mention given them in the commander-in-chief's dispatches.

CHAPTER 7

The Battle of Ypres—Final Phase

In its final phase the great battle lasted for another eleven days. Holding now the main ridge of hills from Zandvoorde to near Wytscheate on the Ypres-Lille road, a distance of five miles, and in possession of the village of Hollebeke, or rather of its site, the Germans appear to have decided that the effective direction for their attack was through Wytscheate and the sector of the Allied front following the Lille road from near Wytscheate through the village of Messines to Armentières. And this decision on their part was without question strategically sound. Could they have carried it out, they would not only have compelled the British forces to fall back from the west of Lille, but to evacuate Ypres. They would have won the battle.

Moreover the victory must have been decisive, for on the north it would have cut off an important part of the British and French forces, together with the Belgians, from the remainder of the Allied line, and on the south it would have turned the flank of that line. The mistake, a fatal mistake, lay in not having made this the real objective from the first, and in wasting force and incurring defeat, with its inevitable demoralisation, in attempts to break through into Ypres across the belt of woods on the east and the south-east.

There the only lines along which attacks in great strength could be thrown were roads running into Ypres like spokes into the hub of a wheel, but the farther in any one of these attacking columns moved, the more were its flanks exposed. The precaution against flank attack, advance in echelon, was made by the character of this woodland belt out of the question. We have seen that, appreciating these capabilities of defence, the British commander-in-chief had crushed a gigantic onset. It is manifest now that the Germans had believed that by weight of numbers they could prevail over the difficulties, and the chances those difficulties gave of holding this sector with a comparatively small force, but that had merely involved them in enormous losses, a risk inseparable from their tactics.

Having now realised their mistake, they attempted to throw an immense wedge of troops against the two miles of British line between Wytscheate and Messines. Here again, however, they found themselves anticipated. The front was no longer held merely by a single rank of cavalry. The bemudded, dirty, unshaven ragged, and almost unrecognisable yet victorious survivors of that band of heroes had been relieved. Part of the 16th French Army Corps, General Conneau's cavalry, a division of the Indian Army Corps, and a part of the British 2nd Army Corps were on or behind it. Sir John French was taking no unnecessary risks. To these troops, some 50,000 in all, therefore, he added as a reserve units of the Territorials recently arrived from England. It was certain that they would have to meet German forces four if not five times as numerous, and it was certain that those German troops would fight to the last gasp.

The Germans lost no time. Their attack against Wytscheate and Messines was made concurrently before daybreak. They had taken advantage of the darkness to carry out mass movements which could not be sighted from aeroplanes. The onset was both heavy and sudden, and it formed probably the greatest night operation on record. Darkness, it was now held, afforded the best protection against British rifle power. As this was an attack which had to succeed at all costs, the enemy took the heavy punishment inflicted by a furious resistance. A proportion of these German troops were lads of 17 and even younger. They had been used to fill up the gaps left by casualties, and mingled with the older men drove forward on the order of their officers and faced death at the muzzles of British rifles and the massed guns of the British Horse Artillery by hundreds.

Both Wytscheate and Messines fell into the enemy's hands. At the same time with the evident object of arresting the movement of reserves assaults were made along the British line to the south of Messines past Armentières and along the valley of the Lys. This part of the attack was, of course, no more than strategical. For the purpose it was useless. Round both Wytscheate and Messines the enemy found himself confronted by quite unexpected forces. He could make no further advance from either. So costly indeed had been his attack upon Wytscheate, that the French infantry, launched upon a counter-attack with the aid of a British cavalry force, cleared him out of the place at the point of the bayonet.

It was during the fighting on this day, a Sunday, that there occurred the episode which earned for the London Scottish Territorials the special acknowledgment of the commander-in-chief. Transported in motor omnibuses from the base at Boulogne to Ypres, where, on arrival, they were quartered for the night in the Hotel de Ville, they had been sent forward in the first instance to Neuve Eglise, and then to Messines to support the front line. This was during the crisis of the German attack on October 31. The battalion fought its way forward from Messines to a position east of the Ypres-Lille main road. There, under heavy fire, it dug itself in, and for five hours repulsed a series of determined assaults. Resolved at any price to be rid of these fellows in kilts who had thrown themselves right athwart the line of advance upon Messines, the Germans, at two o'clock in the morning of November 1, renewed the onset with a crushing superiority of numbers.

While the battalion was resisting the attack in front, another force of the enemy developed an attack in flank. Others, getting between the first and second British lines of trenches opened an assault from the rear. These set on fire an adjacent house. The flare from this building lit up the combat and the bayonet charges in which the companies of the reserve dashed into and defeated the Germans who had got round the position. By their gallantry the reserve prevented the battalion from being surrounded.

Unable to carry the position by assault, the Germans now tried to wipe out the battalion by an enfilade fire from machine guns. This had now at length made retirement imperative. The corps had to cut its way out with the bayonet. Inevitably the losses were heavy. The striking fact, however, is that the first unit of the Territorial Force which had taken part in battle had saved itself in a situation and in a manner which would have done honour to the most famous and veteran regiment in the service. Indeed there are few episodes in British military annals more dramatic or more brilliant. Naturally this episode, apart from its immediate military effect, attracted great attention because it afforded a proof of the quality of the Territorial Force, a proof which that force has since amply upheld.

The effect of the delay opposed to the German advance by this unlooked for and obstinate resistance was serious. Without question it upset their plans and prevented the attacks upon Wytscheate and Messines from being, as they had been designed to be, simultaneous.

The result was both that the attack upon Wytscheate failed to stay, and that the attack upon Messines effected nothing more than the occupation of the ruins of that village. That trifling outcome needless to say was not the German aim.

The upshot of the German operations for this day proved for all practical purposes negative. On November 2 the effort to break through was renewed. Wytscheate was once more attacked and carried. This time the place was set on fire, and as night fell at the end of the short dim November day the burning ruins cast round a mighty glare, lighting up the fierce and repeated bayonet charges with which time and again the French infantry threw back the efforts of the enemy to make headway.

Meanwhile, finding that strong forces of the Allies had been ranged against them, the Germans to the south of Messines tried to open up a road for their columns with an artillery fire of great intensity. On the other side the British and French ranged a powerful force of guns in a wide arc, and concentrating the fire of these towards one comparatively limited fire-zone on the German front, moved that fire-swept area up and down the hostile line. The effect may be compared to playing the point of a ray of sunlight focussed through a burning glass. In face of such a fire no advance could be along this section attempted. The Germans had to retire their troops out of range to save them from annihilation.

And this in effect was the defeat of their scheme. Next day (November 3) the attack was towards Hollebeke, in combination with another attempt to debouch from Wytscheate. The diversion was tantamount to a confession of failure.

In face of it Sir John French knew that he had definitely won the battle. His first step was to issue an Army Order thanking the troops. Every word of this historic document is justified. It ran:

> I have made many calls upon you, and the answers you have made to them have covered you, your regiments, and the army to which you belong with honour and glory.
>
> Your fighting qualities, courage, and endurance have been subjected to the most trying and severe tests, and you have proved yourselves worthy descendants of the British soldiers of the past who have built up the magnificent traditions of the regiments to which you belong.
>
> You have not only maintained those traditions but you have

materially added to their lustre.

It is impossible for me to find words in which to express my appreciation of the splendid services you have performed.[1]

But though in truth decided, the battle was not yet over. The Germans refused to accept defeat. They now adopted different tactics. These were a tremendous bombardment of the British lines alternating with repeated attacks. The latter were not as before directed against one or two decisive points of the front, but distributed all round and included the part of the front to the north of Ypres. There four hostile army corps were employed. The attacks were not only made with smaller masses and more numerous, but they were delivered both by day and by night and almost without cessation. It was, in fact, a tactic of wearing down. This went on for six days and nights without cessation. The struggle was marked by many remarkable episodes due to the fact that the Germans, conscious of defeat, now fought with redoubled bitterness and with much of the spirit of bravado and revenge.

One instance of this was the extraordinary attempt to carry a French trench by a charge of cavalry. This, of course, was no better than suicide. "Eye Witness," says in recording the affair:

> Every horse, was killed, but those riders who were not hit continued the charge on foot. The last survivors were slain on the very parapet of the trench.

At another point, where the bodies of a company of Germans enfiladed by machine-gun fire lay as they had fallen in a regular row, a second body of the enemy advanced at nightfall, and along the line of corpses dug themselves in.

By dint of these attacks, and while the British troops were strengthening their line, turning their hasty pre-cover into trenches of systematic make, with zigzag communication ways, and supports trenches and "dugouts" in the rear, the Germans in many places advanced their positions so close that the occupants of the trench on one side were

---

1. To the 2nd British Army Corps Sir John French issued on the same date a special Army Order in these terms: "The Field Officer Commanding-in-Chief has watched with the deepest admiration and solicitude the splendid stand made by the soldiers of the King in their successful effort to maintain the forward position which they have won by their gallantry and steadfastness. "He believes that no other army in the world would show such tenacity, especially under the tremendous artillery fire directed against it. "Its courage and endurance are beyond all praise. It is an honour to belong to such an army."

within earshot of those on the other. It became the enemy's practice to bring up heavy artillery in the night, to shell a British position, and while the troops were sitting tight under the bombardment to "dig in" close by.

This closeness of the opposing entrenched positions in many places led to repeated night raids; a form of activity in which more especially the Indian troops proved adepts. An Indian night raid, which recovered a line of trenches the enemy had taken, is thus described by those who witnessed it:

> In the afternoon it began to rain heavily, and the rain continued to fall as the night darkened. British troops in the trenches, knowing of the massing of the enemy, were keenly on the alert amidst the most depressing circumstances, and none were allowed the comfort of a sleep.
>
> But, all unknown to them, behind a thin line of trees some short distance to the rear, there silently gathered together many hundreds of figures, which, by reason of their lithe, gliding movements and their practical invisibility might have passed for a mysterious aggregation of spirits from some other sphere. Not a word was uttered, and such orders as were issued seemed to pass down the long lines as the wind whispers through the grass.
>
> Shortly afterwards a score of these grey figures detached themselves from the larger body and stealthily, like Red Indians on the trail in an enemy's country, moved up to and beyond the advanced line of the British trenches. Down these, under the breath, was passed the word, "The Indians are going out," and the already alert Tommies craned their heads forward into the misty night to watch events.
>
> The score of ghostly figures suddenly disappeared from their view, and, python-like, crawled noiselessly to the first German trench. Here were the German look-out men.
>
> What happened there exactly is not known. There was no shout or sudden cry, but in a few minutes the British soldiers saw one of the score reappear like an apparition and go back to his comrades in the rear. Then the hundreds waiting there filed past the trenches just as silently as had the advanced party before them, and also disappeared in the direction of the German lines.
>
> For five minutes there was perfect quiet. Then came a few shots,

followed by a wild splutter of musketry, intermingled with cries and groans.

Three or four light-balls were thrown in the air, and by their means the British troops could see, some 600 yards to their front, a mass of wild and struggling men, the gleam of steel, and the whirling rush of the rifle-butt. It was the Pathans at their deadly work. For ten minutes they hacked and slew amongst the half-awake and wholly-bewildered Germans, who had laid down in serried ranks to await the order for the night assault on the British trenches.

The score of Pathans who had gone out in advance had silently slain the German pickets, and the main body had thus been enabled to get right amidst the sleeping foe unchallenged. The slaughter was terrible, and only ended when the Germans, thoroughly aroused to their peril, bolted and ran. Then their swarthy assailants, glutted with their night's work, came back briskly, but just as silently, to their original post.

The threatened German attack had been turned into a bloody defeat. For hours afterwards the furious Germans poured a hail of shrapnel and shell into our trenches, in the hope of obtaining some revenge for their terrible punishment.[2]

Besides this a variety of ruses were resorted to. Men dressed in French or British uniforms stole singly through the British lines to cut field telephone wires. Others employed themselves as eavesdroppers. Germans dressed in imitation uniforms of the British staff more than once appeared and tried to give false orders.[3]

On the main ridge to the south-east of Ypres, the Germans massed a number of batteries with which they tried to rake the British lines. The ridge, however, was an exposed position, and both the French and British guns were concentrated upon it with marked effect. Describing this "Eye Witness" states:

---

2. Account sent by Mr. Hodson, correspondent of the Central News, and published in the *Daily Telegraph*. The trenches taken were filled in.

3. "Eye Witness," writing under date November 13, 1914, says: "One remarkable and absolutely authentic case occurred. A man dressed in a uniform which resembled that of a British Staff officer suddenly appeared near our trenches and walked along the line, asking if many casualties had been suffered, and stating that the situation was serious and that a general retirement had been ordered. A similar visit was reported by several men in different trenches, and orders were issued that this strange officer was to be detained if again seen. Unluckily he did not make another appearance."

The south two villages (Kortewilde and Kostzelhoe) which the enemy had captured and their line on the ridge close by were heavily bombarded by the British and French artillery. From the high ground to the west the effect of this cannonade could be seen to some extent, though the villages under fire were partially obscured from view by the smoke of the bursting shells, and resembled the craters of volcanoes belching fire and fumes. At one place the gaunt wreck of the old church tower and the blackened remains of a few houses round it would emerge for a moment only to be again blotted out in the pall of smoke. The long straggling villages, when they became temporarily visible, seemed to melt away and assume odd and fantastic shapes as the houses crumbled and the blocks of masonry were thrown hither and thither by the blasting effect of lyddite and melinite.

There can be no doubt the change in tactics was due in part to the fact that owing to the shock of defeat a continuance of the mass attacks had become for the time impracticable. Of the feeling, at any rate, on the part of some of the enemy the following extract from a German soldier's diary picked up on the battlefield throws a certain light:

2nd November.—Before noon sent out in a regular storm of bullets by order of the major. These gentlemen, the officers, send their men forward in the most ridiculous way. They themselves remain far behind safely under cover. Our leadership is really scandalous. Enormous losses on our side, partly from the fire of our own people, for our leaders neither know where the enemy lies nor where our own troops are, so that we are often fired on by our own men. It is a marvel to me that we have got on as far as we have done. Our captain fell, also all our section leaders and a large number of our men.

Moreover, no purpose was served by this advance, for we remained the rest of the day under cover and could go neither forward nor back, nor even shoot.

It is simply ridiculous, this leadership. If only I had known it before! My opinion of the German officers has changed. An adjutant shouted to us from a trench far to the rear to cut down a hedge which was in front of us. Bullets were whistling round from in front and from behind. The gentleman himself, of course, remained behind.

Still in the trenches. Shells and shrapnel burst without ceasing. In the evening a cup of rice and one-third of an apple per man. Let us hope peace will soon come. Such a war is really too awful. The English shoot like mad. If no reinforcements come up, especially heavy artillery, we shall have a poor look-out.

The first day I went quietly into the fight with an indifference which astonished me. Today, for the first time in advancing, when my comrades right and left fell, felt rather nervous, but lost that feeling again soon. One becomes horribly indifferent. Picked up a piece of bread by chance. Thank God! at least something to eat.

There are about 70,000 English who must be attacked from all four sides and destroyed. They defend themselves, however, obstinately.[4]

As the effect of this week of day and night wearing down work, it was apparently on November 10, judged that the British were ripe for the enemy's last effort—the attack of the Prussian Guard. This, preceded by the most intensive artillery fire the Germans had yet achieved, began on November 11 soon after daybreak. They had clearly, in regard to the artillerists, and they tried against the entrenched positions north and south of the Menin-road, the effect which had been successfully used against them at Messines. The way having thus been, as it was supposed, opened up, 1st and 4th Brigades of the Prussian Guard rolled forward.

The line of attack lay diagonally across part of the British front, and on it was turned the united fury of field guns, machine guns and rifles. It has been affirmed by all who saw the onset that the Guard stood against this terrible hail like rock. The grey-green mass, at the outset some 20,000 strong, moved forward in close formation, and almost as though on parade. As one man fell another stepped into his place. Their losses were enormous, but the mass kept its formation and its momentum. At three places despite the desperate resistance of the British they broke the line, and penetrated into the woods. There, however, the British reserves, brought up for the counter-attack, fell upon them. In a bayonet fight with a brigade of Irishmen, the Guards met not only their equals, but their superiors. Those who held together were driven back, enfiladed by the fire of machine guns. The rest broke into scattered bodies; these when rounded up fought to the

---

4. Given in the British official narrative.

last where they stood. Only a miserable remnant of this mass of brave men reached the lines of the enemy.

That was the supreme effort and the end. On the farther side of Belgium beyond the sight of the beaten army flared the monstrous pyres of paraffin-soaked timber in which, tied together, four by four, and standing upright, the bodies of the unfortunate German slain were burned by tens of thousands. Such was the aftermath of this mighty tragedy.

CHAPTER 8

The Battle on the Yser

As we have seen, the gigantic Battle of Ypres presented four phases.

During the first phase, from October ii to October 17, the British Army, pivoting upon Givenchy, drove the Germans from Hazebrouck to Lille.

During the second phase, from October 18 to October 24, the Germans, resuming the offensive, hurled the weight of their attack against the sector of the British front to the west of Lille. The British positions had meanwhile been extended round Ypres to the south and east, and the line of the Allies formed as far as the coast.

The third phase was marked by the effort of the enemy, now enormously reinforced, to break through into Ypres from the south-east, aided by a turning movement from the south. The fighting during the three days, October 29 to October 31, formed the crisis of the battle. It has been stated in the French Army Bulletin summarising the operations from October 21 to November 15, that the Emperor of Germany, who had at this time taken up his headquarters at Courtrai, "announced that he wanted to be in Ypres by November 1, and every preparation had been made for the proclamation on that day of the annexation of Belgium."

In the fourth and final phase of the battle the Germans tried to pierce the Allied line between Ypres and the Lys through Wytscheate and Messines. That defeated, the great mass assault was made against Ypres from the east by the Prussian Guard on November 11.

While German infantry attacks continued to be made until November 15, they were no more than the sullen efforts of a baffled but still bitter foe. The stress of the fighting lasted from October 11 to November 11, that is exactly one month. For a second time in this

Western campaign there had been in a great pitched battle, a trial of strength, and for a second time the forces of Germany had, as on the Marne, gone down.

It is important to keep these phases of the Battle of Ypres in mind. They throw light on the battle which was concurrently, from October 17 to October 31, being fought on the Yser.

From its source in the hills west of Ypres to the sea the whole course of the Yser does not exceed 20 miles. It is a stream, however, of a quite exceptional character. Running through a tract of country for the most part below sea level, it is more like two streams flowing in the same direction, and connected by winding cross channels. On a smaller scale the like effect may be seen in the channels on stretches of flat shore at ebb tide. The Yser was of course nothing more originally than a network of such channels running through the mud flats, and though all this part of the Lowlands was more than a thousand years ago finally reclaimed from the sea, the waters continued to flow along the ancient beds. They have been connected besides by canals.

In the Middle Ages when Ypres was a great centre of trade, and one of the most populous cities of Europe, these canals were busy arteries of commerce. The country between Ypres and the coast, one of the most fertile tracts in the world, was at the outbreak of this war full of quaint and picturesque memorials of its former importance. In modern days, and more especially under the wise and beneficial rule of the present Royal House of Belgium, it was a picture of peaceful and settled wealth.

On the Yser half-way between Ypres and the sea was the old town of Dixmude, with a church and a *hôtel de ville* which were masterpieces of Gothic architecture. Towards the coast, where the line of sand dunes has in part covered the ancient dykes, the river takes a sharp bend to west. A tract about two miles wide and three miles long is thus enclosed on the east between the river channels on the one side and the sea on the other. This was occupied by the little seaside residential places, Lombartzyde and Westende. Nieuport lay on the west bank of the river a mile or more inland. The Yser here becomes one channel, deep enough to be navigated by shipping of moderate draught. It was crossed at Nieuport by five bridges. Between them lay the series of locks dividing the tidal part of the Yser from the inland reaches. The locks were those used to regulate the river overflow at low tide while keeping out the sea when the tide was at flood.

There are two points of some importance on the west bank of the

Yser between Dixmude and Nieuport—the villages of Pervyse and Ramscappel. Both are on the main road connecting the two towns. Five miles farther to the west lies the town of Furnes, already mentioned as the meeting place of the great road from Ypres with that running along the coast from Ostend through Nieuport and on to Dunkirk and Calais. The great roads, and indeed most of the main roads and canals in this part of Flanders are carried along embankments. Before the war these were mostly bordered with trees, affording in winter shelter from the cold winds which sweep over the country from the North Sea, and welcome shade in summer. It was a land of deep repose, and for nearly 100 years and until the coming of the Goth, nothing save the mellow chime floating distantly from some tall and noble spire reared in far off days by pious hands, had broken in upon its dreaming.

General Joffre issued the first orders directed towards his great scheme of military envelopment on September 11. This promptitude was essential. When in the first phase of the battle of Ypres the British drove the Germans back upon Lille, the strategical effect was to tear in the German front a gap from Lille to beyond Thourout, a distance of nearly thirty miles. The Germans had to mass their forces at Lille in order to keep their hold on that place.

Through the gap thus made the French pushed forward four divisions of cavalry, two divisions of their Territorial troops, and a division of marines, 6,000 strong. Already, however, on October 15, the Germans had, north of the gap towards the coast, two army corps, and these were in the course of the next two or three days reinforced by two others. The objective of these troops was to seize Nieuport and the crossing of the Yser.

The Belgian Army reached Nieuport from Antwerp on October 16. That army was, however, not immediately fit for further service. In these circumstances the line of the Yser from Nieuport to Dixmude was held by the French cavalry and marines, while the 1st division of British infantry was thrown forward to Bixschoot, with the 2nd division in support. Later along the Yser and round Ypres, where after November 20 they relieved the British, the French forces on this part of the front were brought up to five army corps. At this date in mid October, however, all that could be opposed to the German mass aggregating 240,000 men detailed to seize the crossings of the Yser, were these French cavalry, one division of marines, and two divisions of British infantry, not 45,000 in all.

The first German thrust against Nieuport was made on October 17, and it must inevitably have succeeded had it not been that the enemy came within range of and were enfiladed by the fire of a British flotilla. This equivalent to a destructive attack in flank wrecked the attempt. The shells of the warships raked the German lines as far inland as Dixmude.

The Germans realised that at Nieuport, in face of the guns of the British ships, they could not succeed. They made ready, in consequence, to throw their attack against Dixmude. For that purpose they waited until their whole force could come up. Their first attempt had been made with two army corps only. The respite enabled the Belgian army to be refitted. Both sides meanwhile proceeded to dig themselves in. In this region the water level is not more than two feet below the surface. No sooner were the trenches cut than the water oozed in. These conditions were aggravated by days and nights of heavy and almost incessant rain. A dense mist overhung the country. The nights, too, were now becoming bitterly cold.

On the side of the Germans the numbers were large enough to afford reliefs. They were not large enough on the side of the Allies. The Belgians passed days and nights in the trenches under these conditions without respite. It was an effort of endurance that has never been paralleled. But for their unconquerable spirit these heroic men could not have come through such an ordeal. They were defending, however, the last few square miles of their country and they were defending that last bit of territory from foes whose pitiless cruelty they had seen in butchery and outrage. Behind them they had the memory of a happy freedom. Before them lay only the prospect of submitting for ever to the odious tyranny which had laid some of the fairest towns and districts of Belgium in ruins. In that mudded and warworn army there was a fire no hardship could subdue.

On October 21 opened the great German drive. It was directed alike and at once to the seizure of Ramscappel so as to compel the Belgians to evacuate Nieuport; against Dixmude; and farther south against the British positions at Bixschoot. The latter point was as far as natural conditions were concerned the easiest crossing of the three. There is here only one channel of the Yser with a line of canal on either side of it. The three attacks were made simultaneously because they brought into play the vast German superiority in numbers.

The enemy had massed along this front a great weight of guns, including the heavy pieces used in the attack on Antwerp, and his plan was to draw west of the Yser an impenetrable curtain of fire while he constructed pontoon bridges. There were difficulties. First the river channels were in flood. Secondly they were commanded by the French and Belgian guns. Thirdly and along their length they were under the cross fire from the warships. This acute spasm of the battle, lasting without a moment's respite for three days and two nights, was therefore in one of its main features a gigantic artillery duel.

Pontoon bridges constructed by the Germans were destroyed by the French gunners or by the shells from the warships time and again. More than once the bridges were struck and wrecked when they were crowded with troops and these miserable men, thrown in a struggling mass into the water, were drowned by hundreds. Time after time the Germans endeavoured to bridge the river, or rather the network of rivers before the effort at length succeeded.

Then from Ramscappel the Belgians were forced to retire. Once across the river with a considerable force of infantry, cavalry, and guns, the Germans seized Pervyse, and pushed forward to Furnes with such speed that the small Belgian reserve force there, surprised by them, had to quit hastily. A surprise, however, was also in store for the Germans. A division of French Algerian troops, who had been sent forward by forced marches to reinforce the Belgian resistance, were already close at hand. They reached Furnes shortly after the German advance force had established themselves there. The attack was as impetuous as it was unexpected. The Turcos cleared the Germans out of the place at the point of the bayonet. Enemy reinforcements, however, hurried up.

In turn the Germans tried to carry the town by storm. The struggle went on from street to street and from house to house. Again and again the Germans were driven out. Again and again they rallied and renewed the fight. As night came on the French commander called upon his men for a supreme effort. It was victorious. Broken by this onslaught, the Germans were not only chased out of Furnes but pursued to Ramscappel and driven out of that village as well. Behind them their bridges over the Yser had in the meantime again been destroyed. Mr. A. Beaumont, special correspondent of the Daily Telegraph, who reached Furnes the following day, has recorded that:

"The roads from Ramscappel to Pervyse, and from Pervyse to Dixmude were lined with the enemy's dead. Many of the fugitives tried to escape by the fields and canals, and their bodies are still found in great numbers. As in many other places in the north, quite a number of these Germans are very young, apparently under eighteen, or else more than fifty years of age.

King Albert of Belgium desired in person to honour the French troops who had helped to reconquer the village (Ramscappel), and an impressive ceremony was held a few days later. The king passed in review the survivors of the gallant companies of Turcos and *chasseurs* in the little square. They were assembled at eight o'clock in the morning, and drawn up in a square in the presence of a French general. The king arrived in a motorcar and alighted at once. Three buglers, who had gone through it all, sounded the call, and the commander of the troops moved forward to salute them. The king likewise raised his hand in a long and silent salute. Then, accompanied by the general in command he passed down the lines, after which the troops in turn defiled in his presence. The buglers did their best, but their shrill notes were not in accord; yet tears came to the eyes of many spectators of this scene, and not the least moved among them was the king himself. The general then rode forward, and in a loud voice said:

> The king desires me to transmit to you his hearty congratulations for your splendid conduct at Ramscappel; this is an honour of which your commander is justly proud.

Of the attack on Dixmude[1] an account was sent by a German who took part in it to *Vorwärts*. He relates:

> We lay for four whole days without anything to eat or drink. Day and night the earth trembled with the reports of the guns. No sleep was possible. Behind us lay a field of roots. Creeping down the bank in order not to be seen by the enemy, we managed to get some of them. We sucked up the night dew on the grass in order to slake our thirst. After four days we had to give up the position in order to attack the enemy from another side.
>
> Next day it began to rain, and we stood up to the knees in water, and replied to the fire of the enemy until the evening came. All was quiet for a time. But the cannons continued their work. We watched by turns while the others sat in the water, and, leaning against the trenches, tried to sleep. A terrible picture faced us. Dixmude was in flames, and the whole sky was blood-red. The enemy's shells exploded with such a report that we

---

1. *Dixmude* by Charles Le Goffic is also published by Leonaur.

thought our ears would burst, and the light was so strong that you could read a paper by it. Dealing death and destruction, the shower of lead sped through the night air over our heads. In the morning the sun rose a fiery red.

It was the death signal for many of us, for Dixmude had to be stormed. At two o'clock we received an order for the attack. We left our firing places, and at once came under fire. By short rushes we approached the strongly held trenches of the enemy. Air and earth shook with the reports of the guns, for the enemy were firing from at least twenty batteries. Many of us were torn in pieces. Amidst it all, the rifles and the machine guns made their peculiar noise. It was a veritable field of death. Right and left of me comrades fell. We reached a small ditch and blazed away, and there a bullet hit my rifle, glanced off, and went through the head of the man next to me.

At last we came within 200 metres of the enemy's position. Their fire grew fiercer, but our rage was the greater. Then the enemy received reinforcements, and brought up three machine guns, which they trained on us. The top of my helmet was shot away, and the bullets pierced my spade.

Next came shells such as we had never seen before. The sand spurted up as high as a house. One shell made a hole at least two yards deep in the ground. The black smoke rendered it almost impossible to see anything. These were the shells of the British fleet which had taken part in the battle. In the middle of a field near us eight horses were suddenly torn into shreds by one. What was that? It was a bugle signal, "Fix bayonets." In a minute we rushed forward another 100 yards. Then we took a breathing-space. What was that? I could neither see nor hear, for I was hurled back three yards with my head against a tree. For a moment I lost consciousness, and when I came to I knew that I had not been hit. I rushed forward to join my comrades. I will not tell you anything about the bayonet charge, for it was a slaughter. Twice we were driven back, but at the third attack we won. When you heard about the victory did you not cry "Hurrah"? But we thought upon the terrible sacrifices that had been made, for many lay dead. I was hit in the pursuit of the enemy, but I need not describe what it looked like in the enemy's trenches. The men lay one over another.

At Bixschoot the Germans succeeded in capturing part of the British trenches held by the 1st Division. These, however, were wrested from the enemy in a brilliantly executed counterattack. To the troops for this service the brigadier-general in command issued a special order of congratulation. This document gives a clear summary of the operation:

> The 2nd Infantry Brigade (less 2nd Battalion Sussex Regiment left at Beesinghe) was allotted the task of reinforcing the 1st Infantry Brigade, and re-taking the trenches along the Bixsencote-Lange-march road, which had been occupied by the enemy.
> In spite of the stubborn resistance offered by the German troops, the object of the engagement was accomplished, but not without many casualties in the brigade.
> By nightfall the trenches previously captured by the Germans had been re-occupied, about 500 prisoners captured, and fully 1,500 German dead were lying out in front of our trenches.
> The Brigadier-General congratulates the 1st L.N. Lancashire Regiment, Northamptonshire Regiment, and the 2nd King's Royal Rifle Corps, but desires specially to commend the fine soldierlike spirit of the 1st L.N. Lancashire Regiment, which, advancing steadily under heavy shell and rifle-fire, aided by its machine guns, was enabled to form up within a comparatively short distance of the enemy's trenches.
> Fixing bayonets, the battalion then charged, carried the trenches and occupied them, and to them must be allotted the majority of the prisoners captured.
> The Brigadier-General congratulates himself on having in his brigade a battalion, which, after marching the whole of the previous night without rest or food, was able to maintain its splendid record in the past, by the determination and self-sacrifice displayed in the action.
> The Brigadier-General has received special telegrams of congratulations from both the general officer commanding-in-chief 1st Corps, and from the general officer commanding 1st Division, and he hopes that in the next engagement in which the brigade takes part the high reputation which the brigade already holds, may be further added to.

In truth the immediate impetus of the German onset had exhausted itself in the violent and costly efforts put forth. After an interval of not more than six hours Dixmude was retaken, and the Belgians, advancing from Nieuport, took and entrenched themselves in Lombartzyde. Despite its frightful cost in life, the second attempt to get across the Yser had tragically failed.

After reorganising the Germans began the third great attempt on October 9. This was even more determined and more wasteful of life than the second. Again it was persisted in for three days. The scenes were a repetition of those of the week before, if anything, they were still more terrible, for the resistance was as unflinching as the attack was bitter. On the evidence of men who had taken part in the battle, Mr. Frederick de Bathe, special correspondent of the *Daily Telegraph*, wrote:

> The Germans tried nineteen times to cross the Yser at one point; on each occasion they were repulsed by the Belgian and French troops, which were massed upon the opposite bank.
> It is said that the enemy lost whole regiments. A wounded German officer who was taken prisoner affirms that of his regiment, which went into action 2,000 strong, only eighty were left unscathed. While claiming that the Belgian and French had suffered big losses, he admitted that these were nothing in comparison to those sustained by the Germans. He added that it was not a battle, it was butchery! A peasant, who came through the German lines, reports that the enemy have no time to bury their dead singly, but are obliged to have them carried away in three-wheeled farm carts by the country people in loads of twenty to twenty-five, and removed to the rear of their positions for burial.
> The cross-fire from the British fleet prevented the Germans from advancing along the coast, obliging them to throw pontoon bridges over the Yser. The pontoons sank time after time with their human burden, shattered by the shells of the Allies. It is no exaggeration to state that the Germans on the Yser alone up to date have lost 75,000 men killed and wounded, and this does not include the prisoners, who have been numerous. Over 8,000 of the enemy's wounded who were being brought to Bruges and Courtrai, via Thourout, were abandoned on Sunday last, and were obliged to make the ten-hour journey on foot.
> The churches of Thourout and in the neighbourhood, as well

as all the farms which are still standing, are crammed with wounded. Hundreds of German wounded are streaming in day and night throughout the region behind the enemy's lines. In certain places close to the Yser between Nieuport and Dixmude the ground is literally covered with corpses of men and horses. The shrapnel from the British fleet has caused more than threeparts of the slaughter in this particular direction. The scene is indescribable.

Three times the Germans fought their way over through the cross fire of the Allied guns, ashore and afloat, and three times they were thrown back. The enemy's expenditure of ammunition was as prodigal as his expenditure of men.

Then began a systematic destruction which has had no parallel in modern war. The Germans set themselves to batter the country into ruins, they bombarded and wrecked not only Nieuport, Dixmude, and Ypres, but every village and hamlet within range of their guns. Of this, after having seen its effect, Mr. E. Ashmead-Bartlett said:

> This part of Belgium, perfectly flat, is studded with picturesque old Flemish homes. Almost every village of any size possesses buildings of historic or architectural interest. The old church of Dixmude was one of the finest buildings of its kind in the countryside, and so also was the *hôtel de ville*. What remains of these buildings would not be worth the while to cart away as old bricks.
>
> As a machine of pure destruction the *Kaiser's* army is unique. I doubt whether any other army in the history of the world has had the knack of laying waste a whole country so completely. They wipe out everything.
>
> These towns and villages play no part in the defence of the Yser. They are merely shell-traps, where no general would think of placing his men.
>
> As a revenge on an innocent civil population, who thus lose their hearths and homes, and are now refugees all over France, Holland, and England, the plan succeeds admirably. On the other hand, the defence is materially aided, because the fire is taken off the troops in the trenches and on the long trains making their way to the front with food, ammunition, and supplies of all kinds. I do not believe the line of the Yser could have been held had the Germans scientifically supported their

infantry attacks with this tremendous volume of shell fire, with which they have laid low Dixmude, Pervyse, Nieuport, and fifty other smaller towns and villages.

The crowning act, however, of this "revenge," deliberately indulged in that the attention of the world might be drawn off the crushing disasters suffered by German arms, was the ruin of Ypres. That act of vandalism was not, it is necessary to remember, done during the battle or for any military purpose. It was begun after the battle, and when the issue, and with it the future history of Europe, had been for ever changed. Of what that ruin was there has been drawn by Mr. Luigi Barzini a picture of enduring reality. He was one of three civilians who visited Ypres while this bombardment was going on. His description appeared in the *Daily Telegraph* of December 2, 1914.

> At a turn of the road, the town appeared in the distance—two mutilated campaniles, a ruin of massive towers, and the ancient belfry, with its vague bluish carvings. In the dull, declining day, the trees at the edge of the plain seemed like a dark mist. They formed, as it were, a sombre border of cloud on the horizon, and above the network of branches rose the remains of the bombarded town, pale and sinister, with something unreal and death-like in their mutilated aspect—phantasms of a massacred glory.
>
> At short intervals the air was shaken by the bombardment, and, urged by the wind, two clouds of white smoke fled between the trees and vanished amidst their branches. Two flashes of livid light burst on high, and for an instant the top of the towers disappeared in a cloud. The destructive fury of the German guns still continued to strike the heart of Ypres. The road had been converted into a desert.
>
> We had left behind us towns and villages crowded with troops, immense parks of carts and motor-lorries scattered over the meadows, extensive encampments at the edges of the road, in which the innumerable piles of arms seemed like black sheaves crowned with points, the general quarters of divisions and brigades denoted by standards. Then, having passed Vlamertynghe, about three miles from Ypres, we came upon the sinister solitude of a modern battle.
>
> There was no other voice, no other sound, than the boom of cannon and the crash of shell. But the flashes of the explosions

seemed to render all the more evident, more profound, and more significant the terrible silence of the town and the fields. It was the silence of resignation, fear, and agony. The sound of our footsteps upon the muddy pavement of the suburb echoed amidst the little houses—the first houses of Ypres.

Not one building remained intact. The hurricanes of steel had battered and penetrated them all.

✶✶✶✶✶✶

At one side of the street three wounded men were waiting for succour, having remained where they had fallen a few minutes before. They were poor inhabitants who had possibly been compelled by the need of obtaining food to come forth from some cellar. They did not call for assistance; they did not say a word, they did not even complain. Pale, stunned, suffering, and mute, they merely looked. The danger seemed to impose silence; there is an unconscious desire not to be heard, not to be discovered by the invisible and monstrous will to massacre which is in the air. Under the bombardment one had the vague impression of being searched for by death.

There were three of us, and we walked in Indian file along the wall towards the famous Grande Place, which only a few days ago afforded one of the most precious and complete visions of the arts of the world.

The route was not always easy. We had to avoid the holes which had been dug by the projectiles, to clamber over heaps of ruins, extricate ourselves from the labyrinths of innumerable fallen telephone wires, and every time we heard the voice of a shell we stopped immediately and irresistibly. We ceased to move with a strange and involuntary suddenness, like the automatic figures of the Three Kings in a Flemish clock when the last stroke of the hour sounds. Then, when an explosion had taken place, our mechanism was again set in motion, and we proceeded.

A little forest of red crosses arose on the edge of the road in a glade; they marked a group of fresh graves in which lay inhabitants who had come out of their places of refuge only to meet with death. In the tragic silence any noise seemed to be enormously exaggerated.

✶✶✶✶✶✶

Long *vistas* of ruins were open at every side street—demolished walls, beams fallen from roofs or stretching across between one house and another, and broken doors. The stricken houses had launched their walls against the opposite buildings, and remained open, empty, unrecognisable.

Having thus traversed the Rue d'Elverdinghe, which seemed as if it would never end, we entered the famous square, and for an indefinable time remained there at the corner, nailed as it were to the ground, stupefied and moved, full of admiration and grief and reverence, incapable of expressing our feelings, overcome by the grandeur and the sadness of that which we saw, intimidated by something that was both prodigious and sacred.

We seemed to be disturbing the solemn mystery of an august end. The life of seven centuries, which was still palpitating yesterday, was being extinguished in a solitude of horror in the pallid twilight of a winter day.

Gigantic and solemn above the mournful crowd of crumbling houses towered the monumental piles—torn, battered, devastated, but erect and still proud. Undermined by the blows of the shells, showing long cracks, breached and broken, the noble stone walls of the Halles, the *hôtel de ville*, and the Cathedral of St. Martin remained standing, indescribable in death, still stretching towards the sky their proud towers without bells and without pinnacles, hollowed at their bases as though by blows of a monstrous axe.

******

We pointed to things with vague gestures, without being able to find words, and forgetting even to bend our backs when we heard the lamenting voice of the shells. None of us had ever seen Ypres, and together with the discouragement, caused by the vision of irreparable ruin, there was created in us the marvel of a revelation.

For the love and devotion of innumerable generations there had kept intact on the earth a wonderful corner of the twelfth century, and we, arriving in front of this marvel, whilst it was dissolving, surprised the dream at a moment when it was vanishing for ever.

All the rest of the world was plunged in the barbarism of the Middle Ages when the Flemish peace had Ypres for its centre. It was the wealthy and serious merchants of Ypres who created the Halles, the market of the world, the capital of business, the incomparable seat of commerce, the parliament of rulers and of people. Dante had not then been born, and already the Halles of Ypres were a century old.

The love of Ypres gave to the Halles and to the old Grande Place a perennial youth. Ypres adored these eloquent and austere witnesses to her past, which told the story of her ancient power. She protected, defended them, never permitted the weight of centuries to do them any injury. Oppressed by famine and pestilence, the people of Ypres rebelled, sacked, and burned; but the Halles remained. The people of Ghent arrived in arms, their Allies the English arrived; they besieged Ypres, entered and laid waste; but the Halles remained. The Iconoclasts sacked the town, but the Halles remained. The Duke of Alba's troops arrived and persecuted Ypres—then fallen into decay—but the Halles remained. Alexander Farnese conquered the town and abandoned it to the excesses of his soldiery; but the Halles remained. Four times in one century the French took Ypres, but the Halles remained. They remained because the most brutal troops were conquered by their age and their potent grace. There was no passion, no ferocity that could resist such imposing severity and harmony. A respectful circle was formed, and the torch and the sword were lowered before that splendour of the past.

But the butcher of ancient glories has come; the blind Teutonic cataclysm has fallen upon unarmed and tranquil Ypres, and the portentous life is now extinct. There remains nothing but the gigantic ruins, isolated walls, the corpses of monuments which preserve a sublime expression of disdainful power.

★★★★★★

The bells have fallen. The last hour they chimed was seven in the morning of Sunday, November 22.

At a quarter past seven the belfry received its first mortal wound.

But the first night, according to ancient usage, from the tumult of the august tower there descended upon Ypres—not yet completely deserted—the notes of the horn of the night watchman, who hour by hour sent to the four cardinal points the announcement that all was well!

All around the gabled houses are abandoned in their last agony. They are those pointed houses, dwellings of a distant epoch, which give an ineffable impression of familiar calm and patriarchal life, buildings with faces inexpressibly benevolent, paternal, sweet and grave. Through the broken windows our gaze penetrates into comers which recall certain interiors of Flemish art. In these interiors, until yesterday, close to the windows, with their little leaded panes, the placid ladies of Ypres wove in traditional calm their arabesques of lace. Their agile and sapient fingers produced white, flowery patterns that were as light as foam. For Ghent had taken from Ypres the industry of its linens, England that of its cloths, Paris that of its damasks, but no country had had the power, the placidity, the patience, and the taste to imitate its lace. Here the old industry lived, modest and silent.

The mediaeval city slept its great sleep amidst the tumult of the outside world as if the Kasteelgracht and the Majoorgracht, the wide canals which encircle it and were its gates, were enchanted and had isolated it from swift innovations.

✶✶✶✶✶✶

In the war between Germany and the Halles of Ypres, in the war between Germany and the Library of Louvain, between Germany and the cathedral of Rheims, it is not possible to remain neutral.

CHAPTER 9

The Winter Campaign

The first purpose of the Allies' scheme of military envelopment was to arrest and eventually to break the German offensive. Even after their losses in the Battle of Ypres and the concurrent Battle on the Yser, the Germans still had on the West a superiority in numbers. The shock of those defeats was bitter. That is sufficiently proved by the proclamation which soon afterwards the Emperor of Germany issued to his troops. A cruel hour, he told them, had struck for them and for the Fatherland. He exhorted them to meet it with a greater determination. For a time Germany became a land of mourning. The German newspapers of this date, the later part of November, appeared day by day with pages of private obituary advertisements. The dream of conquest, except as regarded Belgium, was shattered, and it was realised that even to keep that country as a reward of what were called the sacrifices made, Germany would have to face a struggle to the death with powers whose united superiority was now only too manifest.

That mood, however, soon passed, and feeling, directed at the outset of the war against Russia, was with a redoubled intensity excited against England. The reasons are not far to seek. Extraordinary efforts had become necessary, not only on the East to repair the disaster of the Battle of the Vistula, and to furnish General von Hindenburg with the forces for his great "drive" towards Warsaw, but to make good the wastage on the West.

It is a recognised axiom among military men that for such a scheme as the Germans had in view in France, the lowest superiority in numbers necessary is a proportion of four to three. Even that assumes equal training and equipment, and equal skill in leadership. The last factor, skill in leadership, which is in war the most difficult to estimate beforehand, is, at the same time, as this struggle has proved, tremendously important. In regard to it the odds were heavily against the Germans. The Battle of Ypres, it has become evident, was on their part a series of bad mistakes—mistakes which were not seen until too late. After the defeat at Reims Count von Moltke was removed from his place as Chief of the Staff and Baron von Falkenheyn appointed. The strategical scheme of Baron von Falkenheyn was sound and bold enough if Antwerp had not got into the way of it, and if, too, the tactical blunders of Ypres had not ruined its execution.

Besides defects in leadership, the Germans had to face the striking comparative deficiency of their field artillery, and the fact that their gunnery had not turned out so practically sound as that of the French. It followed that to resume the offensive they must have a superiority of even more than four to three. They had begun with a superiority of two to one. Yet through the unexpected skill in their opponents' leadership they had been foiled and had had their initiative wrested from them. In view, however, of the demands of the campaign on the East, this necessary weight of numbers they could not on the West supply. One resource was to make it up by an appeal to the spirit of the army. That took the form of an unusually liberal distribution of rewards for individual valour.

The Battle of Ypres had at one and the same time brought the second German plan of a Western offensive to the ground, and ensured the accomplishment of General Joffre's envelopment scheme. There was nothing now before the German Staff, therefore, but to attack that envelopment scheme while it remained, as they thought, still in its inceptive stages. If we turn to the day-to-day record of the operations as disclosed in the official reports we shall at once see that there was on the part of the enemy a series of attempted wedging movements. They tried by wedging to break the Allied front simultaneously at Roye and at Arras. This, had it been successful, would have forced out the section of the Allied front lying between those points, and have broken up the Allied position.

The movement was not successful. Another movement of this kind was tried between La Bassée on the one side and the Yser on the other. This time the Germans did get a foothold on the west side of the Yser. They were driven out of it, however, by the Belgians cutting the dykes and flooding the country all along the lower course of the river. When the flood burst upon them large numbers of the enemy caught in their entrenchment diggings were drowned. (See note following). Many of their guns could not be recovered. A third of these wedging attempts was made between La Bassée and Arras. Though they led to desperate fighting, these efforts proved barren of result.

Note:— A correspondent of the Paris *Gaulois*, describing the annihilation of a brigade (nearly 9,000) Wurtembergers by the floods on November 4, wrote:

> At midday, the Wurtembergers, in formidable numbers, had succeeded, under the protection of their artillery, in crossing the Yser on planks,
>
> After a week's fighting the river was choked with sunken boats, trunks of trees, bodies of men, and carcases of horses. It was over a veritable bridge of corpses that the enemy passed.
>
> Meanwhile the Allied troops had taken up a position a little in the rear, some regiments remaining in position to cover this movement. Massed on the left bank of the Yser, the enemy's infantry prepared to attack. Some caps skilfully arranged over empty trenches drew the German artillery, which wasted its shells on the decoy. Then the Wurtembergers advanced, and were astonished to find, instead of bodies of the enemy, nothing but a few caps. Just then a loud rumbling noise was heard in a westerly direction. The noise gradually became clearer, resembling the rush of the tide. Suddenly a flood of seething water burst upon the astonished Germans.
>
> Trees and corpses were carried on the current, which swept everything before it. Cries of rage and terror came from the German lines. It was too late, down came the torrent, and in a few moments the enemy's trenches were filled. The terrified herd of Wurtembergers fled to the high ground, to get clear of the inundation, but from the heights the Allied artillery poured volleys of shrapnel into them. The enemy was taken between water and fire. Those who escaped drowning succumbed to our bullets or shells. A few came to our lines, thus evading death by captivity. This was the end of the Wurtemberg brigade.

Let us turn to the side of the Allies. For them the first necessity was to solidify their front. If they could do that they would:

> (1) Hold these German armies so that they would be able neither to advance nor to retreat whatever might be the develop-

ments of the war on the East front. That meant that the Germans must fight with divided forces, and feed the struggle on the East out of their last reserves.

(2) Bring into fullest play the Allies' superiority in field guns, and by imposing on the enemy the necessity of constant counterattacks, eliminate in the end his advantage in numbers. The effects of this elimination would be that his power in any event of resuming the offensive would progressively disappear, and that, as the process proceeded, the advantage in numbers would pass to the Allied side, and eventually make an Allied offensive both practicable and successful.

Now it is quite certain on the events which have since taken place that the German Headquarters Staff clearly recognised these possibilities. Not only is that shown by the heavy losses they incurred in the wedging battles, which lasted from the middle of November to early part of February, but in the adoption of tactics, designed, as their relative strength in numbers fell, to economise their force. In short, not being able to change the features of the situation, they made a virtue of necessity by trying as far as they could to convert their front into an impregnable barrier of defence, and concurrently doing their utmost to increase the Allies' losses.

Evidently both these means were calculated to delay the accomplishment of the Allied scheme. If at the same time there could be set on foot in the Allied countries the legend, not that the Germans had failed in their great invasion project, as they had, but that they were successfully withstanding an attempt of the Allied forces to push them back, then public opinion in the Allied countries might grow tired of the struggle, and at the finish withdraw from it, leaving Belgium in German hands. The government of Germany well knew that in England more especially, where the misconception of military operations was profound, operations would be estimated on the, for the immediate purposes of this campaign, entirely false basis of a movement of the front from place to place. The object of the Allied commanders, and the conditions of a successful Allied advance would, in all probability, be alike misunderstood. Experience has shown that these calculations were only too well founded. The nearer the Allied scheme approached to accomplishment, the more energetic became the efforts to propagate the notion that it was a failure.

The German plan of defence, which may be dealt with first, had then, apart from political calculations, two main features. The first was the fortification along their front of advantageous points in such a manner that they could be permanently held. The second was an elaboration of the tactics of trench warfare.

From Ypres southwards to the spur of Notre Dame de Lorette near Arras the German front followed approximately the "inland coastline" already spoken of, and the only break in it geographically of any consequence was the valley of the Lys, the flat stretch lying between the hills south of Ypres and the spur at Aubers south-west of Lille.

On the promontories of this "coastline" the enemy proceeded to fortify themselves. They did the same at other points along their front and notably on the ridge across Champagne, and on the hills to the south-east of Verdun, as well as on the eastern spurs of the Vosges. Simultaneously in the trench warfare they revived grenade throwing, and the use of the trench mortar, expedients which had disappeared from military operations for 200 years. These devices were accompanied by systematic sniping. As skill with the rifle is not a strong point with the German army, a prismatic telescopic sight was invented. This reduced sniping practically to a mechanical trick. If the object fired at was centred on the prism a hit became a certainty—wind permitting. Sapping and mining were also persistently carried on, and the front became for mile after mile a monstrous network of pits, barbed-wire entanglements, electric alarm traps, and obstacles of every sort. In short, what the Germans lacked in comprehensive military skill they made up in laborious detail.

If now we glance at the activity of the Allies, we find that the hardest part of their work was that of solidifying their line in order in the first place to make it invulnerable against German counter-attacks. Those counter-attacks were, as we have seen, to begin with heavy. In support of them the advantage which the enemy then had in howitzers was utilised to the full. During the first weeks of the winter campaign the Allied troops had to hold trenches for the most part hastily made in the stress of battle, and hold them both against this prodigal bombardment with heavy German shells, and through bitter conditions of wet and cold. To reach their trenches along the flooded area in Flanders men had in some places to cross stretches of country on planks, the targets in coming and going for the enemy's shrapnel. The weather, too, was sometimes so severe that the water in the men's drinking bottles turned to ice. The trenches were frozen puddles.

Writing at this time the French "Eye Witness" said:

From the sea to the Lys the operations to the north of the Lys have become terribly difficult. The liquid and cold mud from which the men suffered invaded the breeches of the guns, so that they could no longer fire, and they had to fight with the butt-end of their rifles and with their fists. Our soldiers, according to the expression of one of their leaders, have become blocks of mud. The attempt has been successful to provide for them when they leave the trenches a proper bath and a complete change of linen, which they appreciate very much. Their unalterable good humour enables them to endure with the best possible grace the rough life which is imposed upon them."

A vivid impression of Flanders at this time (the end of November) has been recorded by Alice and Claude Askew, who as members of Dr. Hector Munro's Red Cross Ambulance Corps went to the front to distribute woollen comforters, cigarettes, coffee and chocolates:

Up at Furnes the cold was terrible. The picturesque old town has been shelled twice, but as yet no great damage has been done, and the doctors and nurses working up at the Field Hospital—once a college—are hoping that their hospital may be spared, for this hospital, with its hundred beds and capable band of workers, is doing splendid service.

The patients are so cheerful. Those who are well enough smoke—how the soldier loves his "fag" and how lightly they take their injuries.

★★★★★★

Mr. Seeker was operating in the theatre—a patient had just been brought in from the trenches and immediate operation was necessary. A few oil lamps supplied the only illumination; the room was in complete shadow save round the operating table. Outside the wind howled and moaned, and firing could be heard in the distance. We felt very close to the naked heart of war.

The drive back to Dunkirk a few hours later was a strange drive. The road has been broken and battered by the passing of countless military wagons, trodden down by marching feet, it has become a furrow, the plough of war has been over it. On either side gaunt trees lift up gaunt boughs; their branches look like skeleton fingers pointing to the sky, and they look like grim sentinels; the water is half frozen in the dykes.

The whole thing seems unreal—the torn road—those blurred lines of men—the distant gun fire. The effect is that of a dream. We have seen the grim and terrible side of war—the bleeding side.

The moon—a pale sickle moon—shines out of the dun sky—the cold becomes more intense every moment—more freezing.

By continuous labour, however, the entrenchment system developed bit by bit into a vast underground military town. The fire trenches were connected by zigzag communication ways with supports trenches in the rear. From the latter opened the "dugouts" which were the dwelling places of the men on trench duty. Made and furnished out of the wreckage of towns and villages, some of the "dugouts" had doors and windows. Here and there the appointments of these underground quarters included desks and long-case clocks. Trench pumps were installed, and the troops provided with sheepskin coats. Entrenchment kitchens, too, were fitted up. The work of improvement went on in fact without a pause.

By day, where fighting was not in progress, these mazes of trenches seemed unutterable desolations of deserted silence. No sign of movement betrayed the thousands who were in them. At night, however, they were scenes of incessant activity. It was by night that entanglements were laid and defences strengthened. At night took place the changes and reliefs. From their billets in the cellars or lower stories of a ruined farm, the smashed windows barricaded with planks and sandbags, or from quarters in some deserted village or abandoned works, the reliefs moved across a country totally without lights, felt their way along lanes and roads pitted into craters by shells; navigated on planks and temporary bridges, ditches, streams, and canals; or crept under the shelter of partly demolished walls, until the rear communication ways into the trenches were reached. In this manner nearly all movements close to the firing line was made.

Acknowledgment too high can never be paid to the devotion and valour of the men who, through the weeks of an unusually dreary and bitter winter, both withstood the fury of the German attacks, and patiently day by day and night by night, solidified the barrier which was to consummate the enemy's ruin. Dangerous though it was the work may well have appeared unheroic. To some interpreters of public opinion at home it did appear unheroic. The soldiers' devotion, however, is a devotion to duty. This was, in his dispatch of November 20, well expressed by the British "Eye Witness."

> It is difficult to do justice amid comfortable surroundings to the fortitude of those who day and night support the rigour of life in the trenches. It is true that everything is done for them which foresight and experience can suggest. It is true that by universal admission the rations are unlimited in amount and excellent in quality. But no attention and care can make trench life in winter anything but an extreme test of soldierly fortitude.
>
> It is a small thing that it is dangerous, for danger is the condition of a soldier's life; but it is monotonous, it is damp, it is insanitary, it is intolerably cold, and it is a strain upon the nerves. This war, more than any other, is one of unrecorded heroisms.

Not only the British Army, however, but the French and the Belgian Armies had unshaken confidence in their leaders, and with good reason. In time the entrenched front became completely organised, a system of settled communications linked up by telephone wires in every direction. The French trenches formed a seemingly endless labyrinth. In Flanders along the Yser rats, driven out of their usual haunts and starving in the desolated country, took up their abode with the men in the dug-outs, and became domesticated and friendly.

To many whose ideas of war remained based on the marches and counter-marches of earlier campaigns it was puzzling to see armies of hitherto unheard of magnitude thus fortifying themselves against each other. Taken together the combatants numbered millions. Their diggings stretched over more than 500 miles of country. A vast amount of labour is needed to complete a modern entrenched post, yet such posts were to be counted along these lines not by thousands but by tens of thousands.

It has been stated that in face of the hugely multiplied power of modern firearms, and of the destructiveness of modern high explosives as used now in war, there is no alternative save for the fighting hosts of the present day to dig themselves in, and thus to remain locked in a deadly embrace. The explanation is crude. Like the astonishment called forth by this spectacle because it was unprecedented, the idea that all this represented merely a "deadlock" sprang from failure to grasp the realities of this gigantic struggle.

At the back of every operation of war there is a strategic purpose. In this instance, so far from there being no strategy in the so-called impasse, it was wholly dictated by strategy. So far from there being no manoeuvres in it, it was nothing else, from the beginning, but a mighty series of manoeuvres. They were modern manoeuvres, not ancient, but that is all.

To every student of this campaign with a knowledge of military affairs, the strategy on both sides which brought about this situation has been clear. Let it be remembered that entrenchment economises force. The proposition presented to General Joffre was that of arresting and breaking the offensive of an enemy not only superior in numbers, but with traditions which led him to cling to and cherish the offensive as his chief instrument of victory. General Joffre therefore knew that the Germans would struggle to regain the offensive until their power to do so became too exhausted to keep up the effort. He knew further that in the position in which he had succeeded in placing them they must make that effort at a disadvantage, and that that advantage must grow rather than diminish. For these reasons it was that the labour of entrenching was undertaken by the Allied troops. No part of that labour was thrown away.

In enclosing the Germans in an entrenched front he so economised his force that it became, though less in number, equal to that of the enemy in power. The simple proof of that is that the Germans were unable to break the barrier. They did their utmost to break it. Their success or their failure in the war depended upon being able to break it. They sacrificed at Ypres, on the Yser, and in later battles more than half a million of men in the endeavour to break it. It remained firm against every assault.

Nor was the loss of life the only loss. These battles has led to a vast, and as it proved, wasteful expenditure of ammunition. Since the barrier could not be broken, the question now was how to render the envelopment scheme abortive by inflicting on the Allies losses which would delay or make impossible the offensive on the part of the Allies to which the scheme was designed to lead. Expedients to that end had to be devised more effective than the fire of heavy howitzers. They must also be less costly expedients. Thus hand grenades and trench mortars reappeared, and mechanical sniping. The reserve of shells with which Germany had begun the war was used up. Such munitions had to be employed more sparingly. Besides, owing to the scarcity of copper resulting from the British naval blockade, both the cost and the difficulty of manufacturing shells had immensely increased.

The German ordinary grenade was nothing more than the small

iron bomb which had been used during the campaigns in Flanders in the seventeenth century. It was now filled with a charge of guncotton, and hurled into the hostile trenches by hand. Another variety had attached to the globe a short iron stump. This enabled the grenade to be stuck on to the muzzle of a rifle, and fired into the opposing trenches when the distance was too great to allow of the use of hand bombs. The trench mortar fired in the same way an iron globular bomb about a foot in diameter. The bomb was stuck on to the muzzle of the mortar by a short iron stump projecting from it, and filled with a heavy charge of nitro-glycerine, was fired at a high angle, so that it might fall right into a hostile trench and by the tremendous force of the explosion wreck it.

These projectiles, grenades and mortar bombs, were now turned out of the German arsenals in huge quantities. They were both much cheaper than shells, always a primary consideration in German warfare, and the mortar bombs required no copper driving bands.

In addition to these expedients mines were resorted to. Several blind saps—tunnels slightly below the surface—driven towards a hostile line of trench would be connected by a cross tunnel, and in this just in front of the trench the mines would be laid. At the moment chosen for attack they would be exploded from the German position by electricity, and a rush made to occupy the craters so formed. Yet another ruse was to drive an open sap—a narrow zigzag cutting—to a point commanding a hostile trench, and there install a machine gun. For daring in these operations military distinctions were freely bestowed, and it is not surprising that in carrying them out many of the enemy displayed an audacious cunning.

When, however, we consider that the British and Belgians alike were much more expert riflemen, and that all three Allies as time went on steadily emphasised their ascendancy in artillery, the failure of these efforts of German perseverance to make up for the German want of military genius, was, it is not difficult to see, inevitable. The British troops improvised hand grenades out of army jam or beef tins. In grenade throwing they speedily became expert. Every German device was countered and improved upon. Parties engaged in mining met each other underground, and fought it out hand to hand. To diminish the losses arising from rifle and artillery fire, the larger German operations in this stage of the campaign were their night attacks. In these night battles the country before plunged in total darkness would suddenly present the spectacle of flights of star shells and flares, mingled with the play of searchlights, and the lurid flash of guns and rifles.

Attack and counter-attack, varied in every interval of clearer weather by artillery duels, went on during week after week. The lines round Ypres and to the west of Lille, more especially about La Bassée, remained among the main scenes of German activity.

Round Ypres the shot-torn and shell-ploughed woods became those melancholy and unapproachable "zones of the dead" where the German slain lay unburied, and many of the wounded had been left miserably to perish.

The British "Eyewitness" wrote on November 20:

> Frequent allusion has been made to the losses of the enemy. Round Ypres we are continually finding fresh evidence of the slaughter inflicted. On November 15 one of our battalions, upon advancing discovered a German trench manned by seventeen corpses, while there were forty-nine more in a house close by. Next day a patrol discovered sixty dead in front of one trench, and fifty opposite another. In fact, all the farms and cottages to our front are charnel houses. The significance of such small numbers lies only in the fact that they represent the killed in a very small area.
>
> According to prisoners the German attempts to take Ypres have proved costly. One man stated that there were only fifteen survivors out of his platoon which went into action fifty strong; another reported that of 250 men who advanced with him only nineteen returned.
>
> It is believed that one Bavarian regiment, 3,000 strong, which left Bavaria for the front on October 19, had only 1,200 men left before the attack made along the Menin-Ypres road on November 14, when it again suffered severely. The plight of some of the units of the new formations is even worse. One regiment of reserve corps having but 600 men out of 3,000.
>
> If the period since the beginning of the war is considered the numbers are greater. For instance of the 15th Corps one regiment has lost sixty officers and 2,560 men, and another has lost 3,000 men. These figures include casualties of every kind—killed, wounded, and missing.

By dint of persistence the Germans succeeded in establishing on the west bank of the Yser a bridgehead at a point known as the Ferryman's Hut. They lost it, however, on November 27.

The French official account says:

> The action was particularly brilliant. Several German trenches were carried in succession.
>
> The operation was one of the most arduous and difficult tasks which our troops have accomplished. The object was to drive from the left bank of the Yser the Germans who had succeeded in establishing themselves there for a length of over a mile.
>
> The difficulty in the attack lay in the fact that the canal was bordered by marshes which could not be crossed, and the only way of approach was along the bank and on a very narrow front. Moreover, the right bank, where the enemy had taken up his position, dominated the left bank, which was exposed to a machine-gun fire. The assault on the Ferryman's hut was delivered by a detachment of 100 volunteers from the African battalions.
>
> Our men fought knee deep in the water in a downpour of rain. The Germans displayed the greatest courage, and our men had to kill one officer and fifteen men who refused to surrender.
>
> In the ferryman's hut itself, which had been turned into a little fort, there were fifty-three lying dead, two of whom were officers. They had been killed by our 8.6 shells. Close by was the wreckage of their searchlight and their machine guns.

Across the Yser the Germans had tried to push their outposts westward as far as possible. Mr. A. Beaumont, special correspondent of the *Daily Telegraph*, gathered the story of one of these expeditions which reached a ruined village:

> Amid the ruins the church alone was standing, though the belfry was demolished. A score of Germans on outpost duty had taken shelter in the church for the night. They found the sexton, an old man of more than seventy, and mercilessly flogged him because he would not or could not tell them where the enemy was.
>
> He crept out into the fields, found a French company concealed in some trenches, and told them his story. There was an instant rush of picked men into the village, the church was surrounded. The Germans taken by surprise hid in the choir, but to light up the place the old sexton found a bundle of straw, to which he set fire. As he held it up the Germans were slain on the spot.

The efforts of the Germans were directed not only towards gaining a crossing over the Yser, but to driving the British out of the valley of the Lys. This it has already been noted was geographically a weak point in their front. Down the valley of the Lys, besides, lay the railway junctions of Menin and Courtrai, vital to the maintenance of their positions alike between the Lys and the sea, and from Lille to Arras. South of Ypres they had at length succeeded by sapping and mining in getting possession of the Kleine Zillebeke ridge, though they had been unable to capture it in the battle. At the same time they tried to push the British line westward from Lille. Repeated and desperate attacks were made on the British posts at Cuinchy and Givenchy. Cuinchy they captured. Later, however, the place was retaken, and with it a large depot of German bombs and hand grenades. On January 25 the enemy, advancing from La Bassée in two powerful columns, made a furious effort to take Givenchy. Five assaults were delivered against that place. The first attack was in the nature of a surprise.

Unexpectedly in the cold and misty dawn the mass, brought up with secrecy during the night, surged from the German trenches. The British trenches were not more than 100 yards away. Across this space, ankle deep in mud, the attackers ploughed their way despite severe losses. The British trenches were taken, though not without a stiff fight. The resistance enabled the British supports to be called out. Charging into Givenchy village the Germans found themselves confronted at the end of the main street by these additional troops. The fire lasted only seconds. Without further ado the British dashed in with the bayonet. The clash was desperate. It was a *mêlée* of man to man. Not only bayonets were used. Many Germans were knocked out by British soldiers' fists. The remnant who could not get out of the village in time sought refuge in the houses. They were hunted out. One man broke into a house where eight Germans had sheltered themselves, bayoneted four, and made prisoners of the others.

With the defeat of this attack the British regained the trenches lost. The later attacks of the enemy never got home. A determined struggle was all this while being waged to the south of La Bassée in the area of the brickfields. At one point the Germans broke through the British line. Early in the afternoon, however, a combined French and British counter-attack drove them back. Here, too, there was hand to hand fighting.

From October onwards La Bassée remained one of the hottest corners in the war. Perched on an inland promontory which had been elaborately fortified, the German front here formed a salient. It was an important part of their plan to pierce the Allied front at this point. To carry out that plan they made repeated attacks in great force. That these attacks failed was due to the remarkable fighting qualities of the troops opposed to them. About this struggle, of vital importance in its bearing on the campaign, many stories have been told. The two following, both authentic, illustrate the spirit which inspired our men, British and Indians alike:

> In one trench which had become in the course of the fighting more or less isolated, forty of our men continued to hold firm until every one of them was either killed or wounded. Eventually there were only three left capable of firing, and these three continued to hold the enemy at bay. In the meantime word had been brought to those in rear that their ammunition was nearly exhausted, and seven men, the strongest available, were selected to bring up as much ammunition as they could carry. These latter found the three wounded survivors still standing amid the bodies of their dead and disabled comrades and still firing steadily. The support, slender as it was, came in the nick of time, for at that moment the Germans launched another assault, which, like the previous ones, was beaten off, and the position saved.
>
> A very striking instance of resource and presence of mind was shown by a private (Indian) since been promoted from the ranks in recognition of his services. He and another were instructed to creep out of the trench they were defending in order to make observations of a German trench 200 yards away. They advanced, creeping in the dark, with about forty yards laterally between them. When they had covered half the distance a brilliant German searchlight was suddenly flung over the space which divided the two trenches. The flood of light left one of the two fully exposed, while just avoiding with its outer rim his companion.
>
> Concealment was useless for the man so exposed, and he was quick-witted enough to realise that no ordinary resource would save his life. He at once rose to his feet, and, in view of the British trench, advanced, *salaaming* to the German trench. Its occupants, taken aback by so unusual an advance, ceased fire. He still advanced, and, approaching quite close to the trench, was

allowed after some dumb show to enter. A dialogue followed. The Germans, anxious to define his status, mentioned several Indian nationalities. He shook his head until the word Mussulman was mentioned. Then he nodded vigorously. A moment later his questioners mentioned the British. He drew his hand across his throat with a lively gesture of disgust. The Germans, encouraged by this indication, gave him some rations and a blanket.

He spent the night with them. Next morning, by the use of his fingers, he indicated to a superior officer who had been sent for to deal with so novel a case, that there were twenty-five other Mussulmen in his trench, whom, if released, he could certainly bring in. The Germans, completely deceived, gave him a final cup of coffee, and set him on this promising errand. He rejoined his friends, who had long since given him up, with a report of far more than local interest.

These acts of valour are but typical of a thousand like them. By such devotion to the soldier's ideal—his duty—by a courage, a morale, and a disciplined fortitude which have never been surpassed in any armies at any time, the first and essential part, the foundation, of the Allied generals' scheme, the most brilliant and daring stroke of strategy till then attempted in war, was accomplished. The Germans were held as in a vice.

CHAPTER 10

Neuve Chapelle

All through the winter campaign the enemy had been incessantly trying to sap and mine forward, and not only at La Bassée but right across the valley of the Lys to the hills south of Ypres.

He was anxious to make this gap secure. It was the key of his position along the line from Noyon to the sea.

The construction of the Allies' entrenchment barrier was but the first stage of their great plan. At once after that barrier had been made the second stage was entered upon. The second stage was that of drawing one by one the enemy's teeth in the shape of the carefully fortified promontories and ridges, selected by him with an eye to their defensive possibilities. As in the entrenchment stage this was gone about methodically. Neither time was lost, ammunition wasted, nor lives thrown away.

Guns were massed against the position picked out for assault. They were massed without being seen. The present day gunner does not trust to the eye. He uses his gun with mathematical precision. This system the French artillerists had reduced to an exact science. At a given time these guns opened at the same instant, and on a preconcerted plan swept the position with a squall of fire. In this tornado everything, entanglements and obstructions, were cut to pieces; trenches crumbled; concrete redoubts were split into ruins. Amid the hurricane of lead nothing could live. Having swept the position the guns drew a curtain of fire behind it while the infantry advanced to the attack.

More than once it happened that the French infantry charged up to and captured trenches after this treatment without losing a man. None were left to oppose them. In fact, however, no assaults were made until the "lie" of the enemy's trenches and defences was thoroughly known.

The first German "tooth" drawn under this system was their fortification on the spur at Vermelles, four miles to the south of La Bassée. That was on December 7. After that fangs were one by one extracted all round the hostile front.[1]

One of these fangs was the German position on the spur at La Bassée. Along the south side of this spur early in February the Irish Guards and the Coldstreams turned the enemy out of his defences among the brick stacks there, and made the position useless to him save for purposes of defence.

Affairs having reached this stage the plan of assault was decided upon by Sir John French on February 19. It was to be carried out by the British First Army, under the command of Gen. Sir Douglas Haig, with the support of a large force of heavy artillery, a division of cavalry and some infantry of the general reserve.

The attack was to be directed against Neuve Chapelle. Holding attacks, that is practically feints, were to be made at the same time by the Second Army against La Bassée from the south and by the 4th Army Corps and the Indian Army Corps to the north.

The German position at La Bassée formed a buttress of the line which they had been striving to draw across the valley of the Lys. Their line from La Bassée across the flats of the valley as far as the hills south of Ypres had become a maze of diggings and entanglements, and was deemed to be impregnable. It was important to break this barrier. For five months at enormous cost the enemy had fought to build it up and to maintain it.

The village of Neuve Chapelle lay about halfway between the spur of La Bassée on the south and the Lys on the north. The distance between the promontory on the one side and the river on the other is some eight miles. Neuve Chapelle was on the flat. From La Bassée round behind Neuve Chapelle the "inland coastline" curves, forming a bay completed near the villages of Fournes and Aubers by another promontory known as the Haut Pommeau. The distance from La Bassée to Fournes as the crow flies is five miles. Beyond Fournes again the "inland coastline" bends round sharply, and describes a much greater bay in which is situated the city of Lille. Eastward of Neuve Chapelle on the slope of the higher land is the Bois de Biez, and this with the hamlet of Pietre it was one of the British objectives to seize.

---

1. other examples are the Spur at Notre Dame de Lorette near Arras; the ridge north of Beausejour in Champagne; the Crete de Combres at Les Eparges on the Meuse; the Bois de Pietre on the Moselle; and Hartmannsweilerkopf in Alsace.

With these places in British hands the German hold on both Lille and La Bassée would be rendered precarious.

Now let us look, in its general aspects, at the British tactical plan.

A massed force of guns, including batteries of heavy howitzers, was at a given time (7.30 a.m. on the morning of March 10) to open on the German line of trenches, extending across the flat country and half-a mile or so to the west and in front of Neuve Chapelle. Behind these trenches ran the main road from La Bassée to Armentières. For thirty-five minutes the guns were to keep up their squall of fire. By that time it was calculated the German trenches would be knocked to pieces; the entanglements and obstacles cut through; and the defending troops either killed, wounded, or demoralised. At the end of the thirty-five minutes the infantry of the First Army were to rush the position. Meanwhile, the artillery was to alter the range and sweep with a like squall of fire Neuve Chapelle and the German second line of defences to the north and south of the village. Then the infantry were to advance to this second line. In turn the artillery were now to sweep the area beyond the village, and to throw a curtain of fire along the slopes of the higher land. While this was being done the infantry were again to advance from Neuve Chapelle on to the slopes more particularly towards the Bois de Biez and Pietre, while the guns further extended their range.

It will be seen that the infantry rushes had to take place between the artillery squalls. The latter had of necessity to be regulated by time table. It was an application on a large scale of the tactics carried out in Champagne and round Arras, Roye, and at Les Esparges.

Both the massing of the guns and that of the troops intended for this operation was carried out alike with secrecy and success. The batteries during several days preceding the battle had taken up their allotted positions without the Germans becoming aware of it. From the German lines the guns of course were out of sight. The troops had been massed in the first instance at points in the rear. From these they marched during the night before the battle to the British line of trenches. It is remarkable that the movement of these hosts remained undetected. Amid the unrelieved darkness of the ruined country they set out along the shell-pitted roads, regiment after regiment, brigade following brigade. They moved as silently as possible, as silently as only British troops can when silence is called for. At ten o'clock on the evening of March 9 this march began. Through devastated and deserted villages passed the subdued tramp of these legions, men from every part of the British Isles, regiments famous for valour on many a field.

Behind the British lines the corps halted along the roadsides. After their march they were served with hot coffee. They extended for mile after mile—Highlanders and Riflemen; Territorials and Indians; a magnificent army, and in immediate command of it one ol the ablest and most resolute of British generals.

Still, apparently, the Germans suspected nothing. No outward sign of alertness was to be observed along their line. The soughing of the bleak night wind of March alone broke the silence. Then one by one the regiments moved by single files through the communication ways down into the trenches till these were filled with men. From the enemy's front there was yet no alarm, though their trenches were at many points less than 100 yards away.

Towards morning there comes out of the darkness a dull boom. A pause and then another. After a further pause a third. The guns are registering the range.

And now the faint light of dawn begins to break and the white wall of sandbags which marks the German front can be dimly made out, with here and there dark patches where the bags used are blue. Thousands of eyes watch it for evidence of movement. There is none.

From a prisoner afterwards taken it was learned that a German captain, hearing what he thought were unusual sounds, and seeing the British trenches opposite crowded, telephoned the alarm to the artillery. According to this story he was told there were no orders to open fire, and advised to mind his own business.

So at last day broke, and the hands of watches approached 7.30. With the inevitableness of fate the minutes sped. The signal time was reached.

The guns—hundreds of guns—spoke at the same instant in an overpowering crash of intensified thunder. The earth shook as though smitten. The German line appeared as if swept by an earthquake. It became a line of ceaseless explosions. Shells crashed upon it from minute to minute in thousands; the guns went at it at top speed. The wall of sandbags was tumbled and breached in all directions. Amid the spurting fires and the acrid smoke the bodies, or fragments of the bodies of men were hurled into the air. Some of these ghastly fragments were even blown into the British trenches. Back to the British trenches also wafted the sickly fumes of lyddite and cresolite. Shells whistled past only a few feet above the heads of the British infantry. The storm of shrapnel chopped the enemy's entanglements to pieces. The high explosives left his trenches shapeless. His laboriously made fortifications had been literally blasted out of being.

From behind a ragged wrack in the sky where aeroplanes were sailing, the sun came out, making still darker the cloud of smoke and dust hanging like a black pall over the German entrenchments. Where the sunlight touched them the British trenches flashed into rows of gleaming bayonets.

For the allotted thirty-five minutes the rain of fire went on. It paused as it had begun, on the instant. The momentary silence was as stunning as the uproar. It was the signal. The whistles blew for the charge.

The British infantry told off for the attack swarmed out of their trenches. There were five brigades of them : in the first line on the right to the south of Neuve Chapelle, the *Garhwalis* of the Meerut division of the Indian Army Corps; in the centre opposite Neuve Chapelle, the 25th; on the left to the north of Neuve Chapelle, the 23rd; in the second line the 22nd and the 21st.

The leading regiments of the 25th, the Lincolns and the Berkshires, cleared the space to the enemy's trenches with a rush. The German entanglements here had been chopped by the shells into mere litter. To reach the wreckage of the wall of sandbags was a matter of seconds. The enemy's trenches proved to be full of dead and dying. Such survivors as there were, paralysed with fright, surrendered. Then the two battalions swung one to the right, the other to the left and swept in both directions along the line. Against the Lincolns a remnant of the Germans still showed fight. The Lincolns went into them with the bayonet. Though desperate while it lasted, the struggle was brief. The men left alive surrendered. Against the Berkshires two German officers fought a machine gun, and continued to fight it until bayoneted.

In the track of the Lincolns and Berkshires came the Royal Irish Rifles and the Rifle Brigade. While the Berkshires and Lincolns were rounding up the prisoners, the Royal Irish and the Rifle Brigade moved forward towards Neuve Chapelle.

On the right the *Garhwalis* had equally rushed the German front. There, too, it had been a hand to hand finish, but soon over.

On the left, however, it was not the same story—not by any means the same story. The 23rd Brigade was made up of the Scottish Rifles, the 2nd Middlesex, the Devons and the West Yorkshires. Against the part of the German line they were told off to attack the guns had not done the work thoroughly. The enemy's mass of entanglements here followed a dip in the ground, and the shells had mostly missed.

Let it here be said that an accident of this kind is always liable to happen. It does not of necessity imply remissness on the part of the gunners, and involve blame. Difficulties like this will crop up in carrying out the best scheme of tactics. Indeed no great battle has ever yet been fought in which the unexpected has not been encountered, and had on the instant to be provided for.

At the same time, in a scheme of attack of this kind it is, apart from accidents, the underlying assumption on which the whole is reared that every part of the area under fire shall in the first instance be equally and fully swept. If that be not done then the infantry have imposed upon them a task which no men ought to be asked to face, and which deliberately they would never be asked to face. That was the position in which the Scottish Rifles and the 2nd Middlesex, two battalions who are among the flower of the army, found themselves. Rushing forward, they in a flash saw before them in this hollow the German entanglements standing almost intact. The work in front of them was the impossible.

Imagine the tragedy of it. They were swept by the fire of machine guns, by rifle volleys discharged from second to second, and showers of shrapnel. To go back would have thrown the whole plan of assault into confusion. It might mean the loss of the battle.

On the other hand, it was impossible to re-range the British batteries. The guns were now thundering out their *rafale* upon Neuve Chapelle and the German second line. In Neuve Chapelle and along that line were the enemy's local reserves. These or part of these, if there were any break in the rain of fire, would charge forward to reinforce their first line. They were there for the purpose.

Part of the Scottish Rifles got through. The entanglements in front of them had been wrecked. They reached the section of the German trenches which was their objective and overpowered the defenders. The other part was held up by the barbed wire. Then began a frantic struggle to smash through the webwork with the butts of rifles, to stamp it down, or to crawl through it. The effort was in vain. The bomb-throwers of the company dashed round in the track of their comrades who had already reached and captured the adjacent German trench. Through this trench they reached that still held and daringly bombed the Germans out of it. Meanwhile the others, forced to lie down, were sprayed both by the machine guns and by the enemy's shrapnel. A subaltern and 150 men were all who later answered to the roll-call.

The 2nd Middlesex fared no better. The instant they surged into the open two machine guns, one at each end of the section of the German trench they were to take opened upon them. Under this fire they had to clear a space of more than 120 yards. It was strewn as they raced forward with their dead and wounded. To them also the startling truth was revealed that the enemy's entanglements were still almost undamaged. Like the Scottish they tried to stamp and tear their way through. The effort was speedily seen to be a waste of life. They lay down amid the hail of bullets. A second time, and then a third they tried to break through. A message, however, had been got through to the guns. Relaid on to the German trench the artillery this time cut the entanglements through and the position, aided by a bombing party, was carried.

Such was the attack upon the German first line. But for this disaster to part of the 23rd Brigade, the casualties in this phase of the battle would have been comparatively slight.

The 25th and the *Garhwalis* completed their work before the time allotted for the fire squall against the village and the enemy's second line had expired. When this tornado began Neuve Chapelle was, although damaged, still standing. When the shell storm ceased, it had, save for the broken walls of the church, totally disappeared. This fair-sized place, which formerly had had some 3,000 inhabitants, was now pounded into shapeless ruins. The shells had fallen as elsewhere upon the cemetery. Tombstones had been blown about in all directions; graves torn open; coffins ploughed up and scattered in splinters together with the bones they had enclosed. In the churchyard had been posted a German detachment intended to defend that approach to the village by rifle and machine-gun fire from behind the gravestones. Most of these men lay among their gruesome surroundings dead or wounded. The whole village and its immediate neighbourhood was wrapped in smoke and dust.

Into this the moment that the guns had ceased the Rifle Brigade dashed. The German defence had been smashed. Some of the enemy continued to snipe from behind bits of wall, broken tombstones, or the wrecks of carts. Among the ruins of a few outlying houses which had escaped complete destruction others put up a fight with machine guns and potted at the British from window spaces. They were speedily disposed of. The rest, bewildered by the blast, were collected from the cellars and dug-outs in which they had sought refuge, coming up with their hands above their heads.² From the opposite direction the village had been stormed by the 3rd Gurkhas of the Indian Brigade. On the way they had got in with their *kukris* among a German detachment who attempted with machine guns to defend a group of houses by the cross roads at the south end of the place. The two corps, Riflemen and Gurkhas, old comrades in former fights, and each now equally dirty and blood-bespattered, cheered each other with enthusiasm.

The artillery tornado against Neuve Chapelle and its environs had been timed to last for half an hour. It began at 8.5 a.m.; it ended at 8.35 a.m. At the same instant the infantry advance against this second German line had swung out with a sledge-hammer energy. Within twenty-five minutes the village of Neuve Chapelle was in the British hands.

Thus in the centre this second wave of the onset had been crushingly successful. It was not immediately successful on the flanks. On the left flank, since the 23rd Brigade had been held up on the German first line, the troops of the 25th, who had captured the village, had to face north in order to enfilade the enemy still holding out against the 23rd. It was through this pressure as well as through the redirection of the guns, that these Germans still on that part of the first line were about eleven o'clock in the morning dislodged.

Meanwhile, through the gap in the enemy's first line which had been cleared by the 25th Brigade, the Devons, part of the 23rd, had come on and attacked on the German second line of defence, an orchard, triangular in shape and bounded along each face by a road, which the Germans had fortified. This, one of the strong points of the German second line, the Devons carried by storm. Later, when the Middlesex got through, they occupied the position.

Both the village of Neuve Chapelle and its environs over a con-

---

2. The correspondent who sent to the London News Agency a picturesque story of the battle (published in the *Daily Telegraph* of April 19, 1915), says: "Many strange incidents were observed. In one cellar a portly German was found dancing about in an agony of fear, screaming in a high-pitched voice in English: 'Mercy! mercy! I am married!' 'Your missus won't thank us for sending you home!' retorted one of the men who took him prisoner, and his life was spared. A Rifle Brigade subaltern, falling over a sandbag into a German trench, came upon two officers, hardly more than boys, their hands above their heads. Their faces were ashen grey; they were trembling. One said gravely in good English: 'Don't shoot! I am from London also!' They, too, were mercifully used."

siderable area north and south presented a network of German diggings, and before any further advance could be made it was essential that the whole of these should be in our hands. It was supposed that this area had been completely and thoroughly searched by the shell fire. Unfortunately, as in the instance of the fire directed against the German first line, that proved not to be the case. Just to the south of Neuve Chapelle there is a junction of roads. The main road which runs almost straight as a ruler from La Bassée to Estaires, meets at this point the main road to Armentières.

The two highways join at a rather acute angle, and in that angle there was a group of houses. This position the Germans had elaborately strengthened. Among the British troops it had earned the name of "Port Arthur." Remarkably enough some 200 yards of the German trenches at this place had been missed or practically missed by the fire storm. The attack here was assigned to the 22nd Brigade (British) and the 21st Brigade (Indian). The corps who faced the almost untouched length of German trench were the 59th Garhwalis, one of the finest battalions of the Indian Army. They met with the same experience as the Scottish Rifles, a frightful fire of machine guns, added to repeated rifle volleys. Some of these dauntless and wiry warriors managed to tear or wriggle through the entanglements and went into the Germans with the bayonet. They were overborne by numbers, but fought to the last man.

While this was going on the Leicesters, the entanglements in front of them having been cut, had on the right of the Indian troops carried the opposing German position, though under a cross fire from the enemy still holding out against the *Garhwalis*. They wheeled round to left and bombed the Germans out. Meanwhile the Seaforth Highlanders had been brought up for an attack upon the enemy from the opposite flank, and this was supported by a frontal attack from the 3rd (Territorial) Battalion of the London Regiment. The charge of the "terriers" formed one of the brilliant episodes of the battle. "Port Arthur" was at last finished, and the whole mass of German reserves who had for months inhabited this maze of diggings and fortifications, supposed to be impregnable, were either killed, wounded, prisoners, or on the run.

So much were the survivors on the run in fact, that the British troops were able to form up for the third swing in the advance without any opposition worth speaking about. Indeed, Sir John French states in his dispatch that the 21st Brigade formed up in the open without a shot being fired at them.

It was now about 1.30 in the afternoon. The part of the British line which needed to be strengthened for the further work in hand was the right wing. The 23rd Brigade needed to be reinforced, and in view of the more extended front which had to be covered as the advance proceeded, more troops were necessary. Not only was the front to be covered wider, but the further work on hand would probably turn out the stiffest. This work was an advance towards the slopes on the east and the seizure of decisive positions there.

Concurrently with the British infantry attack on the German second line the artillery had been searching this ground and the slopes, and although the Germans had been rushing up reinforcements and these were beginning to appear in the woods the curtain of fire made it out of the question for them to move farther forward.

Obviously it was all-important that the British line should be re-formed and reinforced for the further advance before enemy reinforcements could be massed.

The 4th Army Corps and the Indian Army Corps had therefore been ordered up in the forenoon. There was a delay in their arrival. Apparently it arose from bad roads. Whatever the exact cause the delay meant that recovering from their initial demoralisation, the Germans had organised several strong points of opposition. One of these points was a bridge on the little River Les Layes, which runs across the flats from just outside Neuve Chapelle to Armentières, where it falls into the Lys. At this bridge the 25th Brigade found themselves held up. The approaches were a nest of machine guns. The third stage of the British advance did not begin until 3.30 in the afternoon. Two good hours had been lost.

Not merely were the 25th Brigade held up, but the Indian troops of the Reserve, advancing towards the Bois de Biez, found themselves enfiladed by the fire of this German position. The Gurkhas indeed reached the wood, and entered it. They were under a cross fire, however, from front and flank, and in the end had to retreat. In the direction also of the Pietre road the 21st Brigade met with greatly superior opposition, and like the 25th could got get forward. This was the situation at nightfall. The British troops dug themselves in along this new line.

At daybreak on March 11 the battle was renewed with an attempt by the Germans to shell the British from their new positions During the night the enemy had brought up strong reinforcements and posted them in the woods and on the plateau. Their positions were energetically bombarded. Two German regiments in the Bois de Biez suffered heavily.

The enemy launched a counter-attack. Their columns were broken by the British fire. In pursuit of these beaten forces the British attack was renewed by the 4th Army Corps and the Indian Corps. The Germans, however, had also on their side established a new line. It was found necessary to deal with this as with the others, by a squall of artillery fire. But meantime the weather had changed. Rain and mist made accurate observation and reliable ranging out of the question.

That night further German reinforcements arrived. They were Saxons and Bavarians, mainly from Tourcoing. Before dawn on March 12 the German artillery opened upon Neuve Chapelle. Then in the dim light of breaking day two immense grey columns of German infantry were seen coming out of the woods towards Neuve Chapelle, one on the north-east, the other on the south-east. What is more they came on in mass formation. The British trenches, needless to say, had as usual been made as nearly as possible invisible. In that uncertain light the line even at quite a short distance away could not be made out. The Bavarians attacking from the south-east were still in column of route. An officer rode in their midst on horseback. Finding that they were close to the British line the charge was sounded. The mass came on in the closest formation. One minute they had uttered a cheer, the next a score or more of machine guns opened upon them. As though struck by lightning, the mass went down as it seemed, together. It changed into a writhing rampart of dead and wounded. Along it men still unhit, could be seen digging themselves in for sheer life, and even using corpses as a shelter.

It was a terrible and ghastly spectacle, the result of a terrible and ghastly blunder. Hardened as they were, even the British troops were sickened by it. From out of the heap wounded Germans crawled towards the British lines. Some of the British went out and helped them in.

The attack from the north-east was also a failure. Whether it was the fate of the Bavarians or not, the heart went out of it. At the beginning it was violent, but it utterly petered out.

These crushing repulses were again followed by a renewal of the British onset. It was directed against the village or rather the group of houses on the ridge known as the Moulin de Pietre. Through a sweeping "curtain" of German fire the British infantry stormed the enemy's trenches with grenade and bayonet. Nothing could stand against their tenacity. They held on to their new positions until nightfall. It was found, however, that to keep these positions in face of the enemy's strength was a game not worth the candle. The line was therefore withdrawn and consolidated.

This work occupied the night, so that when the morning of March 13 dawned the Germans found the British firmly entrenched east of Neuve Chapelle. The bombardment which the enemy at once opened from the Aubers ridge did very little damage. This, the fourth day following upon three days of hard and continuous fighting, was the most trying of all. The men were by this time in the last stage of fatigue. The devotion of the British soldier, however, is not readily fathomed.

Such was the Battle of Neuve Chapelle. It cost the lives of nearly 2,500 British heroes, and casualties to nearly 9,000 others, while 1,751 were listed as missing. The losses of the enemy were some 18,000. In his dispatch Sir John French says:

> The results attained were, in my opinion, wide and far-reaching.

Not only did the British attack breach a part of the German front which had been elaborately fortified, and prove the power to breach it, and at a cost to the attacking force actually less than the force defending, but it set back in a decisive manner a scheme which the Germans had for six months been striving regardless of cost to carry through—the barring of access to the valley of the Lys. That valley is the military main road into Belgium, and as already pointed out, it is along it that there lie the railway junctions vital to the German position between the coast and the Aisne, and vital consequently to their whole position on the West. From their point of view, too, this much more than the crossing of the Yser is the way to the coast. The struggle, therefore, for mastery of the valley of the Lys represents a most important phase of the war.

As to the losses in the Battle of Neuve Chapelle it is now clear that they were due mainly to two things—the parts in the German first and in the German second line of defences which escaped the effect of the artillery "*rafales*"; and the late arrival of the reserve on the first day. If the artillery sweep in each instance was not perfect, it is at once just and necessary to point out that the flatness of the country rendered ranging far from easy, and that in each instance the section missed was comparatively but a very small bit of the line under fire.

We are now in a position to sum up the military results gained in the operations briefly told in this story. They were, as will be seen, of the utmost importance. Had the British troops not been transferred when they were from the Aisne, the whole course of the Western campaign, and with it the whole course of the war, must have been changed. With the vast superiority in numbers which, as events proved, the Germans were able to put into the field even before the end of October, a superiority aggregating nearly a million men, they would have been able, round the uncompleted left flank of the Allies, not only to place themselves between the French and British forces and the coast, but, it is practically certain, to place themselves between the Allied armies and Paris. They would have gained an unspeakable strategical advantage, and possibly also, as a consequence, a succession of decisive victories.

As it was, by the employment of the British troops to extend the left wing of the Allied line, this strategical scheme of the enemy was nipped in its first stages. Not only that, but it enabled the Allied generals completely to turn the tables. In place of enveloping the Allied armies as they had proposed, the Germans found themselves enveloped. To escape from this situation, which they well knew meant carrying on the War East and West with inevitably divided forces, a condition which eliminated their main chance of victory, they were forced to fight the first battle of Ypres. Despite their immensely greater numerical strength, they lost it through a succession of tactical blunders. To that has to be added the brilliant resource shown by Sir John French, and never more brilliantly than in the crisis of the battle on October 31.

Enabling the Allies to maintain their envelopment, the first battle of Ypres, both definitely checked the German offensive on the West, defeated their attempt to re-seize the strategical initiative, pinned down and by degrees wasted their main forces, and what perhaps is most important of all, ensured the necessity on their part of a division of forces between the two fronts. It is absolutely true to say that the later weeks of October were the chief crisis of the war. Only it may be when the events of this war fall in the course of time into a more just perspective shall we appreciate all we owe to the men who fought through that campaign.

To deal with the later and second battle of Ypres is beyond present scope. This little book will have served its purpose if, bringing into light the strictly historic truth of momentous and arresting events which may determine the destiny of Europe for ages, it has revealed at the same time the noble courage and the grand endurance of the British soldier, and has shown the majesty with which, like his fathers, he can do battle for his country.

ALSO FROM LEONAUR
AVAILABLE IN SOFTCOVER OR HARDCOVER WITH DUST JACKET

THE ART OF WAR by Antoine Henri Jomini—Strategy & Tactics From the Age of Horse & Musket.

THE ART OF WAR by Sun Tzu and Pierre G. T. Beauregard—*The Art of War* by Sun Tzu and *Principles and Maxims of the Art of War* by Pierre G.T. Beauregard.

THE MILITARY RELIGIOUS ORDERS OF THE MIDDLE AGES by F. C. Woodhouse—The Knights Templar, Hospitaller and Others.

THE BENGAL NATIVE ARMY by F. G. Cardew—An Invaluable Reference Resource.

ARTILLERY THROUGH THE AGES—by Albert Manucy—A History of the DEvelopment and Use of Cannons, Mortars, Rockets & Projectiles from Earliest Times to the Nineteenth Century.

THE SWORD OF THE CROWN by Eric W. Sheppard—A History of the British Army to 1914.

THE 7TH (QUEEN'S OWN) HUSSARS: Volume 3—1818-1914 by C. R. B. Barrett—On Campaign During the Canadian Rebellion, the Indian Mutiny, the Sudan, Matabeleland, Mashonaland and the Boer War Volume 3: 1818-1914.

THE CAMPAIGN OF WATERLOO by Antoine Henri Jomini—A Political & Military History from the French perspective.

RIFLE & DRILL by S. Bertram Browne—The Enfield Rifle Musket, 1853 and the Drill of the British Soldier of the Mid-Victorian Period *A Companion to the New Rifle Musket* and *A Practical Guide to Squad and Setting-up Dtill*.

NAPOLEON'S MEN AND METHODS by Alexander L. Kielland—The Rise and Fall of the Emperor and His Men Who Fought by His Side.

THE WOMAN IN BATTLE by Loreta Janeta Velazquez—Soldier, Spy and Secret Service Agent for the Confederancy During the American Civil War.

THE BATTLE OF ORISKANY 1777 by Ellis H. Roberts—The Conflict for the Mowhawk Valley During the American War of Independenc.

PERSONAL RECOLLECTIONS OF JOAN OF ARC by Mark Twain.

CAESAR'S ARMY by Harry Pratt Judson—The Evolution, Composition, Tactics, Equipment & Battles of the Roman Army.

FREDERICK THE GREAT & THE SEVEN YEARS' WAR by F. W. Longman.

AVAILABLE ONLINE AT www.leonaur.com
AND FROM ALL GOOD BOOK STORES

ALSO FROM LEONAUR
AVAILABLE IN SOFTCOVER OR HARDCOVER WITH DUST JACKET

THE 9TH—THE KING'S (LIVERPOOL REGIMENT) IN THE GREAT WAR 1914 - 1918 *by Enos H. G. Roberts*—Mersey to mud—war and Liverpool men.

THE GAMBARDIER *by Mark Severn*—The experiences of a battery of Heavy artillery on the Western Front during the First World War.

FROM MESSINES TO THIRD YPRES *by Thomas Floyd*—A personal account of the First World War on the Western front by a 2/5th Lancashire Fusilier.

THE IRISH GUARDS IN THE GREAT WAR - VOLUME 1 *by Rudyard Kipling*—Edited and Compiled from Their Diaries and Papers—The First Battalion.

THE IRISH GUARDS IN THE GREAT WAR - VOLUME 1 *by Rudyard Kipling*—Edited and Compiled from Their Diaries and Papers—The Second Battalion.

ARMOURED CARS IN EDEN *by K. Roosevelt*—An American President's son serving in Rolls Royce armoured cars with the British in Mesopotamia & with the American Artillery in France during the First World War.

CHASSEUR OF 1914 *by Marcel Dupont*—Experiences of the twilight of the French Light Cavalry by a young officer during the early battles of the great war in Europe.

TROOP HORSE & TRENCH *by R.A. Lloyd*—The experiences of a British Lifeguardsman of the household cavalry fighting on the western front during the First World War 1914-18.

THE EAST AFRICAN MOUNTED RIFLES *by C.J. Wilson*—Experiences of the campaign in the East African bush during the First World War.

THE LONG PATROL *by George Berrie*—A Novel of Light Horsemen from Gallipoli to the Palestine campaign of the First World War.

THE FIGHTING CAMELIERS *by Frank Reid*—The exploits of the Imperial Camel Corps in the desert and Palestine campaigns of the First World War.

STEEL CHARIOTS IN THE DESERT *by S. C. Rolls*—The first world war experiences of a Rolls Royce armoured car driver with the Duke of Westminster in Libya and in Arabia with T.E. Lawrence.

WITH THE IMPERIAL CAMEL CORPS IN THE GREAT WAR *by Geoffrey Inchbald*—The story of a serving officer with the British 2nd battalion against the Senussi and during the Palestine campaign.

AVAILABLE ONLINE AT **www.leonaur.com**
AND FROM ALL GOOD BOOK STORES

ALSO FROM LEONAUR
AVAILABLE IN SOFTCOVER OR HARDCOVER WITH DUST JACKET

"AMBULANCE 464" ENCORE DES BLESSÉS by *Julien H. Bryan*—The experiences of an American Volunteer with the French Army during the First World War

THE GREAT WAR IN THE MIDDLE EAST: 1 by *W. T. Massey*—The Desert Campaigns & How Jerusalem Was Won---two classic accounts in one volume.

THE GREAT WAR IN THE MIDDLE EAST: 2 by *W. T. Massey*—Allenby's Final Triumph.

SMITH-DORRIEN by *Horace Smith-Dorrien*—Isandlwhana to the Great War.

1914 by *Sir John French*—The Early Campaigns of the Great War by the British Commander.

GRENADIER by *E. R. M. Fryer*—The Recollections of an Officer of the Grenadier Guards throughout the Great War on the Western Front.

BATTLE, CAPTURE & ESCAPE by *George Pearson*—The Experiences of a Canadian Light Infantryman During the Great War.

DIGGERS AT WAR by *R. Hugh Knyvett & G. P. Cuttriss*—"Over There" With the Australians by R. Hugh Knyvett and Over the Top With the Third Australian Division by G. P. Cuttriss. Accounts of Australians During the Great War in the Middle East, at Gallipoli and on the Western Front.

HEAVY FIGHTING BEFORE US by *George Brenton Laurie*—The Letters of an Officer of the Royal Irish Rifles on the Western Front During the Great War.

THE CAMELIERS by *Oliver Hogue*—A Classic Account of the Australians of the Imperial Camel Corps During the First World War in the Middle East.

RED DUST by *Donald Black*—A Classic Account of Australian Light Horsemen in Palestine During the First World War.

THE LEAN, BROWN MEN by *Angus Buchanan*—Experiences in East Africa During the Great War with the 25th Royal Fusiliers—the Legion of Frontiersmen.

THE NIGERIAN REGIMENT IN EAST AFRICA by *W. D. Downes*—On Campaign During the Great War 1916-1918.

THE AUXILIA OF THE ROMAN IMPERIAL ARMY by *G.L.Cheeseman*

THE MILITARY SYSTEM OF THE ROMANS by *Albert Harkness*

AVAILABLE ONLINE AT **www.leonaur.com**
AND FROM ALL GOOD BOOK STORES

www.ingramcontent.com/pod-product-compliance
Lightning Source LLC
Chambersburg PA
CBHW030217170426
43201CB00006B/118